Russia and Ukraine

To all Ukrainian children kidnapped by Russia.
May they come home soon to their families in free Ukraine.

Russia and Ukraine

Entangled Histories, Diverging States

Maria Popova
and
Oxana Shevel

polity

First published in 2024 by Polity Press

Polity Press
65 Bridge Street
Cambridge CB2 1UR, UK

Polity Press
111 River Street
Hoboken, NJ 07030, USA

ISBN-13: 978-1-5095-5736-3 (hardback)
ISBN-13: 978-1-5095-5737-0 (paperback)

A catalogue record for this book is available from the British Library.

Library of Congress Catalogue Number: 2023932868

Typeset in 10.75 on 13 Adobe Janson
by Fakenham Prepress Solutions, Fakenham, Norfolk NR21 8NL
Printed and bound in Great Britain by TJ Books Ltd, Padstow, Cornwall

For further information on Polity, visit our website:
politybooks.com

Contents

Abbreviations

ATO	Anti-Terrorist Operation
BSF	Black Sea Fleet
CBR	Central Bank of Russia
CCU	Constitutional Court of Ukraine
CEC	Central Election Commission
CES	Common Economic Space
CIS	Commonwealth of Independent States
CSCE	Conference on Security and Cooperation in Europe
DCFTA	Deep and Comprehensive Free Trade Area
DNR	Donetsk People's Republic
ECHR	European Court of Human Rights
EU	European Union
FSB	Federal Security Service
GUAM	Georgia, Ukraine, Azerbaijan, Moldova
KGB	Committee for State Security
KIIS	Kyiv International Institute of Sociology
KPU	Communist Party of Ukraine
LDPR	Liberal Democratic Party of Russia
LNR	Luhansk People's Republic
MAP	Membership Action Plan
MP	Member of Parliament
NABU	National Anti-Corruption Bureau of Ukraine
NATO	North Atlantic Treaty Organization
NAZK	National Agency for Corruption Prevention
NDI	National Democratic Institute

OSCE	Organization for Security and Cooperation in Europe
OCU	Orthodox Church of Ukraine
OUN	Organization of Ukrainian Nationalists
PIC	Public Integrity Council
PLC	Polish-Lithuanian Commonwealth
PR	Party of Regions
ROC	Russian Orthodox Church
SAPO	Special Anti-Corruption Prosecution Office
SBU	Security Service of Ukraine
SMD	Single Member District
SPS	Union of Right Forces
UAOC	Ukrainian Autocephalous Orthodox Church
UGCC	Ukrainian Green Catholic Church
UNESCO	United Nations Educational, Scientific and Cultural Organization
UNR	Ukrainian People's Republic
UOC-KP	Ukrainian Orthodox Church of the Kyiv Patriarchate
UOC-MP	Ukrainian Orthodox Church of the Moscow Patriarchate
UPA	Ukrainian Insurgent Army
USSR	Union of Soviet Socialist Republics
ZUNR	West Ukrainian People's Republic

Illustrations

Tables

Figures

Maps

Acknowledgments

In the frenzied first weeks of Russia's full-scale invasion of Ukraine, the two of us, graduate school friends, who had worked on both Russian and Ukrainian politics for more than two decades, talked every day as we sought to make sense of how Putin could widen this criminal war of aggression when he should have known that Ukraine would resist with all its might. We also strove to counter the prevailing impression that Ukraine's spirited resistance was surprising and, perhaps, futile. Had Louise Knight from Polity Press not approached us, we might have stuck to writing short pieces and op-eds and talking to the media. We are grateful to her for the encouragement to write a book where we could go deeper into the root causes of Russia's war on Ukraine. We thank Louise and Inès Boxman for their guidance, responsiveness, professionalism, and flexibility throughout the entire process – from idea to finished product.

We are incredibly lucky to be part of a highly supportive network of colleagues and friends, who listened to our ideas, read early drafts, suggested relevant literature, helped edit, shared data, and offered constructive suggestions and criticism. Of course, all mistakes and omissions are our own responsibility. We started the book at a writing retreat in Budapest, which was organized by the BEAR Network, headed by Juliet Johnson and Magdalena Dembińska and managed by Sasha Lleshaj. We thank the Jean Monnet Centre Montreal, and especially Anastasia Leshchyshyn, for organizing a book manuscript workshop for us in Montreal, where we received invaluable advice from Dominique Arel, Yoshiko Herrera, Juliet Johnson, Andrew Kydd,

Matthew Pauly, and Lucan Way. Dominique Arel, Juliet Johnson, Marko Klasnja, Mark Kramer, Alexander Lanozska, Anastasia Leshchyshyn, Catherine Lu, Lorenz Luthi, and Matthew Pauly read and commented on various parts of the manuscript and at various stages, and offered great suggestions. The anonymous reviewers also offered helpful advice. We thank Volodymyr Paniotto for sharing Ukrainian polling data. Yoshiko Herrera and Catherine Lu went above and beyond and were immensely generous with their time, knowledge, and friendly encouragement.

We thank our families for patiently bearing with us, while we often worked late nights, skipped family outings, and talked loudly on Zoom for hours. Thanks to George, Emilia, and Miljenko for making it possible for Maria to work around the clock when it was necessary and to Viktor, Anton, and Max for listening to many unsolicited lectures at dinnertime. Viktor also pitched in with some last-minute but much needed research assistance. Isabella wants to know why Putin attacked Ukraine and when she's a little older she can read the book to find out. Sofia made it possible for Oxana to work at all hours and cheered her on. Oxana's family and friends in Ukraine have not only been a source of encouragement but also a living proof of the resilience, faith in victory, and unbreakable spirit of the Ukrainian people.

Introduction:

Russia's invasion and Ukraine's resistance

At dawn on February 24, 2022, rockets rained on Ukrainian cities and the nearly two hundred thousand troops Russia had amassed on Ukraine's borders over months, allegedly for training exercises, rolled into Ukraine. A forty-mile Russian military column headed straight for Kyiv to take over the capital and overthrow President Zelensky's government. In a nearly hour-long speech, Russian President Vladimir Putin justified this "special military operation" as an act of self-defense. The Kyiv government, Putin claimed, was controlled by "neo-Nazis," was "perpetrating genocide" of Russian-speakers in eastern Ukraine, and the Ukrainian military, strengthened through Western training and armament, was posing a security threat to Russia. To reduce the danger, in Putin's words, Russia had to "de-Nazify" and "demilitarize" Ukraine. Anyone trying to stop Russia would face consequences they had never seen in their history, Putin warned, in a thinly veiled nuclear threat.[1] Western intelligence had warned for months about an expected Russian military incursion in Ukraine. But Russia shocked the world by unleashing the biggest land war in Europe since World War II to achieve the explicit and maximalist goal of conquering Ukraine.

The second surprise was Ukraine's spirited and effective resistance. Putin, and many in the Russian army, expected that the "special military operation" would last mere days or short weeks, and that Russian troops would be greeted as liberators from "Nazi" rule by grateful Ukrainian citizens. The West's estimation of Ukraine's capacity and commitment to defend itself was similar. The German finance minister reportedly told the Ukrainian ambassador that Ukraine had just hours before it would be defeated by Russia. Military experts debated when Kyiv would fall, not whether. Pundits started thinking about what Russian occupation of Ukraine would look like.[2] But reality turned out to be dramatically different. On February 26, Western partners offered President Zelensky evacuation options for him and his family to leave the capital but, instead of accepting them, he filmed himself in the center of Kyiv to rally Ukrainian defenders, saying "I am here. We are not putting down arms. We will be defending our country."[3] Volunteers flooded military recruitment centers, the government gave them arms, and civil society sprang into action to support the war effort by crowdfunding military supplies, organizing delivery logistics, and providing humanitarian aid.

By early March, the Ukrainian military and the territorial defense forces, where regular citizens enrolled to defend their home regions, stopped Russian armored columns on their way to Kyiv. By the end of March, Russia lost the battle for Kyiv, and had to withdraw from the capital region. By April, Putin's blitzkrieg to overrun Ukraine was a clear failure, and Russia regrouped and continued to fight in the east and the south. By late May, Russia lost as many servicemen as the Soviet Union did in ten years of war in Afghanistan.[4] In the fall of 2022, Russia tried to formalize its land grab by organizing sham referenda and then annexing four Ukrainian regions into the Russian Federation. Undeterred by nuclear saber-rattling, Ukraine started a counteroffensive, which liberated first areas around Kharkiv in the east, and then Kherson in the south, the only Ukrainian regional center that Russia had managed to capture in the beginning of its invasion. Russia's mobilization in the fall and the recruitment of tens of thousands of convicts into the regime-sponsored private mercenary group Wagner did not help Russia regain initiative in the war, but only led to its mounting casualty counts. In 2023, Ukraine continued to try to push Russia out of all its territory and launched a counteroffensive in June, while Russia held on to its maximalist goal of conquering as much of Ukraine as possible.

The root of the war: Russian re-imperialization vs. Ukrainian independence

The scale of the Russian invasion and the effectiveness of Ukrainian resistance both defied expectations. Why did Russia try to overthrow its neighbor's government and conquer the entire country? How did Ukrainians manage to withstand a full-scale invasion by the world's second most powerful military? Why did diplomacy fail to avert Russia's aggression? We argue that an escalatory cycle between Russian imperialism and Ukraine's commitment to its independent statehood that started in the wake of the USSR's dissolution in December 1991 led to this war. The 2022 Russian invasion was the culmination of this escalatory cycle and the final, destructive phase of the collapse of the Soviet empire. The more Russia sought to fulfill its vision of restoring control over Ukraine, the more Ukraine pulled away and tried to consolidate independence. Ukraine adopted domestic policies emphasizing the distinctiveness of the Ukrainian nation, de-emphasized links with Russia, and gradually shifted to a Euro-Atlantic foreign policy. Each such step was viewed with hostility in Russia and increased its imperial drive. The central place that Ukraine occupied in Russia's national imaginary and its geopolitical centrality to any future Russia-led polity meant that Russia cared the most about Ukraine's political trajectory relative to the rest of the post-Soviet states. The escalatory cycle was therefore the most obvious and the most consequential in Russia–Ukraine relations but it is a generalizable pattern that can be analyzed across the post-Soviet region.

The escalatory cycle produced two dramatically different polities. Russia became a consolidated autocracy led by a revanchist dictator, bent on restoring the empire, and sustained by a passive society, which appreciated great power status more than democracy. Ukraine built a competitive, if imperfect, democracy with a vibrant civil society, a strong sense of its nationhood, and a commitment to its independence. Moreover, by 2022, Russia and Ukraine perceived each other as their antithesis. Unwilling to accept or even acknowledge Ukraine's homegrown commitment to forge its own domestic and foreign policies, Russia viewed its neighbor as a fundamentally anti-Russian project, steered by a hostile West. Having failed to bring the recalcitrant "younger brother" back into the fold through hybrid warfare – disinformation and destabilization through the intervention in the east – Russia escalated to a full-scale invasion. For Ukraine the coerced return to Russia's new supranational project known as the Russian World (*Russkii Mir*) had become an existential nightmare. Resisting Russia's invasion became Ukraine's fight for survival as a state and a nation.

What triggered this escalatory cycle? And did the cycle lead the countries inexorably into a collision course – or could the divergence that it produced have been bridged? The trigger was the misaligned understanding of the 1991 dissolution of the USSR. Although Russian president Boris Yeltsin and his Ukrainian counterpart, Leonid Kravchuk, along with Belarusian leader Stanislau Shushkevich hammered out the Belavezha Accords, disbanding the Soviet Union together, they imagined the aftermath differently. Russia's leadership assumed that the newly created Commonwealth of Independent States (CIS) would be a union of nominally independent states, but united as before in the economic, political, and security spheres, with Russia in the lead. Over time, centripetal forces would bring the former republics back together, the process aided by successful market reforms that would increase Russia's attractiveness as the center of gravity, many in Yeltsin's camp reasoned. By joining other republics' push for independence from the USSR, Yeltsin thought he was reinventing the union state, rather than destroying it.

The Ukrainian leadership, on the other hand, believed that the Belavezha Accords were a starting point on the road toward greater independence and separation between the former union republics in all areas, save possibly economic cooperation. In this sense, the CIS creation was, for Yeltsin, re-written vows for continued marriage, while Kravchuk famously called it a "civilized divorce." In Ukraine, the majority of the political class united behind the idea of an independent state. For some, Ukrainian independence was a long-held dream for which they had long advocated and suffered repression under the Soviet rule. But for many others independent statehood held a practical rather than ideational appeal. Already in the late Soviet period some of the former communist elites in Ukraine decided to back independence, drawn to the idea by perceived economic opportunities, political prestige of being in charge of a state rather than a province, and autonomy to make decisions without Moscow oversight. This alliance between national-democrats ideologically committed to independent Ukraine, and centrist former communists supporting independence for pragmatic reasons was an informal grand bargain that shaped policies in Ukraine. Originally, the push away from Russia was the product of these elite decisions. While Ukrainians overwhelmingly voted for independence in 1991, the economic hardship of the 1990s created political divisions, with the median voter often taking somewhat more "pro-Russian" positions than the elites. Over time and, in part due to Russia's actions, popular preferences evolved – first in the strategically important and electorally sizeable center of the country, and after Russia's aggression in 2014 in the east and south as well.

Since 1991, therefore, Ukraine defied Russia's expectation that it would be tied back to it, but the resistance was originally moderate, unfolding in fits and starts. Successive Ukrainian governments pursued nation-building policies that were more limited than the most committed Ukrainian nation-builders preferred, but still included symbolic statehood-strengthening measures such as Ukrainian-only state language, the rejection of dual citizenship with Russia, and the re-evaluation of shared history. Russia found all these policies objectionable. In foreign policy, Ukraine pushed against Russia's re-imperialization initiatives and initially sought to develop a multi-vectoral foreign policy aimed at balancing between Russia and the West. Russia objected at each step even to modest Ukrainian attempts to craft an independent foreign policy, but reacted with only moderate interference.

Russia's methods included both carrots and sticks: trade barriers, preferential energy prices or price gouging, and diplomatic pressure to sign on to supranational cooperation structures. The interference was moderate for two reasons. First, Russia was constrained by its own state weakness and domestic crises. Second, in the 1990s, it was reasonable for Russia to expect that moderate interference could be sufficient. By pressuring Ukraine through economic levers, obstructing some of Ukraine's separation initiatives such as delimitation and demarcation of the shared border, and using the CIS framework to pursue integration measures, Russia could hope to halt and eventually reverse the separation process. However, the 1990s ended without a decisive re-imperialization success. Successive Ukrainian governments consistently resisted Russian attempts to establish closer political or military integration and committed to maintaining equal partnership with Russia and the West.

The end of the first post-Soviet decade saw a leadership change in Russia when President Yeltsin resigned and handed the reins to Vladimir Putin. Putin immediately embarked on the creation of a power vertical, which entailed regional centralization, strengthening state power over the economy, and consolidation of political power in the hands of the president. He started a second war in Chechnya, which hastened the erosion of civil and political rights. He also moved to impose control over the oligarchs who had emerged and wielded political power during Yeltsin's term. Political competition in Russia rapidly declined.

Meanwhile, in some intended vassals, especially in Ukraine, the political trajectory pointed to strengthening political competition. First in Georgia in 2003, and then in Ukraine in 2004, authoritarian, pro-Russian incumbents lost their grip and ceded power after popular mobilization against electoral fraud. Both color revolutions ("Rose" in Georgia and "Orange" in Ukraine) were significant setbacks for Russia's imperial ambitions. In Ukraine, popular mobilization prevented the pro-Russian candidate, Viktor Yanukovych, from taking office and instead brought to the presidency Viktor Yushchenko, a pro-Western reformist former prime minister. Yushchenko's victory resulted in a Ukrainian government strongly committed to pro-Ukrainian identity politics and more ambitious about Western integration. Russia interpreted the Orange Revolution through its imperial lens, which could not envision a Ukrainian domestic political dynamic and majority popular sentiment that would be different from Russia's. The imperial mindset could only conceive of Ukrainians' mobilization as instigated and backed by the West and ultimately aimed at weakening Russia.

The color revolutions were highly contingent critical junctures. If they had failed, authoritarian regimes across the post-Soviet region would have entrenched. But those revolutions that did succeed in unseating the wannabe authoritarians fostered Russian paranoia that the West was "stealing" or "luring away" Russia's rightful vassals and threatening Russian regime stability too. Russia started seeing the domestic politics of Ukraine as a tug of war between itself and the West, as opposed to a political process determined by the evolving preferences of the Ukrainian electorate and domestic political competition. The Russia–West relationship soured as a result.

In Ukraine, the Orange Revolution ushered in the first decisive departure from Russia's preferred vision of Ukraine's past and future. Yushchenko spearheaded legislation that recognized the murderous famine of 1932–1933 (Holodomor) as a genocide of the Ukrainian people. Russia vehemently objected, insisting on characterizing the famine as "a common tragedy of the Soviet people." To Russia's wrath, Yushchenko also tried, albeit unsuccessfully, to foster the creation of an Orthodox Church in Ukraine, independent of Moscow, and to legislate recognition as war veterans and fighters for Ukrainian independence to members of the Ukrainian nationalist formations who had fought against the Soviet Union during and after WWII. In foreign policy, Yushchenko rejected Ukraine's status as Russia's vassal and moved away from the multi-vector policy of his predecessors. He expressed Ukraine's desire for a European future more forcefully. Under his leadership in 2007, Ukraine started negotiations with the European Union (EU) on a comprehensive and ambitious association agreement – Deep and Comprehensive Free Trade Area (DCFTA) – which could be a stepping-stone on Ukraine's path to EU membership. Yushchenko also applied for a NATO Membership Action Plan (MAP) in 2008, but was rebuffed by NATO, which offered only a vague promise to consider Ukrainian membership someday.

In 2010, Ukrainians narrowly elected as president pro-Russian Viktor Yanukovych, who had lost the Orange Revolution elections. In the first few years of the 2010s, it seemed that Russia's objective to turn Ukraine into a reliable vassal was on track to be realized. Yanukovych embarked on authoritarian power consolidation, bringing Ukraine's political model closer to Russia's. He quickly back-pedaled on the 1930s famine interpretation, revised memory politics to mimic Russia's, elevated the legal status of the Russian language, extended Russia's Black Sea Fleet presence in Ukraine, and reversed Ukraine's expressed interest in NATO membership.

However, the strength of the pro-Western constituency in Ukraine, along with continued, though curtailed, political competition meant that domestic pushback prevented Yanukovych from taking pro-Russian policies too far. Yanukovych continued the Yushchenko-initiated negotiations with the EU, albeit more slowly and tentatively and, by the fall of 2013, Ukraine was ready to sign the association agreement. Russia did not tolerate this manifestation of an independent Ukrainian foreign-policy course. In 2011, Russia launched a competing supranational initiative to the EU (the Eurasian Customs Union, later Eurasian Economic Union) aimed at bringing the vassals closer and cutting off their road to EU integration. To stop Ukraine from pursuing the European integration path, in 2013 Russia mounted a trade war, meant to illustrate, in the words of Putin's advisor, that Ukraine would be making a "suicidal step" by signing the EU agreement.[5] Then, in November 2013, Putin and Yanukovych met in secret and Russia successfully strong-armed him at the eleventh hour to renege on the signing of the EU association agreement. The failed signing triggered a reaction in Ukrainian society that neither the Yanukovych government nor Russia could control. The Euromaidan street protests exploded in November, quickly swelled and, after violence escalated and the regime killed dozens of protesters, culminated in the crumbling of Yanukovych's government and his flight from Ukraine. Like with the Orange Revolution, Russia interpreted Euromaidan through its imperial lens and saw the protest as an American-orchestrated coup "to steal" Ukraine from Russia and lure it to the West. Russia could not recognize it for the domestic mobilization that it was. Following Euromaidan's victory, Russia lashed out against the new government in Kyiv, characterizing it as an "illegal fascist junta." It then initiated a disinformation campaign, targeted at the Ukrainian, Russian, and Western public, claiming that Yanukovych did not flee Kyiv hoping to figure out how to hold onto power as his government crumbled, but was deposed in a US-backed coup.

The escalatory cycle between Russia's desire to control Ukraine and Ukraine's commitment to independent statehood helps us to understand why Russia reacted militarily against Ukraine in 2014, rather than employing the non-military means of pressure at its disposal and waiting for Ukraine's regionally divided electorate again to bring to power a Russia-friendly president in the subsequent round of competitive elections. Euromaidan was a watershed event, as it ushered in a government that was the most pro-Western and, to Russia's eyes, anti-Russian that Ukraine had ever had. To Russia, this fiasco demonstrated that the non-military levers it had used up until then to keep Ukraine in its sphere of influence had been insufficient. Russia concluded that a stronger reaction was now warranted, in order to achieve its goal of controlling Ukraine.

This reaction started with the annexation of Crimea immediately after Yanukovych fled, when "little green men" – Russian troops without insignia – seized state institutions and Ukrainian military bases. The success of the operation was facilitated by the presence of Russian troops and the Black Sea Fleet in Crimea to which Ukraine had agreed when the USSR fell apart, by the sheer surprise and speed of the brazen operation, and by the West urging restraint on Ukraine. Within barely two weeks, Russia staged a "referendum" in Crimea on the peninsula's fate. The vote fell well short of international standards for free plebiscite but officially delivered a majority for Crimea leaving Ukraine and joining Russia.

The next step in Russia's covert military aggression against Ukraine was the so-called "Russian Spring" project. The operation was supposed to drive a wedge between southeastern Ukraine and the new government in Kyiv. In the southeastern regions – Odesa, Kherson, Mykolaiv, Zaporizhzhia, Kharkiv, Dnipropetrovsk, Donetsk, Luhansk, labeled Novorossia in Russia, referencing an old imperial construct – Russia and Russian operatives amplified local dissatisfaction with the change of government in Kyiv hoping to trigger a regional rebellion that would break up Ukraine. This plan failed almost everywhere because Russia misjudged domestic sentiment in these regions. The Kremlin assumed that the Russian-speaking population in the south and east of Ukraine, many of whom had opposed Euromaidan, would also support separating their region from Ukraine. Only in parts of Donetsk and Luhansk oblasts, collectively known as Donbas, did Russia's interference succeed in creating the self-proclaimed Donetsk and Luhansk "people's republics" (the DNR and the LNR) and in fostering an armed insurgency, which challenged the central government militarily. In April, the Ukrainian interim government launched a military campaign to try to restore its control over Donbas. In the summer of 2014, Russia sent in regular troops, as the Ukrainian army was gaining the upper hand against the rebellion on the battlefield. Russia's intervention turned the tide and forced Ukraine to sign two disadvantageous accords in Minsk in September 2014, and again in February 2015, to avoid losing even more territory.

The escalatory cycle between Russian imperialism and Ukraine's commitment to its independent statehood played out by heightening anti-Russian sentiments in Ukraine in response to Russia's 2014 aggression. Instead of scaring Ukrainians out of pursuing a pro-Western policy course and forcing them to accept that they were in Russia's sphere of influence, Russia's attempt to bring Ukraine back into the fold through force boosted support for EU and NATO membership in all regions of Ukraine. A September 2014 survey conducted by Gallup on behalf of the International Republican Institute showed that support for membership in the EU, which stood at 42% in September 2013, rose to 59% by September 2014, while support for joining the Russia-led Customs Union fell from 37% to 17%. Support for Ukraine's membership in NATO, which in the years before Euromaidan hovered around 20%, also increased markedly. By September 2014, a plurality of 43% supported NATO membership. In the following months and years support for both EU and NATO solidified.

Post-Euromaidan elections produced successive, reliably pro-Western governments. Ironically, the annexation and occupation of Ukraine's most Russia-leaning regions by Russia and its proxies took millions of pro-Russian voters out of the voting electorate, dramatically changed the electoral equation, and made the formation of a future pro-Russian Ukrainian government virtually impossible. The new electoral geography and shifting public opinion in Ukraine also meant post-Euromaidan governments adopted more policies which infuriated Russia. They signed the association agreement with the EU, which Yanukovych and Russia had sought to prevent, enshrined the goal of NATO and EU membership in the constitution, accelerated Ukrainization through a series of new legal measures, contributed to the formation of an Orthodox Church independent of Moscow, and launched decommunization aimed at removing a variety of Soviet-era legacies from Ukraine. As part of the new close relationship with the EU, Ukraine also started implementing a series of reforms of its state institutions (police, courts, local government, etc.), which put it on track to meeting membership criteria for the EU, and strengthened its democracy. Rather than returning to the Russian World, Ukraine was drifting farther away with each passing year.

In 2019, democratic competition produced another turnover in power. Post-Euromaidan president Petro Poroshenko lost to Volodymyr Zelensky, a Russian-speaker from the south of Ukraine, who campaigned on readiness to come to an agreement with Russia on Donbas as well as Crimea. Russia expected that its gamble from 2014 would finally pay off and the insurgent Donbas entities it fostered and consolidated after 2014 would serve as Trojan horses inside Ukraine. If given "special status" within Ukraine on the terms reflecting Russia's preferred interpretation of the Minsk peace agreements, the LNR and DNR would wield *de-facto* veto power over the policies of the government in Kyiv, putting Ukraine back on the vassal track. However, even a conciliatorily predisposed Ukrainian president saw the danger to Ukrainian sovereignty that Russia's reading of Minsk posed. Among the Ukrainian public, despite majority support for a negotiated settlement of the Donbas conflict, there was majority opposition to giving LNR and DNR the powers that Russia demanded. The Minsk process deadlocked and, with it, Russia's objective of vassalizing Ukraine.

Russia's response was to escalate its methods for achieving the vassalization of Ukraine yet again. First, it implicitly threatened a full-scale invasion by amassing troops along Ukraine's border, starting in the fall of 2021. Second, in a bid to blackmail the West into delivering a vassalized Ukraine, Russia posed unrealistic demands to the NATO alliance. In December 2021, Russia handed to the US the text of a treaty it wanted the US to sign. The treaty demanded a ban on further NATO expansion, withdrawal of NATO troops and weapons from the post-communist member states, and a ban on all military cooperation between NATO and post-Soviet non-NATO countries, such as Ukraine. Taking these demands only to the US revealed that, just as Russia views its post-Soviet neighbors as vassals, it likewise views European NATO members as American vassals. The US could not agree to these demands, which were essentially an attempt at blackmail, and went against the principle of sovereign states having the right to decide their foreign-policy alliances, as well as NATO's collective decision-making principle. Russia's escalation and attempt to blackmail the West failed.

Ukraine also stood firm because it was committed to resisting reincorporation into the Russian World. Ukraine knew full well that neutrality and Minsk implementation on Russia's terms were interim steps toward Russia achieving its ultimate goal of vassalizing it. Conceding neutrality after the annexation of Crimea and the loss of territory in Donbas would have been a creeping loss of sovereignty.

Acquiescing to separatist entities holding veto power over a swath of state policies would have cemented this sovereignty loss. For the Zelensky government, therefore, meeting Russia's demands either on neutrality or on the implementation of the Minsk accords on Russia's terms, while hypothetically possible, in practice was unrealistic because Ukrainian society would largely interpret the steps as unacceptable surrender to Russia. By early 2022, 62% nationwide and a majority in every region except the east supported NATO membership.[6] Majority opposed concessions to Russia on Minsk – only 11% believed that Ukraine should be implementing the agreements.[7] Had Zelensky tried to push through these measures, street protests and political instability were sure to follow and he would have most likely been unable to put together the legislative majority required to amend the relevant parts of the constitution. A likely failure to impose these measures on Ukrainian society would have denied Russia's goal of vassalization, and thus put the Russian invasion back on the agenda. But Ukraine would be facing the invasion with a less trusted government, a weakened state, and a potentially more divided society.

In sum, over the last three decades, the escalatory cycle that characterized the Russian–Ukrainian relationship led to increasing divergence between the two countries in multiple dimensions: identity conceptions, regime dynamics, and geopolitical orientation. In Russia, the state and the nation became increasingly conceptualized in civilizational-imperial terms, whereas Ukraine solidified a distinct Ukrainian identity committed to independent statehood. Under Putin's rule, Russia consolidated an increasingly repressive and personalistic authoritarian regime, which felt threatened by Ukrainian democracy's progress and resented its increasingly pro-Western foreign policy. The robust civil society and vibrant political competition flourishing in Ukraine looked like a nightmare scenario from the perspective of Russia's authoritarian regime – a dangerous example that Russia's democratic opposition could try to emulate, with Western instigation. In foreign policy, Putin's Russia became increasingly anti-Western and bent on asserting Russia's dominance over the post-Soviet states, first and foremost Ukraine, at the same time as Ukraine committed to a European path. Russia's imperial vision came to dominate policy-making *vis-à-vis* Ukraine, as Ukraine increasingly slipped away from Russia's grasp.

The methods Russia used to push Ukraine to change course escalated from diplomatic pressure, energy flow carrots and sticks, information warfare, and cyber-attacks to military aggression. Each escalation of pressure by Russia prompted an ever-increasing share of Ukrainians to shift from pro-Russian to pro-Western positions, to embrace more distinctly Ukrainian identity, and to support more decisive Ukrainization policies. As a result, while each Ukrainian incumbent sought to balance between a pro-Russian and a nationalizing or pro-Western position, the equilibrium changed over time. Each pro-Western incumbent became more determined to pursue Euro-Atlantic integration, while each pro-Russian incumbent was less in step with public opinion. This trend in turn boosted Russia's paranoia that the West was stealing Ukraine. The result of this escalatory cycle of divergent trajectories was two incompatible domestic equilibria – Russia became committed to resetting Ukraine as a loyal vassal, while Ukraine became convinced that it had to leave Russia's sphere of influence altogether and join the West.

Was the 2022 war inevitable?

War is never inevitable. Russia's President Putin made calculated decisions to invade Ukraine both in 2014 and in 2022. He could have instead continued pursuing the goal of establishing control over Ukraine through other means or he could have grudgingly accepted the reality of Ukraine's distancing from Russia. Ultimately, the heavy moral responsibility for the murder and destruction of the invasion lies with him and his regime.

Our escalatory cycle argument developed in this book addresses whether the divergence between Ukraine and Russia was pre-determined and whether it was pre-ordained that divergence would produce a collision course between the two states, rather than mutual acceptance of the difference. We explain why both divergence and the collision course were the likely outcome but we also show that neither was inevitable and there were plausible alternative scenarios that could have averted the war. The war in 2022 was a logical step in the escalatory cycle, but throughout the post-Soviet period there were critical junctures where either Ukraine or Russia could have swerved and pursued a different trajectory.

The logic of an escalatory cycle between re-imperialization and independence centers on the compatibility between Russia's and its neighbors' foreign and domestic policies. When the vassals pursue parallel foreign policy and refrain from emphasizing "anti-Russian" identities domestically, Russia does not need to exert its imperial power. In relations with Ukraine, this compatibility would have been more likely if they had developed similar regimes. If both countries were autocracies, it would have been easier for Russia to re-establish control over Ukraine. An authoritarian trajectory for Ukraine would have meant a more pro-Russian course in foreign and domestic policies alike. Had Yanukovych prevailed during the 2004 Orange Revolution or successfully crushed Euromaidan, he could have entrenched himself as an authoritarian Ukrainian leader who would look to Russia for backing. As the price for its support, Russia would have demanded aligned identity politics and closer political integration.

If Russia had de-imperialized and accepted the sovereignty of its former vassals, a collision course also would have been unlikely. Russia would have recognized Ukraine's right to formulate domestic policies without input or pressure, without taking Russia's preferences into consideration. Even if Russia found such policies objectionable it would not have tried to change by force the domestic policies of a state whose sovereignty it accepted. Acceptance would have prevented Russia from perceiving itself in a zero-sum game with the West for control of Ukraine. This way, "either we control it, or they do; Ukraine as nobody's vassal or proxy cannot exist."

If Russia had managed to establish a democracy, even without de-imperialization, its imperial impulses may not have taken it all the way to military aggression either. Regular competitive elections could have empowered a variety of voices which, even if for the most part sharing imperialist goals, would have disagreed on the ways to achieve them. Minority voices advocating a non-imperial identity would have played a greater role in a democratic environment than in an authoritarian one. In this environment, military aggression would have become less likely also because advocates of alternative methods could have voiced their criticisms in public and influenced the policy-making process. Even among the imperialists who favored restoring the USSR or the Russian empire, the proponents of military aggression would have had to win over those favoring milder means toward similar goals, with Russian society further being in a position to affect the outcome of elite disagreements through electoral politics. Russia could have tried to build a liberal economic empire across the former Soviet region, as some Russian politicians have advocated. Such an empire might have been attractive to Ukraine, and Russia may not have had to resort to bullying, blackmail, and aggression to keep Ukraine in its orbit.

Neither of these things happened. Ukraine did not end up as a pro-Russian autocracy and Russia did not maintain political competition. Democratic competition in Russia peaked in the 1990s and only went downhill from there. By 2014, Ukraine was fully committed to independence and increasingly leaned West, while Russia came to see Ukraine's full independence as an anti-Russian project engineered by the West, ultimately aimed against Russia, and was determined to destroy it. In several chapters, we discuss various windows of opportunity during which the escalatory cycle could have been broken and the processes, by design or by fiat, that slammed them shut.

Could the West have prevented the war?

Western containment of Russia may have stood a chance of averting the war. After Russia invaded Georgia in 2008 and Ukraine in 2014, some argued that the West should have concluded that it pushed Russia too much and disregarded its legitimate concerns about its waning influence in its neighborhood. But the West should have drawn the opposite lesson. Instead of worrying about provoking Russia, the West should have recognized that Russia sought to restore the vassal status of its neighbors left out of the EU and NATO, and 2008 and 2014 were just the beginning of an aggressive re-imperialization campaign. Redesigning Europe's security architecture against, rather than with Russia could have preserved peace.

A Western containment strategy could have included sustained efforts to counter Russia's efforts to undermine Western democracies through disinformation campaigns, illegal party financing, and electoral meddling. Instead of a "reset," the US could have championed extensive sanctions after the 2008 Russian invasion of Georgia. A robust Western response to the intervention in Georgia could have deterred Russia from its opportunistic land grab in Ukraine in 2014. Instead, the equivocating Western response in 2008 led Russia to perceive the West as weak and declining, divided, and not committed to preventing Russia from re-establishing dominance over its neighbors. The 2008 financial crisis and the West's introspection and focus on overcoming it through domestic reforms only boosted Russia's perception that the opportunity costs of re-Sovietizing its neighboring region were going down.

In 2014, the West again decided against trying to contain Russia. More far-reaching sanctions and Western unity to isolate Russia could have made the costs of Russian imperialism high enough to deter the 2022 invasion. Europe, and especially Germany, should have reduced its energy dependency on Russia instead of proceeding with Nord Stream 2. The US under both the Obama and the Trump administrations should have provided more extensive military aid to Ukraine to drive home to Russia the message that it cannot hope to easily overrun Ukraine militarily. Instead, the West prioritized engagement and de-escalation, fearing that arming Ukraine would provoke Russia and rationalizing that arming Ukraine would not make a difference on the battlefield. We now know that engagement did not work. In hindsight containment seems like the better strategy to prevent the war.

The narrative of an aggressively expansionist West luring Eastern Europe into NATO and then setting its sights on Ukraine and other post-Soviet states is unconvincing and not supported by facts. On the contrary, the West prioritized a cooperative relationship with Russia and strove to include it in Europe's security architecture, often over the objections and security concerns of the East Europeans. The West did not push the East Europeans into NATO. On the contrary, those who did make it into NATO campaigned hard and overcame initial Western skepticism to achieve it. The West was not only cognizant of Russia's preferences, but tiptoed around them because it sought Russian cooperation more broadly on the international scene. The West hoped that engagement with Russia through trade and other forms of cooperation would be beneficial to all. After 2001, the West also solicited Russia's cooperation in the management of conflicts in the Middle East and Afghanistan, in containing Iran's nuclear program, and in counteracting Islamic terrorism. Even after Russia's 2014 aggression against Ukraine, the West sought a solution that would be acceptable to Russia by backing the Minsk process, offering Ukraine modest military aid, and no security guarantees. The 2022 full-scale invasion is surely Putin's fault, but the West should have tried harder to deter him.

Book outline

This book argues that the key to understanding Russia's attack on Ukraine and Ukraine's fierce resistance lies in examining the trajectories Russia and Ukraine pursued since the collapse of the Soviet Union, and how an escalatory cycle between Russia's re-imperialization goal and Ukraine's commitment to its independence produced increasing divergence. The 2022 aggression was a surge by an autocratic Russia increasingly confident in its ability to re-imperialize the former Soviet region, rather than the desperate reaction of a Russia, scared and cornered by the West. Ukraine's resistance was a determined stand against its Russia-ascribed fate. Ukraine surprised not only Russia, which, seeing Ukraine as not a "real" nation, denied it any agency, but also many Western observers and analysts, who viewed the post-Soviet region through a Russocentric lens or focused on "great powers" dynamics.

The next chapter starts with a summary of Ukraine's and Russia's entangled histories and competing interpretations of this entanglement. These interpretations can present historical events as either justifications for "organic unity," thus strengthening contentions that Ukraine and Russia have always been destined to be together, or, conversely, as evidence of Ukraine and Russia's distinctions going back centuries, and Russia's repeated attempts to suppress independent Ukrainian identity and its quest for political autonomy. The chapter then surveys the trajectory of identity formation in post-Soviet Ukraine and Russia, which were in large part informed by competing interpretations of history. The chapter explains how and why in Russia the search for a post-Soviet identity was a competition between a civic-territorial ideal and an imperial-expansionist one, with the latter one eventually gaining the upper hand. In Ukraine, there were also competing intellectual constructs of a "true" Ukrainian nation, but already in the late perestroika period, identity politics resulted in state elites embracing a conception of national identity that underscored Ukraine's distinctiveness from Russia. The chapter explains how national-democrats ideologically committed to independent Ukraine and centrist former communists supporting independence for pragmatic reasons formed an informal Center-Right grand bargain, which shaped identity policies in Ukraine.

Chapter 2 focuses on the regime divergence between Ukraine and Russia. Why was Ukraine able to establish a competitive, if messy democracy, and why did Russia, after a period of political openness in the 1990s, revert to authoritarianism under Putin's tenure? The chapter traces the parallel political and economic trajectories in the 1990s, pinpoints the beginning of decisive divergence to 2004 in the wake of Ukraine's democratizing Orange Revolution, and then identifies the last opportunity for breaking the escalatory cycle and resuming parallel regime paths in the early 2010s. 2010 to 2014 could have brought about either collapse of Ukraine's democracy and a decisive re-orientation away from the EU and toward Russia, or a democratization breakthrough in Russia, which could have put it on a de-imperialization path. Neither happened, but we discuss some counterfactuals to illustrate how things could have turned out differently.

Chapter 3 discusses how the divergence in identity politics in Russia and Ukraine discussed in Chapter 1 led to divergence in the specific identity policies that the two states adopted. As this chapter shows, starting already in the late Soviet period, Russia and Ukraine pursued increasingly contrasting policies in the sphere of historical memory, language, and citizenship. On the logic that the legitimacy of an independent state rests on the presence of a distinct nation, Ukrainian state elites – including those who themselves were Russian-speakers – pursued nation-building policies that legitimized and fostered a distinct Ukrainian nation. Russia disliked, regularly objected to, and sought to change Ukraine's identity policies. Russia's opposition to Ukraine's nation-building agenda intensified with Putin coming to power and a re-imperialization of Russian identity followed. The persisting and growing divergence in identity policies illustrates the reinforcing cycle of Ukraine's pull away from Russia and Russia's unsuccessful attempts to reverse the process. The chapter also discusses how, originally, Ukraine's identity policies were the product of these elite decisions taken within the logic of the Center-Right grand bargain, while popular opinion was divided, with the median voter position often more "pro-Russian." Over time popular opinion evolved – first gradually, starting in the geographic center of the country, and after the 2014 Russian aggression more rapidly, and now unfolding in the east and south as well.

Chapter 4 discusses the geopolitical interaction between Russia, Ukraine, and the West until 2014. It explains that the domestic politics divergence between Russia and Ukraine gradually strained the relationship between the two countries. The harder Russia tried to reinvent a new supranational arrangement that would keep the two countries together geopolitically, the more Ukraine resisted and tried to break free. As Russia's methods of pressure escalated, so did Ukraine's commitment to a Euro-Atlantic foreign policy. And, as the confrontation between the former vassal and the wannabe suzerain intensified, the Russia–West relationship soured as Russia accused the West of trying to lure away Ukraine. Meanwhile, the West attempted to strike a balance between accommodating Russia's concerns and helping Ukraine democratize and pursue the European integration path it had chosen. 2013 to 2014 would become a fork in the road for all three.

The fork in the road was the Euromaidan revolution, which opens Chapter 5. The popular uprising, known in Ukraine as the Revolution of Dignity, was triggered by Yanukovych's last-minute attempt to reorient Ukraine away from the EU and toward Russia, but was sustained by fears of the regime's growing autocratization and radicalized by the violent attempted suppression of the protest. After Euromaidan culminated in Yanukovych's ouster, Russia lashed out against the new Ukrainian government, intervened and annexed Crimea, and spurred and backed an anti-Kyiv insurgency in Donbas. The chapter traces the momentous events of 2013 to 2014 and analyzes Russia's goals in launching military aggression against its neighbor. We argue that, paradoxically, the Donbas war was not really about Donbas. Rather, by helping to jump-start and by supporting the separatist proxy statelets of Donetsk and Luhansk "people's republics," Russia was planning to use Donbas as a tool to bring about the vassalization of all of Ukraine. The Minsk peace accords were a Trojan horse that Russia sought to use to keep control of Ukraine. Russia wanted the proxy republics it controlled to get a *de-facto* veto power over policies of the central government through the Minsk accords.

Chapter 6 analyzes the consequences of Euromaidan, Crimea's annexation, and the war in Donbas. 2014 was a watershed moment in Ukraine's political trajectory, but not in the way Putin calculated. All the processes he aimed to reverse – Ukrainian identity consolidation, democratization, and a pro-European foreign-policy orientation – accelerated like never before. Rather than turning on each other, Ukrainians leaned into their independent statehood and distinctive identity. Rather than falling into political instability and dysfunction, Ukraine accelerated political reforms and made progress in democratic consolidation, the rule of law and anti-corruption reforms, and growing state capacity. Instead of accepting destiny as a Russian vassal, Ukraine's government and society looked toward Europe and the West with increased enthusiasm and ambition. Instead of acknowledging that its own actions were pushing Ukraine further away, the Putin regime doubled down on the narrative of Western meddling in Ukraine. As the Minsk process failed to deliver a paralyzed and vassalized Ukraine, Putin eventually decided to escalate to the full-scale invasion of 2022.

The concluding chapter recaps the 2022 to 2023 war and illustrates that the invasion was another step in the escalatory cycle, one which has turbo-charged the divergence between Ukraine and Russia. The two countries are now decisively disentangled and Ukraine wants to win the war and complete its geopolitical, economic, and cultural rupture from Russia. The chapter also asks what lessons we can draw from the war for the broader security of Europe and the world, and argues that the West should not return to pre-war cooperation with Russia and the dominant pre-war Western vision of Ukraine as a buffer zone between the West and Russia. Those who argue that Russia is too big and important to be isolated are wrong. Stable peace in Europe requires the realization that as long as Russia remains governed by an autocrat and wedded to an imperialist reading of its history and its destiny, it will remain a threat to its neighbors and to European and global security and stability. Russia should be contained for as long as it takes for Russian society to bring about regime change and democratization. Ukraine should be integrated into the West through EU accession and NATO membership.

1

Entangled histories and identity debates

In his February 21, 2022 speech, days before announcing a "special military operation" in Ukraine, Putin listed his vision of Ukraine's past, present, and future. He claimed that Ukraine is "an inalienable part" of Russia's "own history, culture and spiritual space." "Since time immemorial, the people living in the southwest of what has historically been Russian land have called themselves Russians ... Modern Ukraine was entirely created by Russia or, to be more precise, by Bolshevik, Communist Russia."[1] This theme of Ukrainians being "really" an organic part of a Russian pan-nation and an independent Ukrainian state being an artificial construct existing at the expense of "historical" Russia, or at the pleasure of contemporary Russia, is at the core of the current war. It has been a central tenet of Russia's intellectual thinking even if it has not always driven post-Soviet Russia's state policies. Ukraine and Russia's entangled histories can be told through competing interpretations. One version presents historical events as justifications for "organic unity," thus trying to strengthen modern-day contentions that Ukraine and Russia have always been destined to be together. An alternative view emphasizes evidence of Ukraine and Russia's distinctions going back centuries, and Russia's repeated attempts to suppress independent Ukrainian identity and crush Ukraine's quest for political autonomy and its own state.

In the post-Soviet period, interpretations of history informed debates over national identity in both states. What were the "true" Russian and Ukrainian nations? Competing views of shared history came to inform alternative nation-building projects, which offered different answers to this question. In post-Soviet Russia, several intellectual constructs of a "true" Russian nation have co-existed, but only one of these intellectual imaginaries is compatible with the notion that Ukraine is a distinct nation and a legitimate independent polity. Later in this chapter we discuss how, by the middle of the 1990s, multiple factors prevented this option from becoming a guide to Russian state policies. Instead, Russian identity progressively imperialized, as the Russian state embraced the idea of Russia as a supra-national civilization, which included Ukraine.

In Ukraine, there were also competing intellectual constructs of a "true" Ukrainian nation but, already in the late perestroika period, identity politics resulted in state elites embracing a conception of national identity that underscored Ukraine's distinctiveness from Russia. Over time, the Ukrainian state's commitment to this identity option only strengthened, increasingly coming into tension with the re-imperialization of identity in Russia, both reinforcing each other in an escalatory cycle. The Yanukovych presidency in 2010 to 2014 was the period when the escalatory cycle could have been halted and potentially even reversed, but this option was foreclosed by Yanukovych's ouster. In subsequent years, divergence accelerated – this post-2014 divergence will be discussed in greater detail in Chapter 6. Battles over identity were not the only cause of Russia's 2022 full-scale invasion of Ukraine, but the war cannot be fully understood without the escalatory cycle generated by diverging identity projects in the two states informed by divergent interpretations of history.

Entangled histories

From Kyivan Rus' through tsarism

Ukraine and Russia both trace the origins of their statehood to Kyivan Rus', an early medieval state that formed in the ninth century. Centered in Kyiv, Kyivan Rus' was one of Europe's largest and most powerful polities. It consisted of many principalities and many different tribes speaking different languages, including a variety of Slavic dialects. Though highly diverse, Kyivan Rus' had certain things in common: a dynasty, a writing system, and a religion. In 988, Prince Volodymyr (in Russian Vladimir) adopted Christianity from the Byzantine empire. Different principalities often fought each other, especially following Volodymyr's death. Rus' was not one nation in a modern sense. Many historians consider Rus' to be like the empire of Charlemagne, which was an ancestor to both France and Germany.

After Kyiv's fall to the Mongols in the thirteenth century and the eventual fragmentation of the Mongols in the mid-fourteenth century, western Rus' principalities, as well as Kyiv, came under the control of Poland and Lithuania. In the late fourteenth century, the former lands of Kyivan Rus' constituted nine tenths of the Grand Duchy of Lithuania's territory.[2] The northeastern Rus' principality of Vladimir-Suzdal eventually moved its center to Moscow, which became the capital of the Grand Duchy of Muscovy. Muscovy remained the longest under Mongol suzerainty, becoming fully independent only at the end of the fifteenth century. Most historians consider the political divisions that arose after the Mongol invasion to be instrumental in the formation of separate Ukrainian and Belarusian nations on the one hand and a Russian nation on the other. Historians also generally refer to the people of the Kyivan Rus' in the Polish–Lithuanian political sphere as "Ruthenians."[3] The Latin-derived exonym "Ruthenian" designated not ancestors of modern-day Russians but ancestors of modern-day Ukrainians and Belarusians.

In 1569, the Union of Lublin created the Polish–Lithuanian Commonwealth (PLC), at that time the largest and most powerful state in the eastern part of Europe. The Ukrainian lands of Volhynia, Podolia, and Kyiv were incorporated into Poland proper and administratively divided into six palatinates (provinces) of the PLC. Under Lithuanian rule, the Ruthenian nobility intermarried with the Lithuanian aristocracy and exercised power as military commanders, administrators, and landowners. The PLC had a single ruler elected by the nobility. It was a quasi-federal state but dominated by the Kingdom of Poland. The Ukrainian palatinates, incorporated one by one and not as a group, were not given guarantees pertaining to the use of Ruthenian (Middle Ukrainian) language in the courts and administration and the protection of the rights of the Orthodox Church.[4] A closed system of social "estates" in the PLC and the social prestige of Catholicism caused assimilation of the Ruthenian nobility, although some historians argue that the Ruthenian noble families functioned as a national elite until the early seventeenth century, ensuring continuity of social and cultural structures from the time of Kyivan Rus'.[5]

In the PLC, Ukrainian territories had exposure to influences from the West that the Muscovy did not experience; most consequentially Renaissance and Reformation. In this fertile intellectual climate, Orthodox magnates founded schools and established presses. The first complete text of the Bible in Church Slavonic was published in 1581 in Ostrih in Volhynia. In 1632, the Orthodox Metropolitan Petro Mohyla established the first modern institution of higher learning among the eastern Slavs, the Kyiv–Mohyla Academy.[6] There were substantial social and religious tensions between Orthodox Ruthenian peasants and local nobility, and Catholic Polish ruling elites in the PLC. In the sparsely populated Ruthenian lands in the Dnipro valley, threatened by Tatar raiders from the south, runaway peasants settled since the fifteenth century. In the mid-1500s, a Cossack fortress was founded on the lower Dnipro – the Zaporozhian Sich. By the late sixteenth century this territory came to be known as Ukraine (meaning "borderland").[7]

When the Polish crown began the colonization of these lands in the sixteenth century, Cossacks developed as a distinct social group. The word Cossack comes from the Turkic word *kazak*, meaning "free man." The Polish kings granted Cossacks certain rights and freedoms in return for defending the frontier from Tatar raids, but also attempted to limit their numbers. Cossacks soon emerged as defenders of Ukrainian social, political, and religious rights. Tensions between the Cossacks and the Polish ruling elite of the PLC (which included assimilated Ruthenian nobility and magnates) grew, as Cossacks aspired to recognition as a distinct social estate with guaranteed social, political, and religious rights and freedoms.[8]

The early seventeenth century saw several Cossack uprisings against the Polish authorities. In 1648, in what was the seventh major Cossack insurrection since the end of the sixteenth century, a united army of Cossacks and peasants, now allied with the Tatars, twice decisively defeated Polish troops.[9] The Cossacks were led by the Cossack leader (Hetman) Bohdan Khmelnytsky. Khmelnytsky, who spoke about the liberation of the "entire Ruthenian people," in contemporary Ukrainian historiography would come to be considered as a fighter for his ethnic group's political independence. In 1649, the Polish rulers of the PLC agreed to the creation of the Hetmanate – an autonomous Cossack state. The Hetmanate was created on the territory of today's central Ukraine as a self-governing Ukrainian state, which developed its own administrative military apparatus and foreign policy. Three of the six palatinates of the PLC (Kyiv, Chernihiv, Bratslav) were put under the authority of the Hetman and Polish officials were banned from governing there.[10]

To secure the political and religious autonomy for the Hetmanate against Polish power, Khmelnytsky sought alliances with neighbors such as the Tatars, the Ottoman empire, and Moldova, eventually drawing closer to Muscovy as well. In 1654, Khmelnytsky recognized the suzerainty of the Russian tsar, which was formalized in the Treaty of Pereiaslav. The exact meaning of this act – whether Khmelnytsky intended it as a temporary diplomatic maneuver and a military alliance, or as the unification of two states – was controversial from the beginning. But what it clearly was not was a reunion of two "brotherly peoples." As one historian put it, "no one in Pereyaslav or Moscow was thinking or speaking in ethnic terms in 1654." Language-wise, the two sides needed interpreters to understand each other.[11] Following their oath of allegiance to seal Pereiaslav, the Cossack leaders expected the Muscovite envoys also to take an oath in the name of the tsar to observe the Cossacks' traditional rights, but the Muscovite boyars refused. The tsar was an absolute monarch who would not be accountable to his subjects in this manner.[12] Within the Russian empire, the Hetmanate at first continued to function as a largely self-governing entity but the empire progressively curtailed Cossack freedoms. In the 1780s, the Russian imperial authorities under Catherine II abolished the Hetmanate and established direct rule of its territory, arranging it into three provinces of the Russian empire. Much of the Cossack officer class was assimilated into Russian nobility and peasants were turned into serfs.[13]

The Kyivan Rus', the history of Ukrainian lands in the Polish–Lithuanian Commonwealth, and the 1654 Treaty of Pereiaslav have been hotly debated. Competing interpretations present historical justifications for unity, or, conversely, emphasize Ukraine and Russia's separate paths. Was the Kyivan Rus' the common cradle of a united eastern Slavic supra-nation, which in turn "proves" that Ukrainians objectively belong together with Russians as members of one nation, or was Kyivan Rus' a proto-state of a distinct Ukrainian nation? Was the 1654 Treaty of Pereiaslav Khmelnytsky's fateful mistake since Russia betrayed the original agreement, which ushered in centuries of Russian domination of Ukraine? Or was it a joyous occasion that formalized the historically predetermined reunification of Russians and Ukrainians, divided for four centuries since the fall of Kyivan Rus' to the Mongols? Similar questions can be raised about subsequent key developments. How to characterize the 1709 Battle of Poltava, when Peter I's armies defeated Charles XII's Swedes and the Ukrainian Cossacks under Hetman Mazepa? Was Mazepa, vilified in Soviet and Russian historiography and excommunicated by the Russian Orthodox Church, a traitor who betrayed the Russian tsar, or was Mazepa's decision to side against Peter I a national uprising against the tsar's growing encroachment on Cossack autonomy? Rather than a traitor, was Mazepa in fact a hero of Ukrainian national liberation?

Following the Treaty of Pereiaslav, most of left-bank Ukraine, i.e. the territories east of the Dnipro river, along with Kyiv, came under the rule of the Russian tsars, although the Cossack Hetmanate kept a degree of autonomy until the 1780s. Russian rule came to right-bank Ukraine, i.e. the territories west of the Dnipro, more than a hundred years after Pereiaslav, as a result of the 1772–1795 partitions of Poland. By the nineteenth century, the territory of Ukraine was largely divided between the Russian and Austro-Hungarian empires, with the latter controlling the western and southwestern regions of today's Ukraine (Galicia, Volhynia, Bukovyna, Transcarpathia). When the ideology of mass nationalism reached Ukraine's intellectuals during the first decades of the nineteenth century, this set in motion processes that again would come to be viewed very differently by the proponents of "organic unity" with Russia and believers in Ukraine's distinct national and political identity.

Through the nineteenth and early twentieth centuries, Ukrainian intellectuals and writers, like their counterparts in other stateless East European nations, described the ethnographic characteristics and defined the geographic extent of the Ukrainian people to justify the existence of a distinct Ukrainian nation and its right to cultural and political autonomy and eventually statehood. Within the Austro-Hungarian empire, Habsburg rulers generally tolerated, and even encouraged, the Ukrainian national movement. In the nineteenth century, the Russian empire initially allowed a "Ukrainian idea," but only while it presented Ukrainians as "Little Russians" – ethnographically distinct in points of detail from Russians ("Great Russians"), but still belonging to the single Orthodox nation descending from Kyivan Rus'. The authorities saw this idea as countering Polish claims to the lands west of Kyiv, which had only recently been incorporated into the Russian empire.[14]

The "Little Russia" movement would ultimately split into Ukrainian political nationalism and Russian imperial nationalism. Over the course of the nineteenth century, the tsarist government increasingly grew suspicious of "Ukrainophiles" (Ukraine lovers – a term the authorities invented and the Ukrainian patriots accepted), seeing "Ukrainophilism" as subversive to the empire and Ukrainophiles as agents or allies of Polish separatists.[15] In the second half of the nineteenth century, the tsarist regime aggressively suppressed the Ukrainian movement and banned publishing and education in Ukrainian. One of the

Ukrainophiles harshly punished by the tsarist regime was the poet Taras Shevchenko (1814–1861), who in his literary works portrayed Ukraine as an independent nation subjugated by Polish and later Russian oppressors. He has been revered ever since as the national bard and a martyr for the national cause. In 1863, Minister of Internal affairs Petr Valuev issued a secret letter to censors, known as the Valuev Edict, banning the publication of religious and educational books in Ukrainian. In 1876, Tsar Alexander II issued the Ems Decree banning the publication of all Ukrainian books, their import from abroad, as well as the use of Ukrainian on stage.

The intelligentsia-inspired Ukrainian nation-building of this period was a process typical for any European "stateless nation." Russian proponents of the "organic unity" construct saw the idea of distinct Ukrainian nationhood as both unacceptable and a result of foreign meddling – first Polish, then Austrian. This argument has strong echoes in contemporary claims by Putin and other Russian state leaders that beliefs in distinct Ukrainian identity and a path for Ukraine independent from Russia are "artificial" views, imposed on Ukrainians by the conniving West to undermine the supposed natural unity of Ukrainians and Russians and to weaken Russia. Instead, we will show that today, like in the earlier historical periods, such views are the result of complex domestic processes within Ukraine.

The turbulent twentieth century

At the turn of the twentieth century, Ukrainians were Europe's largest national minority and second-largest Slavic people after the Russians. Of more than 26 million Ukrainians in 1900, 22.4 million lived in the Russian empire and 3.8 million in Austria-Hungary. Ukrainian activists engaged with the ideological trends of the time such as Marxism and socialism, and some gave priority to social liberation issues, while others to the Ukrainian national cause.[16] The first attempt at modern Ukrainian statehood took place in the early twentieth century, following WWI and the collapse of both the Russian and the Austro-Hungarian empires.

During the turbulent revolutionary era between 1917 and 1920, there were competing and evolving Ukrainian ideas, such as an autonomous Ukraine within democratic Russia, an independent socialist Ukraine, a nationalist dictatorship, a conservative Ukrainian monarchy, and others. On March 17, 1917, two days after Tsar Nicholas II abdicated, the Central Rada (Ukrainian for "council") was established in Kyiv.

Practically all Ukrainian parties sent their representatives to the Rada and Mykhailo Hrushevsky, an influential historian, was chosen as its chairman. Originally, the Rada wanted just territorial autonomy within the Russian republic.

After the Bolsheviks in Petrograd seized power in November 1917, the Rada announced the creation of the Ukrainian People's Republic (UNR, its Ukrainian acronym) and claimed supreme authority over the nine Ukrainian provinces of the Russian empire.[17] In the Ukrainian lands of the Austro-Hungarian empire, an independent Ukrainian state, the West Ukrainian People's Republic (commonly referred to by its Ukrainian acronym – ZUNR), was proclaimed in Lviv in November 1918, and united with the UNR in Kyiv in January 1919.[18] Over the next three years, a struggle for Ukraine unfolded within the broader context of civil war in the former Russian empire, marked by varying support and dynamics of Ukrainian nation-building across different parts of Ukraine and in big cities populated by non-Ukrainians and the predominantly Ukrainian countryside. A Ukrainian state in the form of a national republic managed to survive in different configurations until 1920.[19] The short-lived state was recognized by 25 countries and accepted into several international organizations before it was crushed by the armies of Soviet Russia and allied militias.[20]

These historical developments of the early twentieth century have been similarly questioned in debates over entangled history. Was the brief Ukrainian statehood a fleeting and unfortunate civil conflict within a single community, possibly instigated by foreign powers? Or was it the culmination of centuries of struggle against Russian imperial dominance, crushed by the Bolsheviks? In December 1922, the Bolshevik leadership in Moscow decided to create a federation of "national" republics. The 1923 implementation of the union brought together Russia, Ukraine, Belorussia, and Transcaucasia to form the Union of Soviet Socialist Republics (the Soviet Union, or USSR). In the 1920s, a policy known as *korenizatsia* (indigenization) was pursued in the USSR. In Ukraine this program was known as Ukrainization, which entailed promotion of Ukrainian language and culture and cultivation of local cadres for the Communist Party and Soviet state institutions. Its strategic goal was to legitimize the authority of the Communist Party of Ukraine by attracting the local population.[21]

Almost exactly a century later, Putin would present the formation of the Ukrainian republic as Lenin's folly, and Ukrainization policies as the creation of a Ukrainian nation out of nothing, if not the outright brainwashing of Russian people to believe themselves to be Ukrainians. In reality, historians have shown that the Bolshevik leadership recognized the actual and latent strength of Ukrainian national feelings, having had to fight the Ukrainian national movement that managed to mobilize hundreds of thousands of troops to die for their country – Ukraine – only several years prior. Ukrainization overall turned out to be highly successful. Publications and cultural institutions using the Ukrainian language flourished and, by the late 1920s, three-quarters of students attended schools where Ukrainian was the language of instruction.[22] There was also resistance to Ukrainization, which made implementation challenging and uneven, and the Communist Party leadership didn't have full trust in the policy.[23] The Bolshevik leadership in Moscow and Stalin personally started to fear that the policy was bolstering Ukrainian nationalism, which they viewed as a threat to Soviet rule, and Moscow reversed course.

The 1920s were followed by decades of mass repressions, deportations, famines, and Russification perpetuated by Moscow against the Ukrainians. In 1932–1933, Ukraine and other grain-producing regions of the USSR such as the northern Caucasus, the Volga region, the southern Urals, western Siberia, and Kazakhstan were devastated by famine brought by the forced collectivization campaign launched by Stalin in the late 1920s. The Soviet leadership deemed that to ensure the survival of the communist regime in a hostile capitalist global environment, twin policies of industrialization and collectivization were necessary. Industrialization, a government-funded and state-run program to increase industrial production, was of central importance, and its success was in turn dependent on collectivization. State-run collective farms were to be created. These were expected to be more efficient economically, able to feed the growing cities more reliably under state control, and produce grain to be sold abroad for hard currency necessary to fund industrialization.

The creation of collective farms necessitated peasants returning back to the state the livestock and land plots the state had distributed to them after the 1917 Bolshevik revolution to win their support for the Bolshevik cause. The peasants resisted dispossession, and the state responded with mass repression to enforce the policy.[24] After a wave of peasant uprisings in the Ukrainian countryside in 1930, up to 75,000 families were deported to Kazakhstan and Siberia.[25] As peasants continued to resist collectivization, the authorities accused the peasants of sabotage to starve the cities and undermine industrialization. Ukraine was singled out for particularly harsh treatment as it was critical for the fulfillment of the regime's economic plans: historically a breadbasket, it produced 27% of Soviet grain.[26]

Ruthless collectivization in Ukraine began in the fall of 1930 and included measures such as unrealistically high grain delivery quotas, confiscation of all grain produced by individual farmers, including seed stock, and almost complete confiscation of all produce from the collective farms. State policy brought mass starvation to Ukraine already by early 1932 but, after the Ukrainian Communist Party leadership described the growing starvation in their letters to Stalin and asked him to provide Ukraine with relief, Stalin denied the reality of the famine and banned the word itself from correspondence.[27] In the second half of 1932 and into 1933, the famine was aggravated further by Moscow policies when Stalin came to attribute the failure to extract unrealistically high procurement quotas from starving peasants, not only to peasant resistance but to covert resistance on the part of the Communist Party of Ukraine. In Ukraine, unlike in other famine-affected areas of the USSR, the state interpreted failures of collectivization not only through the lens of class struggle but also through an ethnonationalist lens, and blamed Ukrainian nationalism for standing in the way of collectivization's success.

In his August 1932 letter to Lazar Kaganovich, whom Stalin put in charge of implementing collectivization in Ukraine, Stalin spoke of the Ukrainian Communist Party being full of "committed and latent Petliurites" (supporters of Symon Petliura, one of the leaders of the short-lived independent Ukrainian republic of 1917–1920), and "outright agents of Piłsudski" (Józef Piłsudski was the Polish minister of defense and earlier, the president). Stalin's letter spelled out a plan for avoiding the "loss" of Ukraine and turning it into "a real fortress of the USSR, a truly model republic."[28] In December 1932, a Politburo meeting on grain procurement attacked the Ukrainian party leadership. Thousands of Ukrainian party officials were dismissed and arrested, Ukrainization policies were halted, and an attack on the Ukrainian cultural intelligentsia followed. The physical elimination of the Ukrainian cultural intelligentsia by the Stalin regime would later be named the "Executed Renaissance."

In December 1932, Stalin sent two top Soviet officials to Ukraine to ensure that the unrealistic grain procurement quotas would be met. The authorities cut off supplies of all goods and confiscated not only grain but also anything else that could be used for food from villages that didn't meet their quotas. By the spring of 1933, death from starvation became a mass phenomenon.[29] Overall, out of the six to seven million victims of the famine in grain-producing regions of the Soviet Union between 1930 and 1933, 3.5m to 3.8m died in Ukraine,[30] with the death toll being the highest in late spring and early summer of 1933 when food supplies completely ran out.

As millions were dying from starvation, Soviet authorities went to great lengths to conceal and deny the famine's occurrence – even refusing offers of foreign aid – determined as they were to promote the USSR as a socialist paradise abroad. Nevertheless, efforts to raise awareness of the famine and to advocate for international intervention were undertaken, including by Ukrainians living outside the USSR and conscientious foreigners such as journalists, diplomats, and businessmen on assignment in the USSR who witnessed famine conditions. Many such accounts asserted that the famine was a man-made phenomenon and not a largely unintended outcome of Stalin's modernization drive, and that in the Ukrainian SSR the famine was aimed at punishing the Ukrainians.[31]

The tragic developments of the 1930s have been questioned in debates over entangled history. Most historians today agree that the famine was a man-made phenomenon and in Ukraine had a clear "ethnonational coloration,"[32] although historians continue to debate whether the ethnonational element in Soviet collectivization policies in Ukraine makes the 1932–1933 famine a premediated act of genocide against Ukraine and its people. As we discuss in Chapter 3, in the post-Soviet period Ukraine and Russia would clash over interpretations of the 1932–1933 famine, with this clash being one of the key examples of divergence between the two states in identity politics.

Until USSR's victory over Nazi Germany in WWII, millions of Ukrainians lived outside of Soviet Ukraine – most of them, some 5.9 million – in interwar Poland in historic Galicia. More than a million others lived in their historic lands in what used to be the Austro-Hungarian empire and what in the interwar period became Poland, Romania, and Czechoslovakia. After ZUNR armies were defeated by the Polish armies at the end of 1919, Ukrainians in Galicia formed several underground Ukrainian political and military movements. From the 1920s and ultimately into the early 1950s some of these movements fought against Poland, Nazi Germany, and later the Soviet Union with the goal of creating a non-Soviet independent Ukrainian state. Two of these organizations, the Organization of Ukrainian Nationalists (OUN) and its military wing, the Ukrainian Insurgent Army (UPA), would later become a focal point of the debate about entangled history.[33] For a period of time the OUN collaborated with Nazi Germany, hoping for German support for an independent Ukrainian state that never came. Some members of the OUN and the UPA participated in the Holocaust and the killing and ethnic cleansing of Poles. But, as historians point out, the prosecution of fascist collaborators in the Soviet Union was "massively politicized and used to detain all kinds of political enemies," and, in the case of Ukrainian nationalists in western Ukraine, "whether or not a person had committed war crimes often mattered less … than membership in or support of an anti-Soviet movement."[34] Within the "organic unity of Russia and Ukraine" paradigm, the cardinal sin of the OUN and the UPA was not blood crimes against civilians committed by their members but their fight against the Soviet Union and their goal to establish an independent Ukrainian state. For the USSR and later Russia, these groups and their leaders – most notably Stepan Bandera, leader of one of the two factions of the OUN, who was assassinated by a KGB agent in Munich in 1959 – would remain first and foremost traitors of the Soviet state. However, within the paradigm that emphasized the distinctiveness of the Ukrainian nation and its centuries-long national-liberation struggle, the OUN and the UPA could be presented first and foremost as fighters for Ukrainian independence. As we show in Chapter 3, in the post-Soviet period the dispute between Russia and Ukraine over the "correct" way to characterize these groups would become another key issue in the divergence between the two states in identity politics.

WWII ended with Soviet victory, accomplished with the efforts of more than seven million Ukrainians who fought in the Soviet army.[35] Of the Soviet Union's wartime losses of some 26.6 million, Ukraine lost up to seven million people – more than 15% of its population. Approximately 700 cities and towns and 28,000 villages lay in ruin, ten million of the 36 million remaining population were homeless, and Ukraine's industrial base was devastated by the fighting between the Soviet and German armies, Soviet scorched earth tactics, and the deindustrialization policies of the Germans.[36] As the Allies decided the fate and borders of post-war Europe, Stalin insisted on extending USSR's borders west. Ukrainian-inhabited territories in interwar Poland (eastern Galicia and Volhynia), Romania (northern Bukovyna and parts of Bessarabia), and Czechoslovakia (Transcarpathia) with some eleven million inhabitants were added to Soviet Ukraine. For the first time in history, the vast majority of ethnic Ukrainian-inhabited lands, as defined by Ukrainian scholars, were within the borders of a single, albeit Soviet, Ukrainian state.[37] The post-war map of Europe would make Soviet Ukraine look like one of the main beneficiaries of the war, but Ukraine was also one of the war's main victims.

The last four decades of the USSR, from the 1950s through the 1980s, also have competing characterizations. According to the "organic unity" paradigm, Ukraine was benefiting from modernization, development, and even international prestige now that it occupied its rightful place as a "younger brother" in a union with Russia – a junior partner who faithfully followed Russia's lead. Membership in a common state brought economic development after wartime devastation. Soviet Ukraine became one of the 51 founding members of the United Nations and had its own Permanent Mission to the UN, where it was represented as nominally distinct from the Soviet Union. It was a member of numerous UN agencies and signatory to over 120 international treaties.[38] The Soviet government even "gifted" Crimea to Ukraine in 1954. In short, Ukraine could not possibly have any complaints against the Soviet state.

But an alternative interpretation of post-WWII reality in Ukraine is equally plausible. The imposition of Soviet rule on western Ukraine brought mass repression. More than ninety thousand nationalist rebels were killed and over 200,000 people – family members and alleged supporters of "Ukrainian nationalists" – were deported to Siberia. Khrushchev later claimed that Stalin wanted to deport all Ukrainians as an unreliable ethnic group but there were too many of them.[39] The Ukrainian Greek Catholic Church (UGCC), the national church of Galician Ukrainians, was destroyed – its bishops imprisoned and the church "reunited" with the Russian Orthodox Church (ROC) at a staged council in 1946. Ukraine's membership in the UN was Stalin's strategic move to add an extra vote in the organization to the Soviet bloc, and the nominally separate Ukrainian representation had no authority to decide anything without the approval of the Soviet government in Moscow. The transfer of the Crimean peninsula to Ukraine was not a "gift" but a calculated move by Moscow, given that Crimea was tied to Ukraine by its economy and water supply and the Soviet Ukrainian government was given the task to revive Crimea's post-war economy. Ukraine also suffered from intense Russification in the 1970s and 1980s, leading to the disappearance of the Ukrainian language from many of its urban centers. By the end of 1970s, more than half of school-age children attended Russian-language schools, up from 30% in 1958. Large cities such as Kharkiv, Odesa, and Donetsk didn't have a single Ukrainian school.[40] By the late 1980s, only 40% of Ukrainians used Ukrainian as their language of convenience.[41] Those who dared voice concerns about Russification suffered repression. A Ukrainian dissident movement first formed during the period of cultural liberalization and somewhat relaxed ideological control in the 1960s during Khrushchev's reforms.[42] After Khrushchev's ouster, the Communist Party cracked down on the dissidents and, in the 1970s and 1980s, the Ukrainian dissident movement was the one most severely repressed by the KGB. According to the Moscow Helsinki Group, by the early 1980s Ukrainian dissidents constituted the largest single group of political prisoners in the USSR, more than the much more numerous ethnic Russians, while another study estimated that Ukrainians accounted for between 60 and 70% of political prisoners in some Gulag camps.[43]

The perestroika and glasnost reforms, started by Soviet leader Mikhail Gorbachev in the second half of the 1980s, had major consequences for Ukraine. Gorbachev's reforms created opportunities for political mobilization from below, and several political organizations and movements were formed to express grievances over Ukraine's treatment by Moscow. The ecological movement formed in the wake of the Chornobyl (Chernobyl) nuclear power plant disaster was the first, followed by the Ukrainian Helsinki Union in 1988, and the Society for the Protection of Ukrainian Language in 1989. Dissidents released from Soviet gulags and a new generation of Ukrainian intellectuals considered Ukrainian language and culture – the very foundations of the Ukrainian nation – to be under threat due to the Russification policies of the preceding decades. The narrative of Ukraine as a victim of Russian and Soviet imperialism though history, which pre-perestroika would send one to the Gulag, was now entering public discourse. In the summer of 1989, the People's Movement of Ukraine for perestroika (popularly known as Rukh) was born. It adopted a liberal-democratic, pro-Western, and anti-communist ideology. Rukh initially advocated for greater autonomy and cultural rights for Ukraine but, already in October 1990, during its second congress, Rukh dropped the word perestroika from the organization's name and declared as its primary goal the achievement of independence for Ukraine.[44]

Gorbachev's reforms also had a major impact on the Ukrainian Communist Party, as they undermined the loyalty and shared interests between party leaders in Kyiv and Moscow. Gorbachev and reformers in Moscow were encouraging democratic movements in the republics, and the Ukrainian Communist Party, staunchly conservative even by Soviet standards, felt threatened by mass protests. Gorbachev's personnel policies also closed the long-standing pipeline that was bringing Ukrainian functionaries to Moscow and making them influential there.[45] This made the Ukrainian party elites feel "betrayed, abandoned, and angry. The center was now bringing them nothing but trouble."[46]

The dual dynamic of pro-sovereignty mobilization and dissatisfaction of the Ukrainian communist elites with Gorbachev's policies would soon lead to a split within the Ukrainian Communist Party, and ultimately would result in a grand bargain between the national-democrats and a part of the formerly communist elites that will be discussed later in this chapter. Within this grand bargain, the leadership of independent Ukraine would commit to a national identity conception that saw Ukraine as a distinct nation rather than a "younger brother" of Russia or its constituent part and would support independent statehood. A critical step in the process that led to the split of the Ukrainian communists and the emergence of the grand bargain were the March 1990 elections – the first competitive elections held in the Soviet Union for the local councils and legislatures (Supreme Soviets) of the fifteen Soviet republics. Unlike in the Baltic republics, Ukrainian pro-sovereignty forces did not win a majority in the Ukrainian republic's parliament (Verkhovna Rada). Rukh-supported candidates secured about 25% of the seats, virtually all of them won in the races held in the west of Ukraine and in Kyiv.[47] But the presence of a sizeable group of pro-democratic and pro-sovereignty deputies in the parliament, which itself became the new locus of political power in Ukraine, dramatically changed the strategic calculus of Ukraine's communist majority in the Rada and led many of them to side with the pro-sovereignty movement.

Until the failure of the anti-Gorbachev coup in August 1991, the Ukrainian Communist Party nomenklatura would not openly challenge the leadership in Moscow but, after the 1990 elections, Ukraine's communists *de facto* split between hard-liners, who wanted to return to the pre-Gorbachev status quo, and pro-sovereignty communists, who wanted political and economic autonomy for Ukraine. Most of the pro-sovereignty communists were motivated not by an awakened sense of nationalism. Instead, they wanted to preserve their power in an environment where their political standing was simultaneously challenged by the weakening hold of the Communist Party in Moscow and the rapidly growing national-democratic movements in the republic that challenged local communist elites from below. One such pro-sovereignty communist was Leonid Kravchuk, a 56-year-old second secretary of the Ukrainian Communist Party, originally from western Ukraine, who made a career as a party ideologue specializing in the national question. In July 1990, Kravchuk was elected speaker of the Ukrainian parliament and, in the run-up to the Soviet collapse, he would prove highly skillful in maneuvering between national democrats and communists in Ukraine and powerful figures in Moscow, such as Gorbachev and Yeltsin. Kravchuk would adopt delaying tactics on the union treaty that Gorbachev wanted to sign to keep the common state from disintegrating, would outmaneuver Yeltsin who, after emerging as the most powerful figure in Russia following the abortive anti-Gorbachev August 1991 coup, was interested in preserving the Soviet Union with Ukraine in it rather than ending it – developments we analyze in Chapter 4, which discusses the Russo-Ukrainian relationship after independence.

A new page in the Russo-Ukrainian relationship

The dissolution of the Soviet Union in December 1991 opened a new page in Russian–Ukrainian relations, now formally independent sovereign states. From the very beginning, different visions of a future relationship formed in Kyiv and in Moscow. On December 8, 1991, the leaders of Russia, Ukraine, and Belarus met at the Belavezha forest in Belarus and formally dissolved the USSR. At the same meeting they formed the Commonwealth of Independent States (CIS), but Russian and Ukrainian leaders saw the future of the CIS very differently. Kravchuk, elected Ukrainian president on December 1, called it a means toward a "civilized divorce." But Russian leaders did not see the separation of Ukraine from Russia as inevitably final nor the CIS as mere window dressing of an otherwise decisive parting of ways. In the waning months of the USSR, as Yeltsin found himself in a position to take over the union and its institutions, reformers in Yeltsin's government expected that once Russia instituted successful economic reforms, other republics would rally to it and the union could be reconstituted.[48]

In the early 1990s, hopes for reintegration did not seem far-fetched. After all, earlier attempts at independent Ukrainian statehood proved to be short-lived, unlike the centuries-long reality of Russia and Ukraine being one polity. Ukraine and Russia were deeply connected economically within the highly centralized Soviet economic system, family and cultural ties ran deep, and the narrative of historical unity and common destiny perpetuated by the state during the tsarist and the Soviet times was ubiquitous. Even the overwhelming vote in favor of the Declaration of Independence during the December 1, 1991

Table 1.1 December 1991 independence referendum vote in Ukraine, and ethnic Russians and Russian-speakers in Ukraine's regions, 1989 vs. 2001

Region	*% yes vote for independence (Dec 1991 referendum)*	*% ethnic Russians (census data)*		*% Russian speakers (census data)*	
		1989	**2001**	**1989**	**2001**
West					
Chernivtsi	92.8	6.7	4.1	10.5	5.3
Ivano-Frankivsk	98.4	4	1.8	4.8	1.8
Khmelnytsky	96.3	5.8	3.6	8	4.1
Lviv	97.5	7.9	3.6	7.9	3.8
Rivne	96.0	4.6	2.6	5.6	2.7
Ternopil	98.7	2.3	1.2	2.5	1.2
Volyn	96.3	4.4	2.4	5.1	2.5
Zakarpattia	92.6	4	2.5	5	2.9
Center					
Cherkasy	96.0	8	5.4	10.3	6.7
Chernihiv	92.8	6.8	5	13.6	10.3
Kirovohrad	93.9	11.7	7.5	15.1	10
Kyiv City	92.9	20.9	13.9	41.1	25.3
Kyiv region	95.5	8.7	6	10.9	7.2
Poltava	94.9	10.2	7.2	13.2	9.5
Sumy	92.6	13.3	9.4	21.4	15.6
Vinnytsia	95.4	5.9	3.8	8.6	4.7
Zhytomyr	95.1	7.9	5	10.1	6.6
East					
Dnipropetrovsk	90.4	24.2	17.6	37.2	31.9
Donetsk	83.9	43.6	38.2	67.7	74.9
Kharkiv	86.3	33.2	25.6	48.1	44.3
Luhansk	83.9	44.8	39	73.7	68.8
Zaporizhzhia	90.7	32	24.7	48.8	48.2
South					
Crimea	54.2	65.6	58.3	82.4	78.8
Kherson	90.1	20.2	14.1	30.4	24.9
Mykolaiv	89.5	19.4	14.1	33.8	29.3
Odesa	85.4	27.4	20.7	47.1	41.9
Ukraine total	**92.3**	**22.1**	**17.3**	**32.8**	**29.6**

Notes: Russian-speakers refers to those who indicated Russians as their mother tongue (*ridna mova/rodnoi iazyk*) on the census.

Source: Central Electoral Commission of Ukraine, official results (for 1991 independence referendum). 1989 Soviet Census and 2001 Ukrainian Census. 1991 referendum: https://old.archives.gov.ua/Sections/15r-V_Ref/index.php?11. 1989 and 2001 % ethnic Russians: http://2001.ukrcensus.gov.ua/eng/results/general/nationality/. 1989 and 2001 % Russian speakers: Iefimov, S. 2010. "Kuda ischezli russkiie, ili 'soobshchaiushchiesia sosudy' etnoiazykovoi samoidentifikatsii naselenia Ukrainy: 1989–2001," *Ukrainskyi sotsiolohichnyi zhurnal*, 3–4, 86–92.

referendum in Ukraine (90.3% in favor, with 84.2% turnout) could be interpreted as a vote for something other than full separation from Russia.

Not all residents of the Ukrainian republic who voted in favor were motivated by a desire for national revival. Polls conducted one month before the referendum found that 79% of voters saw "escape from economic crisis" as the top priority, 63% "stabilization of the economy and better standards of living," while only 21% listed "the cultural rebirth of Ukraine" and 18% "the securing of political sovereignty of the republic."[49] After the Ukrainian independence referendum, Yeltsin and the Russian leadership recognized the Soviet Union's dissolution as inevitable in the circumstances of the time, but that did not make them see Ukraine's independence as either desirable or irreversible. That Ukrainians would "come to their senses" and rejoin Russia, in one way or another, sooner rather than later, was both a desire and a belief of many in the Russian leadership at the time. To understand why such belief was widespread and deeply held in Russia, including among reformers supporting Yeltsin, one needs to understand how identity politics, to which we now turn, was a formidable obstacle to accepting Ukrainian independence.

Competing visions of the Russian nation

As any new state, post-Soviet Russia had to define the boundaries and membership in the nation, which in the world of nation-states gives legitimacy to the state itself. Most newly independent states that emerged from the USSR's disintegration were far from ideal nation-states where, in the terms of a seminal theorist of nationalism, the boundaries of the nation are "congruent" with the borders of the state.[50] The multinational character of the USSR, Soviet policies of both fostering and suppressing national identities throughout its seventy-year history, problems created by hitherto largely meaningless internal boundaries of Soviet republics in December 1991, overnight becoming international borders separating sovereign states, all made the question "who are we, the people" highly complex for all Soviet successor states.

For post-Soviet Russia this question was especially vexing. History of a land empire – Russian and later Soviet – meant that the post-Soviet Russian state saw its "historic" territory shrink back to its seventeenth-century size. Ethnic Russians, treated as "imperial glue" by the tsars and the communists alike and called to serve the cause of the empire, had a weaker sense of ethnic identity and, in the Soviet era, more readily associated themselves with the Soviet state rather than with the Russian republic. With 25 million ethnic Russians (nearly one-fifth of all ethnic Russians in the USSR) and another ten million Russian-speakers left outside of the new Russian state by the Soviet collapse, the question of their belonging to the Russian nation and the Russian state's obligation toward them loomed large. The independence of Ukraine and Belarus from Russia was an additional major shock, given the long-standing narrative of common origin and continuity of fate of the three eastern Slavic "brotherly" peoples. With the question "who are we, the people" having no one obvious answer for Russia, five broad nation-building projects competed in the public arena – often, as one scholar put it, "in the minds of the same politicians, creating inconsistencies in their views."[51] Although these competing nation-building imaginaries had important differences, only one of these imaginaries was prepared to accept full separation of Ukraine and Russia, and this identity project – imagining Russia as a nation-state within its existing borders – would prove to be short-lived.

The first way to define the nation was by the territory of the former Soviet Union. The vision of the entire USSR as a "true" Russian state has a long history, and the collapse of the USSR became not only a political but also a psychological shock to those in Russia who had internalized such supranational identity. This group included not only communists, who lamented that Russia in its 1991 borders was a "stump of its true self,"[52] but also many who supported Yeltsin during the perestroika years. These reformers sought to dismantle communism but withdrew their support after the USSR collapsed and blamed Yeltsin for it, as they neither anticipated nor wanted the dissolution of the common state. Regarding Ukraine, this way of imagining "true" Russia upheld the narrative of existential unity of Russians and Ukrainians who, together with Belarusians, constituted the "nucleus" of the historic Russian state defined by the territory of the former Soviet Union. Another version of the national imaginary that equated "true" Russia with most of the territory and population of the former USSR was neo-Eurasianism. A successor to the doctrine of Eurasianism born among Russian emigre circles during the interwar period, neo-Eurasianism saw Russia not as a nation-state but as a supra-national civilization. The central tenets of this ideology emphasized Russia's messianic role in the world, its moral superiority to the Anglo-Saxon civilization, and its great power status, and advocated an imperial structure and authoritarian rule at home as the most natural forms of politics.[53]

Two other national identity conceptions that defined the nation as extending past the 1991 borders of the Russian Federation and including Ukraine conceptualized the nation as a community of eastern Slavs, or as a community of Russian speakers. The eastern Slavic conception of the nation also has a long usable past, given that both the tsarist-era and the Soviet-era official historiographies promoted the idea that Russians, Ukrainians, and Belarusians were three "branches" of the same nation, with common origins in the Kyivan Rus'. This narrative also had strong popular support in the post-Soviet period. In a November 2005 poll carried out by the Levada center, 81% of Russians agreed with the "three branches of one nation" conception, while only 17% believed each group was a different nation. The idea of the nation as a community of Russian-speakers also had strong popular resonance. Polls show that the Russian public understood "Russianness" much more in cultural and linguistic than in narrowly ethnic or racial terms. In a February 1995 poll by the Public Opinion Foundation (VTSIOM) that asked about characteristics necessary to be considered a Russian (*russkii*), 80% named native fluency in Russian as a criterion, while only 22% named Russian physical appearance and 24% named "ethnic Russian" passport entry.[54]

Both of these visions – "true" Russia as a nation of eastern Slavs or as a nation of Russian speakers – raised questions about the place of non-Slavic groups living in Russia within the nation. There was ambiguity over whether the language-based definition of the nation was purely about linguistic fluency or ultimately about being Slavic. As one newspaper summed up the dilemma, "if someone speaks Russian but is black, can this person be our compatriot?"[55] The answer was hardly a resounding yes, and "Russian-speaker" was essentially a euphemism (and a preference) for Russian-speaking Slavs. Debates over just who qualified as a "Russian-speaker" did not question the inclusion of Ukraine, however, since Russian-speaking Ukrainians were the "ideal" candidates – and arguably the main target – of this conceptualization of the "true" Russian nation.

The fourth way to imagine the Russian nation was as a community of ethnic Russians (*russkie*). This identity project posited that the Russian state must recognize ethnic Russians as the most important group, acknowledge special obligations to ethnic Russians both inside and outside of Russia's borders, and ultimately take measures to bring the "divided nation" together. Proponents of this national identity conception downplay ethnic diversity of Russia, stressing instead that ethnic Russians constitute more than 80% of the population, which makes the state monoethnic rather than multi-ethnic. This narrative also sees Russians as the main victims of the state policies during the communist period, when ethnic Russians purportedly sponsored the development of other ethnic groups while remaining institutionally underprivileged themselves. In the post-Soviet period, ethnic Russians also were seen as remaining in an underprivileged position within the structure of Russian federalism that benefited ethnic minorities.[56]

Various groups of ethnic nationalists with whom the Russian state had a complicated relationship, ranging from strategic alliance to periodic suppression, have advocated this identity project. Some of these groups' ideas, such as the creation of a designated territorial homeland for ethnic Russians within the structure of Russian federalism, never received state backing, but demands to officially recognize ethnic Russians as the most important ethnic group found their reflection in state documents under both Yeltsin and Putin. The 1996 Concept of State Nationalities Policy highlighted the "unifying role" of ethnic Russians in the state-building project, and the 2012 State Strategy on Nationalities Policy described ethnic Russians as historically serving as the "system forming core" (*sistemoobrazuiushcheie jadro*). As far as Ukraine was concerned, ethnic understanding of the Russian nation – while narrower than the Soviet, east Slavic, or language-based alternatives – still had a way to include Ukraine, on the logic that Ukrainians were not a distinct ethnic group but a sub-ethnicity of the greater Russian ethnic group.[57] Thus, whether Ukrainians were a "brotherly" but separate ethnic group or a sub-ethnicity of the Russian ethnos, their belonging in the "true" Russian national imaginary was mostly beyond dispute.

The final ideational construct was the nation defined by the borders of the Russian Federation. This definition of the nation as a civic political community of state's citizens united by the territory of the state and loyalty to the state's political institutions was without historical precedent. As such, this conception of the Russian nation was a monumental intellectual and political project, which required Russia, to quote one scholar, "to secede from itself, to create a new identity based on the denial of the Soviet past, … to fall into emptiness [and] start its history from a blank slate."[58] This way of imagining the nation was developed by liberal intellectuals and experts during the early years of the Yeltsin presidency. A different word in Russian was used to describe this civic Russian nation – *rossiiskii* rather than *russkii.*

From the very beginning, the civic nation-building project encountered challenges. For one, the *rossiiskii* conception was ambiguous about whether the *rossiiskaya* nation was supposed to be a community of fellow citizens with various ethnic identities or a community of ethnic groups, with ethnic Russians being of higher status than other nations by virtue of playing a "unifying role" and serving as the "basis of statehood."[59] The place of Russians and Russian-speakers outside of Russia, including in Ukraine, was another major dilemma. Defining the nation as a political community within the boundaries of the existing state would exclude millions of Russians – over eleven million of them in Ukraine, according to the last Soviet census – by virtue of them being outside of Russia and being citizens of other post-Soviet states.[60] Such abandonment was not a popular proposal in the context of the geopolitical and psychological shock brought by the USSR collapse and in light of competing conceptions of the Russian nation, all of which offered a broader definition of the Russian nation, to include at least some if not all Russians and Russian-speakers in the former Soviet republics. A commitment to civic nation-building within Russia would have freed Ukraine and Russia from each other, but implementing this identity project was a major challenge.

Identity politics and imperialization

If Russia pursued civic nation-building rooted in the definition of "true" Russia as a political community of the state's citizens, united by the territory of the existing state and loyal to the state's political institutions, Russia's identity project would not have clashed with Ukraine's, since it could have coexisted with the idea of Ukraine as a nation and polity distinct and separate from Russia. Civic nation-building was attempted in Russia in the early 1990s, but from the start it had to compete with alternative ideational constructs, all of which saw Ukraine as in some way a part of "true" Russia. The reasons for the ultimate failure of civic nation-building, which in turn enabled imperialization, were different in different periods in Russia's post-Soviet history. In the 1990s, the failure of this identity project had to do with the larger context of a political struggle between Yeltsin and his communist and nationalist opponents in the parliament. Unlike the communists and nationalists, Russian liberals paid relatively little attention to the national question, prioritizing instead economic and political reforms, with a general expectation that if these reforms succeeded, the national question would solve itself.[61] The collapse of the USSR, conflict over market reforms and over divisions of power between the executive and the legislature locked Yeltsin and the legislature into a bitter power struggle as soon as the USSR ceased to exist. In this conflict each side tried to strengthen their legitimacy by claiming to represent the Russian nation better.

The Russian communists and nationalists, who dominated the Russian legislature in the early 1990s, lamented the dissolution of the USSR and the partition of the "true" Russian nation. They seized the mantle of defenders of a "divided nation" and called for the undoing of the "tragedy" of USSR disintegration brought about by reformers such as Yeltsin. Even though Yeltsin ultimately prevailed in his struggle with the legislature, after ordering tanks to shell the parliament and violently resolving the constitutional crisis in the fall of 1993, after the December 1993 elections, he was again faced with a large communist–nationalist opposition in parliament. The opposition defined the "true" Russian nation either by the borders of the former USSR, as a community of eastern Slavs, or as a community of the Russian-speakers of the former USSR. In a symbolic vote, in March 1996 the Russian legislature overwhelmingly voted to annul the Belavezha Accords, which had dissolved the USSR. Civic identity and state and nation-building limited by the borders of the Russian Federation had little appeal for Yeltsin's opponents.

Scholars have characterized Yeltsin-era policies as moving, under nationalist–communist pressure, from an emphasis on civic *rossiiskii* nation-building in 1991–1992 toward a more cultural and imperial vision of Russia.[62] Speaking for the Russians and Russian-speakers throughout the former USSR was the first step in this direction. Already in his 1994 New Year address, Yeltsin spoke of Russians and Russian-speakers in the former Soviet republics as "compatriots" and an "inseparable" part of the Russian nation. The second half of the 1990s saw an increased rhetoric, not just from the nationalists and communists but also from the Yeltsin camp, about reasserting Russia's influence and power in the post-Soviet region. In December 1994, Yeltsin started a war against Chechnya to crush the Chechen independence movement by force. The war's failures would soon prove to be an embarrassment for the Russian government and would feed into a growing sense of Russia's humiliation about the loss of its former status and influence. Restoring Russia's "rightful" role – controlling at least the post-Soviet states if not the outer reaches of the communist block – was growing in importance. In 1995, in a survey of Russian elites that asked them to state their preferences regarding the territorial status of Ukraine in regard to Russia, 65% favored unification of Russia and Ukraine into a single country.[63] In Russia, the post-Soviet region came to be referred to as "near abroad," distinguishing the post-Soviet states from "truly" foreign "far abroad" states. The "near abroad" concept connoted a diminished type of sovereignty – these countries were "abroad" from Russia technically, but were not quite as foreign as other foreign states. Designation of a truly foreign (*zarubezhny*) state was reserved only for states outside of the former Soviet Union, while the "near abroad" term implied that oversight by Russia would continue.

During the 1996 presidential campaign, Yeltsin promised to strengthen both the CIS and Slavic integration and, after his re-election to a second term, the presidential administration further embraced the notion that Russia had special interests in the former Soviet space. Even liberal members of the government began to refer to the possibility of reviving some form of a union. In May 1996, two members of the Presidential Council published a paper in a large daily newspaper claiming that the revival of the union was feasible and necessary for Russia.[64] A year later, the presidents of Russia and Belarus signed a charter on a union between the two countries that provided, among other things, for union citizenship. Russia would seek a similar arrangement with Ukraine, but without success.

Throughout the first two Putin terms (2000–2004, 2004–2008) and the Medvedev presidency (2008–2012), the narrative that the "true" Russian nation extended past the borders of the existing Russian state saw further development, with state backing. This trajectory has been aptly described as "narrowing in and widening up" to capture the following simultaneous process. The special importance of ethnic Russians (*russkie*) in the Russian state was increasingly emphasized, which "narrowed" state identity relative to the civic (*rossiiskii*) conception of the nation. At the same time, Russianness was conceptualized in cultural and civilizational terms, thus "widening up" the rhetorical expansion of the Russian nation into the territories of the former Soviet republics.[65]

The "narrowing in" ethnic turn in domestic policies began to unfold already during Putin's first term and continued during his second term. Measures were passed, such as the merger of some ethnically designated autonomous ethnic minority regions with their majority Russian neighbors, the end of popular elections to positions of regional governors and presidents of ethnic republics, a shift to Russian monolingualism in education in ethnic minority regions, and the ban on non-Cyrillic alphabets for Russian ethnic minorities. This produced rapid linguistic Russification. If in 2002 all ten largest ethnic minorities had at least two-thirds titular language proficiency, by 2010 only five of the ten did.[66] In a historic reversal of a decades-long trend, the 2010 census showed the share of ethnic Russians in the population rising for the first time since 1979, leading some scholars to conclude that Russia was transforming into an "assimilationist nation-state."[67]

Putin's January 2012 article on the national question published in the run-up to the March presidential elections, which was followed later the same year by the adoption of a "State Strategy on Nationalities Policy for the Period Through 2025," also illustrated this ethnic turn in domestic nation-building. In his article, Putin singled out ethnic Russians for a special role within the Russian state project, characterized them as "the state-forming nation,"[68] and declared Russianness to be the ethno-cultural core of the state. The state was still described as a "multi-ethnic country," but Putin argued that Russians are a "state-forming people," whose "great mission" is to "unite and bind" Russia, which in turn was defined as a "unique civilization" to which traditional notions of the nation-state do not apply.[69] The December 2012 State Strategy on Nationalities Policy singled out ethnic Russians (*russkii narod*) as historically playing the "system forming core" of the Russian state.[70]

The "widening up" of Russianness – the definition of *russkii* in cultural and civilizational terms, which extended the "true" Russian nation beyond just ethnic Russians and past the borders of the Russian state – was encapsulated by the Russian World (*Russkii Mir*) concept. The Russian World project followed the "Russian Project" (*russkii*) launched by Putin's United Russia party in 2007 before the legislative elections, with the aim of taking the initiative on speaking for ethnic Russians away from the nationalists.[71] The process of autocratization and imperialization were interconnected and mutually reinforcing. If democratic competition had survived in Russia, alternative national identity conceptions and political forces advocating them would have had a chance to compete for state power. The ethno-civilizational vision of Russia may not have become the dominant one – its proponents could have lost power in the next election cycle, or the conception itself could have undergone moderation in the process of democratic competition of ideas. Instead, coopting nationalist rhetoric, while simultaneously curtailing political competition led the entire Russian regime on a nationalizing path, while disempowering all possible challengers.

Illustrating the dual dynamics of "narrowing in and widening up," United Russia's definition of *russkii* was broadly civilizational, extending to those "who speak and think in Russian and consider themselves belonging to Russian culture."[72] In his annual address to the federal assembly in April 2007, Putin spoke about a "multimillion Russian [*russkii*] world which is, of course, much larger than Russia."[73] In subsequent years, the Russian World concept would become the ideological foundation of Russia's policy toward the neighboring former Soviet states, and the Russian Orthodox Church would become the key ideological champion of this project.[74] The Russian World project was not just an expression of nostalgia for the shared past. It questioned both the legitimacy and desirability of post-Soviet political realities. As articulated by ROC's leader Patriarch Kirill, the Russian World was a fundamental rejection of Ukrainian socio-cultural distinctiveness and the Ukrainian state's legitimacy and permanency. Russia, Ukraine, and Belarus are "all Rus'," the Patriarch declared, and "remain spiritually one nation," while "state borders are an unnecessary obstacle between the peoples of the Russian World."[75]

Despite this growing dual ethnicization and imperialization of Russian identity, there remained a substantial degree of ambiguity over who exactly belonged to the thus defined nation, and who exactly was to be the target of state policies, since competing intellectual constructs of a supranational Russian nation disagreed on the specifics. Was Belarus "in"? Northern Kazakhstan? Other former Soviet territories with large Russian (or Russian-speaking?) populations, such as northern Estonia or Transnistria? All or some parts of Ukraine? Crimea and southern and eastern Ukraine were definitely "in," as was Kyiv, but westernmost Ukraine, especially Galicia, where a substantial part of the population was Greek Catholic rather than Orthodox, perhaps could be left out. But, despite this ambiguity, the Russian World represented an imperial vision and, as Chapters 3, 4, and 6 will discuss, increasingly came to inform Russian policies toward Ukraine in different areas – from foreign relations to historical memory. Russia's growing imperialization ultimately made the prospect of "losing" Ukraine after Euromaidan unthinkable, and would lead to full-scale invasion, after attempts to leverage insurgency in eastern Donbas to control the government in Kyiv failed.

As long as the Russian state remained weak, however, projecting power to realize any of the supranational identity imaginaries was a challenge. In 2000, when Putin took over as president, he presented a program for dealing with the challenges facing Russia, where he outlined three key pillars of Russian resurgence: a strong state, an effective economy, and a consolidation of the "Russian (*rossiiskaia*) idea."[76] Originally the first two were prioritized.[77] The civic territorial definition of the nation better served the goal of strengthening the existing state and avoiding ethnic tensions domestically, but this conception was in perpetual tension with identity conceptions that saw Russians and Russian-speakers in Ukraine and other neighboring states as belonging to the "true" Russian nation and the "Russian World."

All in all, contradictions in the intellectual constructs of the "true" Russian nation made them a challenging – but also a flexible – guide to state policies. Ambiguity as to the exact boundaries of the "true" Russian nation served a functional purpose, as it allowed state elites room to maneuver and pursue different policies, targeting different groups in line with various policy interests domestically and internationally.[78] Indeed, throughout the 1990s and into the 2000s, until Putin's third term, ambiguity was a notable feature of Russia's identity policies. The compatriots law, first adopted in 1999 at the end of Yeltsin's presidency and revised in 2010, offers one of the best legal illustrations of this ambiguity.

The compatriots law envisaged the "true" Russian nation extending past the borders of the Russian state but remained vague on what specific group or groups were included in the thus imagined nation. The law defined compatriots as people living outside Russia, who share "common language, religion, cultural heritage, customs, and traditions" and who "made a free choice in favor of spiritual and cultural connection with Russia." Without conflict with the letter of the law, compatriots could be defined as anyone – narrowly, as just ethnic Russians by descent, or most broadly, to all former Soviet citizens. Ambiguity over the exact boundaries of the "true" Russian nation continued during Putin's third term, although the notion of Russia as a nation-civilization with an ethnic Russian (*russkii*) core was increasingly becoming the dominant identity narrative.[79] In official rhetoric, usage of the term "*russkii*" rather than "*rossiiskii*" became increasingly common, but with *russkii* defining what is Russian, not narrowly in ethnic terms, but broadly in cultural and civilizational terms.[80] With regard to Ukraine, the *russkii* term was applicable to Russians by blood and to Russian-speaking Ukrainians.

Identity politics did not make the invasion of Ukraine preordained. At the same time, as the notion of Russia as a state-civilization, the Russian World, grew in prominence, Ukraine's attempted departure from the Russian World became increasingly hard for Russia to accept or explain away. The civilizational imaginary of Russia was imperial and thus fundamentally incompatible with the conception of Ukraine as a distinct nation pursuing policies of its choosing in an independent Ukrainian state. Post-1991, Ukraine could have imagined itself as a member of the Russian World, which would have avoided the escalatory cycle. If Ukraine had agreed to belong to the Russian World, Russian re-imperialization could have proceeded smoothly and swiftly, in line with the wishes of the Russian leadership. But this is not what happened. To understand why, we need to examine identity politics in Ukraine and how it resulted in Ukraine developing and defending an identity that imagined Ukraine as distinct from, rather than as a natural part of the Russian World.

Competing visions of the Ukrainian nation

Like Russia, newly independent Ukraine faced the challenge of nation-building and had to define the boundaries of the national community underpinning the Ukrainian state. Like in Russia, there were competing conceptions of national identity. Had the Ukrainian political class embraced the one that saw Ukraine and Russia as organically belonging together, conflict with Russia could have been avoided because Ukraine would have willingly submitted to Russian political dominance or even reunification. But Ukraine chose a different path. Why and how did this happen? We start with a summary of competing identity conceptions present in post-Soviet Ukraine.

If Russia had five broad alternative ways to define the nation, Ukraine had two. The first one, which would end up largely guiding state policies after 1991, emphasized Ukraine's distinctiveness as a nation, the historic existence of a sovereign Ukrainian state in various forms, starting from the time of Kyivan Rus', and a centuries-long struggle for stable independent statehood. This conception of the nation saw Ukrainians as an ethnic group that throughout the centuries developed and maintained a language, culture, and religious traditions distinct from their neighbors. Powerful neighbors such as the Polish–Lithuanian Commonwealth and the Russian and Austro-Hungarian empire – and, later in the twentieth century, the USSR and Poland – sought to control the Ukrainian lands, which made Ukrainian history a constant struggle for political autonomy. Given their tumultuous history with Poland, for western Ukrainians Poland has been an important "other." For Ukraine as a whole, however, in the post-Soviet period Russia (imperial, and later Soviet) would be cast as the main "other."[81]

The second national identity conception was profoundly different. It shared much with the eastern Slavic national imaginary that was a key element of the tsarist and later Soviet official historiography, and which remained a central element of the state-backed historical and identity narrative in post-Soviet Russia. This conception was centered around the belief in the common origin and continuity of fate of the three east Slavic peoples (Russians, Ukrainians, and Belarusians). Instead of emphasizing each nation's distinctiveness, Ukrainians and Russians are seen as "two branches of one people" and the Ukrainian nation is imagined as an organic part of the pan-national Slavic–Orthodox "civilization." Championed, as will be discussed below, by the Ukrainian political Left (communists and their allies), this conception of the Ukrainian nation echoed Soviet historiography, which admitted ethnographic and cultural differences between Ukrainians and Russians while insisting on their unity and shared historical and political destiny.

Where the first identity conception saw history as consisting of a series of conflicts between Ukrainians and Russians and Russia seeking to control Ukraine while Ukraine resisted, within the second conception there could be no schism between the two. Both peoples shared descent from the Kyivan Rus' and, after centuries of separation, with Ukrainians "suffering under the yoke" of Lithuanian and Polish domination, the two "brotherly" peoples reunited and reaffirmed their "organic" unity in 1654 with the treaty of Pereiaslav. The formation of the Soviet Union and Ukraine's incorporation into a union state with Russia was a tragedy for the former conception, since it followed the destruction of an independent Ukrainian state that existed in several different forms between 1917 and 1921. Within the latter conception, the Soviet Union, which provided one common political home for the two "brotherly" nations, was the natural political home for Ukrainians. The two competing conceptions of the historical origins and "true" characteristics of the Ukrainian nation and its national identity were thus radically different. To understand why in the post-independence period the Ukrainian state embraced the former rather than the latter – and thus made the nation-building agenda in Ukraine broadly incompatible with all but the civic nation-building option in Russia – the relative political power of competing political forces and their views on the two competing identity projects needs to be considered.

Identity politics and commitment to independence

From the late Soviet period and until the Euromaidan victory in 2014, political competition in Ukraine played out within a threefold division of the political party spectrum. Each political camp featured multiple and often short-lived and poorly developed political parties, so considering broader political camps rather than individual parties is more appropriate. The first camp was the Left, where the unreformed Communist Party of Ukraine (KPU) was the main political force. The Left rejected market capitalism, opposed Western-oriented foreign policy, and embraced the Soviet-era conception of Russians, Ukrainians, and Belarusians as "brotherly peoples" and three "branches" of the same nation. Guided by this conception of the nation, the Left saw Ukraine's future in a union with Russia, whether it took the form of a renewed Soviet Union or some other political arrangement. The Ukrainian Left was thus different from leftist parties in other post-communist states, since it questioned not only state policies from an ideologically leftist standpoint, but also the very legitimacy and desirability of sovereign statehood itself.[82]

Reflecting the idea that "true" sovereignty for Ukraine can be achieved only in a union with Russia, the leader of the Communist Party of Ukraine, Petro Symonenko, argued that the real independence day for Ukraine was not August 24, 1991, when the Ukrainian parliament adopted the independence declaration, but November 7, 1917, the day of the Bolshevik takeover of power.[83] The 1998 electoral program of the KPU endorsed the recreation of "the criminally destroyed Soviet Union," seeing as "the first step in this direction the creation of the union of Russia, Ukraine, and Belarus."[84] By the late 1990s, Ukrainian communists began to supplement their nostalgic Soviet nationalism with east Slavic nationalism that emphasized the unity of Russians, Ukrainians, and Belarusians in particular, rather than all Soviet nationalities in general. The Communist Party's 2002 program defined the "union of brotherly peoples" as one of the party's goals.[85] The communists were a force to be reckoned with, winning substantial electoral vote shares (some 40 to 50% in the 1990s and over 20% in the 2000s) and being represented in the Ukrainian parliament until 2014. They did not have, however, an outright majority and thus could not formulate state policies independently.

The main ideological opponent of the Left was the national-democratic and nationalist Right. This political camp, originally centered around the Rukh political party, which emerged out of the pro-sovereignty movement in the perestroika period, favored a pro-Western foreign policy and market reforms, and fully embraced the first of the two national identity conceptions described above. The Right saw Ukrainians as a distinct nation, historically oppressed by

Russia, struggling for political sovereignty for centuries, and finally achieving it by escaping Soviet/Russian subjugation in 1991. For the Right, Ukrainian state independence was a paramount value and it opposed policy measures that could blur the boundary between the Ukrainian and Russian nations and Ukraine and Russia as states. The Right thus opposed any forms of integration with Russia on either a bilateral or multilateral level within the CIS. The Right also favored policies of the "national revival" of ethnic Ukrainians whom the Right saw as the "core" of the Ukrainian state.[86]

For the Right, democratic Ukraine would recognize and respect the rights of national minorities but would also seek to undo the legacies of Russification. Measures such as Ukrainian-only state language, promotion of historical memory emphasizing the distinctiveness of the Ukrainian nation and historicity of the Ukrainian state, and opposition to dual citizenship with Russia, all logically followed from the conception of national identity that the Right embraced. The Right was instrumental in promoting a sovereignty and independence agenda and organizing popular mobilization for these purposes in the perestroika years, but until 2004 it was politically weaker than the Left and numerically smaller in the legislature, controlling at best a third of the legislative seats in the 1990s and 2000s. The Right therefore also was not in a position to control the state policy-making agenda single-handedly. This made the position of the third political camp – the self-styled Center – critically important.

The Center consisted of a patchwork of parties and political-economic interest groups comprised of former party apparatchiks and the new business and regional elites. A defining feature of the Center was its ideological amorphousness. As one study put it, the Center "never had much of an identity of its own ... occupied by virtual politics, a shifting kaleidoscope of clan groups, shadow businesses, and old *nomenklatura* interests."[87] The Center was not strongly wedded to either the Left's or the Right's competing national identity conceptions and visions of Ukraine's past and future that these conceptions informed. At the same time, as discussed earlier, since the late perestroika era, after the 1990 local elections shifted the locus of power from Moscow to the union republics, a part of the Communist Party nomenklatura in Soviet Ukraine began to see advantages of greater sovereignty versus continued subordination to Moscow. After 1991, the Center was interested in independence from Moscow, since this allowed the seizing of political and economic opportunities stemming from running an independent state. The vast economic opportunities to be gained from privatization of formerly state-held economic resources were especially appealing.

With neither the Left nor the Right powerful enough politically and electorally to rule the state by itself, the Center was a critical player in determining what identity policies could and could not materialize at the state level. Had the Center sided with the Left, Ukraine could have followed the path of Belarus, acquiescing to a Russia-favored identity conception of "brotherly nations" destined to be together, and to Russia's political control more broadly. Instead, already in the late Soviet period, the Center and the Right formed an informal coalition, which has been described as a "grand bargain."[88] In the post-1991 period the essence of this bargain was that the Right, aware of its weakness and inability to govern alone, would let the Center decide economic policies and essentially allow it to take control of the state's economic resources. In return, the Center would firmly support state independence and pursue "Ukrainization" of the state in areas such as national symbols, state language, education, and cultural policies. The Center was interested in preserving state independence, albeit more in order to capitalize from it than due to romantic nationalist attachment to the idea. Not only the Right but, critically, the Center came to perceive dangers to statehood in many of the Left-favored policies on issues such as citizenship and language. Because the Left could not be considered a trustworthy custodian of a state for which it held little affection or ideological commitment, a Center-Right rather than a Center-Left grand bargain emerged.

The Center-Right bargain goes a long way to explaining the seeming paradox of post-1991 Ukrainian politics of presidential candidates campaigning on a "pro-Russian" identity politics platform, only to abandon these promises once elected. Ukraine's second president, Leonid Kuchma, is a case in point in this regard, having campaigned in 1994 on the ticket of reversing Kravchuk-era policies, which Kuchma described during the election campaign as reflecting "romantic Galician nationalism."[89] In his inaugural speech, Kuchma asserted that Ukraine's place was in Eurasia: "Historically Ukraine is a part of the Eurasian economic and cultural space ... Ukraine's vital national interests are concentrated on the territory of the former USSR."[90] During his tenure, however, Kuchma largely continued national identity policies within the framework of the grand bargain and even authored a book with a telling title: "Ukraine is not Russia." He also stood firm to defend Ukrainian territorial integrity from Russia's first encroachment during the 2003 Tuzla Island standoff, which we discuss in Chapter 4.

The Center-Right relationship was far from smooth sailing. Over time, the Right grew increasingly critical of the centrist elites' economic corruption and authoritarian politics, and also saw the Ukrainization measures the Center was willing to implement as partial and insufficient. The Right attempted to challenge the grand bargain when Viacheslav Chornovil, the leader of Rukh, ran against Kuchma in the 1999 presidential elections on a platform of greater Ukrainization, democratization, and Westernization of Ukraine. Chornovil's suspicious death in a car accident in the run-up to the vote ended the challenge, and the Center and the Right continued their uneasy alliance during Kuchma's second term. The Center-Right grand bargain was highly consequential, setting Ukrainian identity politics on a course of separation rather than integration with Russia. Chapter 3 shows how historical memory, language, and citizenship policies have been key areas where the bargain left an important mark, and each of these sets of policies pursued by Ukraine collided with Russia's preferences, illustrating the dynamics of an escalatory cycle.

Public opinion and Ukrainian identity

Any discussion of identity politics would not be complete without considering societal responses to elite-level debates. How did Ukrainian citizens imagine the Ukrainian nation and what policies on language, historical memory, and relations with Russia did people prefer? Post-Soviet Ukraine was far from a homogeneous society. Ukraine entered the post-Soviet period with a substantial degree of regional and ethno-linguistic diversity. The 1989 census recorded 73% of the population as ethnic Ukrainians, and 27% as belonging to over 100 other ethnic groups (22%, or 11.4 million, self-identified as ethnic Russians). The Russification process, which accelerated during the last two decades of the Soviet era, had resulted in many ethnic Ukrainians claiming Russian as their mother tongue (*ridna mova*) on the census and even more using it as the language of convenience. The 1989 census showed 12% of ethnic Ukrainians – more than four million people – choosing Russian as their mother tongue.[91] An even greater number of ethnic Ukrainians – estimated at 40% in late 1980s – used Russian as their daily language of convenience.[92]

The widespread perception of Ukraine as a country regionally divided between a more ethnically Russian and predominantly Russian-speaking south and east, feeling loyalty to Russia, and an ethnically Ukrainian and predominantly Ukrainian-speaking west, oriented toward Europe and the West and away from Russia, is a much-used shortcut to understanding popular preferences. Indeed, both ethnic Russians and Russian-speakers were concentrated in the southeastern regions, and election results during the 1990s and 2000s consistently illustrated what looked like a divided and polarized country.[93] The southeast consistently voted for political actors promising closer ties with Russia and, in polls, supported membership in Russia-led alliances such as the CIS, Customs Union, and Eurasian Economic Union over membership in Western institutions, such as the EU and NATO, as well as identity and cultural policies, such as elevated status of Russian language and continuation of Soviet-era policies on historical memory.[94] Until 2014, the Ukrainian public, on average, was slightly closer in its views to the identity conception advocated by the Left rather than the Right.

At the same time, the "east–west divide" binary has limitations as an analytical lens.[95] First, the impact of regional, ethnic, and linguistic differences on political attitudes in Ukraine is very complex and has been a subject of much scholarly debate.[96] Identifying as a Russian, speaking Russian, or hailing from the southeast does not pre-determine one's political attitudes and identities, nor does it guarantee that these attitudes and identities remain unchanged. Second, the "eastern half" and the "western half" of Ukraine are neither clearly bounded, nor homogeneous, nor fixed over time. The east–west divide shortcut obscures the growth in the number of people who came to think of themselves as Ukrainian, connoting identification with the state and not simply with the ethnic group.

After 1991, the number of people who thought of themselves as Ukrainian rather than Russian progressively grew. If in the Soviet period mixed marriages and bilingual families often helped Russification, as they made it easier for Ukrainians to choose the socially and politically prestigious Russian identity, in the new political realities of sovereign statehood the same factors allowed many Russians to (re)identify as Ukrainians.[97] In annual polls conducted by the Institute of Sociology of the National Academy of Sciences of Ukraine, the percentage of those who self-identified as Ukrainians increased from 68.9% in 1992 to 84.7% by 2010, while the number of self-identified Russians declined from 24.4% to 12.2%.[98]

The progressive growth of Ukrainian self-identification has favored independent statehood rather than vassalization under Russian power. It was accompanied by shifts in electoral geography and voting patterns which pushed in the same direction. In the 1991 presidential elections, the unambiguously pro-Western candidate Viacheslav Chornovil won only in the three westernmost regions that were incorporated into the Soviet Union last in 1944; in each subsequent legislative and presidential election, the vote for presidential candidates and parties campaigning on a pro-Western and Ukrainian cultural message shifted further and further east (Map 2.1). In 2004, when Yushchenko beat Yanukovych in the presidential contest on a platform of pro-Western orientation and a Ukrainian cultural agenda, the "western half" for the first time surpassed the "eastern half" in relative size – for the first time some regions to the east of the Dnipro river voted with the "western half." Yushchenko's bid for re-election failed due to a combination of ineffective leadership and insufficient progress in fighting corruption. While his identity policies aimed at maximally distancing Ukraine from Russia were unpopular in the east, during his tenure the geographic center of Ukraine moved closer to the west, which reduced domestic support for Russia-favored policies – even after Yushchenko lost re-election.[99] The east–west divide was evolving in a direction that favored continued independence rather than Russian rule.

Just like at the level of the state elites the political Center was a pivotal actor for determining Ukraine's identity policies, so was Ukraine's geographic center for determining majority popular support for competing identity narratives and the identity policies these narratives informed. If most of western Ukraine shared the Right-advocated national identity and most of the southeast shared the Ukraine–Russia "organic unity" imaginary advocated by the Left, the Center was always more ambivalent. Demographically sizeable and electorally important, the geographic center was the area where in the 1990s and 2000s popular attitudes on many issues often fell between the "extremes" of the east and west. Furthermore, over time, attitudes in the center evolved. If the center had moved to the east in its attitudes this perhaps could have made it possible for Russia to bring Ukraine back into the fold during the Yanukovych presidency. But attitudes in central regions moved in the opposite direction, especially during Yushchenko's presidency. This evolution of the center complicates the east–west binary as a useful analytical lens, and it also worked against Russia's expectations of re-integration. Chapter 3 will present survey data on attitudes to the Holodomor and WWII-era Ukrainian nationalist rebels to illustrate how views in the central regions fell between the "extremes" of east and west and evolved toward greater acceptance of the Right-advocated national identity conception.

Map 2.1 Regions where pro-Western parties won the party list vote in parliamentary elections, 1998–2019

Notes:

1. Left of each line indicates where pro-Western parties came first.
2. 1990 and 1994 elections are not shown on this map, as they were held under a different electoral system without a party list component.
3. In 1998, pro-Western parties also won in Kyiv city.
4. In 2012, pro-Western parties did not win in Zakarpattia.
5. In 2014 and 2019, elections were not held in Crimea and Eastern Donbas due to Russian occupation.

Source: Central Electoral Commission of Ukraine, official results.

What were the implications of these patterns of popular attitudes and identities for the prospects of continued sovereignty versus return to Russia's control? Hypothetically, had the Ukrainian political class chosen to pursue identity policies favored by Russia, until at least the 2004 Orange Revolution, such policies would have received substantial popular support. In 2004, nearly 63% supported the idea of Ukraine joining a union with Russia and Belarus, while 48% supported Ukraine's membership in the EU.[100] When, in the early 1990s, the Ukrainian political class chose to decouple Ukraine from Russia within the parameters of the grand bargain, this trajectory choice was not driven primarily by public opinion. In the turbulent political environment of the early 1990s public opinion was volatile and ambiguous. In the spring of 1991 a majority in Ukraine backed a reformed union state in the Gorbachev-organized referendum, but months later an overwhelming majority backed Ukrainian independence in the December 1991 referendum. As discussed above, those who supported independence did it for different reasons, and after the economy tanked in the 1990s many came to see some form of a reconstituted union with Russia as a salvation from economic woes. As time went by, however, popular support for a pivot to Russia was gradually declining, whereas commitment to independence solidified. By the mid-2000s, popular attitudes in Ukraine evolved, especially in the geographic center, thus placing the Center-Right elite bargain on stronger social footing.

After Yanukovych's autocratization and pivot to Russia antagonized even more Ukrainians, by the time the Euromaidan protests prevailed and the new government set a decisive course westward, it was not because the West somehow "stole" Ukraine by influencing its elites against the Ukrainian population's wishes. The identities and preferences of Ukrainian citizens had evolved, and the drivers of this process were domestic, not external. How this process unfolded is detailed in Chapter 5. Centrist elites' selfish desire to be in charge of an independent state may have safeguarded Ukrainian independence in the 1990s and early 2000s but, over time, public opinion evolved in ways that made commitment to independence the choice of a progressively larger share of the Ukrainian electorate.

2

Regime divergence

The dissolution of the USSR produced Russia and Ukraine as independent states under international law. While both embarked on a path toward democratization, early similarities soon gave way to divergence in their political development. Ukraine's democratization unfolded slowly, in fits and starts, while Russia's attempt to build a democracy stumbled early in the 1990s, ushering in a long period of creeping autocratization, which eventually produced Putin's post-2012 personalist dictatorship. In this chapter, we discuss key turning points that led to Ukraine and Russia's divergent political trajectories, such as the 1993 confrontation between Yeltsin and the Russian parliament, the transition from Yeltsin to Putin and the quick marginalization of the Yeltsin-era oligarchs, the 2004 Orange Revolution in Ukraine against manipulated elections, Yanukovych's attempt to reverse democratic gains in 2010–2014, and Putin's protest crackdown after the 2011–2012 manipulated electoral cycle. The most consequential event was Ukraine's Orange Revolution. It put Ukraine on a democratic and pro-European path and triggered fears in Putin's Russia, which accelerated the descent into authoritarianism and the consolidation of Russia's imperial vision. The significant regime divergence between Ukraine and Russia went hand-in-hand with an escalation of Russia's coercion against Ukraine and set the stage for the 2014 start of Russia's military aggression. We also consider some counterfactuals. What if Ukraine's democratic trajectory had ended in the failure of the 2004 Orange Revolution? Could regime similarity between Ukraine and Russia have reduced the likelihood of war?

Presidents vs. parliaments amid economic crisis

Russia and Ukraine started their journeys as independent states with nearly identical state institutions and incumbent leadership. In addition to the nation-building imperative discussed in Chapter 1, the new states faced two other monumental tasks – to transition from the collapsing command economy to the market and to build the institutions of an independent and democratic state. Both tasks turned out to be tall orders, both states hit similar obstacles, and elites committed similar mistakes. For much of the 1990s, the political and economic trajectories of Ukraine and Russia unfolded somewhat in parallel.

In both cases, the first elected president was a popular Soviet-era republican leader – Yeltsin in Russia, Kravchuk in Ukraine. Each president also inherited a boisterous parliament with similar parties and factions: an unreformed and retrograde Communist Party, a market reformers' faction, a nationalist faction, which was aligned with the reformist camp in Ukraine but in Russia formed a red–brown coalition with the communists, and a centrist "swamp" of ideologically muddled independents.[1] The fragmented parliaments did not represent institutionalized party systems, but the *zeitgeist* of political competition they had carried over from the perestroika period. The same applied to debates in the media – there were a variety of viewpoints represented and intense discussion. Media pluralism and freedom were not institutionalized and guaranteed but existed *de facto* and *ad hoc*.[2]

Both states needed to adopt a new constitution to replace the 1978 Soviet constitution, but intra-elite competition complicated the process. Instead, the legislatures adopted and then overrode dozens of constitutional amendments to the existing constitution and the presidents often governed through decree powers. As in the waning years of the USSR, political elites constantly rearranged the institutional landscape, forming and disbanding councils, ministries, and agencies and moving prerogatives among them to try to get the upper hand over political rivals. The air of ungovernability was strong and it negatively affected the other existential task – the economic transformation.

Economic reform in both countries followed a similar blueprint: price liberalization, macroeconomic stabilization, privatization, and the creation of market-regulating institutions, although Russia proceeded through the stages more quickly than Ukraine. Yeltsin zeroed in on the economic reforms that his arch-rival Gorbachev had vacillated on and he aimed to "leap into post-Communism" as quickly and as irreversibly as possible.[3] Kravchuk, on the other hand, prioritized nation- and state-building, while his economic reform strategy was cautious and reactive.[4] For the first year of independence, Russia proceeded with bold reforms under Prime Minister Yegor Gaidar's team, while Ukraine's Vitold Fokin cabinet dragged its feet. Both economies were inextricably linked through a common currency (the ruble), issued by Russia's Central Bank, which led to tensions between the two countries, as Ukraine's policy of subsidizing losing state-owned enterprises to keep them afloat fuelled inflation in Russia as well. Price liberalization increased inflation even more, eventually to over 2,500% per year in both countries.

Efforts at macroeconomic stabilization eventually produced results – Russia had inflation under control by 1995, Ukraine by 1996 – but in the meantime multifaceted economic hardship hit both mass publics hard. Between 1990 and 1996 both economies were contracting by double digits every year. Industrial production plummeted. New businesses were slow to appear due to slow legislative reforms and regulatory changes. Unemployment increased as many state-owned enterprises went through painful restructuring or closed. Other sectors were plagued by "wage arrears," i.e. employees went to work but received no wages for months, sometimes years.[5] The deep depression precipitated a collapse of living standards. Comparative data show that both countries experienced steep negative changes in nearly all indicators of human development – the poverty rate increased dramatically, the death rate increased, life expectancy plummeted by 3–4 years, the fertility rate nearly halved, and crime rates soared.[6]

At the same time, the distortions of the economic transition and the uneven pace of reforms opened multiple loopholes for people with political connections, shadowy start-up capital, or both, to make enormous windfall profits. The privatization process was non-transparent and often resulted in handing over major state enterprises to private owners. The winners then either stripped the assets and destroyed the enterprises or made fortunes without much risk or investment. Through this process, both countries saw the emergence of a group that came to be called the oligarchs, who used their political connections to create financial-industrial groups, which also often included media holdings that served their political interests. Meanwhile, trade unions and civil society were feeble and marginalized from the political process that produced economic policies.[7] In Russia, oligarchic networks took over the natural resources industry. In Ukraine, the big prize was the industrial base in the east and the energy transport network. The absence of an appropriate legal framework or an independent and powerful judiciary to enforce what laws did exist on the books meant that the creation of the oligarchic class was accompanied by gang-style wars as different groups competed for turf and lucrative deals. In both countries, by the mid-1990s, nearly half of economic activity took place in the shadow economy.[8]

Russia's and Ukraine's rough road toward marketization had less to do with the choice of reforms, their sequence, or their pace and everything to do with the weak post-Soviet state. The state lacked institutional control over its money supply. It could not administer its regional and local bureaucracies non-arbitrarily. And, most of all, it could not constrain rent-seeking because it did not have the proper self-regulation mechanisms and institutions.[9]

Predictably, the economic freefall, societal malaise, lawlessness, and ungovernability resulted in political crisis. In both countries, resurgent communist parties used the economic crisis to decry not just the market transition, but also the Soviet Union's collapse. In Russia, not only the communists, but a variety of nationalist forces preferred re-imperialization over building a state within Russia's borders and reforming the economy. In Ukraine, the grand bargain between the national-democratic and centrist elites produced an autarchic economic policy,[10] aimed, in part, at resisting Russia's re-imperialization efforts, but also deepened the economic crisis. Both countries saw a rise in tensions in disaffected regions. In Russia, sovereignty movements emerged not only in ethnic minority regions (Chechnya, Tatarstan, Bashkortostan, and others),[11] but in ethnically Russian regions as well that constructed economic grievances against the center.[12] In Ukraine, the industrial region of Donbas was the locus of economic discontent.

Yeltsin and Kravchuk attempted to push through new constitutions which aimed to establish a strong presidency and increase governability. Both leaders hit a snag due to intensifying intra-elite competition and an increasingly hostile legislature. Kravchuk's main political rivals were his prime minister, Leonid Kuchma, and the chairman of parliament, Leonid Pliushch, while Yeltsin's challengers were the chairman of parliament, Ruslan Khasbulatov, and the vice-president, Aleksandr Rutskoi.

The crises of governability during the economies' nadir in 1993–1994 offer the first sign of divergence between the two independent states and foreshadow that Ukraine would maintain and entrench political competition, whereas Russia would see its gradual stifling. In both countries, 1993 was marked by parliaments trying to adopt institutional and constitutional reforms aimed at constraining the president's decree powers and enshrining a more limited role for the chief executive. Expectedly, the incumbents wanted to prevent the hollowing out of their offices. The maneuvering through the spring and summer of 1993 in both countries included wrangling over early elections for both branches, impeachment and referendum votes and threats, as well as constant tension between the president and parliament over who would be prime minister and whether the president would be able to appoint his own regional representatives.

The conflict between Yeltsin and parliament over a new constitutional draft escalated throughout the spring and summer of 1993 and eventually led to a dramatic standoff. In March, parliament almost managed to impeach the president. In April, Yeltsin squeaked a victory in a non-binding referendum, which he used as a tool to discredit parliament with the public.[13] As Yeltsin and parliament both dug into their positions and conflicting interpretations of a popular mandate, a real crisis brewed. Yeltsin pulled the trigger on September 21, 1993 by disbanding parliament by decree and ordering new elections. The new elections would be for a new bicameral legislature – a State Duma and a Federation Council – tasked with adopting a new constitution. Two days later, parliament defied the presidential decree and voted to remove Yeltsin as president and swear Vice President Rutskoi into office, as well as a new provisional government. After ten days of desperate mediation attempts and some mobilization by nationalists and communists in support of Khasbulatov and Rutskoi, the crisis ended swiftly through military action. On October 4, at Yeltsin's orders, the Army dispersed the protesters by force and opened fire on the parliament building, and Khasbulatov and Rutskoi were arrested and taken to jail.[14] Yeltsin then suspended the Constitutional Court and banned nationalist newspapers and organizations that had supported the challengers.

Once Yeltsin had taken control of the situation, he reneged on parts of his September 21 decree. Entrusting the new legislature (to be elected in December) with voting on the new constitution presented a risk that he might again face a hostile parliamentary majority that would try to curb presidential powers. To avoid a repeat of the stalemate, Yeltsin had his own team write Russia's new constitution, presented it to the Russian people by publishing the draft in national and regional newspapers, and submitted it to a referendum to take place simultaneously with the parliamentary elections. On December 12, Yeltsin's strategy narrowly paid off. 58% of the Russian electorate supported the new constitution, but again elected an anti-Yeltsin legislative majority. While Yeltsin did not campaign for any party, it was clear that a breakthrough first-place showing for Vladimir Zhirinovsky's radical nationalists, a modest 16% vote share for the reformists, and a close third-place result for the communists represented electoral failure for Yeltsin's team.

In Ukraine, the spring and summer of 1993 saw Kravchuk and Kuchma trying to one-up each other as they vied for effective control of the country's executive and hence the course of policy. Kravchuk tried to dismiss Kuchma as prime minister, to abolish his office, to claim the most important portfolios for himself and leave Kuchma only in charge of economic policy. Parliament, in turn, helped Kuchma remain in office through the summer by refusing to accept his resignation, then brought forward parliamentary and presidential elections by a year, thus shortening Kravchuk's term. Parliament's chair, Pliushch, who also seemed to harbor presidential ambitions, tried to reduce Kravchuk's power by sabotaging the constitutional process. Parliament also dismantled Kravchuk's system of executive-appointed regional representatives, which also was one of the bones of contention between Yeltsin and parliament in Russia. Though Kuchma finally resigned in September, Kravchuk continued to face a hostile parliament. In January 1994, shortly before attempting re-election, Kravchuk faced impeachment threats over the decision to give up Ukraine's nuclear weapons.[15] In 1994, both parliamentary and presidential elections took place as planned. The parliamentary elections were a victory for the Left and other forces critical of the direction the country was going in and foreshadowed problems for Kravchuk's re-election. In the summer presidential election, Kravchuk won the first round in a crowded field, but lost the second round narrowly to Kuchma, who ran on a platform of restoring the economy through closer ties and better relations with Russia.

The contrast between the denouements of the two turning points is significant. While in Russia executive-legislative confrontation amid a failing economy culminated in a coup attempt and the bombing of parliament, the Ukrainian confrontation amid similar economic crisis included all sides making compromises – Kuchma resigned as prime minister and Kravchuk agreed to pre-term presidential elections. While Yeltsin used tanks to remain in office, Kravchuk conceded defeat to Kuchma in the 1994 presidential election and returned to politics as a regular member of parliament. Many see Yeltsin's decisions as a gambit that prevented a communist–nationalist coalition from taking control of Russia's government and reversing course on both economic and democratic reforms. "Democrats" both among the elites and in society were, after all, not a majority.[16] Only a presidential system where Yeltsin and parliament checked each other had a chance of maintaining democracy, whereas a parliamentary republic would have descended quickly into dictatorship.[17]

However, in 1993–1994, Ukraine's political future hung in the balance as well and Kravchuk could have tried to impose himself on parliament just like Yeltsin did. Not only was Kravchuk's power constantly challenged by domestic pro-Russian and communist revanchist elites who sought power, but fears that Russia would intervene to suppress or compromise Ukrainian sovereignty were not unreasonable. As Chapter 3 will show, Russia resented Kravchuk's Ukrainization policies as it felt they were aimed at strengthening a distinct Ukrainian identity and driving the two "brotherly" nations apart. Both Crimea and Donbas had pro-Russian constituencies that Russia could have used to foment civil strife just as it did in Moldova and Georgia in the same period. In the 1994 election, Russia reportedly supported Kuchma's campaign financially and Yeltsin even went on TV to ask Ukrainians directly to support Kuchma.[18] In this context, Kravchuk, and his nation-building-focused allies, could have decided that suppressing political competition and preventing the election of a pro-Russian president was essential for the survival of the new state. Yet, Kravchuk allowed early parliamentary elections and then lost his re-election bid, thus setting a precedent for Ukrainian democratization – a turnover in power after a competitive election. Russia has not had this happen to this day.

New constitutions and crony capitalism

In the mid-1990s, both Russia and Ukraine finally adopted new constitutions which bore significant similarities. Both states established an ostensibly semi-presidential form of government with a divided executive – a president and a prime minister. However, both presidents were endowed with significant constitutional powers – they enjoyed security of tenure as impeachment by parliament was prohibitively hard; parliament could not call pre-term presidential elections, but the president could call pre-term parliamentary elections; the president not only picked the prime minister without much input by parliament, but also could sack the government without parliament's consent; finally, both presidents had broad decree powers they could use to make appointments, take policy initiatives, or aid the implementation of laws.[19] The size of parliament's lower house (450 seats) and the electoral system were also identical – 225 deputies were elected in single-mandate districts (SMDs) using majoritarian voting; the other 225 seats went to party lists through proportional representation. The second half of the 1990s saw Ukraine and Russia continue along parallel trajectories, though Ukraine had more intense political competition, which took diverse forms, including ideological polarization among the main political actors, electoral volatility, government instability, and contestation between the executive and the legislature. Kuchma's first term and Yeltsin's tenure were both characterized by further development of crony capitalism. A coterie of oligarchs divided the economic pie and dominated the political process at the expense of the creation of parties which could represent the ideological spectrum.

In 1996, Yeltsin won re-election in part thanks to the loyal support of the oligarchs he had created. The 1996 election was competitive and presented a stark choice – either an ailing Yeltsin continued his corrupt and unpopular marketization of the Russian economy or an unreformed communist, Gennady Zyuganov, would get a chance to try to undo it all. The oligarchs, who had acquired some of Russia's largest export-oriented enterprises cheaply, predictably threw their lot in with Yeltsin. The oligarchic domination of the media and the use of state resources to effectively buy support for Yeltsin without consideration for campaign finance rules meant that the election was free, but not fair. Yeltsin narrowly won. During his second term, the oligarchs consolidated their political and economic grip. They continued to expand their holdings in the oil and metallurgy sectors in non-transparent, politically manipulated privatization tenders.[20] They used their media market clout to stifle investigative journalism that was looking into growing corruption and mismanagement. They backed hand-picked regional political elites, so that across the country, where political competition existed, it pitted various oligarchic networks, rather than parties with ideological programs against each other.[21]

In Ukraine, Kuchma also provided political opportunity for various oligarchic networks to prey on the state. Graft became the glue that held the political system and the state together.[22] Those who drew rents paid back in political loyalty; those who stepped out of line were quickly exposed as corrupt and driven into exile or, in the case of the former prime minister Pavlo Lazarenko, eventually into American prison. While economic reform had been slow under Kravchuk, who opposed painful shock therapy reforms for fear of destabilizing the country and instead focused on nation-building, under Kuchma the market transition moved forward, but the measures were in service to the oligarchs rather than to small businesses.

The 1990s ended with Russia and Ukraine both as hybrid, competitive authoritarian regimes. Sufficient political competition and freedom of speech co-existed with a presidency that wielded power through oligarchic allies. The president remained largely unaccountable to a fragmented parliament with weak parties. An uneven playing field meant the presidential administration marginalized and undermined the opposition.

The last year of Yeltsin's second term, 1999, brought the height of democratic political competition in Russia. Major politicians credibly eyed a post-Yeltsin presidency. Who would win the succession competition was unclear, but the expectation was that it would happen through a competitive election. The main contenders were Moscow mayor Yuriy Luzhkov, whose wife Elena Baturina was a state-created oligarch, and the former prime minister Evgeny Primakov, who moderately leaned toward both communist nostalgia and nationalism. Yeltsin, though, wanted to anoint someone other than Luzhkov or Primakov and kept trying out young, liberal-leaning successors. Nizhniy Novgorod governor and former deputy prime minister Boris Nemtsov, Prime Minister Sergey Kirienko, and then Prime Minister Sergey Stepashin each had a turn at being the flavor of the month, but none managed to establish either sufficient elite backing or popular support.

In the late summer of 1999, Yeltsin appointed yet another young and relatively unknown figure as prime minister. The new guy was a Federal Security Service (FSB) officer by the name of Vladimir Putin. The FSB was the successor institution to the infamous Soviet spy agency the KGB. Putin's post-Soviet political career had started from the entourage of the liberal St. Petersburg mayor, then went through various positions in the presidential administration and the Security Council and included a brief stint as FSB chief. Putin was young and presented as a liberal, so he seemed to fit the successor mold that Yeltsin had been trying for the past year. Within only a couple of weeks, the Russian electorate concluded that the successor had been found. The moment Russia fell for the new PM is macabre. In early September, four apartment bombings, two in Moscow and two in smaller cities, killed over 300 people and injured over 1,000. Prime Minister Putin blamed the shocking violence on Chechen separatists and threatened to hunt down every last one of them, even in their outhouses. The Chechen president Aslan Maskhadov and rebels, who had just taken their insurgency to neighboring Dagestan, vigorously denied the allegations, but PM Putin stuck to his message. The public bought it and rewarded him handsomely as he launched Russia's second war in Chechnya. His leadership style resonated so well that his popularity rose to stratospheric levels – from around 30% to close to 90%.[23] The succession struggle was effectively over before either the parliamentary or the presidential elections were held. Putin had won it and Luzhkov's and Primakov's ambitions were dashed. Even if Yeltsin had wanted to change his mind about Putin, after October, sacking him would have been near impossible.

Competitive authoritarianism's end (one way or another)

The parallel political trajectories continued in the new century to the extent that both Russia and Ukraine were within the hybrid regime category. In 1999–2000, Yeltsin installed Putin as acting president in a New Year's Eve surprise resignation, a move that allowed Putin to go into the presidential campaign with incumbent advantage and took all the suspense out of the March 2000 election. In 1999, Kuchma was re-elected to a second term in an election that was reminiscent of Yeltsin's 1996 re-election. Though quite unpopular, due to corruption scandals and the underperforming economy, Kuchma managed to put together a winning coalition with the use of administrative resources, oligarchic support, and a heavy dose of fear-mongering about a return to the USSR, as his closest competitor was Petro Symonenko, a hardline communist, who was even less charismatic than Russia's Zyuganov. Western and central Ukraine, which had overwhelmingly backed Kravchuk in the 1994 contest with Kuchma, now had to hold their noses and vote for Kuchma in order to prevent a Symonenko presidency.

In the early 2000s, it was plausible to conclude that Russia was progressing better toward democratization than Ukraine. Kuchma appeared determined to consolidate power through dirty tricks, abuse of administrative resources, and suppression of free media and protest, and he appeared to face little resistance from civil society. In other words, Ukraine seemed to be sinking deeper into bad governance and corruption and trending toward autocratization.[24] In Russia, by contrast, the new, young, and, unlike his predecessor Yeltsin, sober president appeared to be making positive changes, even though early signs of autocratization were also there. He curbed oligarchic excess, created a centrist party, streamlined the chaotic relations between federal units and the center, vigorously pursued market reforms, and even laid some foundations for the rule of law through judicial reform. During this time, he maintained partnership with the West. The picture seemed mixed, but with grounds for cautious optimism.[25]

But a more careful look at both countries' politics shows that in the early 2000s regime divergence accelerated, but with Ukraine, rather than Russia, laying the groundwork for further democratization. In Russia, what appeared as moves to strengthen state capacity and the rule of law were actually part of Putin's aim to establish a power vertical – the backbone of his future autocracy. In Ukraine, Kuchma's authoritarian consolidation tactics strengthened viable democratic and liberal opposition (as opposed to the revanchist communist opposition of the 1990s) and reinvigorated civil society networks that had emerged during the student protests in 1990, which furthered democratic causes such as freedom of speech and association. Indeed, scholarly indices tracking multiple layers of democratic governance start displaying divergence between Russia and Ukraine in 2000. According to the *Varieties of Democracy*, a leading expert index of democratic governance, starting in 2000, Ukraine became more democratic than Russia in terms of horizontal accountability, liberal democratic politics, societal engagement in public deliberation of policies, and provision of civil liberties (Figure 2.1).[26]

With the war in Chechnya maintaining his ratings at stratospheric level, Putin took on the Yelstin-era oligarchs. He admonished those who harbored political ambitions, telling them that they had either to pledge political allegiance to him or to leave politics. The biggest fish who did not heed the warning, Boris Berezovsky and Vladimir Gusinsky, went into exile amid escalating legal harassment. Most others submitted to Putin. Mikhail Khodorkovsky tried to balance. Some oligarchic media outlets were subjected to legal harassment and had to close but, through the prism of Putin's tussle with the oligarchs, the move was not considered an assault on freedom of the press. Perhaps the attack on the satirical show *Kukly* soon after it portrayed Putin as an evil dwarf should have been more of a wake-up call that Putin had the thin skin of an autocrat.

Political competition started to decline. The 2003 Duma elections were relatively freer from legal harassment and manipulation than the 2002 Rada elections in Ukraine, but that was, in large part, because they were considerably less competitive, i.e. Putin's hold on power was not seriously challenged.[27] United Russia won a plurality of the vote share and almost a majority of the seats (223 of 450) and the rest of the votes were divided among a wide range of parties which could not work with each other to challenge Putin: communists, nationalists, liberal reformers, and centrist formations who hoped to work with United Russia rather than challenge it. No individual politician had stature and name recognition approaching Putin's. In 2004, Putin coasted to re-election victory. With 72% of the votes, Putin trounced his nearest competitor, communist Nikolay Kharitonov, who received only 14%. The opposition was able to contest and win gubernatorial elections, but Putin took measures to curb the *de facto* power of regional governors by appointing presidential representatives as intermediaries between the center and the federal units.

In Ukraine, by contrast, political competition intensified. Re-elected Kuchma appeared more driven than his Russian counterpart to consolidate an authoritarian regime only because he faced more obstacles. Ukrainian opposition journalists faced more legal harassment than their Russian counterparts,[28] but their exposés of corruption at the heart of Kuchma's regime went further than Russian colleagues'. In the fall of 2000, Heorhiy Gongadze, an investigative journalist working on oligarchic corruption in Kuchma's circle, was murdered, and the opposition uncovered secret tapes made in the president's office which strongly suggested that Kuchma had ordered Gongadze's disappearance. In part, the leaking of the tapes indicates that Ukrainian political elites were fragmented, rather than consolidated, and capable of challenging each other. The societal reaction to the Gongadze murder also reveals an engaged civil society. The initial outcry and shock of the "Kuchmagate" scandal didn't die down gradually, but triggered a grass-roots protest movement, "Ukraine Without Kuchma," which maintained presence in Kyiv during the whole winter.

In the spring of 2001, the political crisis both deepened and widened. A major politician, Yulia Tymoshenko, joined the protest after Kuchma dismissed her from cabinet. Almost immediately, Tymoshenko's husband and later Tymoshenko herself were arrested as part of an investigation into malfeasance. However, in a sign that Kuchma didn't control the courts reliably, a judge released Yuliya Tymoshenko, and the legal case stalled. Also in the spring, Kuchma dismissed his prime minister, Viktor Yushchenko, in whose cabinet Tymoshenko had been energy minister, despite Yushchenko's support for the president during the "Ukraine Without Kuchma" protests. Yushchenko, a liberal reformer appointed by Kuchma in 1999, had grown significantly popular as his cabinet had finally started to take Ukraine out of the deep economic crisis of the 1990s. Yushchenko had directed a series of successful economic reforms, such as the introduction of a national currency, and Tymoshenko had overseen a substantial increase in tax collection from oligarchs. Yushchenko's reforms alienated both the communists and centrist oligarch-gravitating MPs, who united in April to support a no-confidence vote. Once out of government, Yushchenko and Tymoshenko became allies and started preparing an opposition coalition ready to challenge Kuchma's party of power in the upcoming 2002 Rada elections.

The Rada election campaign was marred by a long list of manipulations. Yushchenko's party, Tymoshenko's party, and Oleksandr Moroz's Socialist party each challenged Kuchma's centrist "party of power" from different, moderate angles. All proposed to continue economic and democratic reforms, as well as a pro-European foreign policy, but to do it better than Kuchma and without corruption. Unable to scare voters again with the specter of communist restoration, Kuchma tried to paint Yushchenko as a western Ukrainian "Nazi" (even though Yushchenko hails from the northeastern Sumy region) and a "traitor" whose wife was not only from the Ukrainian American diaspora, but also served in high positions in the US government. The opposition was almost completely shut out from the most-read newspapers and most-watched TV channels, while pro-government channels routinely trashed all opposition leaders.[29] The regional authorities, fearing presidential retribution, sabotaged the opposition's attempt to rent space for campaign events. In SMDs, Kuchma's coalition ran "clones" of popular opposition candidates. The clone candidate had the same name as the popular candidate and registered only to syphon off votes by confusing the electorate. Voter suppression and ballot stuffing techniques abounded. Opposition candidates were deregistered on technicalities and had to devote resources to mount a legal challenge, which they often lost as judges had been pressured too.[30]

Despite Kuchma's efforts, Yushchenko's party won the party-list vote and Tymoshenko and the Socialists did well too, and Kuchma had to cohabitate with a hostile parliament. Unlike the 1990s situation when the main challenge was on the communist revanchist Left, now the opposition were reformers aiming to take Ukraine on a path toward Europe. The Center-Right grand bargain hung in the balance, as the nationalists and reformers on the right were no longer in alliance but in opposition to the elites around Kuchma, whom they saw as increasingly authoritarian and corrupt. The electoral success of Yushchenko's and Tymoshenko's parties in the 2002 elections indicated growing popular support for a reformist and pro-Western agenda. Russia never had a moment where reformers were a significant political force able to win elections. Most of Russia's well-known reformers – Gaidar, Chubais, Kasyanov – were never popularly tested politicians, but rather executive creations. Only Nemtsov tried to build an independent political base, but he never attracted a sizeable following the way Tymoshenko and Yushchenko did.

Veto statistics illustrate just how much more politically constrained by parliament Kuchma was than his counterpart Putin. While Putin vetoed only 5% of Duma's laws, Kuchma vetoed twice as many – 10%; moreover, while parliament overrode Putin's veto only in a couple of cases, the Rada overrode almost two dozen (20%) of Kuchma's vetoes.[31] In the run-up to the 2004 presidential election, Kuchma engineered a Constitutional Court-sanctioned loophole to run for a third term, but eventually decided against the idea, selected a designated successor, and threw his political weight behind him. He chose his latest prime minister, Donetsk native Viktor Yanukovych. The scene was set for a hotly contested fall 2004 match-up between two PMs, both Kuchma appointees, who nonetheless could not be more different – liberal reformer-technocrat, Ukrainian-speaking, pro-Western Viktor Yushchenko and pro-Russian, Russian-speaking oligarch with a criminal rather than technocratic record Viktor Yanukovych.

Ukrainians expected a campaign full of dirty tricks, but reality exceeded predictions. In early September, Yushchenko was poisoned with dioxin, probably at a dinner with the deputy chief of the Ukrainian secret service, got treatment in Austria, and returned to the campaign trail with the ravages of the poison etched into his disfigured face. The panoply of manipulations used during the 2002 Rada campaign came back for an encore. The Yanukovych campaign had a "Stop Yushchenko" media strategy, which included censorship on news about the opposition's campaign in the main media outlets and coordinated anti-Yushchenko narratives in the main analytical and current affairs shows.[32] Pro-regime figures and Yanukovych supporters in Donbas again branded Yushchenko a "Nazi," a now eery precursor to the "de-Nazification" narrative Russia has used since February 2022. State employees and small businesses were pressured into providing free advertising and labor for the Yanukovych campaign. State funds were distributed to buy support. In the run-up to election day, voting lists were padded with dead souls and on election day "carousel voting" meant people were bussed to different precincts, where they cast multiple ballots, ballot boxes were stuffed with extra bulletins for Yanukovych, etc.[33]

On October 31, Yushchenko and Yanukovych came out nearly tied in the first round and the electoral map was almost the same as the Kravchuk–Kuchma contest – western and central Ukraine overwhelmingly supported pro-Western, Ukrainization supporting Yushchenko, eastern and southern Ukraine went for pro-Russian Yanukovych. In the three weeks before the runoff, polls indicated that Yushchenko would win the second round convincingly (~53% to ~44%) even though the Yanukovych campaign had gone into overdrive to pay pundits to predict an extremely close runoff and to use all its administrative resources to push maximum turnout in its stronghold regions. But they went even farther; on election night, November 21, the Central Election Commission (CEC) dragged its feet amid exit poll figures suggesting a Yushchenko victory, and then announced that Yanukovych had come out the winner with 49.5% to Yushchenko's 46.9%.

Yushchenko's campaign, however, had evidence that electoral protocols were falsified and immediately challenged in court the result announced by the CEC. Yushchenko's voters and civil society mounted mass protests, first in Kyiv, then around the country. Within a couple of days, the Yushchenko campaign set up a huge stage and 1,500 tents in Maidan Nezalezhnosti (Independence Square) and hundreds of thousands of people protested around the clock, demanding the Supreme Court cancel the fraudulent result and order a re-run of the run-off. In addition to capturing the nation and the world's attention with its denunciation of stolen elections, the protest aimed to keep an eye physically on the Supreme Court, where the figurative ball now was. The protesters watched those who came in and went out of the court building, thus simultaneously pressuring and protecting the justices from coming under political influence by Kuchma or Yanukovych.

As the Supreme Court examined the evidence, the Orange Revolution became the focus of attention in Europe, the US, and Russia due to the geopolitical importance of the outcome. Europe and the US made strong statements in support of the Yushchenko campaign's demand for due process and a just outcome. Russia, in turn, congratulated Yanukovych on his victory and wanted to see the protest suppressed and Yanukovych inaugurated. Kuchma, who was still the incumbent president, played a big role in the denouement. He talked to Putin, who reportedly hinted that the government should use force to suppress Maidan.[34] Instead, consistent with his foreign policy of balancing Europe and Russia, Kuchma decided to invite both to send representatives to help him to mediate talks between Yushchenko and Yanukovych.

The choice of mediation team suggests that Kuchma distanced himself from Yanukovych and wasn't planning to yield to Putin's demands to ram through Yanukovych's inauguration, but instead wanted to hammer out a compromise. The mediation team included three European representatives (the Polish and Lithuanian presidents and the EU foreign-policy chief) and only one Russian one (the speaker of the Duma). The talks officially deferred the final decision to the Supreme Court, but the discussion of electoral reform and a transition to a parliamentary form of government from the current super-presidential system sent a subtle signal to the justices that delivering a ruling that paved the way for a (weakened) Yushchenko presidency was acceptable.

On December 3, under the still-watchful eye of hundreds of thousands of protesters, the Supreme Court upheld Yushchenko's petition, canceled the results of the November 21 run-off due to irregularities, and ordered a re-run of the run-off on December 26. On December 8, the Rada adopted the compromise reached through mediation – constitutional changes to make Ukraine a parliamentary republic, electoral system switch to full proportional representation, and the dismissal of the CEC head who had overseen the fraud and manipulation. The compromise paved the way to Yushchenko's victory – on the high of the massive popular mobilization in his favor and the wide understanding that he would have already won had the result not been manipulated, his victory in the December 26 run-off was much more likely. However, the nod to Yanukovych was that he could return to parliament as opposition leader and face an institutionally weakened president. On December 26, Yushchenko defeated Yanukovych 52 to 44% and was inaugurated as Ukraine's third president on January 23, 2005.

The Orange Revolution was a fork in the road for Ukraine's democratization. Ukrainian civil society harnessed the power of peaceful protest and achieved unprecedented victory. As the unofficial anthem of the Orange Revolution went (in Ukrainian): *razom nas bahato, nas ne podolaty* "together we are many, we cannot be defeated." Yushchenko's swearing-in as the third president in Ukraine's independent history also represented a second turnover in power, which, according to Samuel Huntington's famous "two-turnover" test,[35] made Ukraine officially a democracy. Perhaps most importantly, the Orange Revolution compromise ushered in major institutional changes and set precedents that put Ukraine firmly on a democratizing trajectory. While Yushchenko became president, he was not the only politician who won. His allies, who led the opposition to Kuchma in the Rada,

Yuliya Tymoshenko and the Socialists, as well as the oligarch Petro Poroshenko, the only one who allowed the opposition access to his TV channel, all came out of the revolution on the winning side and with increased political clout. Ukraine began 2005 with a ruling coalition of sorts, rather than a new super president.

The Orange Revolution was a turning moment not only for Ukrainian political development, but also for Russia's, where it accelerated Putin's autocratization efforts. Its outcome came as a shock to Putin. Russia had reportedly spent hundreds of millions of dollars on Yanukovych's campaign, had sent political technologists to advise him, and Putin personally drummed up support for Yanukovych before the first round in lengthy interviews and public meetings, including a trip to Kyiv days before the vote.[36] Putin likely not only felt humiliated by Yanukovych's defeat, but also interpreted it as a threat to the stability of his regime and his own political longevity, as well as a Western plot against Russia.

As a result, Putin pushed through a color-revolution-proofing package of legal measures that further suppressed civil society and independent media and eroded electoral rights. He also set out to create a pro-regime constituency by launching the Nashi youth movement, which imitated Ukraine's Pora movement active during the Orange Revolution, and by stoking anti-Western sentiment and narratives.[37] A false conspiratorial narrative about the Orange Revolution emerged in the Russian press. According to this narrative, Ukrainians neither organized nor pulled off this mass mobilization themselves. The protests were not organic action by Ukrainian civil society, but a staged event by Western-funded groups. The compromise that Ukraine's competing politicians managed to arrive at was nothing but successful installation of American proxies in Ukraine. A pro-Russian president was prevented by the West from taking office and a western-Ukrainian nationalist, married to an American woman of Ukrainian descent who must surely be a CIA spy, was put in office illegitimately and would now push in Ukraine an anti-Russian, pro-American agenda dictated to him directly by Washington.[38]

The Orange-era divergence

After the Orange Revolution, Russia and Ukraine went from subtle gradual divergence to full-blown movement in opposite directions. Russia's regime plunged into authoritarianism, while Ukraine's made strides toward democratic consolidation. This contrast is captured by different cross-country indices that seek to assess the level of democracy around the world. One of the best known, Freedom House's Democracy Index, moved Russia from the "partly free" to the "not free" category in 2005 and pushed it down even further in 2006; that same year, Ukraine, on the other hand, moved from the "partly free" to the "free" category. The *Varieties of Democracies* project, which produces the most comprehensive measures of different layers of democratic governance, also shows that a big gap opened up between Russia and Ukraine in 2004–2006. On each of the five democracy indices, but especially on electoral, liberal, and deliberative democracy, Ukraine became more democratic, while Russia became less so. Once parallel regime development was no more.

The Orange Revolution itself could be seen as an example of deliberative democracy. Deliberative democracy is public debate about the common good, dialogue, and compromise shaping both the actions and preferences of political actors. The Orange Revolution's resolution was peaceful, legal, and negotiated and it was possible because participants, even Yanukovych, put narrow interests aside. During Yushchenko's presidency, this trend continued, buttressed by the constitutional curtailing of presidential powers. The president could no longer choose his own prime minister but was required to appoint whoever parliament put forward. This change institutionalized co-habitation between president and prime minister from different parties, which boosted deliberation opportunities. After the 2006

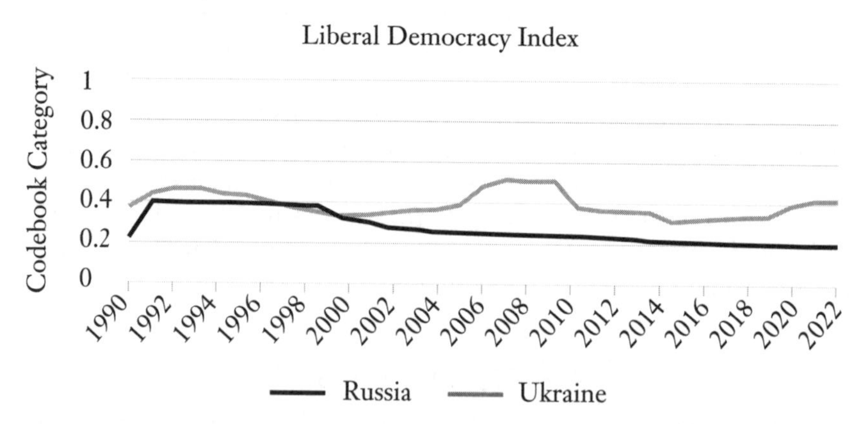

Figure 2.1 Political regime divergence in Russia and Ukraine
Source: Michael Coppedge, et al., 2022. "V-Dem [Russia and Ukraine, 1990–2022] Dataset v12" Varieties of Democracy (V-Dem) Project. https://doi.org/10.23696/vdemds22

parliamentary elections returned Yanukovych's Party of Regions as the biggest faction in parliament, Yushchenko had to appoint his former rival in the Orange Revolution as prime minister and governed, though very uneasily, with a Yanukovych cabinet.

Electoral democracy increased as elections became both clean and fairer, and freedom of the press and freedom of assembly were entrenched both *de jure* and *de facto*. A new electoral law adopted in 2005 strengthened the foundations of free and fair elections by providing guarantees for domestic election observers' unobstructed participation. Two parliamentary elections – in 2006 and in 2007 – featured the intense, polarized competition characteristic of previous Ukrainian elections, but took place without the manipulation and fraud of the 2002 elections. The absence of electoral manipulation in the 2007 elections was especially encouraging because they were called through a constitutionally debated Yushchenko decree. By calling these pre-term elections, Yushchenko tried to find a way out of deep political gridlock, a constitutional crisis that pitted Yanukovych's Party of Regions against an infighting Orange coalition, and afterwards, Yanukovych tried to trigger social mobilization similar to the Orange Revolution (a Blue Maidan) with allegedly paid attendees. Against this backdrop, the free and fair 2007 election was a clear improvement from the pre-Orange period. In addition, government censorship ended and the media market diversified further. Ukrainian journalists were increasingly free to provide balanced coverage of current events with diminishing political pressure and interference.[39]

Liberal democracy, which adds the elements of individual and minority rights, due process, and the rule of law to electoral democracy, increased under Yushchenko's presidency. Legal harassment of the media and the opposition was largely abandoned as a political competition strategy. Yushchenko attempted judicial reform measures aimed at rooting out corruption and set Ukraine onto a path toward meeting the EU's Copenhagen criteria for accession. EU accession was, after all, a lynchpin of Yushchenko's political agenda.[40]

While it strengthened democratic institutions and allowed civil society to flourish, the Orange coalition failed to deliver on its revolutionary promise to clean up Ukrainian politics, which cost it dearly. The state weakness that characterized the competitive authoritarian period persisted and oligarchic networks maintained their corrupt practices. There was also no rule of law breakthrough toward a cleaner and more trusted judicial system. Yushchenko's weakness and the Orange coalition's infighting disappointed Ukrainians, and Yushchenko's ratings fell to the single digits.

The main achievement of the Orange Revolution was the systemic transformation of the rules of the game and, thus, the political regime. Ukraine was still characterized by regional divisions and it still had fractious political elites and an underdeveloped party system. But the fragmentation transformed from competitive authoritarianism, where incumbents tried to crush the opposition, into democratic dysfunction, where political competitors undermined each other's governance agenda, which led to volatility, instability, and mud-slinging but no longer crossed into blatant authoritarian tactics. The entrenchment of crucial democratic institutions – free elections, free media, civil society participation – scaffolded further democracy-building. Against this backdrop, the argument that the Orange Revolution did not bring about durable or fundamental change to Ukrainian politics but was a flash-in-the-pan social mobilization, followed by more of the same,[41] misses the mark.

Russia, by contrast, slid further down into authoritarianism. Electoral manipulation and barriers to participation increased significantly in the mid-2000s. Electoral reform aimed to marginalize and weaken small parties, strengthen Putin's party, and opposition-proof against independents. Election monitoring by independent organizations was limited. Gubernatorial elections were eliminated in December 2004. Putin's Unity party merged with the other candidate for a "party of power" – Luzhkov and Primakov's coalition – into a new party called United Russia. In the 2007 Duma election, a newly introduced 7% electoral threshold, an unusually high barrier comparatively speaking, reduced the number of parties to only four. In addition, the elimination of single-mandate districts and their replacement with full proportional representation meant that independents, such as Boris Nemtsov, could no longer run for the Duma. All parties gradually fell into line to support the president. The nominal opposition in the Duma, including the extreme nationalists of the LDPR, who routinely challenged Yeltsin, the communists, and the once liberal reformers Yabloko and the Union of Right Forces (Russian acronym SPS), kept their opposition rhetoric, but became indistinguishable from United Russia in terms of legislative behavior. A study of legislative voting patterns in the 2003–2007 Duma showed that all "opposition" parties voted with United Russia.[42]

Civil and political liberties were curtailed. The regime consolidated media control.[43] It became exceedingly hard and risky for journalists to investigate the war in Chechnya or the handling of the terrorist incidents connected to Russia's war on Islamic separatists in the Caucasus. The murders of journalists Anna Politkovskaya in 2006 and Natalia Estemirova in 2009 got significant attention abroad and sent a chill through the Russian media space, but the problem was broader and more systematic. The legal persecution of Russia's richest oligarch and potential Putin rival Mikhail Khodorkovsky in 2005 and the systematic destruction of his business empire Yukos through the courts clearly illustrated that liberal democracy was plummeting.

By 2008, meaningful electoral competition virtually disappeared. That year, Putin left the presidency, but did not leave power. Instead, he became prime minister and his close ally Dmitry Medvedev assumed the presidency. The tandem seemed to be governing together, but, in reality, Medvedev was nothing but a stand-in for Putin. In theory, Medvedev might have gotten a taste of power as president and sidelined his mentor, but that did not come to pass. In a way, Putin's personalist dictatorship continued consolidating, even while he was out of the presidency.

Last chance for regime convergence

The 2010–2013 period was the final possibility for reversal of the divergent regime trajectories and realignment of the Russo-Ukrainian relationship into the reintegration Russia wanted. In Ukraine, aided by the infighting within the Orange camp between Yushchenko and his one-time-ally-turned-rival Yulia Tymoshenko, Yanukovych was narrowly but democratically elected to the presidency in a free and fair presidential election in 2010. Upon taking office, Yanukovych set out on a last-ditch attempt at autocratization, but underlying conditions worked against him. In Russia, by contrast, the last couple of years of Medvedev's figurehead presidency were marked by a desperate attempt by civil society to break Putin's looming authoritarian consolidation, but underlying conditions greatly favored Putin victory. Both countries came out of these years of upheaval even more different than before.

Yanukovych's assault on the democratic gains made during Yushchenko's tenure started almost immediately with the reversal of the Orange Revolution's constitutional reform, which had created a parliamentary system of government. In October 2010, the Constitutional Court, yielding to executive pressure, repealed the constitutional amendments and reinstated the vast presidential powers of the pre-Orange period. The move signaled Yanukovych's ambition to aggrandize the presidency, which was the first sign of democratic backsliding.

Eroding liberal democracy, Yanukovych moved to establish firm control over the judiciary in order to weaponize it against the political opposition. First, the president pushed through legislative changes which gutted the jurisdiction of the Supreme Court – the same court that had asserted its independence during the Orange Revolution. Yanukovych used his decree powers to create a High Specialized Court for Civil and Criminal Cases and appointed members from his Donetsk political machine.[44] The restructuring of the judiciary soon revealed its purpose. Scores of Orange-era politicians faced criminal charges, some were imprisoned, others went into exile. The biggest trial was Yulia Tymoshenko's in 2011, which ended in a seven-year sentence. The young judge, who was plucked from obscurity to preside over her case, became deputy chair of the biggest Kyiv court within a year of convicting her.[45] When Tymoshenko appealed her sentence to the judicial hierarchy, the last instance was no longer the relatively independent Supreme Court, but the Yanukovych-created High Specialized Court. Predictably, the Yanukovych appointees to the bench upheld her sentence.

Deliberative democracy regressed as Yanukovych's Party of Regions (PR) increasingly dominated state institutions, which were supposed to function through inter-party collaboration. In the Rada, Yanukovych's consolidation of power started with a technical rule amendment to allow individual members of parliament (MPs), instead of only factions to form coalitions. After the rule was changed, PR bribed some MPs from other factions and strong-armed others to cross the floor and, through this tainted process, created a PR parliamentary majority.[46] PR then took over all parliamentary committees and increasingly resorted to procedural irregularities to ram through preferred policies.[47] Civil society repression and curbs on freedom of association and protest also made a comeback, albeit in an *ad hoc* way, rather than through legislative changes. The Tax Maidan in 2010 and the Language Maidan in 2012 were social mobilizations against a new tax law and a new language law adopted by Yanukovych's parliamentary majority. Each ended in police violence and was followed by legal repression of activists.

Despite his efforts, however, Yanukovych could not dismantle previous democratic gains quickly. Civil society was too developed and mobilized already to accept curbs on freedom of protest and association and protests were frequent and well organized. Parliament was boisterous and occasionally constrained his initiatives. The media market and the oligarchy were both fragmented and resisted consolidation under the control of "The Family." The Family included his son Oleksandr as well as a coterie of loyalists from Yanukovych's home region of Donetsk. Yanukovych systematically appointed "The Family" to important decision-making positions.[48]

As Yanukovych pursued authoritarian restoration in Ukraine to mixed results, in Russia, 2011–2013 saw the last opening for disrupting Putin's tight grip on power. As Medvedev's term drew to a close, Putin prepared to return to the presidency in another swap. In the fall of 2011, he associated himself more directly with United Russia and thus the party's vote share in the December Duma election was seen as crucial – any drop might signal Putin's weakness, so the regime machine worked in overdrive to prevent it. Official results showed that United Russia's 2007 result of 64% had dropped to 49% – still giving it a governing majority, but way weaker than expected. On top of this, the numbers reported by the Central Election Commission looked falsified.[49]

The manipulated election triggered protests under the slogan "For Fair Elections" and soon hundreds of thousands rallied in Moscow and other cities, but the protest was both short-lived and insufficiently large to achieve a breakthrough. The protests were non-violent and organized largely through social media.[50] They were spontaneous rather than meticulously planned and represented the activation of politicized and opposition-leaning citizens, many of whom had not actively protested before.[51] Some opposition politicians joined forces – anti-corruption activist Alexei Navalny, liberal politicians Ilya Yashin and Boris Nemtsov, former prime minister Mikhail Kasyanov – and tried to lead a mobilization, which might have grown into the full-blown color revolution Putin so feared. Unlike in Ukraine, however, none of these politicians had a significant electoral base or enough elite support behind them. Navalny may have had a potential electoral base, but it was untested in elections and he decided against testing it in 2012, when he did not try to register for the presidential election. He justified his decision by arguing that the elections would be fraudulent anyway, but this position only further eroded the legitimacy of elections as a democratic institution.[52] The crowds also emphasized a reform path over a revolutionary one.[53] In hindsight, this choice may have been a missed opportunity to stop Putin's regime from further consolidation.

The Russian protests revealed that opposition to Putin's regime existed, but they did not achieve the mass reach of a color revolution. In contrast to the Orange Revolution, which had the clear goal of stopping Yanukovych from stealing Yushchenko's electoral victory, the Russian protesters had difficulty uniting behind a clear, achievable goal. The government waited out the post-Duma protests. Pussy Riot's anti-Putin performance in the run-up to the presidential election attracted attention, but the group members' swift arrests did not trigger a renewed protest wave. On March 4, Putin won a third presidential term, in an election that did not feature any credible opposition candidates. In May, Putin's inauguration brought protesters back to the streets. The March of Millions attracted significant numbers but, after scores were beaten and arrested at Bolotnaya Square, the protests slowly petered out. Marches continued until 2013 but were sporadic and increasingly desperate actions, mostly organized by a small minority of motivated, long-standing regime opponents.[54]

Oligarchic elites and the siloviki, the cadre of the repressive apparatus, including Putin's old employer the KGB/FSB, remained loyal to Putin throughout, and there were no significant signs of defection, which could have aided the opposition's chances to destabilize the regime. Committed regime opponents maintained organizational networks they could draw on and decentralized links between different groups existed, but they did not reach enough people to spur mass mobilization or to sustain it. The regime was not sufficiently constrained by society and did not have to meet its demands or yield to its pressure, which spurred a vicious circle and suppressed civil society development even further.[55] Navalny's attempt to turn his virtual anti-corruption movement into a grassroots political force did not produce significant success. He ran for Moscow mayor in 2013 and barely got a fifth of the votes. He and his brother were then prosecuted for corruption and malfeasance in politicized trials, which was an effective means of removing Navalny from the electoral arena of competition for the long run.

In sum, the 2011–2013 period confirmed what had become increasingly obvious since 2004 – Ukraine was a democracy, Russia was an autocracy. With Putin safely back in the driver's seat for another presidential term and Yanukovych facing increasing instability because of his attempt to reverse democratization against the grain, the stage was set for confrontation between the two diverging states.

Was regime divergence inevitable and would regime similarity have made war less likely?

Ukraine and Russia were not pre-ordained to end up with such contrasting political regimes, and political regime similarity would have probably prevented the war. The logic of an escalatory cycle between re-imperialization and independence centers on the compatibility between Russia's and its neighbors' foreign and domestic policies. When the vassals pursue parallel foreign policy and refrain from emphasizing "anti-Russian" identities domestically, Russia does not need to assert its imperial power. This compatibility could have arisen if Ukraine ended up as an autocracy like Russia. Or it could have arisen if Russia persevered as a hybrid regime or became a democracy, even a dysfunctional one. If either of these counterfactuals came to pass, regime similarity could have unwound the escalatory cycle and Russia's persistent re-imperialization pressure *vis-à-vis* Ukraine might have produced a different outcome from that of military aggression in 2014.

The counterfactual for the breakdown of Ukrainian democracy was the emergence of an authoritarian regime. An authoritarian trajectory for Ukraine would have meant a more pro-Russian course in foreign and domestic politics alike. An authoritarian Ukrainian leader would have been more likely to yield to Russian pressure across policy areas because he would be more insulated from public preferences. In addition, he would have used strategies like those of Russia's authoritarian regime to mold public preferences into an acceptable form. Without political competition and public deliberation, the preferences of average Ukrainians might not have evolved over time closer to the Europeanization position and away from the Russian World position. Simply put, given the contrast between an authoritarian Russia and a democratic Europe, an authoritarian Ukraine is more likely to have veered toward the former and away from the latter. Russia would have gradually vassalized Ukraine, cutting off its road to Europe in exchange for cheap gas and cooptation of oligarchic networks. Achieving imperialist restoration *de facto*, Russia could have left Ukraine nominally independent, as it did with Belarus, but would have set the framework of Ukrainian identity, language, memory politics, as well as controlled its geopolitical orientation and foreign economic policy. Western Ukrainian electorate and political and intellectual elites favoring a pro-Western course and pro-Ukrainian cultural agenda, a minority constituency on the national level, would have been suppressed, marginalized, or coopted in the context of broader authoritarian repression. As Chapter 1 showed, identities and their salience are constructed politically, and systematic efforts by an authoritarian state to inculcate a pro-Russian identity could have further reduced the constituency opposed to *de facto* vassalization of Ukraine. Also, identity diversity is not a guarantee of democratic competition, as Russia itself demonstrates – the elites representing different groups can be coopted into the authoritarian coalition.

There are at least three hypothetical possibilities of how Ukrainian democracy could have broken down and a pro-Russian authoritarian regime could have taken hold. One possibility is Kuchma consolidating an authoritarian regime in the early 2000s and foregoing the risk of trying to transfer power to a chosen successor. In formal terms, he made this option available to himself. The Constitutional Court signed off on his plan to seek a third term. In fact, he may have been more electable than the boorish Yanukovych. While Yanukovych was clearly unacceptable to western and central Ukrainian voters, Kuchma had a track record of winning both, based on western/central and eastern/southern support. He could have played this to his advantage. In addition, to prepare for re-election, he could have solicited more help from Russia in the form of preferential energy prices and other trade concessions. Instead of pursuing a balanced foreign-policy course, he could have steered Ukraine into the CIS integration process and thus left the can of worms that came with the prospect of European integration unopened. Finally, an authoritarian Kuchma could have pursued the creation of a power vertical using Putin's strategy as inspiration, but also following in Lukashenka's or Nazarbaev's footsteps. The western Ukrainian voters could have been marginalized or coopted economically in a Kuchma dictatorship. The Kuchmagate tape scandal that suggested the president's involvement in Gongadze's murder made this scenario less likely, but, of course, the leak was not inevitable.

A pro-Russian autocracy in Ukraine could have also emerged had Kuchma and Yanukovych prevented Yushchenko's victory or quashed the Orange Revolution. There are several ways in which the Orange Revolution could have been prevented. If Yushchenko had died from the poisoning, it is unclear that Tymoshenko would have won the election with such a short campaign period. If the regime had been more effective at electoral manipulation, at ballot stuffing, or at protest-proofing Kyiv, at silencing the media that supported the protesters (for example, by taking Poroshenko's Channel 5 off the air), they could have gotten away with stealing the election. The Orange Revolution was only the second of the color revolutions in the post-Soviet region and the regime was taken by surprise to some extent. Authoritarian learning on how to protest-proof hadn't taken place. The Orange Revolution protesters could have failed to achieve their goal of obtaining an election re-run and a clean vote if the Supreme Court had been effectively bought or intimidated to reject the opposition's lawsuit. The Supreme Court's decision was quite creative and relied on the interpretation of the spirit of the law to rule in Yushchenko's favor. A technical decision could have rejected the lawsuit and then the European negotiators, and the US behind the scenes too probably, could have pressed Yushchenko to stand down and concede defeat to preserve the rule of law. Alternatively, if Russia had escalated its reaction to military threats, Europe, at least the EU, if not the Polish and Latvian presidents, may have pressured the Orange camp to concede. Once installed as president in 2005 and with the full power of the super-presidential constitution behind him, Yanukovych could have pursued autocratization.

A third possibility for authoritarian consolidation in Ukraine, though less likely, is Yanukovych successfully completing the consolidation of an authoritarian regime in 2010–2013 that would have prevented Euromaidan. With Tymoshenko and a number of other opposition figures in prison, the judiciary under firm control, parliament subdued, Yanukovych could have more effectively pursued a coordinated strategy to dismantle the competitive media market and re-introduce censorship. Following Putin's example, he could have introduced civil society-curbing legislation and anti-protest laws to protect himself pre-emptively from the kind of mass social mobilization that happened during Maidan and was his eventual undoing. While plausible, this counterfactual did not materialize because several factors worked against it. Civil society had already developed the capacity to maintain its networks. The Orange era had resulted in significant fragmentation of the oligarchic class, which meant that opposition figures had an economic power base. Finally, society's commitment to Ukraine's independence had evolved to a point where a decisive turn toward Russia would not go unnoticed and would be politically destabilizing, which is what happened after Yanukovych backtracked in 2013 on the association agreement with the EU at the eleventh hour.

Another set of counterfactuals envisions Russia's gradual democratization. Had Russia developed a democracy, even a dysfunctional one, or at least sustained a substantial degree of political competition under a competitive authoritarian regime, war could have been avoided. Democratic Russia was less likely to invade Ukraine because the decision would not be that of one person, and the party of war would have to compete with a plethora of domestic actors whose preferences or at least preferred methods for "dealing with" Ukraine were different. A politically competitive Russian regime may not have respected Ukrainian sovereignty by tolerating a diverging domestic and foreign-policy course produced by Ukraine's own democratic process. Democracies can, of course, be imperialist, expansionist, and aggressive in foreign policy, so Russian democratization is far from a silver bullet against Russian revanchism. However, a competitive Russian regime is more likely to have created space for debate around both Russian and Ukrainian national identity. Even if political actors proposing a civic Russian nation and Russian non-interference in Ukraine would not have won the day, their presence in a competitive regime may have constrained the gradual move toward the ethnicization and imperialization of Russian identity described in Chapter 1. For example, politicians like Boris Nemtsov, who vehemently opposed Russia's annexation of Crimea in 2014, may have raised the political costs of Putin's opportunistic land grab and prevented it. Instead of being able to shape policy, Nemtsov was gunned down in 2015.

Ukraine and Russia both pursuing a democratization path might also have prevented the collision course because Ukraine may have been more willing to hitch its wagon to a democratizing and open Russia than to Putin's autocratic bully of a regime. Especially in the earlier period, a democratizing Russia may have been an attractive model, the liberal empire that some Russian reformers dreamed of. A democratic Russia may have become an anchor of the post-Soviet region and other post-Soviet states may have gravitated to it voluntarily, rather than as a result of bullying and blackmail. In Ukraine, a positive Russian model could have tipped the political scales toward a grand bargain interested in pursuing reintegration that would have included the Center and the moderate parts of the Left and the Right.

So hypothetically, how could Russia have democratized? One scenario for Russia's democratization is if Yeltsin had called elections at the height of his popularity after the failure of the August 1991 coup and had gotten a majority in parliament that would have been more supportive of his economic reform program. A more workable relationship between the executive and the legislature, even accompanied by the same level of economic hardship, could have prevented the bitter confrontation between Yeltsin and parliament. Alternatively, though less credibly, Yeltsin might have agreed to the compromise Khasbulatov and Zorkin offered before the impeachment attempt in late March 1993 – a coalition government of national accord and restrictions on presidential decrees, among other measures. Either scenario would have prevented the fall 1993 constitutional crisis/attempted coup/military intervention and might have also prevented the adoption of the super-presidentialist constitution and the outsized growth of executive power that followed. Yeltsin's political instincts were not fundamentally authoritarian or power-driven; for example, he seriously considered resigning the presidency in the summer of 1995 when the Chechen war was going badly[56] – so he did not use his excessive presidential powers to the fullest, but the super-presidentialist constitution gave Putin a flying start to consolidate autocracy.

This counterfactual is not very plausible because a pro-reform majority in the Russian parliament was unlikely. Yeltsin's attempt to make a fast and irreversible economic transition was never truly popular with Russian society at large, nor did it have the backing of most Russian elites. The support that Yeltsin enjoyed in the fall of 1991 was based on his charisma and decisiveness during the hard-liners' coup attempt, rather than on any well-formulated political program. The economic hardship that descended almost immediately eroded whatever support existed for radical reforms precipitously. Thus, pulling the 1993 elections earlier may have produced a different set of parliamentarians, but would not have significantly increased the core group of supporters of radical market reforms. A government of national accord with the red–brown parliamentary majority and with Yeltsin's executive powers significantly trimmed is also not a promising recipe for democratization, and even could have exacerbated the Russian–Ukrainian relationship earlier and could have produced earlier confrontation over identity issues.

A second hypothetical scenario for preventing authoritarianism in Russia is that of someone other than Putin succeeding Yeltsin in 2000, and Russia's regime trajectory mirroring Ukraine's once the 1990s economic crisis was over. Perhaps if the next Russian president were not an ex-KGB officer, he could not have counted on the near-guaranteed loyalty of the vast security apparatus. A different Yeltsin successor may have chosen a different path or might have been weak and unable to consolidate an authoritarian regime. Elite fragmentation and balancing rather than the consolidation of a power vertical may have followed as a result, opening the door to democratization in Russia as well.

However, Yeltsin's 1998–1999 revolving door of young, liberal PMs suggests that Russian elites and society were not likely to coalesce behind a genuine liberal figure. Boris Nemtsov, the most politically adept of them all, who fought tirelessly for Russian democracy until his 2015 assassination, had Yeltsin's personal affection, but not a realistic shot at the top job. Luzhkov or Primakov were the more likely Yeltsin successors, had Putin not struck a chord with Russian society and

Yeltsin had nominated a weak liberal dud. Neither of them, however, was a champion of democracy. Luzhkov and Primakov were closer to the red–brown coalition that Yeltsin fought in the early 1990s. Not only had Luzhkov turned Moscow into a "single-company town" under his financial, media, and political control, but his ideological pitch for the presidency was nationalist. He railed against Sevastopol belonging to Ukraine, advocated the incorporation of all Russian-speakers in the "near abroad" back into the Russian state, and talked about arming Serbia to withstand NATO's assault. His ally Primakov leaned more toward the communists. At the same time, it is possible that had one of them succeeded Yeltsin instead of Putin, elite divisions may have lasted longer and Russia could have continued as a competitive authoritarian regime, or even democratized after their tenure.

Regime similarity, whether as two authoritarian regimes or as two democratizing regimes would also have increased the likelihood of Ukraine and Russia maintaining more aligned foreign policies as their national interests may have been more aligned. Two autocracies would have been more likely to see Western democracy promotion as a threat and thus would have been suspicious about developing closer ties with the West. Two democratizing regimes, on the other hand, may have been equally interested in exploring the possibility of closer ties and cooperation with Europe specifically and the West more broadly. A competitive authoritarian or democratizing Russia may have perceived Ukraine's pro-European foreign policy as being in sync with its own goals and, therefore, acceptable. Chapter 4 will show how parallel foreign policies do not mean that Russia refrains from interfering in Ukrainian domestic politics or abandons its re-imperialization agenda. However, the element of paranoia about Ukraine being used by the West to undermine and weaken Russia's autocratic regime would be much weaker, and hence the pressure for finding a military solution would be lower as well.

3

Historical memory, language, and citizenship

Starting already in the late Soviet period, Russia and Ukraine pursued increasingly divergent policies in the sphere of historical memory, language, and citizenship. Within the logic of the grand bargain, successive post-Soviet Ukrainian governments formulated policies that underscored differences rather than similarities between the two nations and states. Ukraine legislated single rather than dual citizenship and Ukrainian as the only state language, and re-evaluated the Soviet-era historical narrative, which emphasized commonalities in identity, interests, and a continuity of fate of Russia and Ukraine – from the ancient past and into the future. Russia disliked, regularly objected to, and sought to change Ukraine's identity policies. Russia's opposition to Ukraine's nation-building agenda intensified with Putin coming to power and the re-imperialization of Russian identity that followed, but the two countries have been clashing over identity policies since the 1990s.

During the Yeltsin presidency, citizenship and language were the main issues of contention. Historical memory emerged as a sore point in the 1990s as well, but would become a real battleground in the 2000s, especially after the 2004 Orange Revolution, when Yushchenko tried decisively to distance Ukraine from Russia in memory politics. While Russia was increasingly presenting the Soviet period as the golden age, including in Russia–Ukraine relations, and developing the cult of Soviet victory in WWII as the central element of a state-supported historical memory narrative, Ukraine questioned Soviet-era narratives of Ukrainian–Russian relations in general, and in the twentieth century and during and after WWII specifically. The two states were increasingly casting their shared past in opposite lights.

The growing re-imperialization of Russian identity during Putin's third term, Euromaidan's 2014 victory, and the subsequent conflict over Crimea and the war in Donbas accelerated the divergence. Originally, Ukraine's identity politics were the product of elite decisions taken within the logic of the Center-Right grand bargain discussed in Chapter 1, while popular opinion on many identity issues was divided, with the median voter position generally more "pro-Russian" than the position taken by the ruling elites. Over time, however, popular preferences evolved – first in the strategically important and electorally sizeable center of the country and, after Russia's aggression against Ukraine in 2014, attitudes to Russia and Russia-favored identity policies began to change in the east and south as well. The Center-Right grand bargain was put on a stronger societal footing.

As with regime divergence, which was discussed in the previous chapter, the Yanukovych presidency was a period when Russia's goal to halt Ukraine's divergence in the sphere of identity politics had the best chance of being achieved, but after Yanukovych was driven out by Euromaidan, the divergence in identity politics accelerated further. The post-2013 divergence discussed in Chapter 6 and in the conclusion shows how Russia's full-scale invasion led to more profound changes in societal identities in Ukraine – a process that now affected also the historically Russia-friendly southern and eastern regions, and drove identity policies in the two states further apart still. Overall, persisting and growing divergence in identity policies illustrated the escalatory cycle of Ukraine's pull away from Russia – for reasons that had everything to do with Ukrainian domestic politics, elite competition, and evolving societal attitudes, not with foreign meddling – and Russia's unsuccessful attempts to reverse the process.

History and memory

As Chapter 1 explained, the history of Ukraine and Russia could be narrated from two radically different perspectives. One narrative would emphasize the common origins and resulting joint identity, shared interests, and continuity of fate of the two "brotherly" peoples. The other would stress differences in identity, political traditions, and national aspirations. The former approach gives historical justification to Russia–Ukraine political unity, while the latter to Ukrainian state independence. After 1991, Ukraine and Russia increasingly diverged in their approach to interpreting their entangled histories, and this divergence resulted in an escalatory cycle, which reinforced and exacerbated the divergence. Ukraine began to question Soviet-era interpretations of history, many of which continued in Russia or were replaced with imperial-era narratives, all of which saw Ukraine and Russia as destined by history to be together rather than apart. Russia resented these developments in Ukraine, tried to halt them, but ultimately could not. In Russia, especially from mid-2000s onwards, the state increasingly controlled historiographic research, legislated correct ways to interpret the past, especially the WWII period and the Soviet period more generally, and used history as a tool to justify Russia's right to dominate its former vassals. In Ukraine, these developments only heightened the determination to keep highlighting Ukraine's historical separateness, and the two states, including respective presidents, accused each other of "falsifying" history.

This collision course was, in principle, not inevitable. Had Russian state elites imagined the Russian nation as a political community within a state defined by the existing borders, a historical narrative seeing a distinct Ukrainian people and a sovereign Ukrainian state would not have clashed with Russia's national and historical imaginary. Conversely, if the politics of identity in Ukraine resulted not in the grand bargain between the Right and the Center, but in the Ukrainian Left controlling the state – by itself or in an alliance with the Center – and determining historical memory politics, the Russia-favored narrative of historical unity and continuity of fate of the three eastern Slavic peoples would have been adopted in Ukraine as well and a collision of the historical narratives and memory politics could have been avoided. But this is not what happened.

As discussed in Chapter 1, in Russia a conception of the "true" Russian nation as a supranational civilization encompassing Ukraine progressively gained prominence at the level of the state, especially with the rise of the Russian World project in the late 2000s. The Russian World project was not only about culture, religion, and language but also about collective historical memory. Belonging to the Russian World presupposed shared collective memory, and inculcation of a view that would highlight the historical continuity of the fate of the people of the Russian World was of utmost importance for the Russian state elites. The imperialist vision of the Russian World project and the re-imperialization process informed by it were fundamentally incompatible with the idea of Ukraine as a distinct national and political community and the independent Ukrainian state as a legitimate political home for this nation. In Ukraine, the state supported and institutionalized a reading of history that emphasized Ukraine's national and cultural distinctiveness and the legitimacy of sovereign Ukrainian statehood. The two approaches were fundamentally at odds with each other, and the two state-supported historical policies clashed.

From the start of independence, the Russia-favored historical paradigm of three "brotherly" Slavic nations was replaced in Ukraine by the framework of history developed by Mykhailo Hrushevsky.[1] Hrushevsky was an academic and a prominent politician in the early twentieth century – the inaugural president from 1917 to 1918 of the short-lived independent Ukrainian republic that existed between 1917 and 1920. Hrushevsky's framework saw a coherent and distinct Ukrainian national history stretching back centuries. Ukrainian–Russian relations were not based on harmony and unity between brotherly nations but were a tumultuous and tragic history, punctuated by repeated attempts by Ukraine to acquire political freedom and Russia's coercive actions to prevent it. Post-1991, the adoption of this framework led to state-endorsed rethinking of key historical events in a way that radically diverged from interpretations favored in Russia. The divergence affected virtually all pivotal events in Ukrainian–Russian history from Kyivan Rus' through the twentieth century.

The extent to which the Ukrainian state pushed for historical re-evaluation of the Russian–Ukrainian "Slavic unity" paradigm varied in consistency and strength under different Ukrainian governments, and sometimes also across time under the same government. Still, the process began already in the late perestroika period and continued, even if with some variation in intensity, from then on. Russia was broadly unhappy with this departure from its preferred reading of history unfolding in Ukraine, especially the reading of the Soviet era, and attempted to halt this process. In 2003, which was declared "The Year of Russia in Ukraine" by Kuchma, an announcement was made after a meeting of the two countries' prime ministers that a joint working group would be created, headed by the deputy prime ministers of the two countries, to "harmonize" Ukrainian and Russian historical narratives and work on new history textbooks.[2] A group of Ukrainian historians, intellectuals, and civil society activists swiftly issued an open letter addressed to the Ukrainian president, prime minister, and speaker of parliament protesting the commission's formation. The authors of the letter stated that the Russian deputy prime minister believed it necessary to reconsider historical interpretations developed in the late perestroika and early post-Soviet years because they were supposedly unduly influenced by the "political situation" at the time. However, the letter authors argued that it was exactly during this period when in Ukraine historical research finally became independent of the "dominant political situation of the Soviet era." The commission was announced, the letter writers continued, after the Russian government expressed dissatisfaction with the analysis of the 1932–1933 famine in Ukraine.[3] The commission was not disbanded but its work did not result in either "harmonization" of historical narratives or Ukraine changing its approach to history. All in all, the incident with the commission illustrates that Russia was not prepared to accept Ukraine's right to differ in its interpretations of history but it was also not able to establish such control.

Divergence in historical interpretations between Russia and Ukraine unfolded in an escalatory cycle. Russia resented all historical "revisionism" by Ukraine. The re-evaluation of some historical events generated especially vehement objections in Russia and put the escalatory cycle in overdrive. Two examples of Ukraine and Russia clashing particularly severely over historical memory pertain to two twentieth-century historical events: the 1932–1933 famine and interwar and WWII-era Ukrainian nationalism.

Holodomor

In the aftermath of the devastating 1932–1933 famine, and throughout the Soviet era, the subject was suppressed and the very fact of the famine remained a taboo within the Soviet Union. When the ban was lifted during glasnost, the famine was portrayed as Stalin's crime against the peasant class. This largely remained the approach in post-Soviet Russia, where the state and state-sponsored historians present the famine as a "common tragedy" of all people of the Soviet Union, denying any differences in state treatment of different ethnic groups – as Russian president Medvedev did in his November 2008 letter to his Ukrainian counterpart Yushchenko.[4] In Ukraine, however, already during glasnost, the anti-Ukrainian nature of the famine, and not only its anti-class nature, emerged as a subject of public discourse. This interpretation was advocated by the Ukrainian Right and was broadly as follows: Ukrainians constituted a disproportionate number among famine victims and, with peasants being the core of the Ukrainian nation, Stalin's use of famine to break the resistance of the Ukrainian peasants to collectivization was also a policy aimed at breaking any national resistance by the Ukrainians against the Soviet state. The Soviet state applied particularly deadly measures disproportionally or even exclusively in Ukraine, such as the blockade of settlements to prevent starving peasants from fleeing the countryside to the cities, the confiscation of anything of value, and the policy of "blacklisting," which subjected villages to a range of repressive measures for not fulfilling impossibly high grain-procurement quotas. Advocates of this interpretation also highlighted that the famine was followed by a terror campaign eliminating a swath of the Ukrainian cultural intelligentsia and political cadres. The famine was thus an act of deliberate destruction of the Ukrainian nation – an act of genocide committed by Stalin's regime to enable the transformation of the Soviet Union into a new imperial state. As wider circles of the Ukrainian population became attuned to these discussions, a groundswell of eyewitness testimony emerged. Domestic realities in Ukraine shaped the discussion of the 1932–1933 famine and set it on a trajectory that would soon clash with what the Russian state wanted to define and defend as a "common" memory of the tragedy.

The logic of the grand bargain shaped state policies on the famine under presidents Kravchuk and Kuchma. In early 1993, two years into independence and on the 60th anniversary of the tragedy, Kravchuk signed a decree creating a program of official events to commemorate the anniversary of the famine that for the first time introduced the term Holodomor (death by starvation) into official use to describe the 1932–1933 famine. In subsequent years, state-sponsored nationwide commemorations were regularly held, but the Left in parliament blocked attempts by the Right to legally define Holodomor as a genocide of Ukrainians committed by the Soviet communist regime. For the Right, Holodomor became one of the fundamental symbols of Ukrainian national history – a national catastrophe that also symbolized Ukraine's victimization by the regime in Moscow. For the same reasons that the Right sought legal acknowledgment of the famine as an ultimate crime perpetrated by the Soviet state against Ukraine, the Left opposed it. The communist period and joint statehood with Russia was something the Left wished to restore rather than condemn. In the early 2000s, political changes in Ukraine enabled the legal recognition of Holodomor as genocide in 2006.

The 2004 Orange Revolution that brought pro-Western president Viktor Yushchenko to power was a turning point in Ukrainian political history, although the beginning of this turn can be dated to 2002, when for the first time the Center-Right – Yushchenko's

Our Ukraine party – won the party list vote. In February 2003, parliamentary hearings on the famine, previously obstructed by the Left, finally took place. Three months later, following recommendations from the hearings, a special session of parliament approved an address to the nation, where Holodomor was described as "one of the biggest acts of genocide in world history."[5] After Yushchenko won the presidency in 2004, he devoted considerable attention to identity issues in general and to the recognition of the Holodomor as genocide, specifically. Yushchenko spoke about the Holodomor in his inaugural speech and, in November 2006, submitted to parliament a draft law that defined Holodomor as an act of genocide against the Ukrainian people. By that point, the pro-presidential majority in parliament had collapsed but parliament nevertheless approved a modified version of the bill. Critical votes came from the Socialist party, whose voter base was in the rural areas and which, after a decade and a half of independence, was no longer as committed as the communists to a reading of history that saw the Soviet past in exclusively positive light. Socialist party leader and speaker of the parliament Oleksandr Moroz proposed a compromise draft that used the term *narod* (people) rather than *natsia* (nation), signifying a political rather than an ethnic designation of the group subjected to the genocide in Ukraine; added a clause acknowledging "other nations of the Soviet Union" as victims of the famine; and dropped the clause on administrative liability for public denial of the Holodomor. This compromise law was narrowly adopted, with 233 out of 450 deputies in favor, in November 2006.[6]

Russia was outraged by the law. The law did not directly blame Russia for the Holodomor but could be construed as implicating Russia in the genocide since Russia cast itself as the successor state of the Soviet Union. The law also ran fundamentally counter to the notion that being in a common state with Russia was where Ukraine "naturally" belonged, if such a state committed the ultimate crime of genocide against the Ukrainian people. In 2006, the Russian Duma passed a resolution denying that the famine was genocide. Since the passage of the Holodomor law, the Russian government increasingly came to portray Yushchenko, specifically, and the Ukrainian authorities, generally, as hostile and accused them of fostering "provocative actions" by "radical nationalist forces" which went against, in Russia's interpretation, the will of the majority of the Ukrainian people.[7] Russia took it upon itself to define what were the Ukrainian people's true interests, but as opinion polls show, Holodomor was perhaps the first example of identity politics, when the public quickly aligned with the position of the Ukrainian state.

As discussed in Chapter 1, among the realities complicating the oft-used east/west shortcut for analyzing public opinion in Ukraine has been the presence of a strategically important and geographically sizeable center of the country, where opinions often fell between the "extremes" of the east and west. The center was also the region where, after the Orange Revolution, attitudes began to tilt toward the west. Polls on the Holodomor law illustrate both of these dynamics. In November 2007, a survey by the Kyiv International Institute of Sociology (KIIS) on attitudes to the law on Holodomor as genocide of the Ukrainian people, nationwide 63% supported the law, with percentages of support by region as follows: 85% in the western regions, 76% in the central regions, 55% in the southern regions, and 35% in the eastern regions.[8] Between 2010 and 2012, according to Rating Group polls, opposition to the recognition of Holodomor as genocide declined nationwide from 34% to 22%, and the center became virtually identical to the west in its attitudes on the question – nearly 80% in the center regarded Holodomor as genocide of the Ukrainian people.[9]

Since the 2006 Holodomor law was passed, top state officials in Russia took it upon themselves to contest the interpretation of the 1932–1933 famine in Ukraine. In 2008, President Medvedev refused to pay an official visit to the opening of a memorial in Kyiv to the victims of the Holodomor, and wrote a letter to Yushchenko accusing him of politicizing what Russia considered the shared tragedy of Soviet citizens and "attempting to maximally separate our nations, united by centuries-long historical, cultural, and spiritual connections."[10] Russia also took its fight against the Holodomor interpretation in Ukraine to the international level and was able to swat the Yushchenko government's attempts to gain recognition from the international community of the Holodomor as an act of genocide against the Ukrainian people. In Ukraine this campaign was carried out under the slogan "Ukraine Remembers, the World Recognizes" and was particularly intense in 2008, on the 75th anniversary of the 1932–1933 famine. In international organizations such as the United Nations and UNESCO, Russia blocked all Ukrainian initiatives to recognize the Holodomor as an act of genocide targeting Ukrainians.[11] Within Ukraine, however, the divergence continued and strengthened. As Chapter 5 will illustrate with the post-Euromaidan polling results on this issue, there is now a virtually universal agreement within Ukraine on the famine as a genocide of Ukrainians.

The OUN and the UPA

Revisiting the history of Ukrainian interwar nationalist groups and their leaders was another area where the narrative of existential unity and common enemies and allies got challenged in Ukraine, to Russia's ire. The frame of "brotherly unity" and commonality of interests of Russians and Ukrainians demonized or downplayed all figures and events that suggested the legitimacy of attempts to establish independent Ukraine separate from Russia. Within this frame the Ukrainian nationalism of the first half of the twentieth century, and in particular the two controversial World War II-era nationalist organizations: the Organization of Ukrainian Nationalists (OUN), a radical right-wing group founded in 1929 that sought to secure Ukrainian independence, and its military wing, the Ukrainian Insurgent Army (UPA), which fought against the Poles, Germans, and Soviets during and after WWII – were unambiguous villains. This was the case within the commemorative cult of the WWII (Great Patriotic War) which was created already in the Soviet period, continued in Russia, and intensified after the 1990s.

After 1991, the memory of WWII was adapted to the Russian nation-building agenda, but the way it was done differed significantly in the 1990s and afterwards. In the early 1990s, there was an attempt to re-narrate the Soviet victory as a great feat of the people accomplished not due to the communist leadership but rather in spite of it, echoing the attempted contrast between the new "democratic" Russia and the old "totalitarian and autocratic" Russia. After Putin rose to power, the emphasis in the official discourse shifted from the contrast between the "old" and the "new" Russia to the status of Russia as a "great power" over its "thousand-year-long" history.[12] The state-propagated narrative of the Soviet Union as a great state saving the world from absolute evil has served to strengthen the legitimacy and status of Russia as a great power. It also aimed to boost the legitimacy of the Putin regime, which presented itself as the successor of the USSR and the guardian of sacred history that could not possibly be narrated in any different way from how it was done by Russia. The narrative of sacred Soviet victory in WWII also served to bind former Soviet states to Russia, since during WWII all Soviet people were one whole, fighting for a common holy goal. Challenging this WWII myth from any perspective – including a national perspective that a post-Soviet state might develop – became sacrilegious. This was essentially an attempt to limit post-Soviet states' sovereignty since Russia's WWII cult disallowed these states to remember WWII specifically, and the Soviet period more generally, in ways that would contradict state-sanctioned historical memory in Russia.

As discussed in Chapter 1, in the Soviet period, from the perspective of the Soviet state, the cardinal sin of the OUN and the UPA was not the participation of some of their members in the Holocaust and the ethnic cleansing of the Poles, but fighting against the Soviet Union and seeking to establish an independent Ukrainian state. Continued demonization of the OUN and the UPA made sense within the post-2000 triumphalist narrative of the Soviet victory in WWII as a key pillar of Russian identity. For Russia, these groups, which sought to destroy the Soviet state in order to create an independent Ukraine, could have no redeeming value. However, within the frame that emphasized the distinctiveness of the Ukrainian nation and its centuries-long national-liberation struggle, a recategorization of the OUN and the UPA as fighters for Ukrainian independence, rather than exclusively Nazi collaborators and enemies of the common Soviet state, was possible. The Ukrainian nationalist movement and its determined partisan guerrilla campaign against the Soviets could be presented not as treasonous activity against the USSR but as the apogee of the national liberation struggle against domination by Moscow.[13]

Even though legal recategorization of the OUN and the UPA as fighters for Ukrainian state independence would not take place until after the Euromaidan, a movement away from the Soviet/Russian reading of history of interwar Ukrainian nationalism was jump-started much earlier within the framework of the Center-Right grand bargain. In 1997, Ukraine's second president, Leonid Kuchma, a centrist who was elected by the predominantly Russian-speaking regions of Ukraine on a ticket that rejected the "nationalist" platform of the first president, Kravchuk, created a government commission to re-evaluate the Soviet-era approach to the OUN and the UPA. The commission's conclusions, published in 2005, were ambiguous and did not result in legal changes then, but the very questioning of the Soviet/Russian narrative about interwar Ukrainian nationalism was setting Ukraine and Russia on opposing trajectories.

Attempts to undo the Soviet/Russian narrative about interwar Ukrainian nationalism intensified in Ukraine under Yushchenko, who tried to get the OUN and the UPA legally defined as fighters for Ukrainian independence. During Yushchenko's tenure, fifteen draft bills were tabled in parliament, seven of them during his first year in office, to recognize the OUN and the UPA as participants in Ukraine's "national liberation struggle" and grant their members status as war veterans.[14] These attempts failed as Yushchenko could not secure enough support for this radical re-evaluation of what in the Soviet period were the most vilified groups. Unlike with Holodomor, when, by 2006, state policy to define Holodomor as genocide came to be supported by a majority of the public (with notable regional variations), it would take Russia's aggression against Ukraine after Euromaidan before the reconceptualization of the OUN and the UPA as fighters for Ukrainian independence would become the majority view (as we will show in Chapter 5 with polling data). Still, public opinion was neither static nor uniformly against reconceptualization and attitudes to the OUN and the UPA began to shift after the Orange Revolution. From December 2006 to December 2007, the share of those who opposed OUN and UPA recognition declined from 52% to 46% nationwide, according to polls by the Democratic Initiatives Foundation. The center again was less opposed to the policy than the south and east. In December 2007, equal shares – 38% – were for and against recognition in the center, while in the southeast only 22% were in support (and even fewer in Donbas and Crimea).[15]

Re-evaluation of the WWII history in Ukraine was a domestic political process, and Russia's reaction to it was telling of Russia's determination to take measures at the highest state level to prevent what Russia cast as "falsification" of common history. In May 2009, under President Medvedev, Russia took legal steps to fight any such "falsifications of history." The National Security Strategy of the Russian Federation declared the need to protect the dignity of Russia's historical narratives, and a presidential commission was created to counter attempts to "falsify history to the detriment of Russia's interests."[16] The 28-member commission, headed by the chief of Medvedev's administration and Putin loyalist Sergei Naryshkin, was tasked with analyzing "information about the falsification of historic facts aimed against Russia" and preparing "recommendations on adequate reactions to falsifications that hinder Russian interests and to neutralize their possible negative consequences."[17]

Prime targets of the commission were neighboring states and their attempts to question key narratives and to doubt the positive role of Russian and Soviet rule in these nations' histories. Days after the commission was formed, Russia accused the Georgian authorities of falsifying history by arguing that Georgia was annexed by imperial Russia rather than that it voluntarily agreed to join the Russian empire.[18] Ukraine and its re-evaluation of WWII history was a particular target of the commission, which was formed at the time Yushchenko was pushing for legal recognition of the OUN and the UPA as "fighters for Ukrainian independence." Russian state actors and institutions also objected to a host of other memorial initiatives during the Yushchenko period, pertaining to events as long ago as the seventeenth century, such as the 1659 Battle of Konotop, when Ukrainian forces under Hetman Ivan Vyhovsky defeated the Russian army, or the 1709 Battle of Poltava, when Peter I's armies defeated Charles XII's Swedes and the Ukrainian Cossacks led by Hetman Ivan Mazepa. Both Vyhovsky and Mazepa turned against the tsar and were seen as traitors by Russia, but from the Ukrainian perspective they were being reconceptualized as leaders of a struggle against the tsar's growing encroachment on Cossack autonomy. The Russian Foreign Ministry decried Yushchenko's March 2008 decree on commemorating the 350th anniversary of the Konotop battle as anti-Russian nationalist manifestations.[19] Yushchenko adopted a March 2009 decree to honor Hetman Mazepa by making his birthday a state holiday, instituted a state award in his name, and named one of the central streets in Kyiv after him. The move produced official condemnations from the Russian Foreign Ministry, the State Duma, and Russia's ambassador to Ukraine, who outlandishly compared plans to erect a monument to Mazepa in Poltava to the hypothetical erection of a monument to Hitler in Stalingrad.[20]

Russia's determination to define and defend one correct reading of history, not just for Russian society but for the neighboring states, first and foremost Ukraine, was elevated to the level of state policy with the formation of the state commission. It showed that Russia would not accept a process that had been going on in Ukraine since independence – the dismantling of a historical narrative about existential Eastern Slavic unity and continuity of fate of Ukraine and Russia. It was a Ukrainian domestic affair but this rethinking of history stood in the way of Russia's re-imperialization, which was aimed at regaining and keeping influence over Ukraine.

Could the process of Ukraine drawing away from the Russia-favored historical memory frame informed by the "brotherly nations" narrative have been reversed at any point after 1991? The general logic of a nation-state where an independent state derives legitimacy from representing a distinct nation made the Russia-favored historical narrative centered on the organic unity of Ukraine and Russia broadly incompatible with – and threatening to – independent Ukrainian statehood. To reverse the process of distancing from Russia in the area of historical memory, the politics of identity in Ukraine had to change first. In the 1990s and 2000s, despite electoral turnover, the politics of identity sustained the distancing: the pro-Russian Left did not manage to capture the state and the Center sided with the Right in support of a reading of history that legitimized the Ukrainian state as the political home of a distinct Ukrainian nation. The presidency of Viktor Yanukovych, who came to power in 2010, was the period when a Russia-favored reversal could have possibly taken place.

After being denied victory by the Orange Revolution in 2004, Yanukovych was elected in 2010 on the platform of undoing the "nationalist" legacy of his predecessor and bringing Ukraine closer to Russia. Yanukovych embraced the Russian–Soviet–East Slavic identity to a greater extent than had either Kuchma or Kravchuk.[21] From the start of his presidency Yanukovych tried to reverse state policy on the interpretation of the Holodomor. Immediately after his inauguration, the links to the Holodomor on the president's official website were deleted.[22] Yanukovych quickly abandoned the interpretation of the famine as a genocide of Ukrainians, recasting it instead – echoing Russia's position – as a "common tragedy of the people of the USSR."[23] School history textbooks, revised by the Yanukovych-appointed minister of education, known for his pro-Russian stand, dropped references to the man-made nature of the Holodomor.[24] Yanukovych also undid the only tangible – and controversial – legacy of Yushchenko with regard to the OUN and the UPA. In the final weeks of his presidency, after it became clear that parliament wouldn't pass his OUN/UPA legislation, Yushchenko awarded posthumously the Hero of Ukraine title, the highest state honor, to the leader of the OUN, Stepan Bandera. Earlier he had conferred the same honor to the UPA commander-in-chief Roman Shukhevych. Three months into the Yanukovych presidency, a local court in Yanukovych's home region repealed Yushchenko's decrees.[25]

Whether Yanukovych, had he stayed in power longer, would have been able to fully reverse the state policies on history and historical memory pursued by his predecessors in the direction favored by Russia will remain unknown. During his nearly four years in office, he attempted a substantial but not a wholesale reversal of historical memory policies. He did not, for example, attempt to repeal the 2006 law on the Holodomor, and the Yanukovych-controlled Constitutional Court refused to rule on the question of whether Yushchenko's decrees on Bandera and Shukhevych were unconstitutional.[26] Yanukovych had legislative majority, but the full compliance of his coalition was not a given in the environment of diminished, but still existing, political competition during his years in office. Civil society resisted measures aimed at re-harmonizing Ukraine's historical narrative with Russia's through the creation of a common instructional book for history teachers.[27] Had Yanukovych violently prevailed over the Euromaidan, he possibly could have succeeded in establishing an authoritarian regime, where the president could push through any policy. Such authoritarian consolidation, and Yanukovych's inevitable increased dependence on Russia in this scenario, could have been accompanied by wholesale reversal of memory politics in Ukraine in the direction favored by Russia. Euromaidan's victory, which drove Yanukovych from power, closed this possibility and ended prospects of a hypothetical harmonization of Ukraine's historical memory policies with Russia's.

Citizenship policy

Citizenship was another policy area where the escalatory cycle played out, resulting in divergence between Ukraine and Russia, informed by different conceptions of identity. Citizenship as a legal institution defines the formal boundaries of the nation in whose name the state is constituted and, as such, the citizenship institution is a key element of statehood. In Ukraine, political elites came to believe the institution of Ukrainian citizenship to be critical for first attaining and then strengthening state sovereignty for a distinct Ukrainian nation. To serve this purpose, the institution of Ukrainian citizenship had to be distinct, not subsumed into any other citizenship – first that of the Soviet Union, and later that of the CIS or a dual citizenship with Russia. From the start, the politics of citizenship centered around the implications of Ukrainian citizenship for political union between Russia and Ukraine. Russia wanted to use citizenship policy as a way of diluting Ukrainian sovereignty and reintegrating Ukraine. As Russia pushed Ukraine to acquiesce to dual citizenship or common CIS citizenship, which it saw as a step toward a common political future, Ukraine's ruling elites stayed firm. Ukraine's ruling class, including Russian-speaking Centrists from the southeastern regions, shared the belief that Volodymyr Lytvyn, speaker of the parliament and once chief of staff of President Kuchma, expressed succinctly as follows: "if we have dual citizenship, we will not have a state."[28]

In the Soviet period, legal citizenship was a union-wide institution: all citizens of the USSR had only Soviet passports and Soviet citizenship. Administrative units, including Ukraine and the fourteen other union republics, did not have their own citizenship. The May 1990 Soviet law on citizenship introduced citizenship of the union republics as a legal possibility, to be set up through republican citizenship laws. Legislatures in the union republics thus gained the authority to create the institution of republican citizenship and define its principles. In Ukraine the controversy over citizenship first arose in July 1990, when the Supreme Soviet of the Ukrainian republic debated the sovereignty declaration.[29]

A draft of the declaration contained the clause "Ukrainian SSR has its own citizenship." This proved to be the most contentious part of the declaration – taking more time during the debate than any other clause, even such controversial ones as the Ukrainian republic setting up its own armed forces.[30] Ukrainian politicians saw the citizenship clause as directly impinging on the question of Ukraine remaining in the union or leaving it. As the then-leader of the Ukrainian Communist Party Stanislav Hurenko put it during the June 28, 1990 debate of the declaration: "each of us has to take a position: sovereignty of what state are we talking about? Is it sovereignty of the republic that exists outside of any union, or a republic that is a full-fledged member of a voluntary union of sovereign socialist states?" The anti-communist opposition ideologically committed to Ukrainian sovereignty saw separate citizenship as a critical sovereignty-building institution, and favored the wording "Ukrainian SSR has its own citizenship." The Left wanted this clause supplemented with the statement "citizens of the Ukrainian SSR remain citizens of USSR." This wording subsumed Ukrainian citizenship into Soviet citizenship and, as such, was a mechanism to preserve a union state.

The consequences of separate republican citizenship for the prospects of the union state was also well understood in Russia. When legislators of the Russian republic debated a republican citizenship law in the fall of 1991 they added a separate article to the draft to ensure that the Russian law would not invalidate the Soviet citizenship law and threaten the prospects of saving the union state. Yeltsin assured legislators that he was "not giving up hope of concluding a political treaty" with other republics on the preservation of the Soviet Union.[31] In Ukraine, however, the Left didn't manage to subsume Ukrainian citizenship under Soviet citizenship. The Center-Right bargain that was emerging already then stood in the way. A segment of the communist nomenklatura was coming to see the potential benefits of greater sovereignty, and ultimately full independence, of Ukraine. For its own political and economic prospects, that segment sided with the

Right over the Left. The Ukrainian sovereignty declaration established Ukrainian citizenship as a distinct legal institution. In a compromise wording of the citizenship clause, all citizens of the Ukrainian SSR were granted "the right to retain" Soviet citizenship, instead of the communist-favored formulation that citizens of Ukrainian SSR "remain" Soviet citizens.

In June 1991, when the first citizenship law came up for discussion in the parliament of the Ukrainian republic, the debate again centered on the implications of citizenship for Ukraine's future – in a union with Russia or on the road to full independence. In June 1991, the anti-Gorbachev coup had not yet taken place, Gorbachev-led negotiations over the new union treaty were ongoing with Ukraine's careful participation, and few could imagine the total collapse of the USSR. But would Ukraine be drawing closer or pulling away from a union state? "There can be no sovereignty without a law on citizenship," stated a pro-sovereignty Ukrainian legislator.[32] The institution of citizenship was seen as strengthening sovereignty and bringing possible future independence a step closer, while its absence dimmed prospects for state sovereignty. In June 1991, the communist majority successfully killed the first attempt to pass a citizenship law of the Ukrainian republic. A few months later, following the collapse of the anti-Gorbachev August 1991 coup, political reality changed dramatically. With prospects of the USSR continuation diminished by the coup, the first Ukrainian citizenship law was adopted in October 1991.

The law followed the so-called "zero option" for defining the initial body of citizens: all Soviet citizens who had permanent residency registration in the Ukrainian republic at the time of the law's entry into force in November 1991 were recognized as Ukrainian citizens. This made the Ukrainian law a lot less controversial than citizenship policies in Latvia and Estonia, where most of those who migrated from elsewhere in the Soviet Union during the time Estonia and Latvia were under Soviet occupation did not receive citizenship automatically. In Ukraine all residents received citizenship, but a controversy quickly developed over dual citizenship – first with the USSR and, after the USSR was no more, with Russia and the CIS. Unsurprisingly, the Left and the Right sharply disagreed on the issue, with each side's position informed by their national identity conceptions and associated preferences for fully independent statehood or one somehow united with Russia.

Conceiving of Ukraine as a distinct nation and viewing Russia as Ukraine's main "other," the Right opposed dual citizenship with Russia. The Left, embracing the frame of Slavic unity, favored dual citizenship as means to foster a political union/joint state, first with the USSR and later with Russia and/or the CIS. The grand bargain between the Right and the Center in Ukraine again proved consequential in rejecting dual citizenship as a policy that would have served to blur the distinction between the Ukrainian and Russian nations and states. In Ukraine, dual citizenship with Russia was supported only by the Left. The Right and the Center opposed both dual citizenship and common CIS citizenship, fearing its consequences for Ukrainian state sovereignty.

In Russia there was an elite consensus over the desirability of dual citizenship with Ukraine for the same reasons – diluting the actual and symbolic boundaries between Russia and Ukraine. From the early 1990s, Russian state elites, including liberals around Yeltsin, favored dual citizenship with Ukraine, and later also common CIS citizenship, and pushed for the institution of such policies. Yeltsin postponed several times the signing of the Treaty on Friendship, Cooperation, and Partnership between Russia and Ukraine, due to Ukraine's resistance to including provisions on dual citizenship. Due to Ukraine's unyielding position, the treaty eventually was signed in May 1997 without any provisions that mentioned citizenship.[33]

When the Ukrainian legislature debated the first citizenship law in the fall of 1991, dual citizenship dominated the debate. By then, the August 1991 coup and Ukraine's declaration of independence undermined the hopes of preserving the Soviet Union, but dual citizenship was still a mechanism to enable the creation of some form of political union with Russia in the future. The Right, opposing any such union, proposed an article: "in Ukraine there is single citizenship." The Left wanted either to remove this article altogether, or supplement it with the clause "dual citizenship is allowed." During the October 8, 1991 debate, the clause "dual citizenship is allowed" came just two votes short of being passed but, ultimately, the Center-Right grand bargain again produced an outcome closer to the position of the Right than of the Left. Kravchuk, then speaker of the parliament and soon to be elected the first president of Ukraine, proposed a compromise clause: "in Ukraine there is single citizenship; dual citizenship is allowed on the basis of bilateral agreements." Ukraine would never conclude any such agreements despite Russia actively pushing for a dual citizenship agreement with Ukraine, and other former Soviet republics, through the 1990s.[34]

The Ukrainian political class – not just the Right but also centrist elites – regarded dual citizenship as fundamentally threatening to Ukrainian state sovereignly. Centrist elites were opportunistic and sought electoral mileage from promising dual citizenship with Russia at election time, but never delivered on this promise. In 1994, Leonid Kuchma campaigned for president with a promise of dual citizenship with Russia, only to abandon it after he got elected. A few months into his tenure Kuchma announced that he would not sign any agreements with Russia if they mentioned dual citizenship, which led to the postponement of the signing of the comprehensive treaty between Russia and Ukraine, which we discuss in greater detail Chapter 4. In the 1990s, dual citizenship remained popular among the Ukrainian public. In 1995, 52.3% supported the idea of dual citizenship, 30.9% opposed, and 16.3% were undecided. Therefore, like with other areas of identity politics such as re-evaluation of the OUN and the UPA, the Center-Right elite grand bargain rather than popular preferences drove state policies in the 1990s and early 2000s. But, just as with other identity policies, popular preferences evolved over time in a direction that put the Center-Right bargain on a stronger social footing. By 2010, a plurality of Ukrainians (43.8%) opposed dual citizenship, 39.3% supported, and 16.7% were undecided.[35]

Once a clause that Ukraine had single citizenship became enshrined in the 1996 Ukrainian constitution adopted on Kuchma's watch, the prospects of dual citizenship with Russia or a CIS-wide citizenship dimmed further. Communist MPs advocated for dual citizenship in 1997, when amendments to the 1991 citizenship law were discussed, but with constitutional prohibition of dual citizenship the communists' proposals were rejected as unconstitutional. The Left pushed for dual citizenship, also unsuccessfully, in 2001 when a new edition of the citizenship law was adopted.[36]

As with historical memory, there was a possibility that a more Russia-friendly president could come to power and be persuaded to satisfy Russia on the citizenship issue. In the run-up to the 2004 elections, Yanukovych agreed to work out a dual citizenship agreement with Russia. It is uncertain whether Yanukovych could have delivered on this promise given constitutional prohibition against dual citizenship and substantial opposition to dual citizenship with Russia not only among the national-democrats, who opposed him, but also among the centrist elites in his camp. But, despite these obstacles, the chance was there and Russian federal agencies even started to draft a treaty on dual citizenship with Ukraine.[37] The Orange Revolution ended these plans, and, unable to secure cooperation from Ukraine, Russia eventually opted for unilateral actions and engaged in the policy known as passportization, or distribution of its passports, despite Ukraine's objections, to Ukrainian residents.

In hindsight, the concerns of Ukraine's political class about dual citizenship being a tool for Russia to undermine Ukraine's sovereignty proved well founded. As Chapter 6 details, Russia engaged in systematic distribution of Russian passports and citizenship to ethnic Russians, Russian speakers, and other minorities in neighboring states. This policy reflected Russia's re-imperialization trajectory, which sought to "maintain neo-imperial influence over and regain territory in the former Soviet republics."[38] Unilateral allocation of Russian citizenship would be used to justify Russia's claim that it had the right to protect these newly minted Russian citizens, to the point of intervening militarily and annexing territories where such citizens resided.[39] Putin would do this first in Georgia in 2008, then in Crimea in 2014, and also when announcing the "special military operation" and invading the rest of Ukraine in February 2022. One of the justifications of the operation was protection of Donbas residents, who, since 2019, were passportized *en masse* by Russia.

Language policy

Policies on state/official language was another area where after 1991 the grand bargain of the Right and Center resulted in measures that pulled Ukraine and Russia apart rather than closer together – a divergence that Russia opposed and tried to halt. The Left in Ukraine advocated for giving Russian the status of second state (or official) language in Ukraine, while the Right was adamant to have Ukrainian as the only state language. The outcome of the Center-Right grand bargain in the sphere of state language policy was legislation that defined Ukrainian as the only state language.

The first language law was adopted in 1989, during the late perestroika period when glasnost allowed the cultural intelligentsia united around Rukh to voice grievances over decades of Russification. In the 1989 law, Ukrainian was designated as the sole state language, while Russian was given status of the "language of inter-ethnic communication" within the then still-existing union state. The Right's support for the one-state-language policy was informed by a two-fold concern: implications of state language policy for the future of the Ukrainian language, including its very survival, and implications of state language policy for the prospects of a fully independent state. The Right often pointed to the example of Belarus, where the policy of two state languages eliminated any incentives for learning and using Belarusian, which perpetuated and accelerated Soviet-era Russification policy. Language policy also had implications for the future of the state. As a symbol of statehood, a one-state-language policy underscored the distinctiveness of the Ukrainian nation, which in turn legitimized distinct Ukrainian statehood. By contrast, two state languages served to blur the difference between Ukrainian and Russian nations and states, correspondingly weakening the symbolic foundation for a separate Ukrainian state.

Centrist elites, most of them Russian-speakers themselves, were not nearly as animated, if at all, by the revival of the Ukrainian language cause but they were interested in ruling an independent state. Consequently, the Center supported the one-state-language policy as a symbol of independent statehood. The Center-Right grand bargain also enabled the codification of the one-state-language principle into the 1996 constitution. While consistently supporting one-state-language policy in practice through the 1990s and the 2000s, the centrist elites regularly speculated on the "language question" at election times by campaigning with a promise to make Russian the second official or state language. Pointing to the prevailing bilingualism of Ukraine, in his 1994 electoral campaign Kuchma promised to propose changes to the 1989 law on language to grant the Russian language official status alongside Ukrainian. Until Yanukovych actually tried to deliver on this promise after his 2010 elections, all prior presidents had abandoned this promise after the elections – their behavior informed by the logic of the grand bargain.

Language policy in Ukraine was a constant focus of attention for Russia. Russian politicians routinely complained about the "persecution of Russian-speakers" in Ukraine and pushed for two state languages, with the argument that most Ukrainians are Russian-speakers. For example, Moscow mayor Yurii Luzhkov claimed during his visit to Ukraine in 2001 that 75% of the Ukrainian population "thinks in Russian," and that therefore Russian should be the second state language and ethnic Russians should be given the status of "state-forming nation."[40]

Appeal to the size and alleged interests of the Russian-speakers in Ukraine has been a persistent Russian tactic but, in reality, the linguistic landscape and attitudes to competing language policy options were highly complex and dynamic. A substantial share of Ukrainians employ both Russian and Ukrainian in daily life. In the 1990s, for example, survey questions on language spoken at home documented between

36 and 39% of respondents claiming to use Ukrainian only, between 29–36% claiming to use Russian only, while 24–32% claimed to use both regularly.[41] Preferences for one- or two-state-language policies were likewise complicated and, over the years, preferences were slowly shifting in favor of Ukrainian as the only state language.

In annual surveys conducted between 1994 and 2000 by the Institute of Sociology of the Academy of Science of Ukraine, Socis-Gallup, and the Democratic Initiatives Foundation, preference for the official status of the Russian language in Ukraine declined from 52% in 1995 to 44% in 2000, while those in opposition to this policy grew from 33% to 36%. A substantial share of the population was undecided: between 13% and 20% during 1995–2010.[42] There were regional differences as well, with the south and east more in support of official or state language status for Russian, but overall attitudes were complex and someone who spoke Russian on a daily basis was not necessarily in favor of giving Russian the status of state language.

Bifurcated linguistic practices and ambiguous attitudes had implications for language policies, as well as Russia–Ukraine disagreements over them. On the one hand, widespread use of Russian – especially among self-identified ethnic Ukrainians – was decried by the national-democrats as evidence of Russification by the Soviet regime, which the independent Ukrainian state had both the right and the responsibility to reverse. In 1989, when the first language law was adopted, only 44.6% of all school children in Ukraine were enrolled in Ukrainian schools, while 72.7% self-identified as ethnic Ukrainians in that year's census.[43] This means that nearly 40% of ethnic Ukrainian children nationwide were receiving education in Russian, with the proportion being even bigger in the east and the south.

At the same time, widespread use of Russian also generated concerns that rapid Ukrainization would face societal opposition and could become politically destabilizing. Therefore, despite the designation of Ukrainian as the only state language in 1989, the implementation of one-state-language policy and actual Ukrainization was rather lackluster. Even though many schools teaching in Russian before 1991 were switched to Ukrainian instruction, this process was uneven across regions and substantially less extensive in heavily Russian-speaking regions such as Donbas and Crimea in particular.[44] If in the 1991–1992 school year in primary and secondary schools 49% of students were taught in Ukrainian and 50% in Russian, by 2000–2001, the respective figures were 70% Ukrainian and 29% Russian. A majority of students received Ukrainian-language instruction in all regions of Ukraine, but with the notable exceptions of eastern and southern regions: 47% of students in Odesa region; 45% in Zaporizhzhia; 17% in Luhansk; 14% in Donetsk; and just 0.8% in Crimea were taught in Ukrainian.[45]

Russian retained its dominant position in media and business and even in the government sector, where documentation was switched to Ukrainian, but interactions among state officials and between officials and the public often remained in Russian. Russian also remained widely used in nominally Ukrainian-language schools, where it routinely dominated outside of classroom instructional time, and also in university teaching and administration (outside of official paperwork) in the Russian-speaking regions. Some officials openly disregarded the language law and continued to use Russian in their official capacities, without many consequences, even in cases of open defiance. Judges who continued to issue decisions in Russian were sometimes called to a disciplinary committee established by the parliament but would defy the committee and address it in Russian and avoid disciplinary consequences.

The inconsistent implementation of the one-state-language policy served to defuse the potential mobilization of those Russian-speakers who were dissatisfied with the policy, in general, and Ukrainization in education, in particular. The *de facto* policy also gave Ukraine arguments to counter the Russian narrative that Russian is "banned" in Ukraine and Russian-speakers are being subjected to "forced Ukrainization." Importantly, a substantial number of Russian-speakers in Ukraine did not object, and even actively supported policies aimed at strengthening the Ukrainian language. Political attitudes rather than linguistic practices often drove attitudes to language policies. A substantial number of Russian speakers in the capital city and other areas of central Ukraine voted for Center-Right parties and supported their policy agenda, including the one-state-language policy, for the same symbolic reasons the political class did – recognizing one-state-language as a marker and a support pillar of state independence.

Ukrainization of education met with varying degrees of discontent in the east and the south of Ukraine,[46] but much less so in the capital Kyiv, or other cities in central Ukraine, which remained predominantly Russian-speaking. In Kyiv, for example, by the mid-1990s, 90% of first grades were enrolled in Ukrainian-language schools, which was three times more than in the late 1980s and five times more than the proportion of city residents who used Ukrainian as their language of convenience at home; but such drastic changes did not provoke public controversy or debate in the media.[47]

In addition to political support for Ukrainian as the only state language as a marker and a symbol of state independence, another reason why many Russian-speakers did not oppose Ukrainization of education and state language policies generally was a change in the cost–benefit calculation of learning (or not learning) Ukrainian. In the Soviet period, given the dominant position of Russian politically and socially, there were no social opportunities linked to Ukrainian language knowledge. Once Ukrainian became the sole state language in a sovereign state, this new political reality affected cost–benefit calculations. As the Organization for Security and Cooperation in Europe (OSCE) High Commissioner of National Minorities, Max van der Stoel, concluded, following his investigation into the situation of Russian-language education in Ukraine conducted at the request of Russia in 2000, "the conviction of many parents [is] that in independent Ukraine it might be advantageous for the future careers of their children to go to Ukrainian-language schools."[48]

All in all, the implementation of state language policy left political actors who were sparring over it dissatisfied. For Russia and the Ukrainian Left, Ukrainization, even if measured, was still objectionable – they wanted state language policy to change and Russian to be granted the status of second state language, which would in turn perpetuate the Soviet-era reality of Russian as a dominant and "superior" language and Ukrainian as a marginalized, "backward," and unnecessary one. The Right, on the other hand, favored comprehensive Ukrainization in all spheres of public life and argued that the state language policy implementation process did not go far enough. The Right complained, for example, that in the educational sphere the number of students taught in Russian still exceeded the percentage of students who were ethnically Russian,[49] as well as criticized the continued dominance of Russian in the media, business, and in urban centers outside of western Ukraine.

With much of the Ukrainian political class interpreting the one-state-language policy as a symbol of independent statehood, a "meeting of the minds" between Ukraine and Russia on the issue was challenging. Russia was not prepared to acknowledge the legacy of Russification and presented any attempts to reverse the Soviet-era status quo when Russian was both a *de facto* high-status language and the language symbolically and practically associated with a common state as unacceptable "discrimination" against Russian-speakers. For Russia, Ukraine's policy of one-state-language was fundamentally unacceptable. The symbolism of state language policy was at the heart of the Russia–Ukraine disagreement. Just as the Ukrainian political class regarded one-state-language as a symbolic marker of distinct statehood, if Ukraine made Russian a state language this would symbolically dilute the difference between the two states. Thus, even if, for much of the population, language policy was primarily about the convenience or inconvenience of daily life, in the minds of elites in both states, Ukraine's language policy bore directly on the prospects of political independence or political unity.

From the time the first language law was adopted in the late perestroika period, Russia consistently pressured Ukraine on the language issue and saw it as very high priority – more so than many other political, economic, and even geopolitical issues in the relations between the two states. In July 2000, the lower house of the Russian parliament adopted a resolution "On discrimination of Russian language in Ukraine" addressed to the Ukrainian president Kuchma, the Ukrainian parliament, and the Russian president.[50] The resolution repeated an inaccurate assertion that "more than half of Ukrainians" consider Russian to be their native language, complained about Ukrainization of the educational sphere and the media, accused Ukraine of trying to foster the "spiritual separation of brotherly peoples," and called on Ukraine to give Russian an official status and on the Russian president and government to "take necessary measures" to end the purported discrimination of Russian language in Ukraine. In October 2002, the Duma again appealed to the Ukrainian parliament to give Russian the status of second state language and, in December, the Speaker of the Duma, during his visit to Kyiv, reiterated the appeal.[51] The Ukrainian leadership remained steadfast, however, and President Kuchma told members of the Russian Duma that Ukrainian "was, is, and will be the main language of communication in Ukraine," while Ukraine was committed to doing "everything possible" to ensure the normal development and functioning of Russian as one of the "minority languages."[52]

Language policies did not change much from Kuchma to Yushchenko's tenure, and Russia continued to object to perceived "discrimination" and to demand elevation of the status of the Russian language. In a 2006 meeting with the speaker of the Ukrainian parliament, Russian foreign minister Lavrov singled out the status of Russian language as "one of the two grave problems" in relations between the two states, the other one being Ukraine's interpretation of the 1932–1933 famine, which changed significantly during Yushchenko's tenure, as discussed above.[53] It is telling that for Russia identity issues, not strained economic relations or the Euro-Atlantic foreign-policy aspirations of the Yushchenko government, constituted the top two concerns.

Like with historical memory policy, the presidency of Viktor Yanukovych was the time when Ukraine's move in the direction favored by Russia could have been expected, and Yanukovych tried to deliver. After Yanukovych jailed Yulia Tymoshenko, the main opposition leader, and through bribery and intimidation cobbled a pro-presidential majority in the legislature, he was in a position to push through – with support from the Left – identity policies that in previous years were unfeasible within the logic of the Center-Right grand bargain. In July 2012, after several failed attempts and amid accusations of violations of the parliamentary procedure that culminated in fistfights in the chamber, pro-Yanukovych parties, with support from the Left, pushed through the law "On the Principles of the State Language policy," which recognized Russian as an official regional language in Ukraine. The law, which became known as the Kivalov–Kolesnichenko law, after the two members of parliament who submitted the draft, established that in administrative units, where native speakers of a minority language constituted ten or more percent of the population, minority language can be used in local government and all spheres of public life. Even though the law technically applied to eighteen minority languages, it was first and foremost about the status of Russian. Of the 24 regions (oblasts) of Ukraine, 11 oblasts in the south, east, and northeast of Ukraine, the capital city Kyiv, and over a dozen urban centers in central Ukraine met the 10% threshold for the number of Russian speakers set by the law.[54] The passage of the law triggered street protests, dubbed the Language Maidan, but the protests did not succeed in preventing the law's entry into force.

The Kivalov–Kolesnichenko law, which followed the controversial extension of the Black Sea Fleet deal, purging of references to Euro-Atlantic integration from state legislation, and other foreign-policy steps discussed in Chapter 4 that pivoted Ukraine to Russia, was widely perceived by the anti-Yanukovych opposition as yet another step in the same direction, as well as an attempt to weaken Ukrainian identity. The year the law entered into force was the first year since independence when the proportion of students studying in Ukrainian decreased. Scholars described the law as "shatter[ing] the political equilibrium by removing state incentives to learn and use Ukrainian,"[55] while the Venice Commission's opinion described the law as unbalanced, giving disproportionate preference to Russian language relative to other minority languages.[56]

The overhaul of state-language policy and the elevation of the status of Russian, if it continued for some years, could have halted modest gains in the reversal of Russification achieved after 1991, and instead accelerated linguistic Russification, ultimately weakening Ukrainian cultural identity, as the law's opponents feared. Yanukovych demonstrated willingness to not only reverse language policies and elevate the status of Russian language at the expense of Ukrainian but also to push Russia-favored policies in other identity policy areas as well as in foreign policy. Had his rule survived the Euromaidan, Yanukovych may have eventually crushed the opposition and consolidated power enough to satisfy Russia's vision of what Ukraine ought to be and put Ukraine on a trajectory compatible with Russia's imperialization goal, rather than going against it. The Euromaidan uprising that ended Yanukovych's rule also put a stop to his attempts to reverse identity policies in Ukraine, ushering in instead a new round of divergence that we discuss in Chapter 6.

4

Ukraine, Russia, and the West

Geopolitical optimism swelled during the waning years of the USSR and at the end of the Cold War the sky was the limit for hopes of European unity and security. In 1989, Gorbachev had proposed the vision of a "common European home" which would unite Europe, despite its diversity of ideological projects and systems of government. After the USSR disbanded and Yeltsin set out to transform Russia into a democracy with a market economy, a "greater Europe" with Russia in it seemed even more within reach. But the high hopes crashed quickly. By the mid-2000s it was clear that Russia would not be integrating into Europe, the continent's geopolitical lines were redrawn as Eastern European states entered the EU and NATO, and confrontation between Russia and the Euro-Atlantic community was growing. In 2023, Europe is again divided, but this time Central and Eastern Europe, from Czechia to Bulgaria to Estonia, are firmly anchored in the West. Ukraine is fighting an existential battle to leave Russia's orbit forever and join the EU and NATO.

Why did the window of opportunity for transcending history close quickly and who was to blame? How did we go from "Europe from Lisbon to Vladivostok" to Moscow bombing Kyiv? Some claim the opportunity was squandered by Western triumphalism. Instead of helping Russia to weather the hard transition toward marketization and democracy, the West purportedly undermined Russia's democratization by offering insufficient economic aid and humiliating Russia every time it asked for more funds.[1] Western neoliberal policy advisors promoted disastrous economic reforms, which spawned an oligarchy

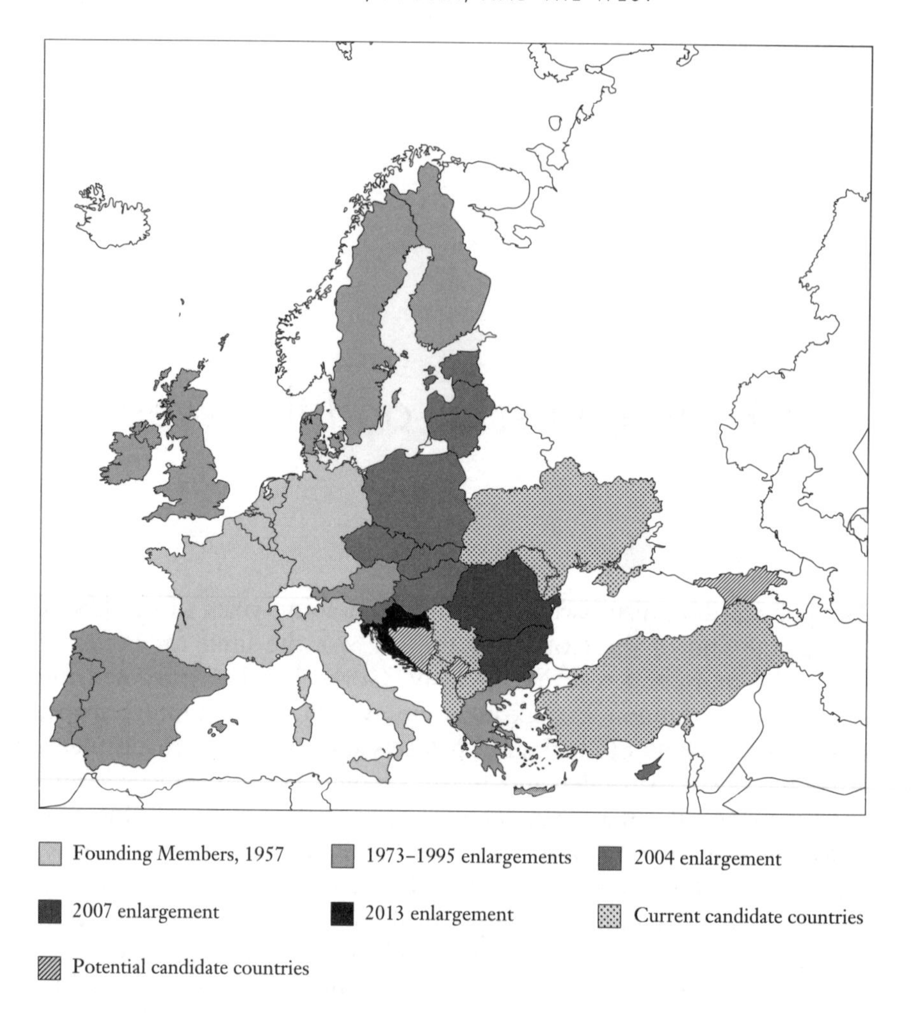

Map 4.1 Waves of EU enlargement

and eventually led to Russia's disillusionment with democracy.[2] The West insisted that its system of government and political culture were superior, that history had ended,[3] and that Russia could enter the "common European home" only if it assimilated and followed the West's rules.[4] Believing itself victorious, the West also disregarded Russia's security concerns. Russia expected NATO to disband or invite it to join. Instead, under US's leadership NATO expanded eastward.[5] Russia tried in vain to communicate its preferences and red lines, became resentful, and then started to worry about its security. It predictably turned anti-Western and lashed out militarily

Map 4.2 Waves of NATO enlargement
Note: Map excludes the United States and Canada, both NATO members.

because the West still refused to scale back its expansionism. The West encircled Russia by adding new NATO members in waves and promising membership to others. It threatened Russia's prosperity by enlarging the EU and its common market ever deeper into Russia's neighborhood.[6]

This view of post-Cold War geopolitical development resonates with many in Russia and with some in the West, but it offers a distorted picture of the processes that led to Russia's conflict with both Ukraine and the West. The focus is exclusively on the international system and on interactions between Russia and the West. The NATO expansion debate, especially, has overanalyzed the US's motivations for choosing this policy course, but understudied the behavior and preferences of NATO's new East European members.[7]

Dismissing the preferences of the more than a dozen countries, supposedly subjected to a geopolitical tug of war between Russia and the West, as inconsequential is Westsplaining. The recently coined term refers to Westerners condescendingly explaining to East Europeans the latter's own interests and history, while failing to take East European perspectives and preferences into account.[8] Tying Russia's regime trajectory or its foreign policy directly to Western policy also smacks of Westsplaining, this time toward Russia. It implies Russia's democratization and foreign policy did not depend on its own agency. Instead, Russia could only react to Western actions in one predictable way – by lashing out.[9]

An even bigger problem than Westsplaining is ignoring the fact that the dynamics of Russia's relationship with its vassals spilled over and exacerbated strains in the Russia–West relationship, as Russia interpreted Ukraine's (and others') gradual attempts to distance from Russia as a Western plot. The root of the difficult Russia–Ukraine relationship is the misaligned understanding of Soviet dissolution – as the end of common statehood or as its reinvention. Russia never saw Ukraine as fully sovereign, but rather as a nominally independent vassal, whom it expected to move in lockstep geopolitically and either to be gradually tied back to Russia or fully reincorporated. Instead, Ukraine resisted Russia's overtures and pressure, initially cautiously. As regime, identity, and domestic policy divergence accelerated, so did Ukraine's assertiveness in foreign policy and its attempts at distancing from Russia. Russia did not respect Ukraine's sovereign choice and turned to energy, trade, and diplomatic pressure to overcome Ukraine's reticence to be tied back to it. As it failed to achieve its goals, Russia gradually developed and committed to two interrelated narratives.

First, Russia started seeing distinct and independent Ukraine as an "anti-Russia," which needed to be either re-educated or destroyed. Second, unable to conceive of the possibility that Ukrainians were pursuing geopolitical distancing out of their own domestic political incentives and as a reaction to Russia's intensifying pressure, Russian elites started blaming the West for "stealing" Ukraine from Russia by influencing its domestic politics. Russian frustration about Ukraine's domestic and foreign-policy choices soured Russia's relationship with the West.

Russia's first narrative, that a type of Ukraine it disapproves of is "anti-Russia," is unadulterated imperialism. It is based on the idea that Ukraine is sovereign at Russia's pleasure and, therefore, any assertions of sovereignty Russia objects to make Ukraine an enemy. The second narrative that the West is manipulating and stealing Ukraine is false as it ascribed a role to the West that the latter actively sought to avoid. Rather than trying to lure Ukraine away from Russia, the West repeatedly moderated its support for Ukraine out of consideration for Russia's sphere of influence. As Russia continued pushing, and Ukraine continued resisting, Russia's methods for establishing control over Ukraine eventually resulted in military aggression in February 2014, first with the annexation of Crimea, and afterwards with the instigation of fighting in Donbas – and the Western response was still moderate and accommodationist to Russian interests.

After detailing the escalatory cycle from independence in 1991 to Euromaidan in 2014, this chapter considers three counterfactuals about how the collision course between Russia and Ukraine might have been affected had the West chosen a different policy toward Russia and its intended vassals. The first one is Russia's integration into the "collective West" early in the 1990s. Some believe this bold action might have prevented the perception of humiliation and resentment, which supposedly eroded Russian democracy and fostered anti-Westernism. We discuss the obstacles that make this counterfactual highly implausible. The second counterfactual is greater deference by the West to Russia through a ban on NATO enlargement. While this scenario is plausible – the decision to enlarge was hard-fought, and the expanders won only narrowly – it would not have produced lasting peace in Europe. We argue that the domestic divergence between Russia and its former vassals would have still led to Russia's escalating desire to reimpose control. The crucial difference is that all East European countries would have been less protected from Russian aggression. Finally, a third counterfactual examines a concerted Western effort to help Ukraine leave Russia's orbit before Russia's re-imperialization pressure escalated to military aggression. While "losing" its vassals decisively would have still been a shock, Russia was more likely to accept such development when its autocracy was less consolidated and Russian identity less hardened around an imperialist conception. This counterfactual is also implausible because neither in Ukraine nor in the West was there majority support for such a path. Tragically, the window of opportunity, however narrow, for facilitating Ukraine's safe and peaceful exit from the Russian World and containing Russia's re-imperialization trajectory closed by 2013.

The collapse of the USSR

In 1990–1991, as centrifugal forces drove the USSR apart, Russia hoped to continue controlling Ukraine in whatever new arrangement followed the union, while Ukraine increasingly pushed for independence. In July 1991, during President Bush's visit to Moscow, Yeltsin announced that the Baltic republics should be allowed to leave the union.[10] That the leader of one constituent Soviet republic would pass judgment on the right of fellow republics with supposedly equal legal status to decide their own fate underscores that Russia saw itself as running the show in the USSR. But this is an aside. Regarding Ukraine, the position of Yeltsin and the Russian democrats supporting him was different from the start. During his meeting with President Bush in Moscow in July 1991 Yeltsin told Bush that "Ukraine must not be allowed to leave the Union," as without Ukraine the union would be dominated by the non-Slavic republics.[11] The Russian population was also unprepared to support Ukraine's separation. An opinion poll conducted in February and March of 1991 found 41% of Russians supporting the independence of Lithuania and just 22% supporting Ukrainian independence.[12]

Far from pushing for Ukrainian independence, the US shared Yeltsin and Gorbachev's goal of keeping the union together and Ukraine in it. On August 1, 1991, American president George H.W. Bush delivered a speech in the Ukrainian parliament that poured cold water on any hopes Ukraine had of leaving the union. In what was mockingly dubbed his "Chicken Kiev speech," Bush spoke of "suicidal nationalism" and warned that the US would not support "local despotism," thus implying that independent Ukraine was unlikely to be governed democratically.[13] If the West was humiliating anyone at that point, it was not Russia, but Ukraine, by dismissing its aspirations and deferring to the imperial center.

As soon as the hard-liners' August 1991 coup failed, informally marking Yeltsin's ascent as the most powerful politician in the USSR, "keeping the union suddenly became one of [Yeltsin's] main concerns."[14] Ukrainian independence was a "nightmare scenario" for most in the liberal camp.[15] Ukraine's parliament, however, moved to declare independence. On August 24, in a vote of 346 to 1, parliament approved the independence declaration and called a referendum on December 1 to put it to the Ukrainian people for confirmation. Both Russia and the USSR scurried to stop Ukraine from leaving. On August 28, delegations from both the Russian republic and the USSR Supreme Soviet flew to Ukraine. The Russian delegation included Yeltsin's vice president Aleksandr Rutskoi and Yeltin's close advisor Sergei Stankevich. The delegation was to inform the Ukrainians, according to the pro-Yeltsin *Nezavisimaya Gazeta*, of Yeltsin's position that Ukraine's exit from USSR would make the article of the bilateral agreement on borders invalid.[16] The treaty between the Russian and Ukrainian republics had been signed in November 1990 and guaranteed the existing border between them. Yeltsin issued a statement reserving the right of the Russian republic to raise the question of the revision of borders, specifically in Crimea and the Donbas region. Raising the question of borders, however, was a strategy rather than an end goal for the Russian leadership. As Yeltsin's press secretary Voshchanov recalled, a member of Yeltsin's inner circle was emphatically clear: "Do you think we need these territories? We need ... Kravchuk to know his place" – the place was in the Union, together with Russia and under its control.[17] Yeltsin used the threat to take away Crimea and Donbas from Ukraine, not motivated by belief that they did not belong in independent Ukraine, but as a strategy to control all of Ukraine politically and convince it not to seek independence altogether. As Chapter 6 will show, Putin implemented a similar strategy after Euromaidan in 2014, when Russia destabilized Donbas, aiming to cause the collapse of Ukraine's central state and to establish Russian control over all of Ukraine.

Kravchuk called the bluff and persisted in pursuing independence. On December 1, 92% of Ukrainians, including majorities in Crimea and Donetsk, voted to leave the USSR. 62% elected Kravchuk as president among six candidates, all of them committed to Ukrainian independence.[18] A week later, newly elected President Kravchuk joined Yeltsin and Belarusian leader Shushkevich at the Belavezha forest retreat near Minsk. Yeltsin's expectation was that whatever the contours of the new agreement, the "three Slav states [... would not ...] split apart, no matter what happens."[19] Having just received a strong mandate for Ukrainian independence, Kravchuk was not willing to agree to a re-constituted union state and pushed for dissolution. Yeltsin needed a deal to finish sidelining Gorbachev. The compromise was the creation of the Commonwealth of Independent States (CIS), which had some of the institutional features of a confederation, on which Russia insisted, but as non-legally binding commitments, as Ukraine had demanded.[20] Kravchuk signed what he thought was a civilized divorce between Ukraine and Russia. Yeltsin, it turns out, conceived of the Belavezha Accords as something closer to a re-writing of the vows of marriage between Russia, Ukraine, and Belarus.

Defining the Russo-Ukrainian relationship

As presidents of now independent states, Kravchuk and Yeltsin shaped the terms of the relationship. The two leaders reportedly did not like each other personally very much, but they had forged a working relationship in the waning days of the USSR and maintained it. Yeltsin, for the most part, did not pay close attention to the Russo-Ukrainian relationship, because he assumed that Ukrainian independence *de facto* if not *de jure* would be short-lived, until a new way of re-organizing the union crystalized. The assumption was common in Russia, and it needed no frequent articulation.[21] In 1993, Russian diplomats were reportedly advising their European counterparts "not to bother building large embassies in Kyiv because within 18 months they will be downgraded to consular sections."[22] Kravchuk, on the other hand, sought to forge a balanced foreign-policy course, which would protect Ukraine's newly acquired independence without antagonizing Russia.

Russia's reintegration efforts were focused on the CIS and its structures, and the aim was to maintain the post-Soviet region as a common economic, military, and political space. In the economic sphere, Russia initially tried to use the ruble zone to govern monetary policy from Moscow. When it collapsed in 1993 because Yeltsin's government wanted to pursue quick marketization but could not make the vassals adopt the same policy, Russia sought to maintain economic interdependence through trade and customs integration. Energy dependence was a major element of economic–political control over the vassals.

Russia provided energy to Ukraine at below-market prices and then used the threat of withholding flows or raising prices as a political weapon against the Ukrainian government if it stepped out of line. For example, in the week before the contentious Massandra Summit in Crimea in September 1993, where Russia and Ukraine were going to discuss the thorny issues of the status of Sevastopol and the Black Sea Fleet as well as the future of Ukraine's nuclear warheads, Russia suddenly cut gas supplies to Ukraine by 25%, citing unpaid bills. The timing indicated Russia's intent to use Ukraine's energy dependence as a bargaining chip.[23] This was the beginning of a long record of energy blackmail, where Russia extracted concessions and limited Ukraine's foreign policy by threatening to freeze Ukraine. During the 2022–2023 winter season, Russia tried unsuccessfully to use the same strategy to bully Europe into withholding military and other support from Ukraine by cutting off gas supplies almost completely.

In security affairs, Russia tied participation in the CIS and its structures to respect for the 1991 borders and dragged its feet as long as possible on legal recognition of these borders. This way, border recognition and secessionism became important instruments in Russia's toolkit for keeping the vassals in line and tying them closer. Often when post-Soviet governments balked at signing onto a new CIS integration initiative, Russia delayed signing of border demarcation treaties, thus implicitly keeping the possibility of border disputes open. Russia also fanned separatist movements across the post-Soviet space and then intervened as a "peacekeeper" or a mediator, which gave it an opportunity to keep various post-Soviet states in a dependent relationship, as they could not afford the destabilization of an unfrozen conflict. Others could not survive without Russia's backing. Moldova and Georgia lost control of parts of their territory to Russia-backed secessionist insurgencies. Armenia relied on Russia's backing in its conflict with Azerbaijan. Tajikistan, Kyrgyzstan, and Uzbekistan also endured Russian interference in local conflicts and disputes. Russia was not shy about asserting its entitlement to a dominant role in the post-Soviet region. In 1993, Yeltsin asserted that "the time has come [...] to grant Russia special powers as a guarantor of peace and stability in the former regions of the USSR,"[24] a statement eerily similar to Putin's statements in 2022–2023. In effect, Russia continued to see itself as the centre and the independent states that came out of the dissolution of the USSR as its "regions."

Ukraine managed to avoid the Transnistria-Moldova or Abkhazia and South Ossetia Georgian scenario in Crimea, but the danger of

Russia fanning centrifugal forces there came up often. Between 1992 and 1994, Crimean secessionism was especially plausible, as Crimean elites pressed for sovereignty beyond the autonomy they were granted within Ukraine. Kravchuk deftly negotiated and defused tensions several times, but the elephant in the room was always potential Russian intervention. The other reason the Crimean question was potentially explosive is that Russian elites across the political spectrum saw it as an affront that the Black Sea Fleet (BSF) and the city of Sevastopol, both situated in Crimea, would be in Ukraine's possession. Russia conceived both entities as imperial Russian, and later Soviet, and thus, Russian because Russia considered itself the successor of the Soviet center. In May 1992, the Russian parliament passed a resolution that sought to legally cancel the 1954 transfer of Crimea to Ukraine by the Soviet government and in response the Ukrainian parliament denounced it. An escalating "war of decrees" between Yeltsin and Kravchuk followed, in which the presidents unilaterally outlined different ways to divide the BSF and define Sevastopol's status. The issue delayed the signing of a Friendship Treaty between the two countries for a few years.

Russia did not achieve Ukrainian reintegration in the early 1990s, not for lack of trying, but because Ukraine put up consistent resistance, both overt and covert. While it did sign up for the CIS as a founding member, Ukraine never ratified the CIS charter,[25] which meant that it resisted being drawn into the increased level of cooperation between the USSR successor states that CIS membership envisioned. Ukraine tried to use the CIS as a forum through which to manage its complete separation from Russia, instead of as a replacement of the disbanded Union state.[26] Complete separation required building national institutions and resisting Russia's pressure to restore a "single national-economic complex."[27] In 1992, Ukraine launched its own currency, so it would have its own monetary policy, rather than be bound by Russia's.[28] It refused to join any CIS common defence structures or to sign the newly launched Collective Security Treaty, which aimed to counterbalance NATO. Kravchuk did not even attend the Tashkent summit where the treaty was signed.[29] In 1992, Ukraine rejected a Treaty on Friendship, Cooperation, and Partnership prepared by Russia, which may have paved the way for a Russian–Ukrainian confederation or union. The treaty envisioned unification in all crucial policy domains – joint customs, taxation, trade, military, and foreign policy – and spoke of nothing short of a "single regional military-strategic space." Concrete provisions called for dual citizenship, the formation of CIS military bases on Ukrainian territory, and a veto on each other's decisions on joining military alliances. In early 1993, similar conditions were outlined in the CIS Charter and Ukraine did not sign on to that either.[30]

On the broader geopolitical scene, however, Ukraine was still largely seen as a vassal of its larger neighbor. While the West could conceive of a new era after the liberation of the Central and East European countries from Moscow's geopolitical domination, it interpreted Ukraine's newly found independence as almost accidental. Few doubted that Ukraine would remain tied geopolitically to Russia. The West perceived Ukraine as an indelible part of Russia's "back yard," which Russia termed "the near abroad" – not quite as foreign as other foreign states. Kravchuk's attempts to orient the country toward Europe and NATO were received in the West with skepticism. Even Ukraine's East European neighbors neither accepted, let alone invited and encouraged it to distance from Russia. Kravchuk tried to define Ukraine as a Central European state, but his efforts were rebuffed. The founders of the Visegrad Group (Czechia, Slovakia, Hungary, Poland) declined Kravchuk's request for Ukraine to join, because they were worried that Ukraine would hold them back from pursuing NATO and EU integration.[31]

The 1994 Budapest Memorandum further illustrates that the West saw Ukraine's future within Russia's sphere of influence. Through this momentous agreement, the US, Western European partners, and Russia successfully pressured Ukraine to drop its claim to Soviet successor status as a nuclear power, transfer the Soviet-era warheads that were stationed on its territory to Russia, and dismantle its delivery systems in exchange for security guarantees from both Russia and the West. Ukraine had asked for security guarantees precisely because its leadership foresaw a potential threat to its sovereignty from Russia.[32] Kravchuk did his best to negotiate strong guarantees, such as a US nuclear umbrella, a promise of NATO membership, or a "Central and Eastern European Zone of Security," but his negotiation leverage was low, because Ukraine also desperately needed economic assistance.[33] The US and Western Europe prioritized Ukraine's accession to the Non-Proliferation Treaty because they estimated the dangers of nuclear proliferation, especially through the black market, to be greater than the likelihood of Russian aggression against Ukraine. The assessment rested on the assumption that Ukraine would continue to be close to Russia, so Russia would not have a reason to threaten it. In hindsight, the position seems naive and, in 2023, former US president Clinton said he regretted his role in convincing Ukraine to sign,[34] but in the early 1990s, this outcome was not surprising. Russo-Ukrainian disagreement over the parameters of Ukrainian sovereignty was there and Ukraine was concerned, but the similarities between Russia and Ukraine were still greater than the differences, and the Ukrainian public did not demand Euro-Atlantic integration. It was easier to believe that any security issues between Russia and Ukraine could be ironed out at the negotiating table.

Looking back, Kuchma's first term and Yeltsin's second term are the era of the smoothest Russian–Ukrainian relationship as independent states and neighbors. For a start, Kuchma and Yeltsin had a better personal relationship than Kravchuk and Yeltsin. But, more importantly, both presidents sought good relations and partnership with the West and moderated domestic demands that would have strained the bilateral relationship. Kuchma steered a balanced course, which he called a multi-vector foreign policy. He tried to foster both a cooperative relationship with Russia and, as a counterweight, a closer relationship with the West. Kuchma's vision was that turning West would be a lever that would get Russia to reduce pressure on Ukraine to integrate in the CIS.[35] The regime similarity and Kuchma's ostensible Russia-leaning positioning in the Ukrainian political spectrum on domestic issues served to allay Russian fears that Ukraine might move away from its sphere of influence. Yeltsin, for his part, moderated the anti-Ukrainian rhetoric coming from the imperialist part of the Russian political spectrum.

An example of the delicate balance of the bilateral relationship was the signing of a bilateral Russian–Ukrainian Treaty on Friendship and Cooperation. It was initialled in February 1995 by Russia's first deputy prime minister, Oleg Soskovets, and Ukraine's prime minister, Yevhen Marchuk, during Soskovets's trip to Kyiv. The treaty provoked outrage in Russia's parliament due to a statement that Crimea was exclusively Ukraine's internal affair. Soskovets was accused of surrendering Russian national interests in negotiations with Kyiv, and enough signatures were gathered to initiate a no-confidence motion in the government.[36] The government pressed on. Yeltsin signed the treaty two years later, and it was ratified eventually in 1999. In March 1999, 45% of Russians objected to the ratification, which stipulated mutual acceptance by both states of their current borders.[37] This episode illustrates the counterfactual discussed in Chapter 2 that domestic political competition had a moderating effect on Russia's re-imperialization drive – Yeltsin and parliament constrained each other, which made policy formation messy and drawn out, but the end result was an imperfect political compromise rather than a radical action.

Still, like Kravchuk before him, Kuchma had to fend off pressure to enter each new institutional initiative, through which Russia attempted to bring the former Soviet republics back into a union-like relationship. In 1995, like Kravchuk in 1993, Kuchma had to manoeuvre out of an energy trap to avoid a Russia-led union – this time the customs union with Russia, Belarus, and Kazakhstan. To force Ukraine's hand, Russia had introduced an excise tax on Ukrainian oil and gas imports, which drove the price of energy that Ukraine paid to Russia above the world market price. Kuchma managed to finagle out of it and keep Ukraine out of the customs union.[38] To balance against Russia, he joined the leaders of Georgia, Azerbaijan, and Moldova, other post-Soviet states also subject to Russia's reintegration pressure, to form GUAM. GUAM's main goal was to create an economic bloc, especially in the energy and energy transportation sectors, which could counteract Russia's frequent energy blackmail. It would connect energy producer Azerbaijan to energy importers Ukraine, Moldova, and Georgia, bypassing Russian control of the pipelines and reducing energy dependence on Russia. In 1999, Uzbekistan, another energy producer, joined the regional grouping.[39]

1997 showcases Kuchma's multi-vector policy. Ukraine held joint exercises with NATO in Crimea and signed a Charter on a Distinctive Partnership and, at the same time, signed a Friendship Treaty with Russia, which had been in the works since 1992. The treaty was an important, though not final, step to Russian recognition of Ukraine's territorial integrity. In addition, the two countries divided the Black Sea Fleet.[40] Ukraine's overtures to NATO were acceptable to Russia because the two states were still developing largely in parallel politically and economically and looking in the same geopolitical direction.

The timing deserves emphasis and broader context. 1997 is the year NATO enlargement to Eastern Europe started rolling out, with the invitation of Hungary, Czechia, and Poland at the Madrid Summit. Russia expressed displeasure at its former Central European vassals recategorizing decisively as Western states. The Yeltsin government protested diplomatically but took no aggressive steps against the Central Europeans and the West more broadly. The Russian leadership must have seen that NATO only arrived at this decision after a lengthy debate and after Central Europeans advocated for themselves. This important nuance is relevant to the Russo-Ukrainian relationship. At the time, divergence between Russia and Ukraine was not significant and Russia had no reason to think Ukraine would be seeking to join NATO unless Russia would be joining the alliance as well. NATO enlargement's first wave may have rattled Russia's imperialist sensibilities,[41] but it did not present a precedent for Ukraine's potential NATO aspirations as a stand-alone candidate.

During Putin's first term and Kuchma's last, Russia managed to pull Ukraine tighter geopolitically through diplomacy and through the first post-Soviet era act of territorial aggression by Russia against Ukraine – the Tuzla Island incident. In 2003, Kuchma announced the "Year of Russia in Ukraine" and began negotiations with Russia, Kazakhstan, and Belarus over the creation of a Common Economic Space (CES), which envisioned a free-trade zone, followed by a customs and monetary union. While the agreement's implementation did not seem feasible or imminent, it was a strong symbolic step toward tying Ukraine to Russia again. Interpretations of why Kuchma took this step differ significantly. On the one hand, Kuchma had selfish reasons to pivot to Russia – he faced large protests at home over the Gongadze murder we discussed in Chapter 2, the West recoiled from him, and to buttress his domestic position, he may have prioritized oligarchic interests in stronger ties with Russia to the detriment of Ukraine's sovereignty. On the other hand, Kuchma's move may have been a bait-and-switch on Russia – by signing onto the unfeasible CES, he avoided joining the Eurasian Economic Union, which would have tied Ukraine more tightly to Russia.[42]

Immediately after the signing of the CES agreement in September in Crimea, Russia challenged Ukraine's territorial integrity. It began building a dam between Tuzla Island, a tiny island in the Kerch straight off the coast of Crimea, and the Russian mainland, which would have effectively given Russia control of the Kerch Straight, the entrance to the Sea of Azov. The Kerch Straight is the very place where after Crimea's 2014 annexation Russia built the Kerch Bridge, which is anchored in Tuzla Island. In 2003, Russia claimed that the island belonged to it, even though the tiny population paid Ukrainian taxes and international borders recognized it as Ukrainian territory. Kuchma and his prime minister, Yanukovych, reacted firmly to protect Ukraine's territorial integrity by sending armed border guards to the island and conducting live-fire exercises not far off in territorial waters. After tense bilateral negotiations, Russia backed off from constructing the dam, but pressured Kuchma into signing a treaty on the Azov Sea, which advanced Russian interests and precluded Ukraine from getting recourse in international law.[43] While Kuchma seemingly won the standoff, his victory was pyrrhic, because he ended up compromising on the text of the treaty and thus Russia got one step closer to tying Ukraine to itself by creating shared, bilateral control of the Azov Sea.

The Tuzla Island incident illustrates both the escalatory cycle between Russian attempts to reintegrate Ukraine and Ukraine's resistance and the futility of an accommodationist approach to Russia's demands. Prior to Tuzla, Kuchma took an important step toward including Ukraine in Russia's project to reintegrate the former Soviet republics. Yet, instead of celebrating this diplomatic success, Russia's President Putin immediately escalated and acted as if Ukrainian territory was under Russian control. This led to swift and decisive resistance even by the supposedly pro-Russian eastern Ukrainian elites – not just Kuchma, but Yanukovych and his future prime minister, Mykola Azarov, leapt to defend Ukraine's territorial integrity. The biggest standoff between Russia and Ukraine since 1991 was thus triggered by the pull–push dynamic of Russia's re-imperialization.

The incident also underscores that Ukraine's gradual re-orientation toward Europe and the West stemmed from Russia's bullying tactics against its former vassal, rather than from any pull from the West. In Kuchma's own words, addressed directly to a Russian audience on the pages of Russia's most-read newspaper: "The closer the dam is to our shores, the closer we are in our moods to Europe and the West in general."[44] And, indeed, what was Ukraine to do to defend itself from Russia's threats to its territorial integrity, but look Westward for protection. Even a Ukrainian president who had come to power on a pro-Russian ticket reacted to protect Ukraine's sovereignty and territorial integrity from a Russian threat.

Orange is the worst color

The rupture in both the Russo-Ukrainian relationship and the Russia–West relationship came from Russian panic at the political divergence marked by the Orange Revolution in late 2004 and increasing Russian resentment of Ukraine's rejection of its vassal status. Whatever attention Russia paid to NATO's second enlargement round in Eastern Europe, the link between it and the Russo-Ukrainian relationship is tenuous. As Chapters 2 and 3 explained, the Orange Revolution deeply unsettled the Russian president and Yushchenko's domestic policies antagonized Russian elites. In foreign policy as well, Yushchenko and his policy course were a bigger irritant than whatever the West was doing. Yushchenko became the first Ukrainian president to pursue a decisively Euro-Atlantic course, rather than attempt to balance Ukraine between Russia and the West like Kravchuk and Kuchma had done before him.

Yushchenko's top priority was EU integration, rather than NATO entry. Not only was he personally committed to the idea that Ukraine belonged in Europe, but he realized that the public was supportive of EU accession but divided on NATO membership.[45] He hit the ground running, courting the EU for a promise to accept a Ukrainian application for candidate status. He imagined that Ukraine could join the EU by 2011.[46] He was fond of saying that his government would reform Ukraine so thoroughly that eventually the EU would come knocking and invite Ukraine to join.

The EU took Ukraine's overtures during Yushchenko's tenure in office cautiously. Successive EU officials and representatives poured cold water on Ukraine's membership aspirations, pointing out all sorts of obstacles – insufficient reforms, geopolitical obstacles, slowing enthusiasm for any further enlargement among Western European publics.[47] Still, things moved slowly forward. In 2007, Ukraine and the EU started negotiations on a new agreement. In 2008, the two parties decided it would be called an association agreement and it would lead to the establishment of a free-trade area between Ukraine and the EU.[48] That is as far as Yushchenko's administration got – short of even a membership perspective.

Yushchenko tried to strengthen cooperation with NATO but achieved limited progress. In 2005, Ukraine received NATO's Intensified Dialogue status, which implied that a Membership Action Plan (MAP) was coming, possibly at the 2006 Riga Summit. However, not only was Yushchenko trying to lead on a policy that had limited backing in Ukrainian society – in 2006 just 12.7% in Ukraine supported joining NATO, 64.4% were opposed, and 22.8% were undecided[49] – but his overall political position was weakened due to infighting in his coalition and the vagaries of Ukraine's electoral process. By 2006, Yanukovych was PM and he pulled Ukraine back from pursuing a MAP.[50] In 2007–2008, Yushchenko re-iterated that joining NATO was the top priority of Ukraine's security strategy.[51] In 2008, he hoped Ukraine would receive a MAP at the Bucharest Summit, but that did not happen – the final memorandum only stated that Ukraine would join NATO at some point in the future. The important takeaway is that the pro-NATO signs coming from Ukraine in the mid-2000s were inconsistent for a variety of domestic reasons and they were not enthusiastically received in the West either.

The Bucharest memorandum is often incorrectly seen as a deep trigger of the 2022 full-scale Russian invasion.[52] But, rather than validating Ukraine's road to NATO, the memorandum suggested that Ukraine's NATO aspirations were far-fetched. The summit demonstrated unequivocally that NATO members were deeply divided on the topic. The US was supportive, but the initiative came personally from President Bush, who was nearing the end of his final term. There were no guarantees of continuity with the next US administration. Poland and some other Eastern European states were on board but, as new members, they had less clout. Many others were opposed – France and Germany continued their record of opposition. The UK – the US's closest ally and currently a strong supporter of Ukraine – was also lukewarm and abstained from supporting a MAP for Ukraine.[53] Ukraine understood from this context that it was not joining NATO any time soon. Russia must have understood it just as well, but it was not in its interest to admit it. Admitting it recognized this reality was not in Russia's interests, either in 2008 or now.

Rather than fearing a realistic prospect of Ukraine joining NATO, Russia was incensed that a Ukrainian president would dare seek accession in the first place. A state that Putin considered "not even a real country," as Putin told President George W. Bush during the 2008 NATO summit, was daring to act on the international scene without deferring to Russia. A 2008 statement by Moscow mayor Luzhkov, a long-standing skeptic about Ukrainian independence, illustrates that Russia was more antagonized by the "anti-Russian" policies of the Yushchenko administration than by Western actions and concerns about NATO admitting Ukraine. In his words, Russia needed to exit the 1997 Friendship Treaty with Ukraine "regardless of whether Ukraine would be joining NATO" because Ukraine was "persecuting the Russian language" and because "Ukraine is *pushing* to enter NATO."[54]

Yushchenko's NATO aspirations were part of a larger pattern, which antagonized Russia. In the run-up to the Georgia war, Ukraine supplied military aid to its fellow NATO aspirant and, after Russia invaded, Yushchenko voiced strong support for Georgia. Ukraine's position drew an angry reaction from Medvedev and a threat from

Gazprom to double the price of gas to Ukraine by January 1, 2009.[55] In 2006, Yushchenko also refused to negotiate an extension of the Black Sea Fleet lease, which was set to run out in 2017.

A longer view of the NATO–Russia–Ukraine nexus emphasizes that Russia's problem with Yushchenko's foreign policy was not the prospect of NATO coming closer to its borders through possible Ukrainian membership. Russia already shared a border with NATO after Baltic membership. Importantly, NATO had no defense plans for the Baltics in 2008 and, even after developing such plans in the aftermath of Russia's war in Georgia, there were no forward deployed militaries until after Russia's aggression against Ukraine in 2014. The multinational battalion formed in the Baltics and Poland after 2014 was modest with under 4,000 troops.[56] Baltic defense budgets saw massive cuts due to the 2008 financial crisis, whereas Russia kept up its defense expenditure throughout the 2000s. Thus, the basic building blocs of a security dilemma between NATO and Russia were missing.

The problem for Russia was Ukraine pursuing cooperation with NATO without Russia's blessing. Recall that in 1997, Kuchma signed a partnership agreement with NATO and Yeltsin saw that as acceptable. In May 2002, it was Kuchma again who was the first Ukrainian president to declare officially Ukraine's wish to become a NATO member.[57] That announcement was also concomitant with a Ukraine–Russia military cooperation agreement, signed by Kuchma and Putin in January 2002, and came in the same week as the announced creation of the NATO–Russia Council. Putin not only didn't threaten Ukraine and speak of red lines in May 2002, but Russia continued to support Kuchma domestically over his rivals and later backed his chosen successor Yanukovych's campaign. In 2002, the Russian–American relationship was at a historic high due to a common fight against the threat of Islamic terrorism. In that context, interest in NATO by a pro-Russian Ukrainian president wasn't seen as worrisome by Russia. Kuchma's move was interpreted as the vassal keeping in lockstep with Russia's own partnership with the West.

By contrast, pro-NATO moves by the "anti-Russian" Yushchenko set off alarm bells in Moscow immediately. Russia resented rather than feared Ukraine's unilateral move toward NATO as it suggested that the Russo-Ukrainian "eternal strategic partnership," as Putin called it,[58] may end someday and Ukraine would no longer be a Russian vassal. A Medvedev letter to Yushchenko in August 2009 conveyed Russia's vision of Ukraine clearly:

> [f]or centuries Russians and Ukrainians have been and remain not just neighbors but brothers who will always hold the best feelings; who share a common history, culture, and religion; and who are united by close economic cooperation, strong kinship, and human relations [...] I would like to inform you that because of anti-Russian Ukrainian government policies we have decided to postpone the appointment of our new ambassador. The specific date [of his appointment] will be determined later when there are genuine improvements in Russian–Ukrainian relations. [...] Russia hopes that the new political leadership of Ukraine will be ready to build a relationship between our countries that will actually meet the genuine aspirations of our peoples and that this will be in the interests of strengthening European security.[59]

The diplomatic language cloaks the Russian president's imperial attitude toward Ukraine: Ukraine has been dominated by Russia politically, economically, and culturally for centuries and any Ukrainian government that tries to weaken or undo this domination is, by definition, anti-Russian. A 2009 veiled threat to Ukraine from Medvedev, who has revealed himself to be among the most extreme hardliners since 2022 and has issued many nuclear threats against the West and genocidal threats against Ukraine, but in 2009 was considered a moderate even "liberal" politician. His perspective was not the exception, but a broadly shared view across the Russian political spectrum.

Angered by Yushchenko's efforts to de-vassalize Ukraine geopolitically, Russia tried to keep the "younger brother" in line by escalating the use of its energy lever. Gas wars marked the whole period of Yushchenko's presidency and Russia cut off supplies to Ukraine twice – in 2005–2006 and in 2008–2009.[60] The January 2009 crisis was particularly acute as not only Ukraine but also European states receiving Russian gas through pipelines going through Ukraine saw supply disruptions. Russia used this leverage to punish the Yushchenko administration for its pro-European foreign-policy course and Ukrainization policies at home, which Russia deemed "anti-Russian." An additional element of Russia's gas war strategy, according to a Gazprom executive who defected to Ukraine after the full-scale invasion, was to paint Ukraine as an unreliable energy transport partner in the eyes of Europe, which facilitated European decisions to try to bypass Ukraine in energy routes.[61] This served the goal of reducing Ukraine's importance to the West and making it increasingly dependent on Russia, which was Russia's long-standing goal.

Yanukovych, Russia's last hope

Yanukovych pursued a decidedly more pro-Russian course than his predecessor, Yushchenko, but even he did not go as far as Russia wanted him to. The European integration process launched by Yushchenko was under way through multifaceted technical negotiations toward the expected signing of an association agreement between Ukraine and the EU. The association agreement did not mean a membership perspective for Ukraine, but it did involve further economic and political integration of Ukraine with the EU. While the Yanukovych administration started dragging its feet on implementation of the various reforms, it did not stop the process.[62] In the summer of 2013, Yanukovych neutralized opposition within his party and from the communists to the association agreement by quashing a referendum proposal on the issue.[63] All the way through the fall, he appeared ready to sign the agreement.

On NATO accession, Yanukovych took more decisive pro-Russian action early in his term. In May 2010, he decreed the closure of the commission working on Ukraine's NATO bid and re-iterated his long-standing position that Ukraine's cooperation with NATO is sufficient and an accession application would not be forthcoming.[64] Then, in June 2010, the Rada adopted a law barring Ukraine from entering any military blocs, which implied permanent neutrality.[65]

While both foreign-policy positions were closer to Russia's desired outcome, it is possible they reflected domestic Ukrainian politics more than Yanukovych taking direct orders from Russia – his position on NATO mirrored the opposition to NATO membership among his voters in eastern and southern Ukraine; he equivocated on the EU's association agreement, perhaps realizing that EU integration was popular with a plurality of Ukrainians. In 2010, 45.5% supported EU membership, 19.1% opposed, and 35.3% were undecided.[66] He was more interested in consolidating his grip on power in Ukraine than in directly serving Russia's interests.[67]

The Kharkiv Agreements, which Yanukovych and Russian president Medvedev signed in April 2010, illustrate how easily Russia would have vassalized Ukraine had Ukraine become a consolidated autocracy. The agreement provided a 25-year extension of the lease on Russia's Black Sea Fleet (till 2042!) in exchange for a gas price discount applied to Ukraine's gas debts to Russia. The economic benefit for Ukraine was much needed, given that its economy was in crisis, and the discount was almost three times bigger than the IMF loan that was Ukraine's other option. The geopolitical decision reversed Yushchenko's foreign policy, jeopardized Ukraine's future Euro-Atlantic integration, and opened the door to escalating Russian demands to establish control over Ukraine's gas production and transmission systems and trade. The Black Sea Fleet lease extension maintained the risk that Russia might use the foothold in Crimea to threaten Ukrainian sovereignty and security. Yanukovych wanted to strengthen his political position by reaping the economic benefits, but getting the agreement ratified by parliament where forces opposed to a pro-Russian pivot still held a substantial number of seats turned out to be harder than he thought. There was mayhem in the Rada – fistfights and pelting the speaker with eggs – and Yanukovych's Party of Regions violated procedure rules and counted votes from MPs who were absent to ram the decision through.[68] For a pro-Russian president, pursuing policies seen as subordinating Ukraine to Russia's interests would have been much easier if Ukraine were an autocracy.

The Kharkiv Agreements also demonstrated again that Ukrainian concessions to Russian demands tend to produce an immediate escalation of Russia's push for ever closer integration. In this case, within less than a month of the agreement's conclusion, Prime Minister Putin demanded the merger of Ukraine's state gas company, Naftohaz, and Russia's Gazprom. In May, President Medvedev visited Kyiv and put on the agenda a package to synchronize the development of Russia and Ukraine's socio-economic relations. In Medvedev's own words: "this is the beginning of a new relationship."[69] Instead of the ever-closer Ukrainian–Russian relationship that Medvedev imagined, the Yanukovych tenure ended with Euromaidan and Ukraine's attempt to forge a European path, away from Russia, to which Russia responded with military aggression in 2014.

Could the West have prevented the collision course?

There are three counterfactuals for how the West might have prevented Russia's attempt to re-imperialize Ukraine through force: (1) the West could have better integrated Russia into the European security architecture as an ally; (2) the West could have deferred to Russia's sphere of influence more; and (3) the West could have sought to define European security against Russia earlier and contained its ambitions *vis-à-vis* Ukraine.

The first counterfactual is Russia's quick integration into the European security architecture at the end of the Cold War. There are various ways this might have taken place. NATO could have dissolved itself, making way for an alternative pan-European organization that would have united Western and Eastern Europe. The Conference on Security and Cooperation in Europe (CSCE, later OSCE) could have played this role, or a new organization could have been launched. Another option was Russia's near immediate entry into NATO, alongside all the former Warsaw Pact members. Whatever the scenario, Russia seemed to expect a proportional response to its goodwill gesture of disbanding the Warsaw Pact and the USSR that would make the Cold War European security architecture a thing of the past. Was that a reasonable expectation by Russia and why did the West not go for such a solution?

The Russian expectation was not prima facie reasonable, as it ignored the fact that the Warsaw Pact members saw the end of the Cold War as the end of Russian domination and were highly skeptical about any future arrangements that would give Russia continued influence over their security. The "NATO should have disbanded" counterfactual rests on the Russo-centric assumption that the collapse of the Soviet Bloc and the USSR were processes largely conducted by the center, that in this process Russia proved itself as a benign actor in the treatment of its vassals, and therefore it should have been reasonably expected to continue to act benevolently toward its now former vassals. Within this Russo-centric perspective, belief in Russia's future benevolence is reasonable, while fears of Russia on the part of the former Soviet Bloc states are unreasonable Russophobia.

However, as instrumental as Gorbachev's perestroika and glasnost policies were in unleashing and intensifying the USSR's demise, the hand of the Soviet leader was forced. The communist regimes were collapsing onto themselves because of decades-old economic and political dysfunction of their subversive institutions, which united society against the repressive communist state.[70] Gorbachev's policies were an attempt to stem the decline. He never intended to destroy the USSR or withdraw from Eastern Europe. His aim was to build "socialism with a human face" and, through this, to strengthen Soviet power by helping it reach its full potential both domestically and abroad.[71] Instead, the command economy's dysfunction was exacerbated, and centrifugal forces of national identity movements in the Baltics, the Caucasus, and Ukraine, made possible by Gorbachev's glasnost, pulled the state apart.[72]

Soviet communism, with Russia at its center, had lost the Cold War not to the West, but to its own periphery, which abandoned it at the first opportunity. Russia did not decisively abandon its desire for regional dominance, but it could hardly sustain it any longer without mass regime violence, which Gorbachev eschewed. While grateful to Gorbachev for inadvertently undoing the Soviet bloc, the Central Europeans – especially Hungary and Poland – immediately moved to join NATO after 1989. By late 1990, all of Hungary's major parties were committed to seeking NATO membership. Their concern was that independent Russia was likely to attempt to restore its control over them. In the early 1990s, Central European intellectuals debated whether Russia was European at all,[73] not whether it should be a guarantor of European security.

Another impediment to NATO's replacement by a different pan-European security organization was the US conception of its role in Europe and its perception of NATO's usefulness. The West's "victory" in the Cold War initially produced a wide-spread expectation that the US and Europe would finally reap a "peace dividend" – i.e. the US would no longer need to be spending billions on European defense to deter the USSR. American troops would withdraw from Western Europe and Europe would take charge and responsibility for its own security. This expectation quickly faded as the US found that the European allies preferred to maintain the Alliance, and the European bases could be used for operations in other parts of the world now that they were free from the task of deterring the USSR. The Gulf War in 1990–1991, during which NATO command in Europe provided crucial support to Mediterranean members close to the conflict zone, cemented the idea that the Atlantic Alliance was not obsolete.[74]

The quick incorporation of Russia into a common European security architecture was unfeasible because Yeltsin did not credibly demonstrate that Russia would continue Gorbachev's geopolitical course. Toward the end of the Cold War, Gorbachev had sent signals that the USSR might durably abandon its desire to control Eastern Europe and become a more trustworthy partner on the international scene.[75] But, as soon as Gorbachev rode into the sunset with the state that he had led, Yeltsin's Russia soon started to re-imperialize. Yeltsin dragged out the withdrawal of Russian troops from both the Baltic states and East Germany all the way until August 1994, and then only complied under pressure because Russia needed loans from the West to stay afloat. None of the borders with Russia's neighbors were decisively delimited in the early 1990s. In the case of the Ukrainian–Russian border, Russia resisted delimiting and demarcating the border all the way until 2003, and issued several threats to dispute borders in eastern and southern

Ukraine. With the Tuzla Island incident described above, Russia sent a clear signal that these were not just rhetorical threats.

The border ambiguity was only one among many reasons there was no window of opportunity during which Russia could join NATO as a full-fledged member. During the Yugoslav wars of the early 1990s, the West consulted regularly with Russia to secure a common approach and thus build the basis for future cooperation; but there was significant divergence of geopolitical interests as Russia leaned heavily to support its traditional ally Serbia, which the US and Western Europe gradually came to see as the aggressor in the region.[76] Russia's democracy and political stability were seriously undermined during the 1993 confrontation between Yeltsin and the parliament and the prospect of Yeltsin losing power to a red–brown coalition gave the West even greater pause. Integrating Russia immediately may have been just too risky.

But, most importantly, at no point did Russia express a desire to join NATO as a member. Joining the alliance would have required levels of transparency to which neither the Russian military, nor Russia's political leadership considered submitting. The political decision is hardly surprising. Russia perceived NATO as an alliance dominated by the US and including its Western European vassals, and joining it as a regular member was beneath Russia and undermined its self-image as a great power on par with the US. Thus, Russia preferred to further cooperate with NATO through the 1997 NATO–Russia Founding Act. The Act billed itself as "the basis for an enduring and robust partnership between the Alliance and Russia, one that can make an important contribution to Europe's security architecture in the twenty-first century." It also explicitly affirmed that Russia would not enter NATO and would not be able to veto alliance decisions, including over enlargement.[77] Russia signed onto this, an act that makes arguments about broken promises regarding NATO enlargement moot.

While the West did not disband NATO and Russia did not want to join, the West did not set out to challenge Russia's role as a regional power in the former Soviet space but deferred to it. As the USSR was falling apart, Russia intervened and backed several separatist insurgencies in the former Soviet space, in Moldova and Georgia. In Azerbaijan/Armenia, and in Tajikistan, Russia backed the government militarily against an insurgency. The West largely deferred to Russia's handling of these conflicts, perceiving them as falling within its sphere of influence. The US also accepted Russia's first war in Chechnya. While the Clinton administration tried to advocate for negotiations over military action, it largely accepted that deciding how to deal with Chechnya was the prerogative of Russia's government. The argument that the West humiliated Russia geopolitically is not convincing, even if Russian elites may have (re)constructed an image of the 1990s in those terms.

The West also treated Russia as a geopolitical and economic partner rather than an adversary and, after each setback, the West sought to restore friendly relations. During the 2000s, the EU and Russia intensified trade and economic ties, especially in energy. They worked on harmonizing trade regulations to remove barriers and Putin was regularly welcomed in Western European capitals as a friendly partner. An overlooked consequence of NATO and EU expansion eastward is that the former Soviet bloc vassals were now secure Euro-Atlantic alliance members and thus could pursue economic ties with Russia without fearing a loss of sovereignty. Most did. The US considered Putin's brutal second war in Chechnya to be Russia's internal issue and accepted the Russian government's claim it was fighting Islamic terrorists, rather than suppressing the Chechen movement of national self-determination. After 9/11, the US turned to Russia for help in its own "war on Islamic terrorism" and forged closer ties. After the relationship cooled in the mid-2000s over Putin's paranoia that the colored revolutions were Western plots aimed at undermining Russia, the US attempted a reset in 2009–2011.

But what if the West had done even more to accommodate Russia's geopolitical preferences? The second counterfactual – that NATO could have rebuffed Eastern Europe's bid to join – is more plausible. Western desire to build a cooperative relationship with Russia was strong and thus the West might have realistically prioritized it over providing security to Eastern Europe. The debate over NATO enlargement in the US was heated and the opponents might have prevailed. Not only did the US not push NATO expansion onto reluctant Eastern Europeans, but their governments had to devise strategies to convince the US that the risk of expanding NATO was worth taking. By the mid-1990s, 72% of Eastern Europeans (ranging from 55% in Bulgaria to 92% in Poland) supported their country's path to NATO.[78] The Baltics jointly declared that their goal was NATO membership in December 1993, but only managed to achieve membership in 2004.[79] The pro-European Bulgarian president Stoyanov saw Clinton's high-profile 1999 visit as an opportunity to make the case that Bulgaria belonged geopolitically in Europe and the West. The US was the main decision-maker on the question of NATO enlargement, so, had the US decided against enlarging NATO, the Eastern Europeans would have been left out in the cold. What would have been the consequences for the Russia–West relationship and the European security architecture?

Keeping Eastern Europe out of NATO would not have solved other thorny issues for Russia–Western cooperation in Europe. Russia would still have disagreed with Europe and the US over the handling of the Bosnian War in 1995 and it would still have resented greatly the NATO intervention in Kosovo in 1999. In fact, analysis of Russian media discourse on conspiracies against Russia suggests that the Kosovo intervention was much more antagonizing for Russia than either wave of NATO expansion, as the former was covered more extensively by Russian media.[80]

A conscious decision by the West to leave Eastern Europe in a security vacuum as a buffer zone between the Euro-Atlantic Alliance and Russia is likely to have been an invitation for Russia to fill that vacuum as soon as it got back on its feet after the economic crisis of the 1990s. The offensive realist paradigm, some of whose authors have criticized NATO enlargement, does not predict that keeping Eastern Europe as a neutral buffer zone would be a stable arrangement. It predicts that keeping Eastern Europe neutral would produce a Russian move to re-establish domination over the area.[81] Russia would not have sat idly by and left Eastern Europe to its own devices, so re-imperialization was inevitable. Russian resurgence in the absence of NATO enlargement would have created a serious challenge not just for Europe, but for the US as well. An insecure Eastern and Central Europe would likely have pursued regional security cooperation to hedge against a potential Russian onslaught and its democratization may have been undermined by an incentive to militarize and fortify against Russia.[82] Alternative alliances would have complicated the process of EU integration. Moreover, the same escalatory cycle that drove Russo-Ukrainian confrontation would likely have been at work in Russia's relationship with most Eastern European countries, leading to the destabilization of all of Europe.

Russian democracy did not decline due to Eastern Europe's Euro-Atlantic integration. As we showed in Chapter 2, Russia's autocratization has domestic determinants and its critical events do not map onto the NATO enlargement timeline. Russian democracy sputtered as early as 1993, which was before NATO had committed to the enlargement path. If NATO's first wave of enlargement in 1999 had been so deeply offensive and triggering insecurity for Russia, then why did Yeltsin select, in that very year, a pro-Western-presenting successor who promised cooperation, not confrontation, with NATO? Moreover, why did Putin's first pivot against the West, during the 2007 Munich conference, come with such a lag after the 2004 second wave of NATO expansion? Because, as we argue here, it is more likely that the Russia–West relationship soured because of the vassals' attempts to leave Russia's sphere of influence than because of Western actions. The spirited attempts by Ukraine's Orange government and Georgia's Rose government to distance their countries from Russia in the mid-2000s are more likely to have triggered Russia's resentment and ontological insecurity as a dominant power, rather than the accession of the Baltics and some of the Balkans to NATO in 2004.

Neither does the NATO enlargement timeline match Russia's aggression toward Ukraine. After the first wave of Eastern enlargement in 1999, Russia did not react aggressively at all toward Ukraine. The tensest moment between Russia and Ukraine came in 2003 over the Tuzla Island incident, before the second NATO expansion wave. When Russia did launch military aggression against Ukraine in 2014, Ukraine's NATO prospects were nil. Some may argue that the enlargement waves created enough of a precedent that any Ukrainian move toward Euro-Atlantic integration could credibly be perceived by Russia as a step toward Ukrainian NATO membership. Ultimately, this argument implies that there could be no Western policy that would credibly reassure Russia. Russia could be paranoid that expansion is coming even without any expansion. It could react to any domestic Ukrainian development it disliked and claim that it was afraid Ukraine is moving Westward. This requires endless appeasement, until Russia establishes firm control over not just Ukraine, but whatever area it unilaterally deems as its sphere of influence and declares itself no longer threatened.

By incorporating all East Central European countries into NATO, the West has extended deterrence to its Eastern European flank and provided huge benefits for European security at a low logistical cost.[83] If NATO expansion was an effective tool for hedging against Russian resurgence in Eastern Europe, then why stop at the Baltics and the Balkans? What if the 1993 idea of Clinton's National Security Advisor Anthony Lake to accept Ukraine into NATO in the first wave had taken hold?[84] What if the Bush administration, which proposed giving a MAP to Ukraine and Georgia in 2008, had convinced reluctant France and Germany that these two countries belonged in NATO? What if, after Russia's war with Georgia in 2008, NATO pre-empted and accepted Ukraine into NATO? Would that have prevented Russia's opportunistic land grab in Crimea in 2014 and the opening of a front in Donbas?

This counterfactual is not very plausible for a host of reasons. Western decision-makers have always taken Russian preferences seriously and have always been reluctant to cross what they perceive as Russia's red lines. Moreover, NATO enlargement happens by consensus of all members and it is difficult to imagine that such consensus could have been achieved either in the 1990s or in the 2000s. Even today as Russia's full-scale invasion of Ukraine rages on, some in France, Germany, and the US remain hesitant to embrace Ukrainian NATO membership as a strategic goal. Only some Eastern European and Nordic countries are fully behind Ukraine's bid. The idea that a neutral Ukraine would be acceptable to Russia and guarantee peace in Europe still has adherents.

More importantly, Ukrainians themselves did not believe in the benefits of NATO membership in the 1990s and 2000s. While Kravchuk may have wanted a US nuclear umbrella[85] and Yushchenko's administration actively sought NATO membership and advocated for it abroad, at home barely a fifth of Ukrainians shared the goal throughout the 1990s and 2000s. The result could stem from a combination of pro-Russian sentiment, an abundance of caution not to antagonize Rusia, and a perception that it is useless to support an extremely far-fetched course of action – the sentiment which might be reflected in a large share of Ukrainians (between 23% and 43%) who in the 2000s in the opinion polls were undecided on NATO membership. But the fact remains that a strong popular mandate for membership in Ukraine would have been necessary to overcome Western caution and skepticism and it just was not there.

This is the tragedy of the current moment. Had Ukraine entered NATO earlier, nuclear deterrence through NATO's Article 5 protection would likely have prevented Russia's opportunistic intervention and land grab in 2014 and the full-scale invasion in 2022. Back in the mid-2000s, Ukraine had no territorial disputes and already had a functioning democracy. Like for the Eastern European countries before it, NATO membership would have been a solid stepping stone to EU integration. Russia's levers of political influence on Ukraine would have been significantly weakened and the chances that Yanukovych would have been able to renege on signing the association agreement with the EU as a consequence of Russian pressure would have diminished. Without the last-minute pull-out from the agreement, the domestic political instability of the Euromaidan protests could have been avoided altogether.

The benefits of NATO membership for Ukraine are obvious, but the big question is whether Russia could have accepted a *fait accompli* either in the 1990s or in the 2000s. If Russia was not able to tolerate even neutral Ukraine and decided to pursue its reincorporation into the Russian World militarily, why would not have it invaded back then to stop NATO membership, just like it invaded Georgia after the 2008 Bucharest summit? If Russia is unwilling to pull out from Ukraine, even after suffering massive casualties and enduring serious sanctions, why would it have accepted losing Ukraine earlier? Control of Ukraine is central to Russia's ontological security, the argument goes.

These are fair questions. As we have shown so far, Russia, indeed, has long viewed Ukraine as a branch of its own nation and expected from the start of the post-Soviet period to control Ukraine politically in some form or another. Ukrainian geopolitical recategorization in the West would be a painful blow to Russia's self-conception whenever it happened. However, there are four reasons to believe Ukraine could have successfully escaped Russia's grip in an earlier period without having to fight a war: (1) divergence between Russia and Ukraine had not yet hardened Russia's commitment to destroying an "anti-Russian" Ukraine; (2) Russia was a weaker state and economy, unprepared for waging a big war; (3) even by the mid-2000s, Putin had not completed authoritarian consolidation and there was still a possibility that, had he chosen military aggression as a response, both elites and society could have constrained him; (4) before the 2008 financial crisis, Russia saw the West as strong and powerful and would have been effectively deterred from challenging its decision to invite Ukraine (and others).

As we show in this book, the escalatory cycle playing out between Russia and Ukraine for the last thirty years progressively hardened commitment to the diverging positions in both Russia and Ukraine and led Russia to move from more subtle to more aggressive means of establishing control over Ukraine. In the mid-late 2000s, Russia had lower economic and state capacity to wage war, as well as a less consolidated authoritarian regime and a more contested imperial identity. While the desire to control Ukraine was there, the willingness to use any means possible to achieve it was not. The vision of Ukraine as "anti-Russia" had yet not become the dominant lens in Russia for seeing Ukraine. In the earlier periods, hardliners like Luzhkov talked mostly about diplomatic and economic pressure, but rarely about military might. Current propagandist Vladimir Solovyev, who now uses genocidal rhetoric against Ukraine on his talk show, in the mid-2000s said anyone musing about a war between Russia and Ukraine was mentally ill.[86] Putin himself insisted that Russia respected Ukraine's territorial integrity and Crimea belonged to Ukraine.[87]

After 2012, Russia's autocracy consolidated into a personalist dictatorship under Putin and after 2014, as the next two chapters show, Russian society went a long way toward imagining Ukraine as a "Nazi regime," Ukrainians as brainwashed by the West, and non-vassalized Ukraine as the "anti-Russia." A process of normalizing military aggression against Ukraine also unfolded. By 2014, it became harder to accept Ukraine's definitive rupture with the Russian World than it might have been in the mid-2000s. Tragically, the opportunity for Ukraine to integrate into the West without having to win a full-scale war was missed.

5

Euromaidan, Crimea annexation, and the war in Donbas

After the divergence of the post-Orange Revolution period, the Yanukovych presidency could have brought Ukraine and Russia closer together and facilitated the vassalization of Ukraine that Russia sought. This possibility was foreclosed when Yanukovych was removed from office in February 2014 at the tail end of a popular mobilization, dubbed the Revolution of Dignity in Ukraine, but more commonly known abroad as Euromaidan or simply Maidan. Almost immediately after Yanukovych's ouster, Russia launched military aggression against Ukraine. Russian forces quickly occupied and annexed Crimea, and then intervened in Donbas, where an armed rebellion arose against the new government in Kyiv. Within a few months, Ukraine lost 8% of its territory and signed two disadvantageous ceasefires in Minsk – the Minsk Agreements – to avoid losing more.

This chapter walks through the chronology of the Euromaidan protests and their aftermath in Crimea and Donbas and addresses crucial questions necessary for understanding Ukraine and Russia's decisive disentangling post-2014. Why did the Euromaidan start and how did it lead to Yanukovych's removal from office? What were the domestic political consequences of Yanukovych's ouster? Why and how did Russia respond with military aggression to what was a Ukrainian domestic development? How did the Minsk Agreements, signed purportedly to facilitate Donbas' full reintegration into Ukraine, become an intractable framework?

Ukrainian civil society's effective mobilization against Yanukovych's creeping autocratization and his administration's attempt to take

Ukraine off the pro-European path was a testament to how much Ukraine had diverged from Russia in the post-Orange Revolution period from 2005 till 2010. Russia's annexation of Crimea, followed by the instigation and backing of rebellion in Donbas, represented an escalation of means, but the continuation of Russia's post-1991 goal to control Ukraine. The Minsk Agreements were Russia's latest instrument for trying to influence Ukraine's domestic and geopolitical trajectory. With Russia and Ukraine envisaging the end goal of Minsk differently, the agreements' implementation came to a stalemate.

Euromaidan (The Revolution of Dignity)

The EU association agreement: a geopolitical fork in the road

After Yanukovych was elected to the presidency in 2010, he reversed many of his predecessor's democratic gains and identity policies but continued the Yushchenko-initiated negotiations with the EU on an ambitious association agreement which would create a Deep and Comprehensive Free Trade Area (DCFTA) between the EU and Ukraine.[1] Support for the agreement at first seemed like a win-win for Yanukovych. By sticking to the EU integration path, Yanukovych did not risk alienating his constituency, disproportionally comprised of voters in southeast Ukraine. Support for the EU, unlike for NATO, was not a polarizing issue in Ukraine and had substantial backing in all regions, though higher in the western and central regions. An EU-supporting Yanukovych could appeal to voters in the center and west of Ukraine, without losing support in the east and south, thus increasing his chances of re-election in 2015. Oligarchs supporting Yanukovych were interested in EU markets, and economic assistance from the EU was also an appealing prospect for Yanukovych. Inflated state procurement contracts and insider privatization channeled state resources to buy political loyalty but, by 2012, the regime was running out of assets to distribute.[2] Furthermore, in the early years of the Yanukovych presidency Russia was not actively opposing Ukraine's EU association process, which remained a pie in the sky rather than an immediate possibility.

As the planned signing of the agreement was drawing closer, though, these calculations changed. The signing of the agreement was scheduled to take place during the EU summit in Vilnius in November 2013. Over the summer of 2013, Russia mounted a trade war on Ukraine. In mid-August, Russia closed its border to virtually all physical exports from Ukraine. The damage of Russia's measures was later calculated to be $500 million.[3] Ukraine joining the DCFTA with the EU would decrease Russian access to European markets, and Russia threatened import tariffs, but Russian opposition stemmed first and foremost from the political and geopolitical implications of Ukraine's possible agreement with the EU. The terms were such that Ukraine could not be simultaneously in an association agreement with the EU and in the Customs Union, which Russia had launched in 2011 as a competing initiative to the EU. Therefore, if Yanukovych signed the agreement with the EU, Ukraine would be "lost" to Russia. Putin was not prepared to accept this. In September 2013, Putin's advisor Glazyev threatened that if Ukraine signed the agreement with the EU, Russia would consider this a breach of the treaty on strategic partnership and friendship with Russia that delineated the countries' borders, and Russia might intervene if the Russian-speaking south-eastern regions rebelled and sought help from Russia.[4]

In addition to blackmail from Russia, other developments were also contributing to Yanukovych's changing calculus. After Yulia Tymoshenko's imprisonment on politically motivated charges of abuse of office, the EU was putting pressure on Yanukovych to release the opposition leader as a pre-condition for signing the agreement. Yanukovych was reluctant but, in addition to the Tymoshenko conundrum, yet another dilemma loomed increasingly large. With state coffers emptied by corruption and economic mismanagement, Ukraine desperately needed financial assistance to avoid default. A loan from the IMF was one option, but it was conditional on economic reforms that Yanukovych did not want to implement as they would have hurt his political-economic model, which centered on enriching his cronies and family. Russia was prepared to throw a financial lifeline to Yanukovych without demanding reforms; all Russia wanted was for Yanukovych to call off the agreement with the EU. In the weeks leading up to the scheduled signing, Putin and Yanukovych met in secret several times, as did their prime ministers. What Russia offered at these meetings was revealed later, in December, when Yanukovych, after jettisoning the agreement with the EU, traveled to Moscow and received his reward: a $15 billion loan, which would allow Ukraine to avoid reforms that the IMF would have required, and a nearly 50% discount on Russian gas.[5]

Protests begin: November 2013

Russia successfully strong-armed Yanukovych to renege. At the eleventh hour, on November 21, the Ukrainian government announced that it was halting preparations for signing the agreement at the Vilnius Summit to "ensure the national security of Ukraine." Ukraine stood at a crossroads, and the road leading to Europe was getting foreclosed. The failed signing triggered a reaction in Ukrainian society that neither the Yanukovych government nor Russia would ultimately be able to control. On November 21, an estimated three to five thousand residents of Kyiv, some responding to a journalist's Facebook call to gather at the Maidan, the site of the 2004 Orange Revolution protests and the 1990 student hunger strike, came out with EU and Ukrainian flags to demand the reversal of Yanukovych's decision.[6] The following Sunday, November 24, an estimated 100,000 came out to protest. The early protests were not led by the parliamentary opposition, whose leaders, broadly seen as unable to stop Yanukovych's political power grab or his pro-Russian identity policies, were not welcomed by the protesters. For a short while, essentially two Maidans existed in two sections of the central square in Kyiv: one where opposition parties gathered their supporters, and another where pro-EU supporters protested without any political party symbols, but only with Ukrainian and EU flags. With paid protests becoming a feature of political competition in the preceding years, the protesters carried signs saying "we are not paid."

When the EU summit in Vilnius ended on November 29 without Ukraine signing the association agreement, about ten thousand protesters turned out. These early protests could have followed the fate of the 2010 Tax Maidan and 2012 Language Maidan, when mobilization against Yanukovych government policies remained modest in size and eventually fizzled out, with activists subsequently criminally prosecuted. But the regime made a fateful mistake. In the early hours of November 30, after most protesters who had come out earlier in the day went home and it was uncertain whether large numbers would return, given that the EU summit had ended, the riot police violently charged a small group of student protesters who had decided to camp on the Maidan for one final weekend. The official reason for the dispersal was to clear the square to install the country's main Christmas tree.

Inconsistent repression, insufficient accommodation: December 1 – January 16

Police savagely beat the protesters on the square and in the adjoining streets, where they pursued them. The violence, caught on camera and aired on the internet and by TV channels not controlled by Yanukovych, led to massive backlash. The next day, on December 1, despite an official ban on further demonstrations, an estimated half a million poured onto the streets of Kyiv. They converged on the Maidan and the Interior Ministry troops, who were placed there the previous day, abandoned their posts. Protesters then reoccupied the Maidan and took over the trade union and the city council buildings adjacent to the Maidan. The first self-defense units were created, using the Cossack principle to organize into "hundreds," and the first barricades went up. After several hundred protesters attempted to break though the police lines near the presidential administration, riot police responded with more indiscriminate violence, beating and arresting everyone in their path, including journalists and bystanders. Videos of people pounded by the police as they were lying on the ground led to more outrage. Police violence was now galvanizing the protests more than the demand to sign the EU agreement. A poll conducted a week after the November 30 to December 1 events found that 70% of protest participants were motivated to protest by police violence, against 54% who were motivated by the non-signing of the EU association agreement.[7]

The next month and a half saw a spiral of increasing yet inconsistent repression by the regime, which sustained the protests and fostered radicalization among some protest participants. Had Yanukovych just waited out the protests, he would have had a good chance of staying in power. Unlike the 2004 Orange Revolution, and despite the Euromaidan name, protests lacked one overarching demand. The key demands between December and February and their relative importance were as follows: end to police repression and release of all arrested Maidan participants (between 82% and 64%); signing of the association agreement with the EU (between 71% and 59%); resignation of the government (between 80% and 75%); resignation of Yanukovych and snap presidential elections (between 75% and 66%); criminal prosecution of the perpetrators of violence against the protesters (between 58% and 51%); dissolution of parliament and snap parliamentary elections (between 56% and 51%); and return to the 2004 constitution, which provided for limited presidential powers (between 38% and 43%).[8] With the opposition fragmented, the ruling party maintaining its cohesion and parliamentary majority, the judiciary and security forces firmly under the president's control, and elections not due until March 2015, there was no obvious institutional pathway by which the main demands of the protesters could be realized.

Instead of ignoring the protests or decisively repressing them, the regime applied repressive and accommodative strategies inconsistently, and used, as one analysis put it, "the wrong amount of violence: enough to provoke but not enough to cow."[9] After beatings, arrests, and extra-judicial persecution of the protesters arrested in late November and early December, in mid-December the government signaled to the courts to release most of the detainees to house arrest. At the same time, in the early hours of December 11 – inexplicably at a time when both the EU Foreign Affairs Commissioner and the US Assistant Secretary of State were in Kyiv – the government sent riot police to disperse the Maidan, only for the police to be called off a few hours later as the crowd on Maidan quickly swelled to 25,000.[10] In late December, just as protest momentum seemed to be dying down again, the West was beginning to lose interest, and Russia's $15 billion loan bolstered the perception of Yanukovych's strength, the regime unleashed another round of repression against the protesters. This time the group that bore the brunt of repression were those who called themselves AutoMaidan. It consisted of several hundred car owners, who drove in mass pickets to government buildings and residences of Yanukovych regime officials, including, on December 29, to Yanukovych's own lavish Mezhyhiria estate north of Kyiv. Yanukovych was reportedly infuriated and, in the coming weeks, over 1,500 drivers were stripped of their driving licenses in court, 129 cars were torched,[11] and over twenty activists were violently detained by police and allegedly beaten in custody.[12]

Repression, radicalization, and violence: January 16 – February 20

In January, as the number of protesters camped out on the Maidan dwindled to a hard core of one to two thousand on rotating duties, plus institutionalized Sunday rallies, which, while remaining sizeable at tens of thousands, were not nearly as large as the early December protests, the authorities tried to bring the protest to an end with a set of laws that became known as "The Dictatorship Laws." On January 16, after parliament returned from holiday recess, the pro-Yanukovych majority passed – by a show of hands and in just seconds – laws which criminalized or introduced harsh administrative penalties for many peaceful protest activities, such as driving cars in groups, protesting while wearing a hard hat, picketing in front of politicians' residences, defaming politicians, collecting information about police officers or judges (i.e. exposing corruption), and distributing vaguely defined "extremist" materials. Participation in a "mass disruption" would now carry a ten- to fifteen-year prison sentence. Copying Russian law, the dictatorship laws stipulated that NGOs receiving money from abroad would have to register as "foreign agents." These laws also authorized the "government" (without defining a specific agency) to prohibit access to the internet, and legislators could be stripped of their immunity without due process.[13] It was reported that Yanukovych decided to fully suppress the protests and adopt repressive laws during his unofficial meeting with Putin on January 8.[14]

The dictatorship laws did not deter protesters but galvanized them. They also increased the probability of violence, as the regime clearly signaled that any protest activity could lead to arrest and a lengthy prison sentence. The political subservience of the judiciary made it likely that anyone participating in protests could be sentenced to years in prison for taking part in "mass disturbances" or distributing "extremist" materials through a social media post. If already in December protesters believed they would face severe repression if the protests did not succeed,[15] this belief now only strengthened. The mood on the streets was radicalizing. As one journalist wrote, "if you can be arrested for wearing a hard hat or writing a Facebook post, why shouldn't you throw a Molotov cocktail or a cobblestone?"[16] Days after the dictatorship laws were passed, the protests turned deadly. On January 19, after a 200,000-person-strong Sunday rally against the dictatorship laws, some protesters decided to march to the parliament building, but were blocked by the police. A four-day stand-off ensued, with protesters throwing rocks, Molotov cocktails, and burning tires at the police. On January 22, two protesters were shot dead. The violence in the capital radicalized protests outside of Kyiv. In some western and central Ukrainian cities protesters began to overrun and occupy government buildings, while in other cities in central and eastern Ukraine the police and pro-regime thugs known as *titushki* attacked and dispersed local Euromaidan protest camps.[17]

The regime's response was again inconsistent. Instead of intensifying coercion, Yanukovych, facing conflicting pressures from his inner circle, Russia, and the EU, chose to back down partially: on January 28 parliament repealed nine of the twelve laws passed on January 16, Yanukovych loyalist Azarov resigned as prime minister, and Yanukovych offered to appoint Yatseniuk, the leader of Batkivshchyna, one of the three opposition parties, as prime minister. A new amnesty law was also passed. But none of these measures were seen as sufficient or credible by the opposition. The opposition in parliament boycotted the vote on the amnesty law, since the law would apply only if protesters left all the buildings they occupied within fifteen days. The opposition saw the clause as a threat rather than a concession. With a presidential majority in parliament and tight executive control of the judiciary, neither the repeal of the January 16 laws, nor the release from jail of hundreds of protesters under the amnesty law, could credibly be regarded as permanent. Protesters reasonably feared that the courts could find ways of not implementing the amnesty law and Yanukovych's parliamentary majority could re-introduce anti-protest measures at any time. Indeed, in early February, parliament reintroduced some parts of the repealed laws as legislative amendments. The cabinet's resignation was also not a credible compromise in the absence of constitutional changes that could guarantee that Prime Minister Yatseniuk would not simply be swiftly fired and prosecuted on trumped-up charges, and join his co-partisan and predecessor Yulia Tymoshenko in prison.[18] Just a day before the above supposedly conciliatory measures were announced, the government adopted plans to increase the size of the police force six-fold and to raise the size of the two main riot police units, Berkut and Grifon, from 5,000 to 30,000.[19]

The protesters demanded the repeal of all dictatorship laws, the return to the 2004 constitution, and the signing of the EU association agreement. Yatseniuk said he would agree to become prime minister under Yanukovych if the 2004 constitution were re-instated and a government of opposition figures were appointed, with assurance that they would not soon be fired.[20] Yanukovych was not willing to meet any of these demands, and Russia was advocating ending the protests by force. On January 29, Russia reimposed export restrictions.[21] Reuters reported that Russia was also withholding a $2 billion loan until the protesters were cleared from the Maidan.[22] The post-Maidan head of SBU, Ukraine's security service, would later allege that dozens of FSB agents arrived in Kyiv in late January and, together with the SBU, made plans for a Euromaidan crackdown.[23]

If in late January and early February there was a glimmer of hope for a compromise, it vanished on February 18. In the morning, an estimated twenty thousand protesters marched to the parliament building to demand the restoration of the 2004 constitution that would curb presidential powers. When the pro-Yanukovych majority in parliament refused to include such a proposal in the discussion agenda, things turned violent. The security forces used live munition, rubber bullets, flash grenades, and tear gas to disperse the protesters. Some of the protesters were also using firearms. Running battles were fought all afternoon and the police pursued the protesters back to the Maidan, where the barricades finally held. By the day's end, at least eighteen people were dead, including several policemen. The government closed the metro and issued an ultimatum to clear the streets by 6pm, after which the Interior Ministry and SBU forces would "restore order by all means envisaged by law."[24] Violence in Kyiv rippled throughout the country, and protesters in several western Ukrainian cities occupied regional administration buildings and attacked police stations, seizing weapons. Some of these protesters then headed to Kyiv to defend the Maidan.

With the 6pm deadline come and gone, in the evening of February 18 security forces stormed the protesters-held trade union building, which was set on fire. *Titushki*, with weapons handed out by the interior ministry, killed six people by the time the police began their attack on the Maidan.[25] Two armored personnel carriers sent by the government to clear the Maidan were stopped and burned by the protesters. The assault on Maidan was surprisingly faltering. The government and opposition leaders met during the day on February 18, and again in the early hours of February 19, to negotiate, with little result. On February 19, Yanukovych left for his Mezhihiria estate and video footage would later show him packing cash and valuables into waiting vans. Russia would ultimately blame the West and the protesters for forcing Yanukovych to flee after, following more deaths on the Maidan, the protesters rejected an agreement negotiated on February 21 between Yanukovych and the leaders of the opposition, with the participation of EU and Russian representatives. But Yanukovych apparently had prepared to flee already on February 19. Later on that day the head of the SBU announced an "anti-terrorist operation" – a state of emergency in all but name. The foreign ministers of France, Germany, and Poland announced that they were traveling to Ukraine to meet with Yanukovych the following day. The opposition leaders met with Yanukovych and announced that the government agreed not to storm the Maidan that night.[26] Yanukovych spoke on television, claiming to believe in dialogue, and announced that February 20 would be a national day of mourning for those killed in the preceding two days.[27]

On the morning of February 20, as three EU foreign ministers arrived for emergency negotiations, the standoff on the Maidan critically escalated. The protesters moved through the police line at one end of the Maidan, reclaiming territory lost to the government forces two days before, as the police retreated up the street after being shot at from the Conservatory building. As protesters moved into the area from which the police had retreated, in a dramatic escalation security forces used live ammunition against the protesters in broad daylight in the heart of the capital city. By the day's end about seventy protesters and several security service forces were killed, and over 500 protesters were wounded.[28] A UN report would later put the death toll at 108 protesters and thirteen law enforcers killed in Kyiv from November through February.[29] Yanukovych's fateful decision to use deadly violence against protesters, something no leader in post-Soviet Ukraine had ever done, set in motion the stunningly rapid collapse of his regime.

Regime collapse and the Yanukovych ouster: February 20–22

The violence on February 20 demolished the government's legitimacy and increased protesters' resolve to remove Yanukovych. Yanukovych's regime, which until then had remained largely united, began to collapse. The mayor of Kyiv resigned from the governing party and reopened the Kyiv metro, which had been shut down to prevent protesters from coming to the Maidan. Police and security forces in several western Ukrainian regions announced their support for the protesters. In the afternoon of February 20, a dozen legislators from Yanukovych's Party of Regions called on the security services to "follow the oath to the Ukrainian people" and not "criminal orders to use firearms," and called for an emergency session of the parliament.[30] By late evening, there were enough defectors from the Party of Regions for parliament to pass a resolution ordering the security forces to return to the barracks and not implement the anti-terrorist operation, which the resolution called unconstitutional.[31] That evening and into the night, the foreign ministers of France, Germany, and Poland and the human rights ombudsman of Russia, apparently included at Yanukovych's request, were negotiating with the opposition leaders and Yanukovych. A deal was announced at noon on February 21. It included the return to the 2004 constitution within 48 hours, the formation of a unity government with opposition members, early presidential elections at the end of the year, and protesters leaving the occupied streets and buildings. A signing ceremony was held with the opposition party leaders, Yanukovych, and the three Western ministers signing the deal. Russia's representative did not sign, although Russia would later blame the West and the opposition for reneging on the deal.

Had Yanukovych agreed to these terms before the February 18–20 violence, the agreement likely would have held. But after the unprecedented violence by the state and amid the ongoing implosion of the regime, the agreement to keep Yanukovych in power was no longer feasible. When in the evening of February 21 the opposition leaders presented the agreement to the protesters on the Maidan, where public funeral ceremonies were held for those killed in the preceding days, protesters booed the opposition leaders. Yanukovych's resignation had become a non-negotiable demand for many. A twenty-six-year-old leader of one of the self-defense "hundreds" took the stage to denounce the deal and presented an ultimatum: if Yanukovych did not resign by 10am the next day, the protesters would start taking government buildings by force.

Had the authoritarian regime been able to hold together, the ultimatum could have led to more violent clashes without achieving the stated goal, but the regime was rapidly dissolving for the second day in a row. In developments described as "astonishing" by the Polish foreign minister, within minutes of the agreement announcement and before Maidan rejected it and presented an ultimatum, security forces started leaving the vicinity of the presidential administration building, "which they did not need to do."[32] In parliament, meanwhile, a large section of the Party of Regions crossed the floor, making it possible to pass several anti-Yanukovych actions with large majorities: return to the 2004 constitution, the freeing of Yulia Tymoshenko, broad amnesty to all protest participants, and the firing of the Minister of Interior. Later in the evening on February 21, the SBU announced that it had stopped the anti-terrorist operation against the protesters started on February 19. That same evening, Yanukovych fled Kyiv, leaving his Mezhyhiria mansion unguarded, and headed for Kharkiv, from where the next day he would travel by car to Donetsk, then Crimea, and from there be taken to Russia by Russian military personnel.

On February 22, the speaker of parliament resigned, claiming ill health, and, with Yanukovych's whereabouts unclear, parliament passed a resolution with an over two-thirds majority (328 out of 450) stating that Yanukovych abandoned his office. On those grounds, Oleksandr Turchynov of Tymoshenko's Batkivshchyna party was elected speaker of parliament and acting president, and early presidential elections were scheduled for May 25. Yanukovych's rule of Ukraine was over.

Russia has tried to paint the Euromaidan as a Western-orchestrated and sponsored plot, the protests as dominated by the far right, and the eventual outcomes as an illegal coup against Yanukovych that brought to power a "Nazi junta." All elements of this narrative are manipulations of the facts. The narrative exaggerates the role of the far right in the protests, mischaracterizes the role of the West, and misrepresents the process by which Yanukovych was removed.

The "Nazi junta" myth builds on the fact that the far-right Svoboda party and new ultranationalist groups that formed during the Maidan, such as Right Sector, were present and active on the Maidan. However, they were marginal at the beginning of the protests and did not dominate even at the end. Right Sector, first heard of in November 2013, in January 2014 claimed around 300 "fighters" and only one of the "hundreds" on the Maidan.[33] At the start of the protests in December, polling data showed that 92% of the protesters acted on their own initiative with just 6% belonging to a social organization or movement (and a mere 2% to a political party). By February, 22% reported belonging to a social organization/movement (from anywhere along the Left–Right or extremist–mainstream spectrum), meaning that at the height of the far-right strength and influence it still represented far less than a quarter of the protesters.[34] It remains unclear to this day who all the shooters were on February 20, and some Maidan activists, including some from the Right Sector, had arms and likely used them. But most of the protesters were not armed and, ultimately, the protesters "won with rocks and Molotov cocktails against snipers."[35]

The "Western-backed coup" myth spins the fact that numerous Western officials expressed support for the protesters into a sinister, but manufactured claim that the West instigated, financed, and directed the protests. Various Western dignitaries, such as Germany's and Canada's foreign ministers and US Senators John McCain (Republican) and Chris Murphy (Democrat), visited the protesters. On her visit to Maidan in December, US Assistant Secretary of State Victoria Nuland handed out cookies to protest participants. As Western officials expressed support for the protesters and condemned violence on either side, however, they supported and preferred Yanukovych's continued stay in power until the very end, in the interest of Ukraine's stability. Only after Yanukovych fled in the early hours of February 22 did the West take his departure as a *fait accompli*. A phone call leaked in early February, where Nuland and US Ambassador Pyatt discuss preference for Yatseniuk over the other leaders of the opposition, Klitchko and Tyahnybok, to join a new Yanukovych cabinet on account of Yatseniuk's perceived stronger economic and governing experience, shows American endorsement of Yanukovych's continued rule, not a plan to end it.[36] Despite escalating regime violence, the West was reluctant to impose sanctions on Yanukovych regime members, belatedly announcing sanctions only on February 20. Even after the worst violence, Western leaders implored protesters to agree to the deal that would have kept Yanukovych in power until at least the end of the year, and quite possibly for another term. The regime collapsed, not because the protesters rejected the deal, but because the Yanukovych party, the police, and security services all abandoned him in the aftermath of the violence, and Yanukovych decided to flee.

Finally, the way Yanukovych was ousted is best described as extra-constitutional rather than anti-constitutional. It was an *ad hoc* legal solution to an extraordinary situation created by Yanukovych's own actions. The Ukrainian constitution, like most constitutions around the world, does not provide for a course of action in the event of the president abandoning his post and fleeing, which is what Yanukovych had done on the night of February 21–22. When parliament later that day voted to remove him from office on the grounds that he had "withdrawn himself" (*samousunuvsia*) from his duties as president, parliament took a political decision in extreme and unprecedented circumstances. Parliament's resolution was within parliament's mandate and an over two-thirds majority of MPs from across the political spectrum freely voted in support. Consequently, parliament's actions do not meet the definition of a *coup*, which refers to an "illegal and overt attempt by the military or other elites within the state apparatus to unseat the sitting executive."[37] The executive was unseated, but through self-removal and not illegally.

With Yanukovych gone, the interim government immediately turned its attention to Euromaidan's goals – putting Ukraine back onto a path to Euro-Atlantic integration and reversing Yanukovych's autocratization steps and pro-Russian policies. Pre-term presidential elections in May and parliamentary elections in October 2014 returned a pro-Western president, Petro Poroshenko, and a broad pro-Western parliamentary coalition. Civil society geared up to push the new government toward fulfilling its promises.

The Euromaidan victory and the decisively pro-Western orientation of the new government were not welcomed across Ukraine in equal measure. If western and central Ukrainian regions supported Euromaidan and, by extension, the new government, in the southeast the views were different. These differences were real and related to the long-standing differences in attitudes, identities, and historical legacies of different regions of Ukraine. But what happened in the southeast was not the Russians and Russian-speakers uniting against the "Nazi junta" to pursue secession of their regions from Ukraine and to unite with Russia, as the Russian state and propagandists sought to present it. How was the southeast different and what did it want (and not want) in the wake of Euromaidan's victory?

The aftermath of Yanukovych's ouster

The southeast and separatism before Euromaidan

There is no doubt that Ukraine's southeastern regions used to be the locus of a pro-Russian political orientation. They were part of the Russian empire for the longest of all of Ukraine's regions, which led to a higher concentration of ethnic Russian and Russified Ukrainians. They were socio-culturally more integrated into the Russian World, and economically more tied to Russia than the rest of Ukraine. Southeastern regions favored a Ukrainian foreign policy oriented toward Russia and wanted Ukraine to be a member of Russia-led organizations such as the CIS and the Eurasian Union rather than pursue Euro-Atlantic integration and membership in the EU and NATO. In presidential and parliamentary elections, the southeast consistently supported pro-Russian candidates and parties. In 2004, the southeast overwhelmingly backed pro-Russian candidate Yanukovych and consequently many rejected the Orange Revolution's argument that the election had been manipulated, rather than free and fair. In 2010, the southeast gave Yanukovych the presidency. While the overall result was very close – 49% for Yanukovych vs. 45% for his rival Yuliya Tymoshenko – the regional election results were highly polarized. In much of the southeast Yanukovych received upwards of 80% of the votes and in his home region of Donetsk he received above 90% in a free election.

That said, the southeast was never a monolith. There are significant differences within the region. Crimea is a special case. Its status within the Soviet Union changed a few times – from an autonomous republic within the Russian Soviet republic, to a regular province (oblast) within the Russian republic, to the now much-discussed transfer of Crimea to Ukraine in 1954, by a resolution of the Presidium of the USSR Supreme Soviet, as a regular Ukrainian region. Contrary to the common trope of Crimea being Khrushchev's "gift" to Ukraine to mark the 350th anniversary of the Treaty of Pereiaslav, which in the Soviet period was celebrated as having produced the "unification of Russia and Ukraine," the move aimed to make Ukraine less Ukrainian by adding many Russians to Ukraine's population.[38] In the 1950s, Crimea had a population of some 1.1 million, 75% of them ethnic

Russians and 25% ethnic Ukrainians.[39] Crimea's demography changed after some 250,000 Crimean Tatars, who in 1944 were deported from Crimea *en masse* by Stalin to Central Asia, began to return in the late 1980s and early 1990s. But still Crimea remained the only region of Ukraine with majority ethnic Russian population (58.3% according to the 2001 census) and also predominantly unilingual Russian-speaking: 77% of its population declaring Russian as their mother tongue in the 2001 census and as a matter of linguistic practice Russian was fully dominant.

The two Donbas regions – Donetsk and Luhansk – have the next highest proportion of both ethnic Russian population (38.2% and 39%, respectively, according to the 2001 census) and Russian-speaking population (74.9% and 68.8%, respectively, identified Russian as their native language). Kharkiv, Zaporizhzhia, and Odesa oblasts have between 20 and 25% ethnic Russians, whereas the inner regions – Dnipropetrovsk, Kherson, and Mykolaiv – all have under a fifth of their populations identifying as Russian. Some big cities in the region (Kharkiv, Odesa, Zaporizhzhia) have similarly high concentrations of Russian speakers as Donbas. For example, Ukraine's second largest city, Kharkiv, has 65.9% Russian speakers, and Odesa and Zaporizhzhia also had significant Russian-speaking majorities. However, outside the cities, most of the southeast, except Crimea, is majority Ukrainian-speaking. The census results indicate that in Kharkiv, Odesa, and Zaporizhzhia regions, between a third and half of the population are Russian speakers and in Kherson, Mykolaiv, and Dnipropetrovsk, the final three regions that make up the southeast, about a quarter to a third of their population identify Russian as their native language.[40]

Politically as well, the southeast has not been monolithic. While it did support the pro-Russian candidate over the pro-Western candidate in each presidential election, the proportion varied significantly. Both in 2004 and in 2010, pro-Russian presidential candidate Yanukovych won all the southeastern regions. However, while he dominated in Donbas and Crimea, in the rest of the southeast he won with a smaller margin. In Donbas, his share of the vote was around 90% in both the manipulated 2004 election and in the free 2010 election. He also received upwards of three-quarters of the vote in Crimea. However, in Zaporizhzhia, Odesa, Mykolaiv, and Kharkiv, his vote share hovered between 60% and 70%, and was even lower in Kherson and Dnipropetrovsk.

Despite their ethno-linguistic and political outlier status, separatism was not a tragedy foretold either for Crimea or for Donbas. Tensions between each region and Kyiv had occasionally flared, but the trendline was toward consolidation of loyalty to the independent Ukrainian state. This applied both to local elites who were well integrated with national elites and competed for national power, as well as to the population in both regions, which increasingly identified with independent Ukraine.

The thornier problem was always Crimea, but not primarily for the reasons a perfunctory look may suggest. Despite having a Russian ethnic majority and shorter history within Ukraine, in the waning days of the USSR, Crimean elites did not straightforwardly seek a "return" of their region to Russia. During the 1990s "parade of sovereignties" in the Soviet Union, Crimea, following Russia and Ukraine themselves, issued its own sovereignty declaration. In response, the Soviet Ukrainian parliament granted Crimea autonomous status to keep it within Ukraine. This accommodation then led a majority of Crimeans (55%) to support Ukrainian independence from the USSR in the December 1991 referendum.

Between 1991 and 1994, Crimea went through a period of contestation to define its place within the new state. All three major ethnic groups on the peninsula saw themselves as a minority.[41] The Russians were the majority in Crimea but were a minority within Ukraine. Ukrainians were the majority ethnicity in the country but were a minority on the peninsula. And then there were the Crimean Tatars, who were the peninsula's indigenous group, since they did not have a homeland state anywhere else, and were only 13% of the population. The Crimean Tatars had just returned to their homeland after spending half a century in Central Asia after a mass deportation by Stalin in 1944. The Tatars' return complicated the local inter-ethnic balance and local politics. Crimean Tatars were more supportive of Ukrainian statehood than Russians in Crimea from the very start, but many of them also wanted Crimean autonomous status recast as a Crimean Tatar national-territorial autonomy, which the local Russian majority opposed, and which Kyiv viewed with suspicion.[42] To sort out these competing interests and claims, Crimean elites and the central Ukrainian government negotiated the terms of Crimean autonomy.[43] In May 1992, Crimea's parliament declared independence, but rescinded the declaration the very next day and instead defined Crimea as an autonomous republic within Ukraine – a status which the Ukrainian parliament recognized the next month.[44]

In addition to the delicate inter-ethnic balance, Crimea's relationship with Kyiv was complicated by the status of the city of Sevastopol, the host of the Black Sea Fleet. After Russia assumed the status of USSR successor, it wanted to claim ownership of the whole fleet, as well as special status for Sevastopol. Finally, as we discussed in Chapter 4, Russia often used the threat of "taking back" Crimea to strongarm Ukraine into various foreign-policy decisions. Kravchuk carefully negotiated and compromised with his Russian counterpart Yeltsin to keep Crimea within Ukraine but accommodate Russian concerns about control of the Black Sea Fleet by agreeing to split the Fleet and allow Russia to lease bases in Sevastopol to keep its part of the Fleet there.

The biggest confrontation between Crimea and Kyiv came in 1993–1994 when the Crimean parliament created a directly elected presidency and a Russian nationalist, Yuri Meshkov, surprisingly won it. Meshkov tried to push for Crimean independence from Ukraine. His timing couldn't have been worse. Barely a few months had passed since Yeltsin's confrontation with parliament and the Russian president was as wary as can be of nationalists, so Meshkov and his nationalist agenda irked him. When Meshkov went to Moscow looking for support, Yeltsin snubbed him and did not even agree to a meeting.[45] Meshkov also failed to rally Crimeans to the cause of challenging Kyiv. In the summer of 1994, nearly 90% of Crimeans had voted in the Ukrainian presidential election for the winning candidate, Leonid Kuchma, so the Ukrainian president had a popular mandate as well from Crimeans. When Kuchma called the separatist bluff, abolishing the Crimean presidency in early 1995, Meshkov had nothing to respond with. A local insurgency could not materialize, as the president in Kyiv was now popular with Crimeans. Meshkov lost the support in the Crimean parliament and left Crimea.[46] Russia was unhappy with Kyiv's power move and postponed the imminent signing of a Friendship Treaty with Ukraine, and foreign minister Kozyrev even made remarks about the use of "military force to protect compatriots abroad,"[47] but, ultimately, the crisis dissipated. 1994 was the last time a Russian separatist won Crimean elections.

Over the next two decades, Crimea's status within Ukraine was legally clarified and entrenched. In 1996, the new Ukrainian constitution enshrined Crimean autonomy. In 1997, the Russia–Ukraine Friendship Treaty recognized Ukrainian sovereignty over Crimea. In 1998, a Crimean constitution defined the terms of autonomy and was accepted by the central government. Crimeans participated in Ukrainian elections and, with the exception of the Crimean Tatars, who voted for Ukrainian national-democratic pro-Western parties, the rest of the electorate usually supported the pro-Russian parties and candidate. During the 2004 Orange Revolution election, Crimeans voted overwhelmingly for Yanukovych, but when the results were reversed by the Supreme Court and he then lost the third round, Crimea remained calm and did not challenge the center. During the Orange coalition years, Crimeans were politically alienated from the center, as they did not support any of Yushchenko's policies – either his Ukrainization identity policies domestically, or his Euro-Atlantic foreign-policy course. This disaffection did not lead to the return of separatism, however. Rather, this was a period of local elite competition, which saw Yanukovych's Party of Regions establish a firm economic and political foothold in Crimea. When Yanukovych finally assumed the presidency in 2010, he won convincingly in Crimea. His "Family" came to dominate the local oligarchs. These processes marginalized and sapped political power from any political actors advocating for Crimean separation from Ukraine and reunification with Russia. In the last Crimean elections before the 2014 annexation by Russia, Crimea's main separatist party, Sergey Aksyonov's *Russian Unity*, received only 4%.[48] Polls also suggested that a growing majority of Crimeans, 49% in 2011 and 53% in 2013, viewed autonomy within Ukraine as the best status for their region, while a shrinking minority, 33% in 2011 and 23% in 2013, wanted annexation by Russia.[49] This trajectory was in line with a decline within Ukraine of the proportion favoring Russian–Ukrainian unification: from around 20% in 2008 to 10% in 2014.[50] Just months before Russia's dramatic land grab, scholars estimated that ethnic claims were not a serious source of instability for Crimea.[51]

Like Crimea, Donbas posed a separatist challenge to Ukrainian statehood only in the early post-independence years. By 2014, the region had no credible separatist movement, either as social mobilization or as political structures. Notably, Donbas support for Ukrainian independence was way higher than Crimea's from the very start, and not much different from support in other regions of the country. While a small majority of Crimeans voted for independence in December 1991, 83.3% in Luhansk and 83.9% in Donetsk regions voted yes. The International Movement of Donbas (Interdvizhenie) had formed in the run-up to the independence vote and aimed to oppose it, but still an overwhelming majority turned out for independence. Donbas elites' use of the separatist card was, thus, even more strategic and instrumental than Crimean elites'. They threatened the center with it to receive concessions, rather than to pursue separation in earnest.

A notable confrontation happened in 1993–1994, at the nadir of the post-communist economic crisis, when Donbas miners, encouraged by local politicians, called a general strike, which paralyzed Ukraine's economy. The miners sought a vote of no confidence in President Kravchuk. While they failed to topple the president, Donbas elites achieved several political victories: (1) they got a chance to hold referendums on self-rule for their regions and managed to get huge majorities to vote yes (80% in Donetsk and 90% in Luhansk);[52] (2) they helped force pre-term parliamentary and presidential elections; and (3) they strongarmed the president into appointing the mayor of Donetsk, Yukhym Zvyahilsky, as prime minister, and another Donetsk official as his deputy. In other words, the separatist gambit was used to ensure an increase in representation in the central government, which Donetsk elites then used effectively to strengthen their political clout nationally and build themselves into the core group of the pro-Russian side of the Ukrainian political spectrum.[53]

The second confrontation between Kyiv and Donbas followed the Orange Revolution. Donbas' own Yanukovych could not ascend to the presidency due to the massive mobilization in Kyiv against his attempt to steal the election. Before compromise was hammered out with the help of international mediators and the Supreme Court, Donbas elites worked with other eastern elites to threaten sedition. On November 28, 2004, the governors of Kharkiv, Luhansk, and Donetsk called for the creation of a "Southeastern Autonomous Republic" and even threatened to ask Russia to intervene militarily on their behalf.[54] The move likely facilitated the conclusion of a bargain, which gave southeastern political elites a consolation prize – while they agreed to cede the presidency to their pro-Western adversary, Yushchenko, the compromise weakened the presidency institutionally and empowered parliament, where they held a solid share of the seats. Within two years of the deal, Yanukovych was back as prime minister and, at the end of Yushchenko's mandate, he won the presidency.

Ideological proponents of Donbas separatism had no participation in any of these rounds of elite bargaining. Rather, Donbas elites sometimes played the separatist card rhetorically to force their elite rivals to compromise and share central power. The separatists, meanwhile, were an insignificant fringe political group. Pavel Gubarev's "Fans of Novorossia Club" in Donetsk was one of several small groups. He established links to Dugin's Eurasian movement and Russian National Unity, a nationalist Russian organization. His members railed against "Nazis" and "nationalists" in Kyiv, starting in the mid-2000s, glorified the Donetsk–Kryvyi Rih short-lived 1918 republic, and called for the federalization of Ukraine. But they were marginal as far as popular support or political influence went, and disconnected from the ruling local elites.[55]

The southeast and Euromaidan

Given the dominance of Yanukovych's Party of Regions in the southeast and low support for Ukraine's Euro-Atlantic orientation in 2014, the southeast electorate largely did not share the values and goals that motivated the Euromaidan protest in Kyiv. But neither did it oppose those goals completely or push strongly in the opposite geopolitical direction. For example, polls conducted in Crimea in May 2013 showed that 17% of respondents said that if Ukraine were forced to choose between EU membership and Eurasian Customs Union membership, they personally would choose the EU; a slim majority of 53% would opt for the Russia-led Eurasian Customs Union. 85% reported holding either a neutral or warm attitude toward the EU, whereas only 15% held a cold attitude. And when asked about their top three most important issues, the top concerns included corruption, state capacity, and economic precarity, whereas only 4% mentioned the status of the Russian language or inter-ethnic relations, and a meager 2% pointed to the Russian Black Sea Fleet status.[56] Similar polls for the Eastern region indicated that about 18% would vote for Ukraine's EU membership in a referendum, while 64.5% would support joining the Customs Union led by Russia.[57]

As the protest temperature rose amid wintertime on Maidan in January–February 2014, the southeast saw some pro-Maidan mobilization as well. The main grievance that fueled Maidans in the big cities of the southeast – Donetsk, Kharkiv, Odesa – was government corruption and abuse of power by law enforcement. Grassroots organizers saw "Europe" broadly construed as an inspiration for seeking solutions to both these injustices. But they clearly represented a minority position. A database of protest events compiled by the Kyiv Center for Social and Labor Research recorded 14.7% of all pro-Maidan protests occurring in the southeast.[58] Polls in December indicated that only 13% of eastern Ukrainians supported Maidan, whereas 81% opposed it.[59] The lack of support did not necessarily indicate universal hostility. Many initially treated Maidan as a nuisance, with contempt, suspicion, or indifference. As the protest escalated in Kyiv and violence spread to western and central Ukrainian cities in the waning days of Yanukovych's regime, the indifference turned to fear. The most common sources of anxiety focused on political instability,

Right Sector radicals coming to take revenge on the southeasterner, repression against Russian speakers, and economic retribution against Donbas and its workers.[60]

Still, a poll conducted in mid-February 2014 did not indicate that majorities in the southeast were so scared of the nationalist uprising in Kyiv that they were clamoring for Russian intervention. The minorities who had supported unification with Russia remained stable – about 40% in Crimea, around 25–33% in Donbas, 23% in Odesa, and 15–17% in Zaporizhzhia and Kharkiv.[61] Even after Crimea's annexation, in a poll conducted by KIIS in early April, less than a third of Donbas respondents embraced support for their region's separating from Ukraine and joining Russia, while 52% opposed.[62]

Crimea's takeover, "referendum," and annexation

Within barely a week of Yanukovych's flight from the country and his replacement with an interim president in Kyiv, a covert Russian special operation replaced the local government in Crimea with Russian proxies and directed them to prepare the region for Russian annexation. In the early morning of February 27, Russian soldiers without identifying insignia, later to become known as "Little Green Men," entered the Crimean parliament and seized power, using tactics familiar from coups around the world. They cut communications, held parliamentarians at gunpoint, and forced them to dismiss the Party of Regions' prime minister, Mohyliov, and install Sergey Aksyonov, the leader of the marginal Russian Unity party, which had gotten only 4% of the votes in the 2010 elections to Crimea's regional legislature and held only three of the 100 seats in it. Parliament was also directed to call a referendum on May 25 about enhanced autonomy for Crimea within Ukraine, without spelling out any details. How many MPs were present and how many of them voted for Aksyonov and the referendum was never definitively established,[63] but what is clear is that the process had neither procedural nor democratic legitimacy, but amounted to a Russian military coup. After initially denying involvement, the Russian government eventually changed its tune and, in fact, boasted that Putin had personally instructed the special operations team on its important mission.[64]

Russia's actions were a brazen and clear breach of international law. There is evidence that they likely followed contingency plans rather than opportunistic improvisation. The contingency plans would kick in in the event of government change in Kyiv, to prevent Ukraine from taking a different political course both domestically and geopolitically. Putin's close aide Vladislav Surkov had visited Crimea in mid-February, reportedly to select Crimea's next leader, and the speaker of the Crimean parliament traveled to Moscow on February 20.

Ukraine could not counteract Russia's aggression in Crimea. Crimean Tatars and other Crimeans loyal to the Ukrainian state staged pro-Ukrainian rallies but they did not prevent either the Russia-forced change of Crimea's government or the referendum. In the annexed Crimea, participants in pro-Ukrainian rallies would later be persecuted. Meanwhile, Russia moved in tens of thousands of troops, ostensibly at the Russia-installed Prime Minister Aksyonov's request to help "normalize the situation." Russia claimed that the Kyiv government was illegitimate and therefore Crimea was in a state of anarchy.[65] The Kyiv government was shellshocked and determined that only a small portion of the Ukrainian army troops stationed in Crimea had any preparedness to fight, so trying military resistance was doomed to failure. In addition, there was a swift cascade of defections to Russia throughout the security and law enforcement agencies.[66] Even if Kyiv had given an order to fight, it is unlikely it would have been followed by most of those stationed in Crimea. Finally, European leaders and the Obama administration pressed the interim government to exercise restraint and not respond militarily to prevent further Russian invasion into Ukrainian territory, as had happened in Georgia in 2008.[67]

Having secured military control of Crimea perhaps more quickly and easily than they had expected, Russia's plan moved toward attempting to put a veneer of legality on the land grab. The referendum originally scheduled for May was moved up to March 16 and would now ask Crimeans to express their opinion on reunification with Russia, rather than on the originally planned issue about enhanced autonomy. The sham "referendum" went ahead on March 16 without any Ukrainian or international observers and under military occupation. In the fall of 2022, Russia repeated this playbook in the parts of Kherson, Zaporizhzhya, Luhansk, and Donetsk regions that it had seized following the full-scale invasion. In all cases, the process lacked any modicum of legitimacy as a plebiscite, since the population could not exercise choice freely. The official results in Crimea were 83% turnout and a 97% vote for reunification with Russia.[68] More realistic estimates, surprisingly reported by the Council for Civil Society and Human Rights under the President of Russia, are that turnout was between 30 and 50% and among them a small majority (50–60%) had voted to join Russia.[69] In any case, the size of the mandate is irrelevant because its basis was illegitimate. Within just 24 hours of the referendum result's announcement, Russia moved to formalize its land grab and annexed Crimea, to the international community's quiet consternation.

Donbas conflict starts

Following the Euromaidan victory and Yanukovych's flight, protests against the new government broke out in various cities in southeastern Ukraine. Most protest activity took place in the regional capitals of the two regions which comprise the Donbas (Donetsk and Luhansk), as well as in Kharkiv, and to a lesser degree in Odesa, Zaporizhzhia, and Dnipropetrovsk. These anti-government protests drew hundreds or a few thousand people and initially occurred simultaneously with the pro-Maidan protests. The largest anti-Maidan protest in Donetsk on March 1 was estimated to number around 10,000 participants.[70] Until pro-Maidan protests in Donetsk came under violent attack by anti-Maidan forces, resulting in the killing of a pro-Maidan activist on March 13, the two largest pro-Maidan protests held in Donetsk in early March were estimated at 6,000–7,000 participants.[71] In early April, shortly after Russia's annexation of Crimea, the situation changed dramatically and a separatist rebellion began in Kharkiv, Donetsk, and Luhansk.

On April 6, pro-Russian militants seized key government buildings in the three regional capitals and proclaimed "people's republics." In Donetsk and Luhansk the militants were armed, having seized firearms from armories in the regional SBU headquarters the day prior. The insurgents sent ultimatums to regional legislatures to adopt resolutions reflecting their demands: non-recognition of the Kyiv government, referendum on secession of the region, official status for the Russian language, and the formation of regional "security forces" to defend against the "fascists" in Kyiv. In Kharkiv, police quickly stormed the regional administration building and re-established control, but in Donetsk and Luhansk the government forces refrained from storming buildings held by armed rebels.[72] Government officials from Kyiv were dispatched to deal with the standoff and Kyiv also attempted to use local heavyweights such as Ukraine's richest man and the long-term "don" of Donbas Rinat Akhmetov, but with no result. Instead, the rebellion accelerated. On April 12, a commando unit of fifty men arrived across the border from Russia, led by Igor Girkin (*nom de guerre* Strelkov), a Russian military counter-intelligence officer. Strelkov's men quickly seized police, Security Service, and other government buildings in the town of Sloviansk, north of Donetsk. In response to the Sloviansk capture, on April 13, the Ukrainian government declared an Anti-Terrorist Operation (ATO) in the eastern parts of the country and moved in to re-establish order by military means. The conflict escalated to a military confrontation.[73]

By mid-May the rebellion in Donbas would result in the Kyiv government losing control over a swath of eastern Donbas. In the two weeks after Girkin seized Sloviansk, government buildings and police stations were captured in 32 more towns.[74] On May 11, sham "referendums" on "state sovereignty" (*samostoiatel'nost*) were held in the localities controlled by the rebels. Supervised by armed men, the referendums were held without access to official voter lists (which the Ukrainian authorities had blocked) and were condemned by Ukraine and international election monitoring organizations, which could not supervise the vote. The announced "results" created a picture of unanimity as in Crimea, with 89% in favor of independence in the Donetsk region and 96% in Luhansk, with turnout 74 and 75%, respectively.[75] Following the referendums, two self-styled "people's republics" (Donetsk People's Republic and Luhansk People's Republic, commonly referred to by their Russian acronyms – DNR and LNR) were promptly proclaimed.

The sham referendums and their results did not reflect popular will in Donbas. Support for separation from Ukraine and joining Russia was a minority view in southeastern Ukraine, even after Russia's annexation of Crimea. A survey conducted during the second week of April by KIIS in eight regions of southeastern Ukraine found just 15.4% supporting the idea of their region seceding from Ukraine and joining Russia, while 69.7% were opposed. In Donetsk and Luhansk, support for secession was the highest, 27.5% and 30.3%, respectively, but it was still a minority view and a far cry from the official near unanimity claimed by the "referenda." Majorities (52.5% in Donetsk and 51.9% in Luhansk) opposed secession.[76]

If the majority of the population in the southeast, unhappy as many were with the change of government in Kyiv, did not support separatism, how did the DNR and LNR come into being and succeed, and why only in eastern Donbas? This question remains debated by analysts and scholars, who emphasize the relative importance of competing enabling factors such as grievances and fears among the local Russian-speaking population and, especially, fears of anticipated Ukrainization cultural policies from the new government; possible violence by radical Ukrainian nationalists; loss of economic ties with Russia; the weakness of the central state and local power vacuum and state implosion in Donbas following the collapse of the Yanukovych regime; strategies chosen by local elites in different regions; and Russia's decision to foster and sustain the anti-Kyiv rebellion.[77]

The exact scope and extent of Russian state involvement in developments in Ukraine in the spring of 2014 and the precise impact of Russian involvement on the outcomes will likely remain unknown until, and unless, Russian security service archives are open. In addition to the circumstantial evidence that Russia was directing the rebellion, such as people bussed from Russia taking part in street protests, Russian citizen Aleksandr Borodai becoming prime minister of DNR as soon as it was proclaimed, and another Russian citizen, Strelkov, declaring himself "Supreme Commander" of the DNR forces, in January 2023 the European Court of Human Rights (ECHR) concluded on the basis of extensive evidence that, starting from May 11, 2014, the date of the rebel-organized "referendum" that established the DNR and LNR, Russia exercised effective control over these areas of Donbas.[78]

With multiple factors at play simultaneously, it is impossible to say for certain if, without Russia's interference and the precedent of Crimea annexation, protests would have died down, or led to civil war. But, regardless of whether Russia instigated anti-Kyiv protests or opportunistically exploited them once they arose, it did interfere early with the intent to affect the course of the protests and lever them toward a specific set of goals. The central goal was to curtail the power of the pro-Western government in Kyiv. The main method by which this leverage would be achieved, and Ukraine's ability to pursue independent domestic and foreign policies would be limited, was "federalization."

From the very beginning of the crisis, Russian demands on Ukraine belied Russia's long-standing view of Ukraine as a vassal and its desire to steer Ukrainian domestic and foreign policy. In mid-March, as the annexation of Crimea was taking place, speaking in the Duma, the lower house of the Russian parliament, Russian foreign minister Lavrov stated that "only federalization" could "stabilize" Ukraine.[79] Lavrov called on the EU and the US to pressure Ukraine to adopt a new constitution that would federalize the country, give Russian the status of second state language, and commit Ukraine to non-block status.[80] The Ukrainian foreign ministry rejected these demands – which also included Ukraine recognizing the annexation of Crimea – as a "fully unacceptable approach to redraw the borders of Ukraine

[and] deny its sovereign rights to domestic and foreign policy."[81] The Ukrainian government then announced decentralization reform to devolve more powers to the regions, but Lavrov dismissed this approach as insufficient: "we are convinced," Lavrov maintained, that devolution of additional powers to the regions "can be done only through federalization."[82]

As leaks from 2016 revealed, Russia wanted to use the spring 2014 anti-government protests as a mechanism by which to force the government in Kyiv to agree to federalization. The so-called "Surkov leaks" – a leak of emails written by Vladislav Surkov, a Kremlin advisor who, in 2014, was tasked with managing Donbas – contained several telephone conversations between Sergei Glazyev, a senior Russian presidential advisor, with Russian and pro-Russian Ukrainian activists involved in coordinating anti-government protests in southern and eastern Ukraine in late February and early March 2014. These "Glazyev's tapes" were made public by the Ukrainian SBU in August 2016. In conversations with activists in Odesa, Kharkiv, and Luhansk, Glazyev outlined the following plan.[83] Street rallies were not enough, Glazyev insisted. Extraordinary sessions of the regional councils had to be convened to declare the post-Maidan government in Kyiv illegitimate and appeal to Russia for help. Some local activists expressed doubt that enough local deputies would come, to which Glazyev responded that they must be pressured or threatened to appear. On March 1, the Russian parliament authorized the use of Russian armed forces in Ukraine, and Glazyev was promising "support" (what exactly such "support" would entail and whether Glazyev was ultimately in a position to deliver it would remain unknown) but a veneer of legitimacy needed to be provided. Decisions of the local councils would provide such legitimacy on the logic that the central government in Kyiv was allegedly an illegitimate entity that seized power in a "coup," therefore the local councils were the only legitimate power, and therefore their decisions – to refuse to be subordinated to the Kyiv government and appealing to Russia for help – would start the process of reversing the center of gravity and political power from the "Nazis" in Kyiv to "supporters of federalism" in the southeast. If local legislatures of southeastern regions formed "people's republics" these republics would have an aura of legitimacy and could pressure the central government to "federalize" the country. Russia would support (and direct) this process.

The overall plan allowed for contingencies, but all options were consistent with an ultimate goal for Russia to hamstring Ukraine's government in Kyiv through puppet actors in the southeast. In April, as protests were going on in several urban centers in the southeast – the process dubbed "Russian Spring" in Russia – Putin introduced the notion of Novorossia when speaking about southeastern Ukraine.[84] Had separatism succeeded across southeastern Ukraine, as Russia hoped, Novorossia – a mega-region covering all of southeastern Ukraine, in reference to the tsarist-era administrative geography and terminology – would have united individual regions in a strongly pro-Russian *de facto* state. Federalization of Ukraine could be forced by the supra-regional entity of Novorossiya but, failing that, individual southeastern "republics" could press for federalization separately. Either way, the pro-Russian entities – and through them Russia – would seek leverage (and ideally veto power) over policies of the central government in a "federal" state. In a federated Ukraine, southeastern "autonomous republics" could ultimately block any domestic and foreign policies of the central government – from educational, language, and cultural policies to foreign-policy alliances and international treaties. Then, even if a pro-Western government were in charge in Kyiv, Russia would still have the ability to reliably limit what this government could or could not do. Later analysis of the Surkov email leaks showed that Russia funded and directed pro-Russian activists in multiple Ukrainian regions to take actions that could result in changes to Ukrainian constitution and federalization.[85]

Based on the "Glazyev's tapes," Russia's preferred pathway was the creation of people's republics by the local legislatures, rather than armed insurgency. A vote by local legislatures had a much stronger appearance of legitimacy than a declaration by armed militants. However, Russia was denied this option because the local elites in the southeastern regions did not break from Kyiv and vote on such resolutions.[86] But even if Russia did not have a reliable partner among local political elites and ultimately played a "behind-the-scenes" role in the formation of "people's republics," it wanted to create such entities (or Novorossia) in Ukraine's southeast, and it wanted to create them in order to seek the "federalization" of Ukraine, rather than annex them outright. Some accounts of the establishment of the "people's republics" in Donetsk and Luhansk underscore the central role of violent street action in the context of profound state weakness, rather than the guiding hand of Russia.[87] But this nuanced account does not invalidate the fact that Russia was involved from the start and had detailed plans – even if it could not always ensure their success – to harness the process in the southeast to force the Kyiv government to agree to federalization.

The day after the May 11 referendum, the DNR and LNR issued a plea to Putin for acceptance into Russia, but it went unanswered. Why didn't Putin follow the Crimean scenario and annex eastern Donbas, where "people's republics" were proclaimed and their leaders appealed for Russia's intervention and incorporation into Russia? Why did Russia not use its military openly to conquer the entire southeastern Ukraine it called Novorossia? In the spring of 2014, the annexation of Donbas by Russia was not a tall order. The Ukrainian army, in the words of a top Ukrainian general, was "literally in ruins" and suffering from "total demoralization."[88] Ukraine had no fighting units stationed east of the Dnipro River and the totality of battle-ready troops in Ukraine numbered just five thousand.[89] One explanation has been that, by not annexing these regions, Putin demonstrated his risk aversion.[90] There is merit to this argument since, by annexing these territories and sending Russian forces to fight the Ukrainian army over Donbas, Putin would have destroyed the fiction that Russia was not involved in the conflict in Donbas, and revealed unequivocally the annexation of Crimea as a Russian military operation before he was ready to do so.

But the annexation was also fundamentally not an effective strategy for Russia's main goal – putting a stop to Ukraine's Euro-Atlantic integration movement and securing control over Ukraine's foreign and domestic policies. Ukraine with a pro-Western government and without Donbas would have continued, and likely accelerated, its move Westwards, as well as further separation from Russia in identity and other areas of domestic policies. This was a far less desirable outcome for Russia than a Ukraine destabilized and kept in limbo through a proxy war in Donbas. The goal of controlling Ukraine could not be achieved by annexation of any given chunk of its territory but could be achieved through the Trojan horse of "federalization" or another agreement, which would give Russia's proxy "republics" in Donbas constitutionally guaranteed veto power over central government decision-making. As long as vassalizing Ukraine could potentially be achieved by other means, territorial annexation and the direct military action it would have required remained a non-preferred strategy for Russia. As we explain below, Russia moved to full-scale military intervention in 2022 only after it, as Putin saw it, had exhausted all other methods for vassalizing Ukraine.

Through April and May 2014, rebels, Russian operatives, and Russian "volunteers," all supported by Russia, fought the Ukrainian forces in the course of the ATO. In the summer, the fighting escalated. The Ukrainian army began to recover from its original disarray and

Russian involvement grew and became harder to deny as rebels were increasingly armed with heavy weapons, such as tanks, which came from Russia and Crimea, as well as artillery and multiple rocket launchers. In late June, newly elected Ukrainian president Poroshenko announced a 20-point peace plan and declared a ceasefire but hostilities quicky resumed. Beginning in June, the pro-Russian rebels declared their intention to hunt the Ukrainian air forces and they shot down several Ukrainian army helicopters and aircraft. The Ukrainian authorities closed the air space over Donbas below 32,000 feet but, on July 17, the rebels shot down Malaysian Airlines passenger fight MH-17, which was heading from Amsterdam to Kuala Lumpur. The airliner was flying at a higher altitude, but the rebels likely mistook it for a Ukrainian military plane and hit it, killing all 298 people on board. The MH-17 downing changed the course of the broader conflict between Russia and the West. As pro-Russian rebels obstructed the crash-site investigation and Russia denied responsibility and came up with a series of lies about who was behind the shooting, widespread outrage in the West eroded the little credibility Russia's claim of non-involvement in the conflict in Donbas had. A new round of sanctions against Russia followed.[91]

Through the remainder of the summer, military fortunes changed, Ukraine gained initiative and achieved a series of battlefield victories, which influenced Russia's political decisions. In early July, Ukraine liberated two strategic urban centers in the Donetsk region, Sloviansk and Kramatorsk. By mid-August, the Ukrainian army and volunteer battalions recaptured substantial amounts of territory that the "people's republics" had seized in the preceding months. On August 20, Ukrainian forces seized Illovaisk, a town between the city of Donetsk and the Russian border. Ukrainian command planned to separate the Donetsk and Luhansk rebel forces from each other and close the border with Russia to prevent the flow of Russian military aid and personnel to the rebels. Had this plan succeeded, the insurgency faced defeat. To prevent this outcome, Russia had to move beyond hybrid tactics of sending only "volunteers" and supplies and sent its regular army forces across the border.[92] The Russian forces encircled a large number of Ukrainian troops in Illovaisk, subsequently killing many after promising them safe passage out of encirclement through a "green corridor." Other Ukrainian soldiers were taken prisoner. In this highly disadvantageous for Ukraine context, as Ukraine sought to prevent the Illovaisk military disaster from spreading, it had to negotiate the first Minsk peace accord, which would become known as Minsk-1.

The Minsk Agreements: Russia's Trojan horse for Ukraine

The "Protocol on the Results of the Consultations of the Trilateral Contact Group" (Minsk-1) was signed on September 8, 2014 by representatives of Ukraine, Russia, and the OSCE. Representatives of DNR and LNR also signed but with their names only, without indicating their status of representatives of proxy "republics." This was a compromise solution. From the start of the conflict, Ukraine has denied that the leaders of DNR and LNR were independent actors acting solely upon their own political agenda and maintained that Russia was the real party to the conflict. Russia has insisted that its role in the conflict was purely humanitarian and Ukraine ought to negotiate directly with the authorities of the DNR and LNR. The Minsk-1 agreement contained twelve points, starting with the immediate bilateral ceasefire and, in the short term, the agreement led to a decrease in violence. On virtually all other points no progress was made and these provisions remained largely unimplemented. The reason, as scholars subsequently pointed out, was that in the Minsk accord "profound differences were papered over with vague language and the two sides interpreted the agreement completely differently."[93]

The key points of disagreement between Ukraine and Russia were the sequence of steps in Minsk implementation and the content of the "special status" which Ukraine agreed to grant to the rebel-held areas. Minsk-1 provided for the withdrawal of "illegal armed groups, military equipment, fighters, and mercenaries" from the territory of Ukraine (item 10); "permanent monitoring of the Ukrainian–Russian state border" by the OSCE (item 4); conduct of early local elections in the rebel-held areas (referred to in the agreement as "certain districts of the Donetsk and Luhansk regions") to be carried "in accordance with the Law of Ukraine "On temporary procedure of local self-government in separate districts of the Donetsk and Luhansk regions (Law on Special Status)" (item 9); and "decentralization of power, in particular by way of adopting a law of Ukraine "On temporary procedure of local self-government in separate districts of the Donetsk and Luhansk regions" (item 3).[94]

Following the Minsk-1 signing, Ukraine would maintain that the security environment needed to be stabilized first, afterwards democratic local elections in accordance with the OSCE standards have to take place, and only after a special status for the regions could be realized. Ukraine maintained that meaningful democratic local elections could not be held as long as "illegal armed groups" (i.e.

armed rebel and Russian forces) remained in *de facto* control of the region and anyone and anything could move across the Ukrainian–Russian border without Ukraine's knowledge or consent. Conducting elections under Ukrainian law meant, from Ukraine's standpoint, that all Ukrainian parties could run, voters would be Donbas residents at the start of the conflict (meaning that subsequent arrivals from Russia would be excluded, but some million and a half who fled from Donbas to other areas in Ukraine since the spring would be included in the electorate), Ukrainian media should be allowed to operate, and the elections themselves would be administered by Ukrainian election authorities. "Decentralization of power" under a law on "special status" would mean extending greater powers to the region but decisively not "federalization" or a *de facto* veto power over central government decision-making. For Ukraine, therefore, withdrawal of illegal armed groups from its territory, OSCE monitoring of the entirety of the Ukrainian–Russian border, and the creation of conditions for a local vote under Ukrainian law were priorities.

Russia interpreted Minsk-1 very differently. It saw adoption of the "special status" law as the top priority and wanted this "special status" to be cemented into the Ukrainian constitution. It also denied its involvement in Donbas, thus muddying the waters around the requirement that "illegal armed groups, fighters and mercenaries" needed to be withdrawn. In subsequent months and years Russia would allow OSCE monitoring of the Russian–Ukrainian border only in a handful of official border crossings, meaning that the broad swath of the border remained under exclusive Russian and rebel control.

In September 2014, Ukraine adopted a law "On Special Procedure of Self-Government in Certain Areas of Donetsk and Luhansk regions."[95] The law reflected measures later spelled out in Minsk-2 (such as regional linguistic autonomy, police and judicial appointments, and provisions for people's militia in the rebel-held regions). The law was designed to come into force after local elections in these areas, held in accordance with international standards and the Ukrainian law, took place. The law set December 7, 2014 as the date for holding elections. But the rebels staged their own sham "elections" in November 2014, which were not conducted in accordance with Minsk accord provisions and were held without international monitoring. All in all, Minsk-1 slowed down the fighting but did not produce a comprehensive resolution of the conflict.

By January 2015 large-scale fighting resumed. The escalation took place around the town of Debaltseve, northeast of the city of Donetsk.

The Debaltseve area was Ukrainian-controlled territory, surrounded by rebel-held territory. As a junction of several roads and railroads, Debaltseve had strategic significance for the ground lines of communication for both sides. At the end of January, rebels launched a large-scale attack to capture the Debaltseve area. After several weeks of intense fighting, they cut off the main road out of the salient, effectively surrounding the Ukrainian government forces, although the fighting continued and lines of control remained contested. In this military environment, disadvantageous to Ukraine, another agreement called "Package of Measure for the Implementation of the Minsk Agreement," subsequently referred to as Minsk-2, was negotiated and signed on 12 February 12, 2015 by the representatives of Ukraine, Russia, the OSCE, and the leaders of the self-declared "republics."[95]

Even though, as the title indicates, Minsk-2 was conceived as a specification of steps to enable the implementation of Minsk-1, Russia and Ukraine contested the precise meaning of many of the agreement's thirteen clauses and disputed the implementation sequence of the agreement's measures. A scholarly study summarized the resulting dilemma thus: "each side expected that the commitments it favored were non-negotiable, while seeking to avoid the commitments that it found unacceptable. The result was an agreement that could not be implemented, but also could not be abandoned."[96] Ukraine, which was forced to sign Minsk-2 with a proverbial gun to its head as its troops were being trounced in Debaltseve, was forced to concede important points, such as the timing of restoration of Ukrainian control over the Ukrainian–Russian border, and specific provisions in the "special status" law. Per item 11 and Notes to the Minsk-2 accord, Ukraine agreed to include in the special status law (Law "On the Special Order of Local Government in Individual Areas of the Donetsk and Luhansk Regions") provisions on linguistic autonomy, participation of elected local authorities in the appointments of heads of local prosecutors' office and courts, and creation of local militia (police) units upon the decision of local councils. The timing of Ukraine restoring control over its border with Russia, which was undefined in Minsk-1, now favored Russia's position. Minsk-2 stated (item 9) that restoration of control over the state border by Ukraine's government would begin on the first day after the local elections were held and would conclude after constitutional reform on decentralization came into force. The constitutional reform was now explicitly mentioned (item 11), and it was supposed to provide for decentralization "taking into account the characteristics of individual areas of the Donetsk and Luhansk regions, agreed on with representatives of these areas." This wording about "agreeing on" constitutional changes with pro-Russian proxies in control in areas of Donetsk and Luhansk essentially gave Russia the ability to demand constitutional changes that would give the self-styled "republics" the kind of autonomy Russia favored. Ultimately, implementing "special status" on Russia's terms, would give separatist entities a veto over Ukraine's future reforms and international orientation. For Ukraine this was an unacceptable outcome, not because it objected to autonomy for Donbas per se, but because the exact degree and content of autonomy could be determined and imposed on it by Russia. This was at the heart of the deadlock over Minsk: as one analysis put it, "the Minsk agreements rest on two irreconcilable interpretations of Ukraine's sovereignty: is Ukraine sovereign, as Ukrainians insist, or should its sovereignty be limited, as Russia demands?"[97]

Minsk-2 was thus clearly disadvantageous to Ukraine, but it nevertheless gave Ukraine a way to avoid the least desirable outcome – a constitutional change that would give Russia-controlled areas veto powers over national policies – by leveraging other clauses in Minsk-2, without formally violating or abandoning the agreement. Specifically, Ukraine leveraged the elections clause (item 12), which stated that in the rebel-held areas local elections "will be held in compliance with the relevant standards of the OSCE" and on the basis of the Ukrainian law. OSCE standards, Ukraine maintained, meant that the vote needed to be free and fair, which in turn necessitated proper security in the region, safe access to Ukrainian media and election authorities, the ability of Ukrainian political parties to campaign and for displaced people to vote. Until and unless such elections took place there were no legitimate "representatives" of these areas, Ukraine argued. For its part, Russia wanted its proxies in charge of LNR and DNR to be considered the legitimate representatives of these regions and for Ukraine to negotiate constitutional changes with them, while Russia would keep the pretense of its non-involvement in the conflict and be seen as a guarantor – on par with Western actors involved in the Minsk process – of the Minsk accords. In March 2015 the Ukrainian parliament amended the law on special status, adding a clause to say that implementation of the main provisions of the law was suspended until free and fair elections, as provided by the Minsk accords, took place on the territories of the DNR and LNR. Since, in the following seven years, Ukraine and Russia were never able to agree on elections that would have returned Ukrainian authority to the Russia-controlled areas, the special status law never entered into force.

Unless either Russia abandoned its goal to control Ukraine through the Trojan horse of the Minsk accords, or the Ukrainian government agreed to submit to such control, the Minsk process was pre-destined for deadlock.[98] Critically, it is the irreconcilable positions over control of Ukraine that were the main obstacle, not disagreements over individual clauses viewed in isolation, or any ethnic tensions or the rights and grievances of ethnic Russians and Russian-speakers in Donbas that Russia claimed to want to address by way of the Minsk Agreements. As an OSCE diplomat involved in the Minsk process summarized in an interview after the Minsk process broke down and Russia launched the full-scale invasion, the Donbas conflict was "fundamentally about Russia wanting to exert influence over the domestic and foreign-policy orientation of the government in Kyiv." In the Minsk Agreements, the diplomat continued, a "fiction of an ethnic conflict was constructed instead, although Russia actually had no particular interest in obtaining any autonomy rights for eastern Ukraine, for Russian-speaking or ethnically Russian Ukrainian citizens." Instead, Moscow was concerned "above all with what was happening in Kyiv. The Ukraine conflict is about the orientation of Ukraine, pure and simple. But the Minsk Agreement addresses completely different issues. That's why the process didn't work."[99] This point cannot be overemphasized. Russia's attack on Kyiv in February 2022 and the wanton destruction of predominantly Russian-speaking southeastern Ukrainian cities and villages during the full-scale war only confirm the insight.

6

The road to full-scale invasion

In a major escalation from its previous methods, in 2014 Russia used military aggression to pursue its familiar goal of vassalizing Ukraine by attempting to control its domestic policies and preventing its geopolitical drift to the West. Putin could not accept the pro-Russian Ukrainian president's loss of power. After taking Crimea, Putin likely hoped that the simmering war in Donbas would cause Ukraine's political and economic collapse or force federalization, which would give Russia an indirect lever over Ukrainian domestic policies. The second expectation was that the "Nazi junta" narrative would delegitimize the government in Kyiv in the eyes of both the West and Ukraine's Russian-speakers, and hasten Ukraine's political disintegration. And, finally, Putin may have hoped that the West would hear his message that Ukraine belonged to Russia's sphere of influence and would abandon any plans to help Ukraine integrate into the Euro-Atlantic structures.

While Putin's swift Crimean land grab turned out to be a boon to his domestic popularity, his overall strategy in Ukraine was self-defeating. 2014 became a watershed moment in Ukraine's political trajectory, but not in the way Putin calculated. All the processes he aimed to reverse – Ukrainian identity consolidation, democratization, and a pro-European foreign-policy orientation – accelerated like never before. Russia perceived each of these domestic Ukrainian developments as slights, which further heightened the tension between the two countries. Meanwhile domestically, Putin's authoritarian regime gradually grew ever more repressive, the imperialization of identity intensified, and Russian elites came to view the West as weak, divided, and afraid of confrontation.

This accelerated divergence between Ukraine and Russia increased the likelihood of a bigger war. First, both countries became increasingly committed to irreconcilable projects. Second, Ukraine's political and institutional reforms, identity changes, and strengthened pro-European geopolitical orientation all diminished Russia's main levers of domestic influence on Ukraine – pro-Russian parties, oligarchic networks, Russian media propaganda, and the Orthodox Church. The flawed Minsk Agreements-devised process had no chance of stopping the collision course that this divergence produced. On paper, the Minsk Agreements attempted to solve what Russia wanted to present as reality – an ethnic conflict between Kyiv and Russians and Russian-speakers in Donbas seeking protection for their rights. But reality was different – Moscow wanted to use the Donbas rebels to control Kyiv. With such a mismatch between stated goals and tacit intentions, Minsk was doomed to failure from the start.

Electoral geography changes in post-Euromaidan Ukraine

Russia's 2014 aggression dramatically altered Ukraine's electoral geography, inadvertently contributing to increased political consensus around identity-strengthening, democracy-boosting, pro-European policies and fueling Ukraine's multi-dimensional distancing from Russia. Crimea and the areas of Donbas that Ukraine lost in the spring of 2014 were home to some 3.75 million voters, or 12% of the voting population. These were the most pro-Russian Ukrainian voters and suddenly they could no longer participate because Ukrainian elections could no longer be held where they lived. This made Ukraine's electoral map decidedly unfavorable to a pro-Russian agenda at the national level.

In addition, Russia's actions alienated many Ukrainians who had previously held pro-Russian positions and pushed them toward a pro-European and pro-Western orientation. In a September 2014 survey conducted by Gallup on behalf of the International Republican Institute, 59% of respondents favored membership in the EU, compared with just 17% who favored joining the Moscow-led grouping. In September 2013, before the Euromaidan protests started, the corresponding figures were 42% and 37%, respectively. Support for NATO for the first time exceeded opposition. In a July 2015 Rating Group poll, 41% said they would vote in favor of NATO membership in a hypothetical referendum, 30% would vote against, and 15% were undecided. Prior to 2013, no more than 25% favored NATO. Positive views of Russia also declined – both nationwide and in the historically Russia-leaning south and east. Nationwide, positive views of Russia dropped from 88% in September 2013 to 34% in February 2015. The east remained above the national average but, even in the east, positive attitudes to Russia nearly halved – from 96% to 55%.[1]

The electoral map changes and attitudinal shifts altered Ukraine's political spectrum. The May 2014 pre-term presidential elections to choose Yanukovych's successor produced results never before seen in Ukraine. The main contenders in the lively and contested campaign were Orange-era heavyweights Poroshenko and Tymoshenko, both running on pro-European platforms. For the first time since 1991, the president was elected without a run-off. Not only did Poroshenko win in the first round with 54.7%, but the electoral map no longer showed a divide into two similarly sized halves. Poroshenko prevailed in every region, except for a small pocket in the east. The east–west dividing line, which had characterized most previous presidential contests, now "jumped" east decisively, after having slowly moved in this direction over the two prior decades (Map 2.1). Poroshenko's success was aided by the implosion of the Party of Regions in the wake of Yanukovych's flight, which left the pro-Russian political field in disarray. Several pro-Russian candidates who ran each got low single digits. The former Party of Regions voters in eastern and southern regions had low trust in the new government and were left disoriented. This contributed to a historically low turnout in the former Yanukovych strongholds in the east and south.[2]

In October 2014, Ukraine held pre-term parliamentary elections, which confirmed that the majority of the Ukrainian electorate now preferred pro-Western parties. The 2014 elections restructured the Ukrainian party system. The election wiped out the Left, as neither the communists nor the socialists cleared the 5% threshold to enter parliament. The result reflected a steep drop in voters' support for Soviet restorationism as Russia's aggression reduced the share of Ukrainians who wanted a union state with Russia. Polls indicated that from February 2014 to September 2014, the share of respondents wanting Russia and Ukraine to be in one state fell from 12% to 5%. Yanukovych's Party of Regions, hastily reconstituted into the Opposition Bloc, also ended up with much lower legislative presence, winning just 9.4% of the vote on the party list nationwide and few single-mandate seats, so it got only 29 seats out of 423 total.

For the first time, the Right held a comfortable legislative majority. Petro Poroshenko's Bloc and four other parties that all campaigned on a platform of closer ties with the West, anti-corruption, market reforms, and opposition to Russia's actions in Crimea and Donbas formed a ruling coalition. The election winners were established mainstream politicians with long political experience, not newcomer radicals. The only new party was Self-Reliance, who described themselves as Christian Democrats and included the mayor of Lviv and young civil society leaders. After it was joined by several candidates who ran as independents, the Poroshenko-backing coalition held a constitutional majority. Notably, the two main far-right parties, Svoboda and Right Sector, failed to clear the 5% threshold, though several of their candidates won in single-mandate districts. Rather than being buoyed by the Maidan revolution, the far right was nearly wiped off the political scene.[3] The results dispelled the manipulative Russian narrative that the Maidan revolution had brought a Nazi junta to power in Kyiv.

Finally, both 2014 elections restored Ukraine's democratic trajectory because they were free, fair, and competitive. In the spring, international observers commended the authorities for running a democratic presidential election in a tough security environment and pointed out that the Central Election Commission, the villain of the 2004 manipulated election, operated "independently, impartially, collegially, and generally efficiently."[4] The fall parliamentary elections further entrenched electoral democracy in Ukraine as they also conformed to international norms for free and fair competition.

Accelerating policy divergence

The implications of the May 2014 presidential and October 2014 parliamentary elections for the political process at the national level were dramatic. The political spectrum was uniting around the idea that Ukraine needed to leave the Russian World decisively and the government made a run for it. With Poroshenko as president and a pro-presidential constitutional majority in the legislature, the policy agenda of those committed to Ukrainization, democratization, and Euro-Atlanticism could move forward.

Deepening Ukrainization

The post-Maidan government's Ukrainization agenda included policies on the decommunization of historical memory, breaking ties with

Russia in the religious sphere, and the strengthened status of Ukrainian as the state language.

Decommunization

The May 2015 adoption of four laws, collectively known as "decommunization laws," was the first major post-Euromaidan policy change in identity politics. These laws were enacted against the backdrop of growing sentiment that Russia's post-Euromaidan aggression against Ukraine was an echo of previous Russian/Soviet moves to subjugate Ukraine and crush its sovereign statehood. Street politics hastened elite actions. Starting with the protesters' toppling of the main statue of Lenin near Independence Square in Kyiv in the early days of Euromaidan in December 2013, hundreds of statues of Lenin around Ukraine came down over the following months in a process termed *Leninopad* (Lenin fall). By December 2014, activists had removed 436 Lenin monuments.[5] Rejecting the Soviet legacy that Russia eagerly embraced was increasingly presented in Ukraine as a matter of state security. The head of the Institute of National Memory, a government body established during Yushchenko's presidency, which drafted the decommunization laws, linked the success of Russia's aggression in Crimea and eastern Donbas to the lack of earlier decommunization and the concentration of the "bearers of Soviet values" in these regions, which he called "islands of Sovietness."[6] The post-Euromaidan makeup of the legislature allowed the decommunization laws to pass quickly, with a comfortable majority.

The laws pivoted Ukraine's official memory regime in a direction sharply away from the Russian–Soviet narrative of the Soviet period in general and, in particular, the World War II era. The Soviet term "Great Patriotic War" was replaced with the internationally used "Second World War." May 8 was designated as Day of Memory, in line with the European practice of commemorating the surrender of Nazi Germany. May 9 remained as Victory Day, a holiday celebrated in the USSR, post-Soviet Russia, and some other post-Soviet states. Decommunization laws also forbade "falsification of the history of the Second World War" and to this end equated communism with Nazism and criminalized "propaganda" in support of these regimes and the display of both regimes' symbols. One of the laws granted the legal status of "fighters for Ukrainian independence in the twentieth century" to members of various groups that fought for Ukraine's independence in the twentieth century, including the OUN and the UPA, and made unlawful "public displays of disrespectful attitudes" toward recognized independence fighters, as well as "public denial of the legitimacy of the struggle for Ukraine's independence in the twentieth century." Another law guaranteed access to the archives of repressive Soviet-era organs.[7]

Opening of the archives was one of the main – and unquestionably positive – consequences of the laws since Soviet archives "became almost fully open to researchers,"[8] even though at the time of the laws' adoptions some were concerned the Institute of National Memory would engage in highly selective opening of the archives to conceal records casting anti-Soviet Ukrainian nationalists in a negative light. With the opening of the Soviet-era archives, Ukraine diverged sharply from Russia, where the Federal Security Service (FSB) had began to curtail access to the archives of Soviet repressive organs shortly after Putin was first elected,[9] and restrictions increased further after Euromaidan.[10] Another practical consequence of the decommunization laws was the state-mandated removal of Soviet-era symbols, monuments, and place names from public spaces in Ukraine. By late August 2016, 987 cities, towns, and villages had been renamed, as well as 26 administrative districts, and the number of dismantled Lenin statues stood at 1,200.[11]

The decommunization laws generated controversy domestically, as well as internationally. Poland strongly objected to the granting of positive official recognition to the OUN and the UPA.[12] Some scholars and human rights groups objected to the laws for their potential to stifle historical study and debate, for exempting from criticism organizations with a history of collaboration with Nazi Germany and violence against ethnic minorities, and for establishing criminal liability and imprisonment for publicly spreading vaguely defined "propaganda" of communist and/or Nazi regimes, displaying their symbols, or denial of these regimes' "criminal nature."[13] In hindsight, these fears did not materialize as Ukraine used decommunization laws mainly to remove Soviet legacy from public spaces rather than to persecute individuals for dissenting opinions. By the end of 2019, more than four years after the laws were enacted, only two individuals were convicted under the decommunization laws for publicly displaying banned communist symbols, both receiving suspended sentences.[14]

Domestically within Ukraine, decommunization laws proved less divisive and controversial than many expected. While there was little explicit support for these laws – as low as 10%, according to an August 2015 poll[15] – the decommunization laws neither aggravated regional polarization, nor mobilized opposition, nor boosted the popularity of pro-Russian parties that vocally opposed the policy. This was in part because among the public much of the opposition to the laws was non-ideological: people disliked the laws, not due to positive views of Soviet-era leaders, or a commitment to the preservation of Soviet-era symbols, but because the financial costs of renaming places and removing monuments was seen as a waste of state resources that could be spent on socio-economic improvements.[16] The laws also contributed, perhaps inadvertently, to the strengthening of civil society. The laws directed municipal authorities to establish toponymic commissions to determine which streets needed to be renamed and to discuss proposals for new names. These toponymic commissions brought together local historians and civil society activists and engaged citizens in debates about local history. The process enhanced local democracy by increasing political participation and citizens' political efficacy as they often successfully influenced local authorities' decisions.[17]

Additionally, attitudes to the OUN and the UPA were gradually changing. In the context of Russian aggression, the OUN and the UPA, demonized by the Soviet Union as well as in Putin's Russia as traitors to the common Soviet state, increasingly came to be seen as past symbols of resistance to Soviet/Russian attempts to subordinate Ukraine. The share of Ukrainians who supported official recognition of OUN and UPA members as fighters for Ukrainian independence increased from 27% in 2013 to 41% in 2015 and 49% in 2017 (after the February 2022 invasion, support skyrocketed to 81%).[18] This symbolic support for WWII-era radical Ukrainian nationalist groups did not mean that Ukrainians embraced radical nationalism and did not translate into electoral support for far-right nationalist parties and candidates. The poor 2014 electoral showing for Svoboda and the Right Sector was followed in the 2019 elections by a near complete wipeout for the far-right nationalists, who won just one parliamentary seat. This did not prevent Russia from fanning the narrative of "fascists" in power in Kyiv, and it predictably decried the decommunization laws as falsifying the "common historical memory" of the Ukrainian and Russian people. The Russian Foreign Minister hyperbolized the laws as "attempts to rewrite the results of WWII and the Nuremberg Trial verdict."[19]

In April 2014, on the heels of Crimea's annexation, Russia passed its own law, diametrically opposed to the Ukrainian laws: if decommunization laws in Ukraine criminalized propaganda and symbols of the Soviet state, in Russia, the Criminal Code was amended to make "dissemination of knowingly false information on the activities of the USSR during WWII" a criminally punishable offense. The same amendment also criminalized public insults to "symbols of Russian military glory" and display of "attributes and symbols" of Nazis and their supporters.[20] In contrast to Ukraine, where decommunization laws resulted in only two suspended sentences in four years, in Russia legislation on historical memory was widely used to punish individual scholars, activists, and private citizens for expressing "false" views of history, as well as to control historical research and publications. By 2019, more than nine thousand people were fined or imprisoned for up to fifteen days for banned symbols. Some of the publicized cases were downright absurd, like that of a person getting fined for displaying on social media a photograph of their family home during Nazi occupation. There were additionally 25 known criminal convictions of individuals, historians, and activists for expressing "false" views about WWII and, among the more than 1,500 individuals convicted under the law against extremism between 2012 and 2017, some were sentences for statements about history. In academic institutions some research topics became *de facto* banned and individual scholars saw their research projects censored and published books removed from bookstores.[21]

Historical memory politics in Ukraine and Russia maximally diverged. In Russia, in the years since Euromaidan, the official historical narrative centered on the sacralization of Soviet victory in WWII became further institutionalized. In 2020, a department dedicated to the investigation of crimes relating to falsification of history was established within Russia's Investigative Committee. The same year, a series of amendments to the Russian constitution proclaimed that as the "successor to the Soviet Union" Russia "protects historical truth" and "honors defenders of the Motherland." The amendments also ruled that "diminishing the significance of the people's heroism in defending the Homeland is not permitted."[22] With criticism of any of the Soviet Union's actions during WWII made unconstitutional and subject to criminal prosecution, Russia instrumentalized USSR's WWII victory to legitimize a neo-imperial reconstruction project and uphold the notion that the Soviet period, when Russia and Ukraine were politically united, was morally and objectively the right order of things. In Ukraine, the designation of individuals and groups who fought against Soviet forces for an independent Ukraine was undoing the narrative of Russian–Ukrainian organic "unity." Those who fought against the Soviet state and continued to be regarded as enemies in Russia were now legally recognized heroes in Ukraine. If sacralization of WWII victory made the Soviet period a historical golden age in Russia and an era when Ukraine and Russia were in a "natural" union, in Ukraine decommunization laws legally designated the Soviet past as a period when Ukraine was subjugated by Moscow.

Religion

Religious politics was another area of post-Euromaidan rupture between Ukraine and Russia. This particular schism was literally of historic proportion: for the first time since the seventeenth century, a Ukrainian Orthodox Church, recognized within global Orthodoxy and independent from Moscow, came into existence. In December 2018, the Orthodox Church of Ukraine (OCU), a Ukrainian Orthodox Church independent from the Russian Orthodox Church (ROC), was formed in Ukraine on the basis of two churches (the Ukrainian Orthodox Church Kyiv of the Kyiv Patriarchy (UOC-KP) and the Ukrainian Autocephalous Orthodox Church (UAOC)) that had functioned in Ukraine since the early 1990s but were considered "schismatic," i.e. ecclesiastically illegitimate, within global Orthodoxy.[23] The following month, the OCU received a *tomos* (decree) of autocephaly from the Ecumenical Patriarchate in Istanbul, thus attaining canonical legitimacy. In both Kyiv and Moscow, the creation of the OCU was considered to be not only a religious matter but also a matter of national security. In Kyiv, President Poroshenko, who tried to bring competing Orthodox churches in Ukraine to form one united church and who lobbied the Ecumenical Patriarch to recognize the OCU, cast the creation of an independent Orthodox Church in Ukraine as the country's "second independence."[24]

In Russia, the emergence of a Ukrainian Orthodox Church independent from Moscow was seen as a severe blow to the ideology of the Russian World project, supported by the state and propagated by ROC, which aimed to keep Ukraine and Russia together. Until the OCU was formed, the only ecclesiastically legitimate Orthodox Church in Ukraine was the Ukrainian Orthodox Church of the Moscow Patriarchy (UOC-MP), which enjoyed a degree of autonomy but was a part of ROC, with the ecclesiastical subordination of Kyiv to Moscow going back to the late seventeenth century. An independent and canonical Orthodox Church in Ukraine destroyed the narrative of the "tri-unite" Orthodox brotherly peoples (Russians, Ukrainians, Belarussians) together constituting a "holy Rus'." As one scholar put it, ROC was acting as a "watch dog of all-Russian unity" and the formation of the OUC dealt this unity a major blow.[25]

Moscow Patriarch Kirill unsuccessfully lobbied the Ecumenical Patriarch Bartholomew to withhold OCU recognition. According to a leaked transcript, during his meeting with Bartholomew in August 2018, Kirill argued that Russians and Ukrainians were a single people and Ukraine's post-Euromaidan government was illegitimate.[26] The Russian political leadership also saw Ukraine's religious future as a highly consequential matter for Russia. Ukrainian autocephaly topped the agenda of an emergency meeting of the Russian Federal Security Council convened in October 2018, headed by Putin and attended by Prime Minister Dmitrii Medvedev and other top officials.[27] Even the Russian liberal opposition lamented the development. Navalny called Putin an "enemy of the Russian World," blaming him for enabling the religious split and the OCU formation in Ukraine.[28]

The Euromaidan victory facilitated the formation of the OCU as it brought to power political forces seeking to secure Ukraine's independence from Russia in the religious sphere, and also led to changes in popular support for the competing churches. During the protests, UOC-KP and UAOC sided decidedly with the protesters, while UOC-MP tried to position itself as neutral.[29] Once conflict started in Donbas, UOC-KP supported the pro-Kyiv side, while UOC-MP again tried to maintain neutrality, describing the conflict as "war among brothers." Incidents highlighted in the media, such as UOC-MP hierarchs refusing to stand in parliament to pay tribute to Ukrainian soldiers killed in the Donbas, or UOC-MP priests refusing to perform last rites for killed Ukrainian servicemen, increased public perceptions of the UOC-MP as a pro-Russian rather than a Ukrainian church, and led to growing support for the OCU in public opinion.[30] In January 2019, 50% supported the formation of the OUC and the tomos of autocephaly, 20% did not, and another 30% were indifferent or undecided.[31] Ukrainian Orthodox politics remained complex and contentious in the following years, and the UOC-MP retained institutional dominance in terms of the number of parishes but its support in society continued to decline.[32] As with historical memory and language, the February 2022 invasion would mark another major step in the cycle of divergence. By July 2022, just 4% of self-identified Orthodox believers would associate themselves with the UOC-MP.[33]

Language

The status of Ukrainian and Russian in Ukraine was another area where Ukraine's push to strengthen state independence and Russia's determination to bind Ukraine to the Russian World collided. As discussed in Chapter 3, within the logic of the Center-Right "grand bargain" successive Ukrainian governments maintained commitment to the Ukrainian-only state language policy, seeing state language as a marker and a pillar of sovereign statehood. In Russia, the continuation of Russian language use throughout the former Soviet space was seen not as a purely cultural, but also a political matter. The "Russian Language Federal Target Program 2006–2010," later extended to 2015, aimed not only to "address the language and cultural needs of compatriots living abroad" but also to support "the Russian language as the basis for the development of integration process in the Commonwealth of Independent States."[34]

The Ukrainization policies conducted by successive Ukrainian governments were measured and varied; Ukrainization went deeper in elementary and secondary education, with regional variation, and in the written documentation of state institutions, while Russian remained widely used in media and business. The Yanukovych administration ended state backing of Ukrainian with the 2012 adoption of a law giving Russian language official status in areas where ten or more percent of the population were Russian speakers. This change significantly reduced incentives to learn and use Ukrainian in nearly half of Ukraine's regions and led to street protests, which became known as "Language Maidan," that did not succeed in reversing the law.

Just one day after Yanukovych's flight from Kyiv in February 2014, parliament voted to annul his 2012 language law. This move aimed to signal the symbolic significance of the one-state-language policy, rather than to change language practice abruptly and force anyone to speak Ukrainian, but the timing was poorly chosen. With the rapidly unfolding annexation of Crimea, the outbreak of anti-government protests in eastern Ukraine, and Russia in a full-throated denunciation of the "Nazis" coming to power in Kyiv after a "coup," acting president Turchynov vetoed the parliament's decision, hoping to diffuse tensions. The 2012 language law remained on the books until 2019, when a new law on state languages was passed.

In 2017, a new education law modified language policy when it mandated all education in state schools, starting from the secondary level, to be only in Ukrainian, with minority languages taught as a subject but not as the language of primary instruction. The law was criticized by the governments of some neighboring states, such as Romania and Hungary, as well as by minority rights advocates for limiting ethnic minority educational rights. In the context of the Russian aggression, however, many in Ukraine saw language policies as having implications for national security and not strictly for minority rights. Some Ukrainian politicians linked Russia's annexation of Crimea to the linguistic isolation of local Russian-speakers from the rest of Ukraine. Unlike elsewhere in Ukraine where many schools that taught in Russian in the Soviet period were switched to teaching in Ukrainian after 1991, Crimea was essentially untouched by this process. Immediately prior to annexation, 90.7% of school children studied in Russian and 6.5% in Ukrainian, with just 7 out of 542 schools teaching in Ukrainian.[35] To address concerns by non-Russian minority civil society groups and Western states speaking for their minorities in Ukraine, the education law was subsequently amended with regard to the "EU languages" but not Russian.

A new language law adopted in April 2019 was another decisive step for the Ukrainization of Ukraine. The law not only affirmed the status of Ukrainian as the only state language but also, for the first time, detailed measures to ensure the practical realization of constitutional obligations placed on the state to "ensure the comprehensive development and functioning of the Ukrainian language in all spheres of social life throughout the entire territory of Ukraine." Under the new law, businesses were allowed to offer services in Russian, but were now obligated to offer them in Ukrainian as well, and media were mandated to have a Ukrainian-language version of their products and could no longer produce content in Russian only. The law also mandated deeper Ukrainization in book publishing, advertising, and TV and radio broadcasting.

The legal measures to strengthen the status of the Ukrainian language in Ukraine predictably angered Russia, and again reflected the cyclical relationship between Russia's determination to control Ukraine and Ukraine's commitment to stick to those policies its domestic politics produced. Russia's annexation of Crimea and the war in Donbas bolstered arguments that Ukraine needed to strengthen boundaries, including symbolic and cultural ones, to protect its nationhood and statehood. Legal measures to increase the use of Ukrainian did not immediately lead to changes in language practices. Surveys showed that most Russian-speakers were not switching to speaking Ukrainian, but with Ukrainian self-identification continuing to increase in the face of Russian aggression, the majority of the population, including many Russian-speakers, supported the post-Euromaidan Ukrainization policies.[36] According to Rating Group polls, support for Ukrainian as the only state language stood at 66% in November 2019, up from 47%

in April 2014, while support for Russian as a second state language declined from 27% to 19%.[37] The majority of Ukrainians, including many Russian speakers, supported state activism to bolster use of Ukrainian. In a KIIS poll held in May 2017, 61% wanted the state "to foster use of Ukrainian in all spheres of public life" – an 11% increase since 2014.[38] These changes in identity and political attitudes help explain why language legislation did not face public opposition, despite a substantial part of the population continuing to use Russian as the language of convenience.

That President Poroshenko, who actively supported the 2019 language law and campaigned under the slogan "Army, Language, Faith," ultimately lost his re-election bid shows that for the majority of Ukrainians identity issues and language policies did not outweigh concerns over the economy and corruption. At the same time, the post-Euromaidan elections were a stark change from pre-2014 elections, when each presidential race had pitted a "pro-Western" vs. a "pro-Russian" candidate sparring over identity politics. The winner of the 2019 elections was not a pro-Russian candidate promising to undo Poroshenko's "nationalist" policies or to re-orient Ukraine toward Russia. Volodymyr Zelensky, a Russian-speaker from the south, swept the vote with a campaign message about pro-European orientation, anti-corruption, and national unity. Politicians promising to pivot to Russia were in the race but in 2019 they stood no chance, due to changes in popular attitudes and electoral geography. The two pro-Russian candidates combined won less than 16% of the vote and were eliminated in the first round, while in the run-off, Zelensky won with 73.2% against Poroshenko's 24.5%. Zelensky "embraced, embodied, and affirmed" Ukrainianness as, first and foremost, a civic identity – a message which resonated with an ever-greater number of Ukrainian citizens.[39]

Even though some Poroshenko supporters tried to portray Zelensky as a pro-Russian candidate, and there was also some hope in Moscow that Zelensky could play this role, in reality the 2019 elections illustrated that Ukraine was likely lost to Russia for good: for Ukrainian society, as well as for the democratically elected state leadership, any subordination to Russia, including in identity policies, was unacceptable. Zelensky's hope to come to an agreement with Putin over Donbas and Crimea that he expressed during his campaign for president would prove unrealistic. Once in office, Zelensky quickly realized that Putin was not interested in solving the conflict, but instead wanted to use Donbas as a lever for curtailing the ability of the government in Kyiv to pursue independent policies.

Building Ukrainian democracy better

In addition to identity shifts, Ukraine's post-Euromaidan political trajectory was transformed by an active civil society sector that pushed for continued Europeanization and democratization. Almost immediately after Yanukovych's ouster, dozens of NGOs came together to form the Reanimation Package of Reforms coalition to advocate legislative changes that would reset major institutions (the judiciary, higher education, local government, etc.) and create new ones (anti-corruption bodies, public broadcaster, etc.) to strengthen Ukraine's democratic state capacity and curb corruption. The reforms aimed to bring Ukraine into Europe as soon as possible.

Reforming the state, strengthening the rule of law, controlling corruption, and meeting conditionality criteria for EU membership are difficult enough tasks, as any Eastern European state that walked the same path before Ukraine could attest. Russia's invasion and annexation of Crimea and the subsequent armed rebellion in Donbas made Ukraine's transformation orders of magnitude harder. One obvious challenge came from the economic and human costs of the invasion. The industrial base in Donbas was disrupted and Crimea's tourist revenue and transportation hubs were stolen by Russia. Roughly 1.5 million internally displaced Ukrainians from these territories had to establish new lives in other regions of the country.[40] Reforming the Army and mounting an effective defense against Russian aggression took resources away from other sectors.

The post-Maidan administrations, first Poroshenko's and since 2019 Zelensky's, led the country with these dual pressures at work – an active civil society expecting reforms and hostile Russia trying to undermine Ukrainian statehood. The results were, unsurprisingly, mixed, but overall positive. Ukraine's significant progress since 2014 is often overlooked and lost within the narrative of deeply rooted, ubiquitous corruption.

Judicial reform

That sweeping legislative and institutional reforms of the judiciary started almost immediately after Euromaidan should come as no surprise, as fair courts and the rule of law were among the top motivating factors of the Euromaidan mobilization.[41] The Yanukovych regime had leaned heavily on the courts and used them as a tool of repression against Euromaidan activists. After Yanukovych's flight, civil society demanded both disciplinary investigations of judges who had delivered questionable rulings and a fundamental restructuring of the judiciary to prevent any future incumbent from using courts as a political instrument. In early April 2014, the Rada adopted a law on judicial lustration which dismissed the judicial leadership at all levels, tasked judges with electing their own court chairs, and created a special commission to investigate complaints against judges who might have violated defendants' rights during Euromaidan.

More new laws and constitutional amendments aimed at Europeanizing and resetting the judiciary followed. The jurisdiction over civil and criminal cases, which Yanukovych had taken away from the Supreme Court, was reinstated, the judicial appointments procedure was streamlined, and three of the main legal codes were rewritten, with an eye toward Ukraine's legal integration into Europe. Individual citizens gained access to the Constitutional Court through constitutional complaint – a common feature of European constitutional judiciaries. The self-government organs of the judiciary were all relaunched and restructured. Each step of the way, draft bills and constitutional amendments were closely vetted by the Venice Commission of the Council of Europe and brought in line with best practices in judicial setup – self-government and institutional insulation.[42]

A notable institutional innovation in 2016 was the Public Integrity Council (PIC), tasked with helping the judiciary's self-government body vet candidates for the bench. PIC members included civil society activists, which aimed to make the process of selecting new judges transparent and accountable.[43] PIC hit the ground running and sometimes clashed with the presidential administration's judicial reform point people. PIC did not win over public opinion fully, as some media praised its activities and others criticized it for political bias. In part, this dynamic perpetuated the judiciary's image as an arena of political competition, but PIC's feistiness also indicated that the judiciary was now closely monitored and no incumbent could hope to use the courts reliably as an instrument for his or her own political aims. This was the beginning of messy judicial independence.

Amid the extensive institutional restructuring, judges themselves seemed more interested in protecting the status quo than in a rule of law breakthrough. The 2014 judicial lustration law innovation, which gave judges the opportunity to elect their court chairs, resulted in the re-election of 80% of old chairs, who were usually the conduit and enforcers of political oppression.[44] Entrenched judicial elites put up a fight every step of the way in the reform process, which solidified society's impression that these elites were protecting sizeable corruption rents. No pro-reform judicial groups or associations appeared and judges who wanted change left the bench and joined the push from civil society.[45] Judges closed ranks and protected those among their colleagues who were accused of violating defendants' rights during Euromaidan. The disciplinary commission, which was founded right after Euromaidan, received over 350 complaints but sanctioned less than 10% of the judges it investigated.[46] Finally, as new politically sensitive cases appeared, the courts tended to stall, drag, and stick to old-school legal formalist rulings, which left room for speculation about possible corruption, behind-the-scenes influence, and political deals. The District Administrative Court in Kyiv, headed by Judge Pavlo Vovk, became particularly notorious as the place where corruption cases were buried and tales of bribery, influence peddling, and collusion abounded.

Poroshenko and other politicians in the reformist coalition also failed to convince society that they were true champions of the rule of law and independent courts, despite the extensive reforms adopted. Each step of the way, civil society had to push hard and monitor carefully to make sure that small, stealthy amendments to new legislation did not hollow out the spirit of the change. Investigative journalists uncovered individual court cases that featured incumbent politicians in familiar roles – attempting to pull strings behind the scenes to obtain a favorable decision. This solidified the impression that political elites had a shallow commitment to the rule of law – they adopted reforms to please the EU and international donors, but perhaps had not fully committed to the spirit of change and intended to circumvent the new rules. The quick stalling of reforms in the Prosecutor General's Office after the ousting of two early reformers (2014–2015) and then a revolving door of appointments by Poroshenko was a major irritant to the anti-corruption and judicial monitoring civil society organizations, who interpreted it as a subterfuge attempt to prevent a full reset of the law enforcement system.[47] If the prosecution remains unreformed, even the best courts cannot deliver justice.

Despite widespread skepticism, progress in judicial performance did take place, albeit slowly and unevenly. Studies showed that Ukrainians who had first-hand experience with the courts assessed the performance of the courts as more satisfactory than public discourse would suggest. The majority of citizens who went to court were satisfied that judges were professional and litigants accepted court decisions as lawful, and reported that no corruption situations occurred. These results contrasted with polls recording only one in ten Ukrainians expressing trust in the courts.[48] Expert indices also record gains in all elements of the rule of law – judicial independence, control of judicial corruption, and access to justice. And politicians and other powerful actors increasingly found themselves losing important cases in court.

The investigation into the 2018 murder of Kherson anti-corruption activist Kateryna Handziuk illustrates both the progress and the shortcomings of judicial reform. A Euromaidan participant, an anti-corruption activist, and a lawyer, Handziuk worked to expose corruption in law enforcement and the regional administration and, in 2018, focused on illegal logging. In July 2018, she was doused with acid and then fought for her life in the hospital for three months before succumbing to her injuries. Media and civil society closely monitored the murder investigation and each Prosecutor General faced extensive scrutiny over it, which underscores the salience of the rule of law-anti-corruption nexus in Ukraine. Civil society pressure pushed the judiciary to deliver some justice – five men were convicted and sent to prison for carrying out the attack, one of the organizers was extradited from abroad to face charges, and a former head of Kherson regional council was arrested on suspicion of ordering the attack.[49] However, anti-corruption activists and Handziuk's family have criticized law enforcement, the prosecution, and the courts for dragging out the investigation and have alleged that two other politically powerful suspects have been protected.[50]

Anti-corruption reform

The centerpiece of post-Maidan reforms was the fight against endemic corruption. As in judicial reform, the main drivers were civil society and the EU, through the conditionality approach built into the association agreement. As in judicial reform, sweeping institutional innovations and legislative changes were introduced. And, again as in judicial reform, progress has been slower than society expected, which is a big reason why Poroshenko lost his re-election bid and Zelensky – an actor and creator of a show about a disaffected, sick-of-corruption schoolteacher who accidentally gets elected president – won in a landslide.

The first anti-corruption institution was the National Anti-Corruption Bureau of Ukraine (NABU), set up in March 2015. NABU is an autonomous institution whose chief is selected and appointed by the president but cannot be easily removed by him. It is tasked with investigating high-level political corruption rather than low-level bureaucratic and administrative corruption, but it does not prosecute cases in court. Cases would be argued in court by a new Special Anti-Corruption Prosecution Office (SAPO), created within the General Prosecution in September 2015. Within the executive, a third anti-corruption institution was set up in the summer of 2016, the National Agency on Corruption Prevention (NAZK), whose mandate was to set anti-corruption policy.[51] Petty corruption in the police was tackled through major institutional overhaul.[52] All these institutions were created with active input from the Reanimation Package of Reforms NGO alliance, the Anti-Corruption Action Centre, and EU experts, and followed institutional best practices.

A High Anti-Corruption Court and an Anti-Corruption chamber in the Supreme Court were also created to rule on the cases built by NABU and SAPO. The court started working in 2019, after years of debate over the exact procedure for appointing the 35 justices who would be hearing the most important political corruption cases in the country. Civil society and the international community wanted to ensure an appointments process to the High Court and the Appeals chamber that was transparent and accountable and pushed to have international experts with autonomy and veto power involved in the appointment procedure. Political incumbents balked at the format. Losing dominance over judicial appointments – incidentally, a power that most democratic executives around the world possess – was a difficult pill to swallow for the incumbents; so both Poroshenko and Zelensky stalled, and eventually Zelensky grudgingly acquiesced.

The anti-corruption reforms achieved some tangible results. In 2015, Ukraine introduced an e-procurement platform called ProZorro, which not only digitized the entire procurement process, but also made it transparent to both participants and the public. The new platform made procurement more efficient and more cost-effective – bids became more competitive, which led to savings, and the time for procuring goods and services was reduced.[53] On the political side, a success story in public procurement, which is often plagued by waste and corruption allegations even in developed democracies, was an encouraging step forward for Ukraine, for local civil society, for international investors, and for the EU and other international partners.

The other success story was NAZK, which in 2016 launched an asset declaration system for state officials, audited the submitted declarations for accuracy, and achieved solid compliance. This innovation increased transparency by forcing no less than one million politicians and state officials to report income, savings, shares, real estate, even art and hard cash in deposit boxes, in a signed declaration.[54] Such a high level of transparency is unusual, even for consolidated democracies in the West. NAZK worked in close cooperation with other anti-corruption institutions (NABU and SAPO) and referred those officials who failed the audits for further, sometimes criminal, investigation. Another newly created institution, an agency that traced and recovered assets derived from corruption and other crimes, also became functional and recovered tens of millions in corruption proceeds for the state coffers.

One could say NAZK's asset declaration system became too successful for its own good and triggered backlash from political actors interested in protecting the old system of kickbacks and corruption rents. In October 2020, the Constitutional Court canceled NAZK's declarations system, as well as the Criminal Code articles on penalties for officials who knowingly provided false information in their asset declarations, or failed to submit such declarations. Citing privacy rights and overreach, the decision in effect suspended the country's best-functioning anti-corruption mechanism. Even more worrisome was that the judge rapporteur on the decision had recently been investigated by NAZK for providing an incomplete declaration, which suggested he had a conflict of interest.[55]

A constitutional crisis ensued. In jeopardy were not only a major element of Ukraine's anti-corruption efforts, but also the achievements of post-Maidan judicial reforms. In response to the Constitutional Court ruling, Zelensky called the justices "devils from political hell," who came to destroy everything that the Orange Revolution and the Revolution of Dignity had fought for – control of corruption and accountability for individual politicians.[56] While he did not spell it out, Zelensky's implication that Russia's shady influence was behind the disruption of Ukraine's anti-corruption process was shared by many Ukrainians, including leading anti-corruption activists.[57] With the benefit of hindsight, this guess seems more plausible and less conspiratorial. The petition which had triggered the Constitutional Court decision was filed by Viktor Medvedchuk, Ukraine's most pro-Russian oligarch and Putin's close friend.

Zelensky tried to end the constitutional crisis by submitting a bill to parliament seeking to terminate the justices, this way himself awakening a devil from political hell that Ukrainians aimed to defeat, namely executive control of the judiciary. Civil society activists and the Venice Commission agreed that both the Constitutional Court and the president were in the wrong – the court for delivering a poorly motivated decision under a conflict-of-interest cloud and the President for trying to resolve the issue through a poorly argued attempt to circumvent judicial independence and punish the justices.[58] The proposed solution was for the Rada to amend anti-corruption legislation in such a way as to address the concerns raised by the Constitutional Court while restoring the anti-corruption mechanism.[59] Neither the president, nor his parliamentary majority took the compromise route, and the Constitutional Court justices did not go quietly but appealed their dismissals. The Constitutional Court chairman, Justice Tupytsky, was then investigated on corruption charges by the prosecution and indicted in May 2021. Meanwhile, he attempted to continue going to work at the Constitutional Court, but security guards stopped him from entering the building.[60] The crisis dragged on and remained unsolved, even after the full-scale invasion. After February 2022, Tupytsky left Ukraine illegally. In May 2022, the head of the Ukrainian National Security and Defense Council, Oleksiy Danilov, alleged that Ukrainian intelligence services had uncovered evidence of a plan for Justice Tupytsky to use the courts to legitimize the reinstatement of Yanukovych to the presidency in a Russia-occupied Ukraine.[61] Zelensky's "devils from political hell" remark sounds even more credible in hindsight.

This episode is another glass-half-full/half-empty situation. The half-empty interpretation underscores that Ukraine needs more work to meet EU's rule of law requirements. The half-full interpretation confirms that Ukraine's judiciary has *de facto* independence from politicians. A popular president with a parliamentary majority could not punish Constitutional Court justices who openly challenged him. In July 2021, the Supreme Court struck down Zelensky's decree which ordered the dismissal of the Constitutional Court justices, i.e. the justices' colleagues protected them.[62]

With anti-corruption institutions fully in place with the inauguration of the High Anti-Corruption Court, by 2020 the wheels of anti-corruption were in motion. In 2021–2022, the High Anti-Corruption Court started delivering verdicts, sending corrupt officials to prison with effective and lengthy sentences, and recovering millions for the state. While a breakthrough in Ukraine's Transparency International ranking or another corruption index has not happened, if positive results keep accruing, the perceptions indices will catch up.

Decentralization reform

In the Ukrainian context, decentralization is not to be confused with federalization. While both could be used interchangeably to describe the devolution of power from the center to subnational/local governments, in post-Maidan Ukraine, federalization refers to Russia's push for Ukraine to transform from a unitary state to a federation, into a polity where Russian proxies in Donbas would wield veto power at the national level. Decentralization denotes the democracy and state-capacity-enhancing reforms that Ukraine's post-Maidan government embarked on in 2014, aimed at empowering local governments and making them accountable to their constituents without hollowing out the powers of central government. Decentralization had long been discussed in Ukraine to accommodate regional diversity. After the instability of 2014, the government adopted decentralization reform quickly to counteract Russia's push for federalization.

The multi-step decentralization reform started in the summer of 2014 and continued over the next eight years. The first step was to merge smaller municipalities into "amalgamated territorial communities," which then had a bigger tax base. Second, the new communities got to keep a considerable portion of tax revenue, received more resources, and got the power to decide how to disburse them.[63] One danger was that the fiscal devolution would lead to local elite capture and the flourishing and entrenchment of local clientelist networks, thus becoming counterproductive to the anti-corruption drive. A related danger was that if some of these local strongmen and women were pro-Russian, they would have greater resources and less central oversight to launch a separatist challenge. For example, one of Ukraine's most pro-Russian oligarchs, Viktor Medvedchuk, was investigated in 2017 precisely for using local authorities in Khmelnytskyi region to attempt to create a secessionist movement.[64]

The consequences of decentralization have, on balance, been positive. The new local governments developed increased governance capacity and became more accountable. Research on local democracy reports that citizens believed that local authorities started listening to them more, informed them better about government services and about how citizens' taxes were spent, and distributed resources more efficiently. Gradually, trust in local authorities started increasing.[65] The emergence of more agile, competent, and trusted local governments through decentralization has been one of the factors that facilitated Ukraine's unexpectedly effective resistance and resilience to Russia's full-scale invasion in February 2022.

Ukrainian democracy and Russian aggression

As if reversing autocratization and reining in a powerful oligarchic class was not difficult enough, Ukrainian democracy faced an additional challenge that no post-WWII democracy has had to deal with. A much more powerful neighbor had not only invaded and occupied parts of the country, but also aimed to cause central state collapse through economic pressure, an information war waged by both foreign sources and domestic provocateurs, and through collaborators and sympathizers within state institutions. How should a liberal democracy protect freedom of the press from a foreign dictatorship that pours a firehose of disinformation on democratic society through long-entrenched and widely watched media outlets? How should a liberal democracy protect political competition and safeguard political rights from a foreign power that has infiltrated its security services, political parties, and business elites?

Liberal democracies have long grappled with balancing national security and civil and political rights, namely, how to make sure national security is not compromised by dissent, but democracy can continue to thrive on pluralism and political competition. The US has maintained a robust debate on this topic. But it bears emphasizing that Ukraine's predicament is far more serious than the US's has ever been, whether it was at the height of the Cold War, during the protracted Vietnam war, or during the "war on terror." The US was always more powerful than its enemies, whereas Ukraine was attacked by a country with purported superpower status. The US also never experienced the level of malicious penetration by its enemies that Ukraine has faced. Imagine how US democracy would have been affected if every third American watched Al-Qaeda TV stations, or if the American government suddenly realized that Al-Qaeda sympathizers and sleeper cell agents were copious among Wall Street elites, in Congress, and in Hollywood, let alone the CIA and the FBI – from rank and file to top leadership.

Post-2014, both Poroshenko's and Zelensky's administrations dealt with the challenge of not only preserving but entrenching the political and civil rights of all Ukrainians, while countering Russia's hybrid aggression. An immediate task was to reduce Ukrainians' exposure to Russian propaganda while preserving freedom of speech. When Russia attacked Ukraine in the spring of 2014, nearly a third of Ukrainians reported that they regularly watched Russian TV stations. Moreover, several major Russian newspapers had subsidiaries in the Ukrainian media market, bearing the same name and tied editorially to Moscow.[66] After Maidan's victory, Russian media's pervasive framing of the Kyiv government as a Nazi junta was reaching significant numbers of Ukrainians.

In the summer of 2014, the Ukrainian government banned Russian state media[67] and over the next few years took other steps to prevent Russian propaganda from reaching Ukrainian audiences, banning certain Russian films, books, and social media platforms, and visits by Russian cultural figures and politicians who had vocally supported the annexation of Crimea. Each of these steps was hotly debated both in Ukraine, with civil society actors split on endorsing or opposing the measures, and among Ukraine's partners in Europe and North America. Russia presented Ukraine's measures as the "Nazi junta in Kyiv" encroaching on the civil and political rights of Russian speakers; but Russia, in fact, first took Ukrainian media off the air in places it controlled. One of the first steps Russia took, in both Crimea and Donbas in spring 2014, was to take over TV stations and take Ukrainian TV channels off the air. It did the same in 2022 in other occupied Ukrainian territories.[68]

Studies have shown that Russian propaganda did represent a threat and that the Ukrainian government's multipronged strategy to counter it was effective. Ukrainians who watched Russian TV were substantially more likely to believe disinformation,[69] and closing down Russian state media and social media made a difference. After the 2017 Russian social media ban, users left Russia's VKontakte (Russia's equivalent of Facebook), even though circumventing the ban was technically simple. More importantly, the most pro-Russian users were just as likely as the average user to abandon VKontakte, which means that the ban worked to reduce both exposure to and further spread of disinformation.[70] The counter-disinformation strategy also included civil society development. Ukrainian civil society founded debunking/fact-checking organizations (e.g. StopFake, Texty), which helped to foster critical thinking and train Ukrainians to recognize disinformation.[71] Ukraine can now advise other democracies on how to devise a national strategy for countering disinformation through civil society, educational campaigns, and institutional reforms.[72]

Another challenge to Ukrainian democracy came from the nationalist far right, which was predictably motivated to counter Russian aggression. In the spring and summer of 2014, several volunteer battalions formed in eastern Ukraine to fight against the Russian forces and their Donbas proxies. The best known were Azov, Donbas, Dnipro, and Aidar. On the one hand, given the unpreparedness of the Ukrainian army in the early days of Russia's aggression, these volunteer battalions were essential for stopping the advance of Russian and Russian-backed forces to capture more Ukrainian territory. On the other hand, some of the organizers and many of the volunteers had far-right, neo-Nazi roots and sympathies. The battalions would pose a danger to the Ukrainian state if they grew in power and were outside its control. Additionally, their contribution to the defense of Ukraine's territorial integrity created the potential to spread their noxious ideology in society. The Poroshenko administration acted to counter these threats. Over the next few years, the battalions were incorporated into the Ukrainian military, pulled away from the front, retrained, and deradicalized. The Azov regiment in the Army became politically and ethnically diverse.[73]

Outside the Army, far-right and neo-Nazi groups formed a political wing and attempted to enter parliament and thus steer policy toward radical nationalism, but their attempt failed, as the movement repeatedly failed to gain parliamentary representation at both the national and the local level. In the 2020 local elections, out of 43,122 seats contested in local councils, the National Corps – the party established by Azov leaders – secured only eighteen.[74] As in other European states, the most radical activists have harassed and perpetrated heinous attacks against minorities and political opponents. Russia's ongoing military aggression made radicals more likely to act on their beliefs, and made it challenging for the state to respond decisively. The year 2014–2015 was particularly fraught, and marked by two high-profile murders of journalists who had long advocated the pro-Russian, re-imperialization narrative and, in 2014, had praised Russia's intervention in Ukraine. Law enforcement and the courts have investigated and prosecuted suspects, although as in other politically salient cases there is disagreement over how effective and impartial the courts have been. While the far right put strain on Ukrainian democracy, on balance the state gradually succeeded in cordoning it off as a marginal political group. If judicial and law enforcement reforms deepen and continue progressing, the state will also become more effective at punishing the perpetrators of far-right violence.

Balancing civil rights and national security was also complicated by Ukrainian governments' track record of politicized justice. Both Ukrainian society and outside observers had a hard time telling when a legal step framed as necessary to counter Russia's threat to Ukraine was genuine and when it was weaponization of law against political opponents. For example, in November 2018, Poroshenko declared martial law after Russia seized three Ukrainian ships in the Azov Sea and captured their sailors. Given the incident and reports of significant military buildup by Russia (up to 80,000 troops), the president expressed concern that Russia might be planning a ground offensive and wanted to start preparing the country for it.[75] The timing, however, appeared suspicious. Ukraine was about to enter a presidential campaign and Poroshenko's popularity was sagging. A *Foreign Policy* article summarized the concern straightforwardly: "Martial Law is a Test. Will Ukraine's Democracy Pass?"[76] Ukraine's parliament resisted Poroshenko's plans and he settled for limited measures only in the border regions with Russia. Over the next month, public debate gravitated toward discounting an imminent Russian invasion and the Rada voted to set the date for the elections. Poroshenko did not try to extend martial law. Ukrainian democracy passed the test – the president followed the public mood, perhaps against his political interests, and the electoral campaign started on time, without any limitations on freedom of speech or assembly.[77] As some analysts warned, Russia probably watched Ukraine's reaction to this provocation closely and the lesson it drew from the weak and tentative response by Ukraine and its Western allies was that it could keep pushing.[78] We now know this pushing eventually led to the full-scale invasion of 2022.

Another example of where things look different in hindsight is Zelensky's steps to weaken Viktor Medvedchuk. Viktor Medvedchuk is Putin's close friend and a long-standing conduit of Kremlin narratives and interests in Ukraine. In February 2021, Zelensky announced that three TV stations owned by Medvedchuk would be shut down. Zelensky reassured the Ukrainian public, media community, and Ukraine's partners that this was an isolated move against a source of Russia's "information aggression," rather than part of a broader attack against media freedom or an attempt to sideline a political opponent, which Medvedchuk styled himself to be. The reaction was mixed. The US was more supportive than the EU, and Ukrainian civil society was split.[79] Those who were concerned about Zelensky's national security credentials generally approved the move.[80] Some who were concerned about his strained relationship with the media worried about a dangerous trend. Ukraine's media freedom ratings took a hit.

Attacks on other media outlets did not follow, but Medvedchuk was soon in deeper trouble. In May 2021, the leader of the "Opposition Platform for Life" party was indicted for treason on charges that he collaborated with Russia on a plan to extract oil and gas in the Black Sea and passed on information about a secret Ukrainian Armed Forces unit to Russia.[81] Some interpreted the prosecution of an ostensible leader of the opposition as continuation of Ukraine's record of politicized prosecutions and a problem for democratic consolidation.

However, by 2021, Ukraine's electoral map indicated that Medvedchuk's pro-Russian platform could never be a winning ticket or have a realistic chance of forming a governing coalition. Of the parties that polled as top ten in October 2020, there were only two pro-Russian parties – Medverchuk's and one other – which together polled at under 20%.[82] All other front runners were pro-European, and a pro-European rather than a pro-Russian governing coalition was assured. Medvedchuk was not a viable political competitor to Zelensky and his party and the political dividend to Zelensky from sidelining Medvedchuk was not electorally meaningful. It is more likely that the indictment was motivated by fears and evidence that the oligarch was undermining Ukrainian national security through his close links to the Kremlin, and developments after the full-scale invasion lend additional credence to this argument. After Russia's invasion, Medvedchuk fled house arrest and hid from Ukrainian authorities, until he was captured trying to flee the country in the spring of 2022. He was then part of a prisoner swap between Russia and Ukraine – Ukraine released him from custody and Russia took him to Moscow, while dozens of Azovstal defenders returned to Ukraine. The swap underscores that his loyalty had been to Russia, rather than to Ukraine. Finally, revelations in 2023 suggest the 2022 "special military operation" plan might have envisioned installing Medvedchuk as Russia's puppet president of Ukraine, which Medvedchuk had assured Putin would be smooth and easy because Ukrainians would greet the Russian army as liberators.[83] Had Russia's invasion succeeded, Medvedchuk would have been Ukraine's Quisling, a traitor and a collaborator.

The more problematic treason indictment was that of Poroshenko, which was heard by a Kyiv court barely a month before the beginning of the full-scale invasion. Zelensky was criticized by Western partners for this move and with good reason. Poroshenko, an MP and the leader of the European Solidarity opposition party, which unlike Medvedchuk's was a viable opponent to Zelensky's party, was accused of facilitating coal sales which helped finance Russia's proxies in Donbas. While the criminal code provision used was treason, Zelensky's comments on the Poroshenko investigation emphasized the rule of law and anti-corruption, rather than national security.[84] While Medvedchuk's indictment appeared long overdue, Poroshenko's indictment appeared problematic for the democratic credentials of the Zelensky administration. But, on the bright side, Poroshenko's decision to return to Ukraine from abroad and fight the charges in court suggests that judicial independence improved from 2011, when Tymoshenko's conviction was a foregone conclusion, to 2022, when Poroshenko had faith that the rule of law would work and he would prove his innocence in court. In January 2022, the court released Poroshenko without bail. Since the beginning of the full-scale invasion, the case against Poroshenko has stalled and he has taken an active part in Ukraine's efforts to solicit military aid and humanitarian support from Western partners.

Moving toward Europe

In the post-2014 period, Ukraine's democratization reforms described above were tightly linked to its European path. Euromaidan had been galvanized to stop Yanukovych from re-orienting Ukraine toward Russia so, after Euromaidan's victory, the new Ukrainian government set out to make Europeanization a reality. On March 21, 2014, the post-Maidan Ukrainian government signed the political provisions of the DCFTA association agreement with the EU, which Yanukovych had refused to sign back in November 2013. On June 27, 2014, newly elected President Poroshenko completed the process in Brussels, to much fanfare, by signing the economic provisions and, on September 16, both the European Parliament and the Ukrainian Rada ratified it. Even though the DCFTA was primarily a trade agreement and did not provide an implied promise of accession, it represented a significant step toward Ukraine's European integration.

The agreement did not just remove tariffs and quotas but sought to facilitate the Ukrainian state's convergence with the EU by influencing its institutional landscape and regulatory environment.[85] As Poroshenko put it, the association agreement was "a *de facto* reform program for Ukraine."[86] It established a free-trade area, which meant that Ukrainian businesses would start adapting to the competitive pressure of belonging to the EU's internal market even before membership. It committed Ukraine to the implementation of comprehensive reforms of its state institutions, especially in rule of law and anti-corruption, which amounted to preparation to come into compliance with EU conditionality for membership. The agreement relied on a conditionality approach,[87] which meant that Ukraine's performance, and hence progress, on the implementation of the agreement depended on its compliance with the fundamental democratic principles and values that the EU aims to maintain among all its members. It put Ukraine on a course toward legal approximation to the EU through the gradual "export of the *acquis*" – the huge body of legislation, regulations, and standards used by all EU members. It institutionalized regular summit meetings for Ukrainian ministers, EU officials, and experts to monitor Ukraine's progress. The institutional structure in place – an Association Council, a Parliamentary Association Committee, and a Civil Society Platform – was the most extensive the EU had with any other state with membership aspirations. It intensified the linkage between Ukraine and Europe and created opportunities for Ukrainian state officials and civil society activists to learn, adopt, and start implementing or advocating European governance methods and principles.[88]

Despite Russia's ongoing military aggression against Ukraine and the sanctions triggered by this international law violation, the EU pressured Ukraine to negotiate a compromise to placate Russian complaints that the association agreement would hurt the Russian economy. Russia argued that the agreement would lead indirectly to cheap European goods flooding the Russian market through Ukrainian re-exports. Despite significant domestic outcry, Poroshenko agreed to the EU's proposal to "calm down the pressure" by delaying the lowering of Ukrainian tariffs on EU goods until the end of 2015.[89]

While immediately renewing Ukraine's course on EU integration, the interim post-Yanukovych government initially refrained from re-affirming Ukraine's commitment to joining NATO. In a March 18 speech, Prime Minister Yatsenyuk tried to reassure both Russia and Ukrainians in the southeast that Ukraine's NATO bid was "not on the agenda."[90] This caution, as we know, did not prevent Russia's spring military aggression against Ukraine, both in Crimea and in Donbas. By the fall, after Russia annexed Crimea and its military openly interfered in the conflict in Donbas to beat back Ukrainian forces, Yatsenyuk's government introduced a bill to cancel Ukraine's "non-bloc" status and to pursue NATO membership again, and in December 2014, 303 out of 450 Rada members voted for the bill.[91] Over the next years, public support for EU and NATO membership grew significantly, reaching 56 and 45% respectively by early 2019, according to Rating Group polls. Shortly after Russia's military buildup in the fall of 2018, which prompted Poroshenko's partial martial law measures, the Ukrainian parliament amended the constitution to enshrine securing EU and NATO membership as the country's goals.[92] This timeline illustrates the escalatory cycle at work – Ukraine was initially mindful of Russia's preferences and tried to forge a compromise but, as Russia stepped up its aggression, Ukraine's commitment to resisting hardened. Rather than submitting to Russia's bid for control, Ukraine's government increasingly looked to the West for security protection.

While NATO emphasized its open-door policy, it was in no rush to admit Ukraine. Compounding long-standing German and French opposition to the idea, the fighting in Donbas ran foul of NATO's policy of not considering candidates with active irredentist disputes. Over the next eight years, the only formal step taken by NATO and Ukraine was the introduction of a Comprehensive Assistance Package (CAP) at the 2016 NATO Summit in Warsaw.[93]

NATO stepped up its cooperation with Ukraine, but the focus was on helping Ukraine reform its armed forces so it could mount an effective defense against Russian aggression on its own, rather than on aligning or preparing Ukraine for NATO membership. NATO members instituted training missions and capacity-building programs, incentivized Ukraine to establish civilian control of the military and increase accountability and transparency in the defense sector, and provided more non-lethal military aid than before. The arms transfers were modest and did not shift the balance of power between Russia and Ukraine on the battlefield. The allies were motivated by both economic and risk considerations, i.e. most NATO members were not eager to commit significant resources to Ukraine's defense and all were cognizant and concerned about the risks of provoking greater confrontation with Russia.[94] Thus, claims by Russia, echoed by some Western analysts, that in the post-Maidan period Ukraine became a "NATO member in all but name,"[95] are hyperbole, at best.

Russia comes to see Ukraine as the "anti-Russia"

Imperialization of identity in Russia

As we discussed in Chapter 1, establishing a non-imperial identity that would leave Ukraine and Ukrainians outside the geopolitical and national imaginary of a "true" Russian nation proved incredibly difficult in post-Soviet Russia. Already in the 1990s under Yeltsin and increasingly in the 2000s during Putin's first two terms, identity policies such as compatriots legislation and the Russian World project blurred the boundaries between Ukraine and Russia and conceptualized Ukraine as a constituent part of a pan-Russian nation, defined not in political or strictly ethnic but in civilizational-cum-imperial and cultural terms. Putin's return to the presidency in 2012 for a third term signaled a turning point in identity politics when state-supported identity narrative and policies became more imperial.[96] Euromaidan's victory and the fear of "losing" Ukraine further fostered these trends.

Putin defined Crimea and southeastern Ukraine as "historic Russian lands" when justifying Russia's claims to these territories, but annexation of Crimea and removal of eastern Donbas from Ukraine's control were not the end of Russia's designs on Ukraine.

After 2014, citizenship policy emerged as a key area where the Russian imperial vision with regard to Ukraine was being actively legislated. After failing through the 1990s to compel Ukraine and other post-Soviet states to agree to either dual citizenship with Russia or to a common CIS citizenship, Russia began to act unilaterally. Passportization (systematic distribution of Russian passports) to residents in the former Soviet states began well before Euromaidan. In Crimea, Russian consular authorities have been handing out passports to Ukrainian citizen residents since the 1990s. This practice met with mixed response from Crimean residents themselves,[97] while successive Ukrainian governments periodically complained to Russia over the practice.[98]

After the Euromaidan victory, Russia stepped up the use of passportization as a tool of political pressure and passed a series of laws aimed first and foremost at Ukraine. In April 2014, the Russian citizenship law was amended to give "Russian-speakers" – a new category – simplified access to Russian citizenship. Russian speakers were defined to include those whose direct ancestors permanently lived on the territories of the Russian empire or USSR, and who regularly used Russian at home and in social, cultural, and other spheres. A special commission was set up for determining one's status as a native Russian speaker, and those who met the criteria could acquire Russian citizenship without meeting standard naturalization requirements such as permanent residency permit, income, and others, although they had formally to renounce their foreign citizenship.

Making Russian-speakers eligible for Russian citizenship was a multi-purpose tool. Citizenship for Russian-speakers could be used as a tool to address the Russian demographic problem by encouraging migration of "Russian-speakers" to Russia. Russian-speakers from Ukraine were an ideal demographic material and were seen, in the words of the head of the Russian Federal Migration Service, as a "good demographic support for our country."[99] But designating a greater number of Ukrainian citizens as Russian citizens could also be used as a tool to legitimize claims over more of Ukraine's territory, as well as intervening to protect them from "discrimination" and "genocide" – charges regularly levied against Ukraine by Putin and other senior Russian officials after 2014. In November 2009, Russian law "On Defense of the Russian foundation" was amended to allow the president to deploy troops abroad to protect Russian citizens from "an armed attack"; so the greater the number of Russian citizens in Ukraine the easier to justify actions to "protect" them.

In 2019, just as Zelensky got elected, Russia stepped up the use of citizenship as a tool of imperialization and instrument of pressure on the Ukrainian government. On April 24, 2019, just three days after Zelensky won the run-off and became Ukraine's president-elect, Putin issued a decree allowing residents of the two separatist breakaway regions in Ukraine's Donbas, the so-called DNR and LNR, to obtain Russian citizenship under simplified rules. In July, by another presidential decree, Putin extended the regulation to the entire Donbas region – including those territories of Donetsk and Luhansk regions under control of the government in Kyiv. Residents of Donbas didn't need either to move to Russia or to forfeit their Ukrainian citizenship. While Russia presented these measures as a humanitarian gesture, Ukraine, unsurprisingly, saw it as a violation of state sovereignty. Ukraine's foreign minister called the these measures a "further step in the occupation" of Ukraine, and the EU concluded that passportization was "contrary to the spirit and the objectives" of the Minsk peace agreements meant to solve the conflict in Donbas.[100]

The timing of the April decree was clearly designed to put pressure on president-elect Zelensky, who, during the campaign, had signaled his willingness to come to an agreement with Putin to end the war in Donbas. By making hundreds of thousands of Donbas residents Russian citizens, Putin was signaling his determination to retain permanent influence on Ukraine via the Donbas. Since Ukraine had no means of either making Russia stop the practice or even determining who and how many of its citizens were issued Russian citizenship, Putin was presenting Zelensky with this violation of Ukrainian sovereignty as a *fait accompli*.

None of Russia's pressures made Ukraine more cooperative, however. During Zelensky's tenure Ukraine's position on how the Donbas conflict could be resolved and how the Minsk peace agreements could be implemented remained at odds with the Russian position. Unable to coerce Ukraine on Donbas, Russia continued to use citizenship policies as a tool to lay symbolic claims on Ukraine. In April 2020, a package of amendments to the Russian citizenship law simplified the application criteria for Russian citizenship for citizens of Ukraine, Belarus, Kazakhstan, and Moldova, as well as those legally recognized as Russian-speakers. Russian citizenship could now be obtained without getting official release from, or even simply renouncing, the citizenship of one's home state.[101] According to Russian official statistics, in 2020 Ukrainians made up the largest group of new citizens – some 410,000, or 63% of the total,[102] and from 2018 to 2019 the proportion of Ukrainians among the newly naturalized doubled from 30 to 60%.[103]

Like earlier measures, the 2020 citizenship measures had more than one objective. Domestic labor market needs and demographic concerns factored in Russia's calculation, and the amendments also paved the way for these newly minted Russian citizens in the DNR and LNR to provide additional votes in the July 2020 constitutional referendum and September 2021 State Duma elections. From the perspective of LNR and DNR residents, Russian citizenship was more appealing than citizenship of the unrecognized "people's republics," and many accepted Russian citizenship as a result of practical calculations as well as pro-Russian attitudes.[104] But the geopolitical implications of these legal changes stood front and center, illustrating Russia's growing imperialization with regard to Ukraine, whose citizens it was now claiming, in larger and larger numbers, as potential if not yet actual members of the "true" Russian nation. After launching the full-scale invasion, Putin signed additional decrees, first imposing Russian citizenship on residents of occupied Zaporizhzhia and Kherson oblasts and, in July 2022, expanding eligibility for fast-track Russian citizenship to all Ukrainians.[105] With such rules on the books, if the invasion succeeds, the Ukrainian nation would cease to exist in a political-legal sense, since all Ukrainian citizens would be rebranded as citizens of Russia. The Ukrainian government dismissed Russia's decrees as legally worthless and as further encroachment on Ukraine's sovereignty and territorial integrity,[106] while in the occupied territories widespread resistance to Russian passportization continues, despite repressive measures against those refusing to accept Russian passports.[107]

Krym Nash and Russian autocratization

What is commonly termed the post-Maidan period in Ukraine, in Russia could be called the Krym Nash period. Krym Nash means "Crimea is Ours" in Russian, which connotes both a claim that Crimea has always belonged to Russia and an expression of enthusiasm that Russia has managed to retake it. In the immediate aftermath of the annexation, the opposition organized a few well-attended anti-war rallies, but they did not spread beyond the big cities and fizzled out quickly. Ultimately Crimea's annexation proved popular with Russian society, perhaps even beyond Putin's own expectations. Putin's approval rating surged from around 60% to over 80% and remained there for years.[108] While rally-around-the-flag effects are common in democracies as well, Russia's rally lasted longer and scholars have argued it cannot be explained by a temporary burst of patriotism. The Russian rally was driven by a TV and social media frenzy that signaled to Russians that rejoicing at the land grab was a socially desirable position. In other words, a significant proportion of the boost may have been insincere, but driven by pressure to conform, which is particularly acute in autocracies.[109] This is an important nuance, but a moot point for the purposes of understanding the effects on Russia's re-imperialization ambition *vis-à-vis* Ukraine. Regardless of whether Russian imperialism was genuinely embraced by an overwhelming majority of the Russian public or performatively expressed because social conformism required it, the outcome was the whipping up of imperialist jubilation, rather than shock and reckoning over Russia's territorial aggression against Ukraine. This also meant that contrary to Putin's assurances in 2014 that Crimea's annexation was a one-off,[110] the public mood was permissive for broader aggression against Ukraine.

For all the talk in Russia about how the "Nazi junta in Kyiv" was allegedly suppressing the political and civil rights of its domestic critics, it was Putin's regime that took drastic steps after 2014 to further reduce media freedom, freedom of expression, and freedom of assembly at home. Censorship in the controlled media and repression of independent media intensified. New legislation against extremism was used to harass independent outlets. The opposition-leaning TV Rain was dropped by 90% of cable providers after the government media regulator launched an investigation into violations of laws about historical memory.[111] The founder and ex-CEO of the biggest social media website (VKontakte) fled the country after pressure on the company to turn over to the Russian government data on the Maidan activists in Ukraine who used the website.[112] The director of Russia's one and only state-run Ukrainian literature library was arrested and eventually criminally convicted for "inciting ethnic hatred," while the fifty-two-thousand-volume library was essentially destroyed.[113] A new law on protest introduced steeper fines and longer prison terms for repeat violators who held illegal meetings, rallies, and pickets. Another amendment increased prison terms to five years for public calls to violate the territorial integrity of the Russian Federation, which subsumed any criticism of Crimea's annexation. The spokesman of Russia's Investigative Committee (a law enforcement organ) explicitly linked the toughening of the laws to an effort to prevent an anti-government protest like Euromaidan in Russia.[114] Navalny spent much of the period under house arrest and facing several politicized criminal cases. In 2020, he was poisoned and, after returning to Russia from treatment in Germany, he was directly hauled off to prison to serve a lengthy sentence. His grassroots organizers around the country also faced sustained repression. In other words, while Euromaidan put Ukraine back on a democratization path, it cemented the Putin regime's commitment to autocracy.

Putinism consolidated as a highly personalist regime, characterized by an emerging ideology, which melded imperialism, great power restoration ambitions, anti-Westernism, and anti-liberalism. In addition, Putinism emphasized emotions such as fear, sensitivity to humiliation, and revenge against traitors and elevated traits such as loyalty, hypermasculinity, and preference for order into values.[115] With economic goals of development and modernization taking a back seat, late Putinism increasingly appealed to Russian society with a symbolic and morality-centered message. The Russian public was being told that post-Soviet Russia had been a victim of enemies both foreign and domestic, but with Crimea's annexation Putin was restoring Russia, a morally superior civilization, to its rightful great power status – a message that resonated with many Russians.[116] In 2020, Putin pushed through substantial constitutional reform, which first and foremost concentrated power in the President and gave him a formal way to stay in office until 2036.[117] The reform also managed to subordinate the judiciary even further, strengthen the power vertical even more, and constitutionally downgrade Russians' civil and political rights, which the regime had not respected in practice for years.[118] Additionally, it enshrined the patriotic legitimation of the regime in the constitution,[119] and exacerbated Russia's already bad governance.[120]

The collision course

With his regime largely secure, the opposition imprisoned or exiled, Russian society docile, and the imperialization of identity further consolidated, Putin set out to bring Ukraine back into the Russian World, which would mitigate the Soviet collapse – in his own words, "the biggest geopolitical catastrophe of the twentieth century."[121] However, instead of increasing its reach over Ukraine, in the 2014–2022 period, Russia progressively lost many important levers of influence it had used effectively since 1991. Ukraine was slipping away from the

Russian World through its re-alignment in identity politics, rule of law reforms, anti-corruption measures, and the curtailment of Russian and pro-Russian media outlets. Russia could no longer count on pro-Russian or Soviet-nostalgia politicians winning significant vote shares, let alone hope that they would come to power in Ukraine through the electoral process. Anti-corruption and rule of law reforms were slowly undermining the power of the oligarchs who had provided Russia with access to both Ukrainian politics and the economy, especially in the energy and industrial sectors. In the fall of 2021, Ukraine's parliament adopted an anti-oligarchization law, which was another sign that the anti-corruption drive would continue. Europeanization reforms re-oriented the Ukrainian economy toward the West and trade with the EU exploded, which made Ukraine less susceptible to Russian economic pressure. Visa-free travel created cultural and business links between Ukraine and the European Union, which further distanced Ukraine from the Russian World. Ukraine also officially removed itself from all CIS structures that it had entered grudgingly or willingly in the earlier periods. On every measure and in every area, Ukraine was slipping away from Russia.

The weakening of the levers of influence seems to have gradually pushed Putin to the realization that if Ukraine was not going to collapse and be up for grabs, Russia would have to achieve its re-imperialization goal either by demanding through aggressive diplomacy that the West deliver Ukraine on a silver platter or by launching a full-scale invasion. Both strategies required a weak, divided, or naive Western alliance which would be willing to yield to Russia's demands.

Russia had good reasons to perceive the West as unwilling to stand firmly with Ukraine. After 2014, the West introduced sanctions against Russia and suspended its G8 membership, but the measures were more expressions of the West's displeasure at Russia's flagrant international law violation than a bona fide attempt to reverse Russia's aggression against Ukraine. The West largely accepted the Crimean annexation as a *fait accompli* and did not forcefully challenge Russia's narrative that the war in Donbas was a purely civil conflict within Ukraine. Neither the EU nor NATO gave Ukraine membership perspectives, which implies that the West continued to see Ukraine either as belonging to Russia's broad sphere of influence or at best as a buffer between the West and Russia. Europe continued its energy relationship with Russia and Germany greenlighted a new pipeline for delivery of Russian gas to Europe. Major European countries like Germany and France still envisioned economic interdependence and Russia's participation in

Europe's security architecture as consistent with Europe's and their national interests. Help to Ukraine was limited to financial assistance and advice on how to reform the military, but no major Western country approved significant lethal military aid to Ukraine. Clearly, the West was still cognizant and respectful of what it perceived as Russia's red lines in Ukraine and there was no major re-evaluation of Russia as an adversary, like the one that took place in Ukraine.

Other geopolitical developments in 2014–2022 likely helped Putin see the West as weak and unwilling to confront Russia. A series of incidents with Russian involvement were not conceived in the West as Russian hybrid warfare against Europe, but as isolated incidents. Arms dealer poisonings and munition depot explosions in NATO members Bulgaria[122] and Czechia[123] in 2014, 2015, and 2020, the Skripal poisonings in the UK in 2018,[124] and the suspicious deaths of Chechen dissidents in Germany and France in 2019 and 2020,[125] did not trigger either a rethinking of Europe's stance *vis-à-vis* Russia or unequivocal responses. In addition, after 2015, Russia challenged the West in the context of the Syrian war, propped up Assad's anti-Western autocracy, and helped the Iranian regime. The US talked about red lines in Syria, but did not enforce them, and Russia felt emboldened geopolitically. Then, as the US prepared to withdraw from Afghanistan, Putin likely saw the US as weak and recoiling from foreign interventions and confrontation with Russia. Of course, achieving the vassalization of Ukraine without a full-scale invasion would have been the lower-cost route for Putin and he tried to achieve it through the Minsk Accords.

Minsk peace process failed

Acknowledgment that Russia's desire to control Ukraine was the main stumbling block of the Minsk process helps us to understand the many failed attempts to implement the Minsk Agreements during 2015–2022. After Zelensky was elected with a promise to reach an agreement with Russia over Donbas there was hope that the Minsk process would get a new lease on life and the Donbas conflict would be resolved. During the campaign, Zelensky expressed optimism about the possibility of a deal with Putin, where the two sides would "meet in the middle" to solve the conflict. As noted above, Russia put pressure on Zelensky over Donbas from the very start of his presidency by passing a law to enable widespread Russian passportization of Donbas residents only days after Zelensky was inaugurated. Nevertheless, Zelensky took steps to try to unlock the Minsk process. He met Russia's pre-condition for a Putin–Zelensky summit when he agreed to incorporate the so-called Steinmeier formula into Ukrainian law. The formula, proposed in 2016 by the then-foreign minister of Germany, Frank-Walter Steinmeier, proposed a sequence for holding local elections in and granting special status to Russia-controlled areas: special status was to come into effect on a temporary basis at the close of the polls on the day of the local elections and, if an OSCE election observation mission concluded that the elections had been held in accordance with OSCE standards and Ukrainian law, the special status would then become permanent.[126] This was a substantial concession by Ukraine, given that public opinion, while broadly in favor of a peaceful solution to the conflict in Donbas, was at the same time against granting special status to Russia-controlled areas. A January 2020 Rating Group poll found that 64% nationwide, with solid majorities in every region, expected Zelensky to end the armed conflict in Donbas.[127] At the same time, a February 2020 Razumkov Center poll found just 21% supported constitutionally enshrined special status for Russia-controlled areas, and 62% opposed.[128]

Opposition by the Ukrainian public to special status or constitutional changes aimed at Donbas, together with the major decline of pro-Russian parties' vote share in the parliament after 2014, had stumped previous attempts at such concessions. In September 2015, then-president Poroshenko, pressured by both Russia and the West, tried to push through parliament a constitutional amendment that would provide for different treatment of eastern Donbas in the nationwide decentralization process. The first reading barely secured a simple majority vote and led to violent protests outside parliament.[129] Final constitutional change requires a constitutional majority support (i.e. two-thirds of the legislature) and was clearly impossible to achieve.

Elections could have unblocked the Minsk process, but Russia was not interested in an election that would bring Ukrainian authority back to Donbas. Over the years Ukraine sought to enable elections through a peacekeeping force. In March 2015, Ukraine sent requests to the UN and the EU for the deployment of an international peacekeeping mission to Donbas but Russia objected to these plans.[130] In 2017, in a surprising development, Putin indicated support for peacekeepers, but it quickly became clear that Russia wanted peacekeepers deployed only along the so-called contact line separating Ukrainian and rebel forces, while Ukraine wanted them deployed also along the 923-km-long Ukrainian–Russian border in Donbas, which Ukraine did not control, and, ultimately, throughout the DNR and LNR territory to prepare the security environment for elections.[131]

A November 2019 Paris meeting between Zelensky, Putin, Merkel, and Macron was the last top-level meeting in the so-called Normandy format, which became the main international forum to address the conflict. The Normandy format was conceived in the summer of 2014, when leaders from Ukraine, Russia, Germany, and France, while gathered in Normandy to mark the seventieth anniversary of D-Day, met to discuss the Donbas conflict. Following the Paris summit, Ukraine made another proposal on elections. In December 2019, the Ukrainian interior minister proposed a scheme whereby conditions for the elections and return of Ukrainian authority to eastern Donbas would occur not at once but incrementally, with joint police presence (Ukrainian, rebel, and international [OSCE]) starting in a select municipality and gradually expanding.[132] Russia had no interest, and the Minsk process deadlocked again.

Military buildup and last-ditch diplomacy

Over the next two years, Ukraine would continue to move toward the West in foreign and toward democratic consolidation in domestic policies, Russia's goal to control Ukraine would not change, and Minsk implementation would remain deadlocked. The central stumbling block – Ukraine's (in)ability to retain sovereignty in domestic and foreign-policy decision-making – has haunted the Minsk process since its inception. As Zelensky would say in an interview after the February 2022 full-scale invasion, in the process of trying to unlock the peace process he had come to the conclusion that the Minsk accords were an instrument "to give Russia back influence over Ukraine that it had over many years," and in the accords "there was no intention to give Ukraine independence."[133] With Ukraine refusing to implement Minsk on the terms favored by Russia and to introduce constitutional measures that would allow the proxy republics to control central government decisions, Russia was running out of options to achieve the vassalization of Ukraine though non-military means.

In February 2021, Russia started a large-scale exercise of tens of thousands of troops along the border with Ukraine. In April, Russia announced completion of the exercises and the withdrawal of troops, but the US Defense Department estimated that around 80,000 troops were left at the borders, as well as much of the equipment, making it easier to start an invasion more quickly.[134] In July 2021, Putin penned a 5,000-word-long essay, "On the Historical Unity of Russians and Ukrainians," where he argued that Ukrainians and Russians are "one people," that the Ukrainian state was an artificial creation by the Bolsheviks on the "lands of historical Russia," and that there is "no historical basis" for the "idea of Ukrainian people as a nation separate from the Russians." "True sovereignty of Ukraine," Putin concluded, "is possible only in partnership with Russia." Any deviations from Russia's vision of Ukraine as a natural part of a pan-Russian nation were a manifestation of historical revisionism, Western meddling, or nationalist aggression by the illegitimate post-Maidan government that came to power in a "coup" supported by "Western powers," and which was now engaged in "forced change of identity" and "forced assimilation" of Russians in Ukraine.[135]

With Russia in open denial of Ukraine's right to sovereign statehood, the war drew another step closer in December 2021 after NATO rejected Russia's draft US–Russia and NATO–Russia agreements, which contained non-starter provisions such as the alliance reversing its long-standing open-door policy and deploying no forces or weapons in countries that joined the alliance after May 1997, with no requirements for redeployment of Russian forces.[136] Even as the US and ultimately all Western allies became increasingly convinced that the invasion was forthcoming, the West continued to pursue diplomacy. In a December 7 video call with Putin, Joe Biden, responding to Putin's complaints about expansion and threats to Russia's security, tried to assure Putin that Ukraine would not become a NATO member any time soon and told him that the US and Russia could come to agreements on Russia's concerns about the placement of US weapons systems in Europe. In early January, the US again offered talks and trust-building measures in various security areas, including the deployment of troops and the placement of weapons on NATO's eastern flank, if Russia would de-escalate its military buildup near Ukraine. At the end of Blinken–Lavrov's fruitless meeting in Geneva on January 21, Blinken purportedly asked Lavrov in private: "Sergei, tell me what it is you're really trying to do? ... Was this all really about the security concerns Russia had repeatedly raised again and again – about NATO's 'encroachment' toward Russia and a perceived military threat? Or was it about Putin's almost religious belief that Ukraine was and always had been an integral part of Mother Russia?" Lavrov walked away without answering.[137]

In February, the UK and France made last-ditch efforts at diplomacy. British Defense Secretary Wallace flew to Moscow to meet with his

Russian counterpart to explore if there was room for negotiation on Putin's demands about NATO expansion and activities in Eastern Europe; but Russia showed no interest in engaging. Macron talked to Putin on February 20, and apparently believed that he may have achieved a breakthrough and gotten Putin to agree to meet in Geneva with Biden.[138] Unfortunately, Macron's "intense courtship" of Putin did not work, as the Russian president set his invasion plans in motion the following day by announcing the recognition of the LNR and DNR. Western diplomatic efforts were extensive, but what the West was willing to offer fell short of what Putin was seeking – a Ukraine restored to its "rightful" place as Russia's vassal.

The subsequent full-scale invasion of Ukraine further showed that what was important for Russia was not control of Donbas, nor any other piece of Ukrainian territory, but control of the country in its totality. After recognizing the proxy republics in the days before the invasion, Russia could have tried to seize just the territory of Donbas, i.e. the remaining parts of the Donetsk and Luhansk oblasts that the proxy republics claimed as their territory but did not *de facto* control. Such strategy would have been consistent with Putin's claim that Russia sought to protect the population there from the purported "genocide" that the Kyiv government was supposedly planning to carry out. But, as in 2014, the drawback of this strategy was that it would still have left the central government of Ukraine free to pursue independent foreign and domestic policies. This is why taking Kyiv was central in Russia's war plans. Had the central government fallen and had Russia managed to install a proxy government in the capital, such a government, Putin hoped, would finally "deliver" Ukraine to Russia. As Putin said when announcing the "special military operation," Russia did not plan to occupy Ukraine. Occupation indeed would have been unnecessary if a proxy regime could have been installed in Kyiv and this regime were able to exercise effective control of the country. But, once this plan failed, Russia got bogged down in the war pursuing its main goal to vassalize Ukraine. This goal increasingly became more remote, given Ukraine's formal status as an EU candidate state that it received in June 2022, and the major rise during that time of anti-Russian attitudes and further increase in those holding a strong Ukrainian identity.

Conclusion

The cause of Russia's invasion of Ukraine was Russia's refusal to accept Ukraine's diverging political trajectory and persistent attempts to leave the Russian orbit. Had Russian democracy survived the tumultuous 1990s, the divergence with Ukraine would not have been as stark. Political competition could have increased the chances of Russia developing a non-imperial national identity conception compatible with the idea of Ukraine as a separate nation and state. The two states could have trodden a pro-European, democratic consolidation path in parallel, with Russia continuing to seek partnership with the West rather than returning to geopolitical confrontation in the late-2000s. Had Ukrainian democracy died in the early 2000s, a Ukrainian autocrat would have been more likely to keep Ukraine as a vassal within the Russian World, in exchange for political and economic backing that would buttress their hold over Ukraine's diverse society, and enable their suppression of political and societal actors committed to Ukraine's independence.

Instead, since the 2000s, Russia and Ukraine embarked on increasingly divergent paths, which gradually increased the potential for a clash. Ukraine's democratic competition led to the gradual strengthening of a Ukrainian national identity, which defined Ukraine as a distinct nation, rather than as a branch of a pan-Russian nation or civilization. Democratization also led to the average Ukrainian increasingly embracing the idea that Ukraine's future lay in European and Euro-Atlantic integration, rather than in the Russian World. European integration promised the consolidation of strong state institutions, the establishment of the rule of law, and faster economic development. Incorporation into the Russian World, on the other hand, offered little more than Soviet nostalgia, cheap energy, and Russian imperialism. As Putin consolidated an authoritarian regime, he came to hate Ukrainian democracy, in part because it might offer a role model for the Russian population, in part because of what Ukrainian democracy produced – an increasingly united and pro-European Ukraine, slipping out of Russia's control.

Moreover, blinded by imperialist condescension, Russia discounted Ukrainian agency, and attributed the divergence to Western perfidy. Even though the West offered neither NATO nor EU membership to Ukraine, Russia complained that the West had even entertained the option of Ukraine's integration as a theoretical possibility. The remote possibility that rattled Russia was not Western aggression against Russia from NATO coming closer to Russia's borders, but the closing of a window of opportunity to reincorporate Ukraine, which Russia's increasingly re-imperializing identity conceived as "theirs" by right and by history.

Over time, as the escalatory cycle between Russia's re-imperialization and Ukraine's commitment to its independence unfolded, Russia's methods for bringing Ukraine back into the fold escalated. The diplomatic pressure and economic carrots of the 1990s gave way to mounting economic blackmail through gas wars and trade barriers in the post-Orange era, and escalated into military aggression after Euromaidan. Throughout, Russia also tried to use pro-Russian oligarchs and the initially sizeable but dwindling pro-Russian Ukrainian electorate as levers to keep Ukrainian governments in line.

After Yanukovych's hapless attempt at reversing democratization gains and abandoning the pro-European path that led to his ouster in a revolution, Putin's regime came to see Ukraine as the "anti-Russia" – a regime that betrayed shared history and, lured by the West, evolved into a cudgel with which the West aimed to destroy Russia. Through its controlled media, the Putin regime cast post-Maidan Ukraine as the worst political regime imaginable – a "Nazi junta" that had usurped power and had to be brought down by whatever methods necessary; and this message resonated with a significant portion of Russian society. Once Russia's Trojan horse method of starting and maintaining an insurgency in Donbas, and then trying to leverage its actors to control central Ukrainian government's ability to pursue independent foreign and domestic policies through the Minsk accords, failed in early 2022, Russia decided to launch a full-scale invasion to bring Ukraine into the fold of the Russian World – come hail or high water.

Ukraine: state and society resilience

The 2022 war represents another iteration of the escalatory cycle that gradually disentangled Ukraine from Russia since the 1990s. Russia's full-scale invasion has produced stronger-than-ever commitment in Ukraine to exit the Russian World. After more than a year of massive Russia-inflicted death and destruction, Ukrainians are determined to win the war – 95% believe in victory[1] and 93% would accept a ceasefire only if Russia left all of Ukraine, including Crimea[2] – and then distance from Russia geopolitically, economically, and culturally. Ukrainians have increased their commitment to strengthening the Ukrainian language, an independent reading of history, religious independence, maintaining a democratic regime, and gaining membership in the EU and NATO.

The Ukrainian state is working toward these goals in a cooperative relationship with civil society organizations, which have mobilized to help the war effort. The Ukrainian state's performance has surpassed expectations, as not just the military performed above and beyond, but local and national institutions managed to keep going under full-scale invasion. Trains run, mail and social payments are delivered, people are evacuated and resettled, the electrical grid is repaired after each missile attack, and "invincibility centers" were set up to keep Ukrainians warm and connected during the Russian onslaught on civilian infrastructure during fall/winter 2022–2023. There is no place for complacency as war, and the martial law it requires, can strain commitment to individual rights due to an emphasis on national defense.

Ukrainians have made their geopolitical choice and they want a future in the West. Strong majorities favor Ukraine's EU and NATO membership as soon as possible. In 2023, between 88 and 94% of Ukrainians in each region want to see Ukraine as an EU member by 2030 and between 80 and 92% want to join NATO.[3] When it comes to Euro-Atlantic integration, the Ukrainian public went from majority opposed or hesitating in the 1990s and 2000s, to increasingly supportive in the 2010s. Each step closer to the current consensus came in the aftermath of Russian threats to Ukrainian sovereignty. That historically pro-Russian southern and eastern regions would come to support EU and NATO membership by large margins was beyond the dreams of most in the Ukrainian Right in earlier periods. In 2021,

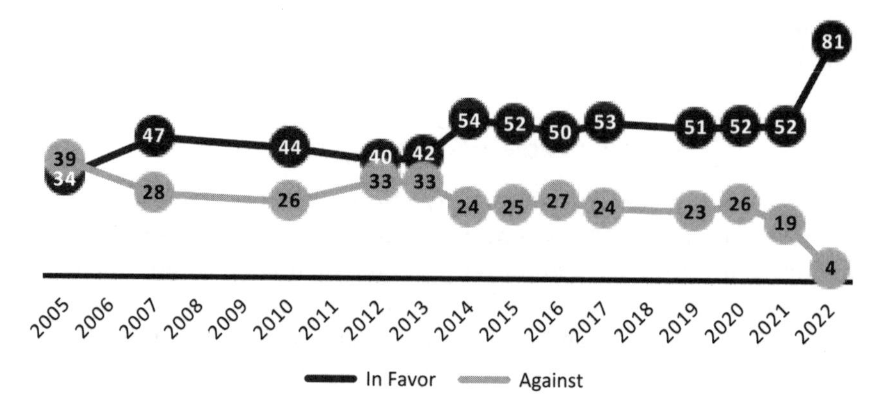

Figure 7.1a Support for EU membership in Ukraine (%)
Source: Kyiv International Institute of Sociology (KIIS).

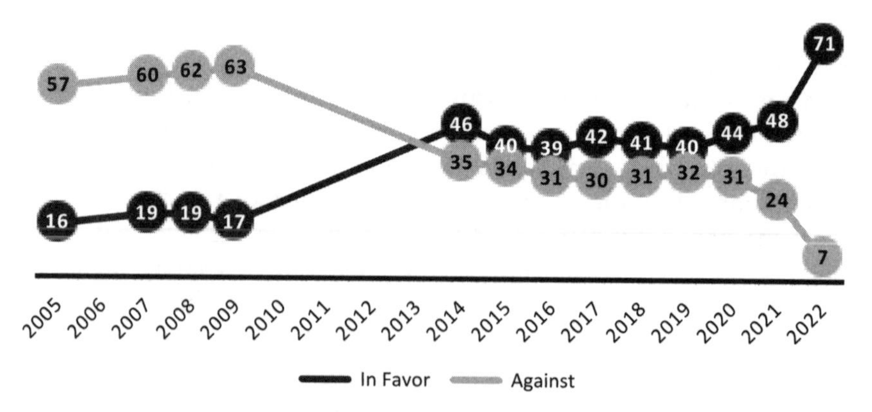

Figure 7.1b Support for NATO membership in Ukraine (%)
Source: Kyiv International Institute of Sociology (KIIS).

virtually no one would have predicted that in 2022 Ukraine would be granted EU candidate status and would have deposited an official application for NATO membership. But the full-scale war made the West more open to the prospects of welcoming Ukraine in its geopolitical ranks and both steps are now facts. Putin has only himself to blame for this geopolitical development.

The war's disproportional destruction and occupation of parts of the eastern and southern regions has nearly wiped out pro-Russian sentiment in Ukraine, both in terms of geopolitical orientation to the Russian state and in terms of warm attitudes toward the Russian people. Even after Russia annexed Crimea and, while it maintained the war in Donbas, many Ukrainians still supported a friendly relationship with Russia and held positive views toward Russians even as positive views toward the Russian leadership plummeted. In a 2018 Rating poll, only 23% held negative attitudes to the Russian people and polling throughout the post-Maidan period showed that 44 to 48% thought Ukraine and Russia should be friendly independent nations. After the full-scale invasion, 92% of Ukrainians view Russians negatively (May 2022 KIIS poll) and only 11% want a friendly relationship with Russia (July 2022 KIIS poll).[4]

The 2022 invasion of Ukraine was Putin's last-ditch attempt to prevent Ukraine from decisively separating from Russia. Russia justified the attack in large part in identity terms: Russians and Ukrainians were one people, Putin argued, and the "special military operation" was supposed to liberate Ukrainian people oppressed by the post-Maidan "neo-Nazi" government bent on denying Russian–Ukrainian organic unity against the wishes of the Ukrainians. His military escalation, however, led to the all but complete separation of Ukraine from Russia. Profound identity changes that began after the Euromaidan and have accelerated since the invasion mean that Ukraine – ironically in large measure due to Putin's aggression – became decidedly more Ukrainian. Since 2000, pollsters have asked Ukrainians what they consider themselves and have given various local, subnational, national, and global identity options. Throughout the last two decades, the share of people who choose to call themselves "citizen of Ukraine" has increased from 41% in 2000 to 65% in the run-up to the full-scale invasion in February 2022. By July 2022, the share jumped to 85%.

Linguistic Ukrainization has also significantly accelerated since the invasion. After 2014, Ukrainians increasingly supported state policy on Ukrainian as the only state language, but regional variations remained, and most of the Russian-speakers, while often supporting state policies to strengthen the Ukrainian language, for the most part didn't change their own linguistic practices and continued to speak mainly Russian. After the February invasion not only linguistic attitudes but also linguistic practices began to tilt toward Ukrainian.[5] The manner in which it has been occurring is another illustration of the escalatory cycle. After Russian troops rolled into Ukraine, it became clear that the ill-defined "de-Nazification" goal Putin articulated at the start of the invasion was about eliminating all manifestations of distinct Ukrainian identity. Russian forces tore down Ukrainian state symbols, changed Ukrainian-language city signs to Russian, destroyed Ukrainian books in schools and libraries, and targeted as "a Nazi" anyone who spoke

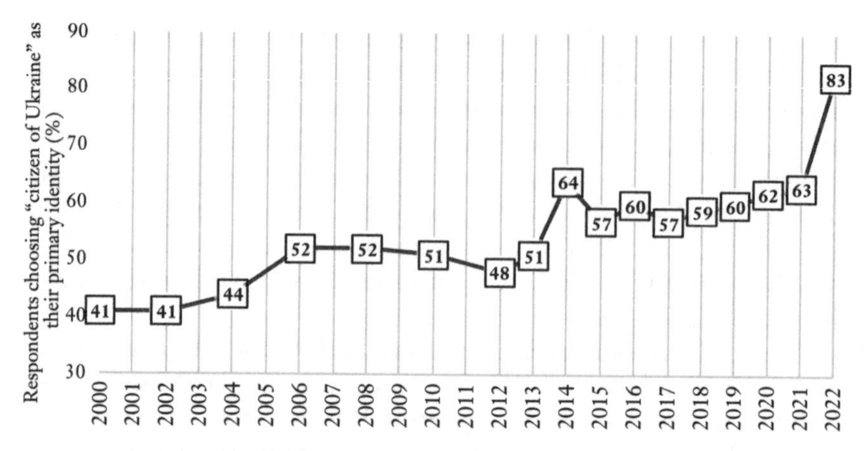

Figure 7.2 Growth of Ukrainian civic identity
Note: The exact wording of the question is: Who do you consider yourself first and foremost? Options: (1) resident of city/village/county; (2) resident of region/several regions; (3) citizen of Ukraine; (4) representative of my ethnic group; (5) citizen of the former Soviet Union; (6) citizen of Europe; (7) citizen of the world; (8) other identity
Source: Kyiv International Institute of Sociology (KIIS).

Ukrainian or opposed Russian occupation. This process is especially evident in the Russian-speaking regions in the east and the south that bore the brunt of the invasion. Many Russian-speaking Ukrainians embraced the Ukrainian language as a way of asserting their distinct Ukrainian identity, defying Russia's claims of them belonging to a Russian rather than to a Ukrainian nation. As one resident of Kherson said after this predominantly Russian-speaking southern city was liberated, "we learned Ukrainian during occupation." In a January 2023 survey commissioned by the National Democratic Institute (NDI), 89% of respondents reported speaking more Ukrainian. A February 2023 Rating Group poll showed that 82% now consider Ukrainian their native language and 60% speak it at home – a 22% increase from before the invasion. The growth in Ukrainian language use is especially pronounced in the east and the south and among Russian and bi-lingual speakers: 45% in this group reported switching to speaking Ukrainian always or frequently.

The invasion plunged the Ukrainian Orthodox Church of the Moscow Patriarchate (UOC-MP) into crisis. While most parishioners and many lower-level priests opposed the invasion, the top hierarchy had many supporters of the Russian World and the Church as a whole was a part of the Russian Orthodox Church (ROC), whose patriarch gave full-throated backing to the invasion. Allegations and evidence of some of the UOC-MP clergy spreading Russian ideological narratives, supporting the invasion, and collaborating with the occupying army, in addition to what many saw as a wait-and-see attitude the UOC-MP leadership took to its continued association with ROC, led to a major drop in societal support. A July 2022 poll by KIIS found that only 4% of self-identified Orthodox declared belonging to the UOC-MP (down from 20% in 2020). Since the fall of 2022, the government took a series of actions aimed at ending UOC-MP's institutional future in Ukraine. SBU searched the offices and religious buildings of OUC-MP to investigate allegations of pro-Russian activities. Following these investigations, the government tabled draft legislation to prohibit the operation of religious organizations affiliated with "influence centers located in the country which carries out armed aggression against Ukraine" (i.e. in Russia).[6] The invasion was a turning point in Ukraine's distancing from Russia in the sphere of religion. If the UOC-MP does not take decisive steps to separate from ROC and gets banned, it would end the institutional presence of the Russian World in Ukraine. Ukrainian society wants the state to address the situation with the UOC-MP – according to the June 2023 KIIS poll, just 6% want the state to do nothing, while 66% support a full ban of the UOC-MP and 19% want the government to control its activity but not ban it.[7]

Russia and Ukraine distanced further in the area of memory politics as well. Re-communization became one of the most visible results of the Russian occupation. On territories of Ukraine seized by the Russian forces, monuments to Lenin were dug out of storage and put up, street and city names changed back to their pre-decommunization equivalents, and the cult of WWII was imposed in education and public spaces. The reaction in the rest of Ukraine was to deepen decommunization. If before decommunization affected vestiges of the Soviet era, now it expanded to manifestations of Russia's imperial legacy in Ukraine. Monuments to Russian imperial figures such as Catherine II came down, as well as monuments and street names commemorating Russian cultural figures such as Pushkin and others whose literary and cultural works celebrated Russian imperialism.

Further distancing also occurred on the rights of women and the LGBTQ+ minority. In contrast to deepening state repression in Russia under the guise of protecting "traditional values," in Ukraine the war increased societal toleration and spurred progressive government policy measures. In July 2022 Ukraine ratified the Istanbul Convention on prevention of gender-based and domestic violence.[8] In January 2023 in an NDI-commissioned poll conducted by KIIS, 56% expressed support for same-sex civil partnerships (24% opposed) and 58% agreed that members of the LGBTQ+ community should have rights equal to other citizens (20% opposed).[9] A draft bill on civil unions that would recognize same-sex partnerships has received surprising support from across the political spectrum, with one conservative MP describing it as "a smile towards Europe and a middle finger to Russia."[10]

The full-scale invasion boosted Ukrainians' commitment to democracy. In 2021, 76% of Ukrainians told pollsters that it was important or very important to them that Ukraine became a fully functioning democracy. By January 2023, that proportion jumped to 92–96% in all regions of Ukraine.[11] To achieve this goal, Ukraine must continue judicial and anti-corruption reforms, safeguard civil and political liberties, and maintain political and electoral competition. The conditionality that comes with EU candidacy and societal commitment to democratization go hand-in-hand to push the government to implement the right reforms. The EU spelled out seven recommendations for Ukraine: three for curbing corruption, two on judicial reform, and one each on media and minorities.[12] The Ukrainian government has raced to implementation, mostly with good results.

In 2022, the government took some positive steps toward bolstering the rule of law and curbing corruption and was criticized for others by ever-vigilant civil society groups. On the positive side, parliament adopted a new National Anti-Corruption Strategy and the anti-corruption institutions have started working in overdrive. A new head of the Specialized Anti-Corruption Prosecutor's Office (SAPO), Oleksandr Klymenko, started his mandate soon after Ukraine received EU candidate status. In 2020, Klymenko had led an investigation into bribery charges against Zelensky's deputy chief of staff, so he was not the president's choice, but he had the backing of the selection panel, which included both civil society and Western experts.[13] It is a positive sign that the president could not push through his preferred candidate. The anti-corruption institutions have produced a record 293 investigations in 2022, among them against an oblast administration chief, 149 people have been charged with corruption crimes, among them the former head of the National Bank of Ukraine,[14] and 34 indictments have made it to court. A corruption investigation also brought down the notorious Kyiv judge Pavlo Vovk, whose District Administrative Court was perceived as the center of a judicial corruption network in the post-Maidan period, as well as the Chair of the Supreme Court, Vsevolod Knyazev, arrested for bribery.

Perhaps encouraged by this flurry of anti-corruption activity, in 2022, Ukrainians reported lower corruption perceptions. While in 2021 only 4% of Ukrainians thought corruption was decreasing, in 2022 the figure grew to 29%![15] Moreover, the proportion of Ukrainians reporting a personal encounter with corrupt practices decreased from half to a third of respondents.[16] On the negative side, the crisis around Constitutional Court (CCU) appointments continued. Civil society criticized the president for failing to veto a new bill on the CCU appointment procedure which the Venice Commission had deemed problematic[17] and one of the CCU appointees was viewed suspiciously by judicial reform watchdogs as a Zelensky ally.[18]

Ukrainian civil society has stepped up to the occasion and is not only instrumental in Ukraine's successful resistance, but essential to Ukraine's democratic development. Civil society groups have sprung into action to raise funds and both provide humanitarian services and aid the military effort. Over 4,000 new NGOs and charities were created in Ukraine in 2022.[19] Over a third of the Ukrainian population volunteers for civil society organizations.[20] Trust in civil society increased dramatically and volunteers in Ukraine are more popular than even the president.[21]

More broadly, Ukrainian democracy is, of course, under strain from the full-scale war. Maintaining unity, fighting disinformation and psyops from the invader, and identifying and neutralizing collaborators and traitors are very real challenges that the political system has to tackle effectively if Ukraine is to maintain its resilience in this existential war. In practice, each of these challenges poses a threat to democratic competition, freedom of speech, and civil rights. Ukraine's government has walked this tightrope since February 2022 and has made some justified and some questionable calls.

The first national security decision with ramifications for democratic competition is the suspension of political parties which espouse pro-Russian positions that justify, legitimize, deny, or glorify Russia's aggression against Ukraine. This process started with a presidential decree in March 2022 and was formalized through law in May. Decisions on individual parties went through the courts. By the end of 2022, twelve parties were banned, most of which had never polled near the 5% electoral threshold. One such party was Nashi, led by Yevhen Murayev, a marginal politician whom shortly pre-invasion British intelligence had identified as a potential Russian puppet in Ukraine. Medvedchuk's Opposition Platform for Life was the biggest banned party and held 43 out of the 450 seats in parliament.[22] Medvedchuk's treasonous behavior was confirmed when Russia exchanged him for Azovstal defenders in a prisoner swap. But is banning his entire party a legitimate move in a democratic system or might Zelensky have done it to consolidate his grip on power, as Ukraine's critics abroad often allege?

First, while the party has been suspended, its MPs are still sitting in parliament, so democratic competition has not been *de facto* curtailed. More importantly, the decisive consolidation of Ukrainian identity, pro-European geopolitical orientation, and the collapse of pro-Russian sentiment among the electorate coupled with Zelensky's skyrocketing popularity among Ukrainians make it obvious that the Opposition Bloc in its pre-2022 format is a thoroughly spent political force in Ukraine. An August 2022 poll showed that support for any party proposing Ukraine's pro-Russian orientation had collapsed from 12% to 2%.[23] Thus, the Opposition Bloc could not pose any threat to Zelensky's party in electoral competition, so the president does not derive electoral benefit from the ban. It is more likely that the ban aimed to draw a thick line between the pre- and post-full-scale invasion eras. While pre-2022, pro-Russian parties could seek links with Russia covertly or overtly and promote Russian narratives about Euromaidan and the war in Donbas, in the post-invasion era loyalty to the Ukrainian state would become a pre-requisite for competing in elections. The individual MPs of the banned parties have the opportunity to reinvent themselves politically, prove to the electorate that they will work for Ukraine's interests, and thus continue their political careers.

Despite the party ban, Zelensky and his government are still democratically constrained by other pro-European parties in parliament, public opinion, civil society, and the media, all of which continue pushing diverse positions. Zelensky's approval is high – the most conservative polls put his approval rating at 76–87% in each region of the country and he is trusted by large majorities of both Ukrainian and Russian speakers, 84 and 79% respectively.[24] However, when it comes to a detailed assessment of the work of the government, Ukrainians see nuance and politics is alive. Big majorities approve of the government's defense (82%), foreign (75%), and energy (80%) policies, but support for health, education, and social policies is lower (50–55%), and majorities expect more from the government in anti-corruption and the rule of law.[25] Moreover, about a third of Ukrainians want to see new political parties (34%) and new leaders (41%) enter politics.[26] Civil society monitors and challenges government decisions, as the discussion of judicial reform and anti-corruption policy showed.

Many of the corruption investigations into high-level malfeasance started with investigative reporting by journalists. A procurement scandal in the Ministry of Defense, which nearly toppled Minister Reznikov and led to resignations, firings, and a NABU investigation, was uncovered by the investigative journalism website Nashi Hroshi.[27] The story that eventually led to charges against Dnipropetrovsk regional governor, Valentyn Reznichenko, was also first broken by investigative journalists.[28]

While investigative reporting is alive and well in Ukraine, the government's broader media policy provides cause for concern and media professional organizations have been vocal in opposition. The first concern is the exclusion of channels tied to former president Petro Poroshenko from the national telethon – a joint news and information channel, which broadcasts nationally 24/7. The telethon was the initiative of five private channels and the public broadcaster in the first days of the full-scale invasion, which was then formalized through a March 2022 presidential decree.[29] The telethon aims at countering Russian disinformation and thus is supposed to unite all national media outlets. Three Poroshenko-connected channels (5 Channel, Pryamyi, and Espreso) were excluded from the telethon and, despite trying to challenge the decision through parliament, the media watchdog, and a popular petition over the course of 2022, they were not included. Given that Poroshenko's European Solidarity is one of the main competitors of Zelensky's Servant of the People for the now-dominant pro-European electorate, this situation is concerning, as it represents a narrowing of the information space. The second concern is a media law adopted by parliament in December 2022, which has drawn criticism from both national and international professional media associations and watchdogs for unduly expanding the powers of the national media regulator.[30] Censorship or suppression of free media have not followed and Ukrainian journalists continue to criticize the government freely, but the effects of the media law should be monitored.

Care is also needed when dealing with the issues of language and religion. In reaction to Russia's invasion, many Ukrainians are choosing to limit or even abandon their use of Russian as they embrace a stronger Ukrainian identity. But the Ukrainian government should be careful to protect the rights of those who want to continue speaking Russian. While decreasing in number, Russian-speakers will not disappear in Ukraine, and speaking Russian should not become associated with supporting Russia. Ukrainian authorities need to proceed carefully and engage with the advice of human rights groups monitoring minority rights. In the area of religion as well, Ukraine needs to ensure that legal measures aimed at countering Russian influences do not violate democratic rights such as freedom of religion.

Although civil society has sprung up to support the war effort and there are many other signs of national unity in the face of Russian aggression, the Ukrainian state is not immune to the dangers of collaboration, both in the occupied territories and in territories under Ukraine's control. In March 2022, parliament adopted a new criminal law on collaboration and collaboration activities. The law provides punishments ranging from confiscation of property to lengthy prison terms of up to twelve years for the most serious violations, for activities that aid Russia in conquering or occupying Ukrainian territory – supplying material resources, voluntarily taking part in occupation activities such as organizing "referenda," or working for the occupation authorities. Moreover, amendments to the Criminal Code adopted at the same time as the law on collaboration criminalized a range of activities that normally would be protected by freedom of speech or freedom of assembly, such as public denial of the Russian invasion, advocating refusal to recognize Ukrainian sovereignty over all occupied territories, promoting the aggressor's agenda through organizing rallies, speaking out publicly, and spreading pro-Russian propaganda in the educational institutions.[31]

Debate on the exact balance between free speech and assembly guarantees and collaboration concerns is important and likely to continue in Ukraine and among its allies, but the Ukrainian situation should be recognized as largely *sui generis.* Both the UK and the US adopted laws on treason in the early days of WWII. Both laws carried the death sentence for activities that aided the enemy and, in the UK, other legal regulations were amended to allow interning of anyone expressing sympathy with the Nazi aggressor.[32] Both countries prosecuted and executed citizens during WWII. However, the relevance of democracies' WWII records to Ukraine's current predicament can be questioned. Neither Britain nor the US were occupied by Germany, so collaboration activities did not carry as direct and immediate a threat as they do in Ukraine today. Continental European states were fully overrun by Germany, so they had no legal means of prosecuting collaborators during the war. Moreover, civil and political rights' guarantees have greatly developed since the 1940s. Ukraine is fighting off an anachronistic imperialist invasion during the most democratic, rights-oriented historical moment. There is no current model of how to tackle collaboration under these challenges while guaranteeing maximum rights. Automatically applying contemporary or historical debates on the politics of fifth columns, collusion with foreign enemies, and subversion[33] to Ukraine risks underestimating the immediacy and potency of the threat that it is experiencing during the all-out war.

Whatever the outcome of the debate, it is crucial for the Ukrainian state, especially for law enforcement and the courts, to implement the collaboration law in line with rule of law standards in a non-arbitrary, impartial process that focuses on solid evidence and due attention to process. How the courts and the prosecution do remains to be seen, but it is an opportunity for these generally distrusted institutions to rise to the occasion. If they do, they will not only be protecting the Ukrainian state from the aggressor, but they will develop *esprit de corps* and a commitment to the rule of law, which is much needed for the renewal of the judiciary.

Russia: genocidal dictatorship?

While Ukraine's state and society have consolidated their commitment to leaving the Russian World and Ukrainian democracy has withstood the test of war so far, in 2022–2023, the escalatory cycle led to Russia digging itself into a deeper hole of autocracy and imperialism. The Putin regime has intensified repression and persecution of domestic critics. Putin's image as a constrained and "competent" autocrat, which many believed in all the way to the invasion, has been shattered.[34] Russia's commitment to great power status and its re-imperialization drive have acquired genocidal intent and rhetoric. The Russian army and the regime's private mercenary group Wagner are systematically committing war crimes and genocidal acts in Ukraine. Russia's international isolation has never been greater, as large majorities of UN member states have repeatedly condemned Russia's invasion, economic ties with Europe have been irrevocably broken, especially in the energy sector, and the International Criminal Court has issued a warrant for Putin's arrest on war crimes charges related to the unlawful deportation of Ukrainian children to Russia.

Intensified domestic repression includes the adoption of new laws criminalizing criticism of the invasion or the armed forces and enforcement of those laws to crush the weak Russian opposition and further demobilize the already atomized civil society. All independent media outlets, though marginal and catering to a very small audience already before the invasion, were driven out of the country into exile. The oldest human rights group, Memorial, which had been legally harassed for years by the Putin regime, was finally closed down for good in December 2022.[35] In March 2022, Alexei Navalny was given an additional and longer prison sentence (nine years) for fraud.[36] Many of the activists from his organization have fled Russia. Other leading opposition figures such as Ilya Yashin and Vladimir Kara-Murza were prosecuted for discrediting the Russian army. In December 2022, Yashin was sentenced to eight and a half years for "spreading false information about the military."[37] Vladimir Kara-Murza, who has already survived two poisonings over the past decade, was sentenced to a whopping 25-year sentence for treason. In his last words before the court, he stated that his trial, "in its secrecy and its contempt for legal norms, has surpassed even the 'trials' of Soviet dissidents in the 1960s and 1970s and [...] the talk of 'enemies of the state' [takes one] all the way back to the 1930s."[38] A study of legal repression in Russia has found that 20,000 people have been detained and 551 of them were political prisoners in 2023. Moreover, legal repression accelerated over the course of the war. While 59 protest-related verdicts and 20 prison sentences were issued in the first nine months of the war, the next three months saw 65 verdicts and 27 prison sentences, and sentence length has also increased, with protesters receiving 6–7 years in prison for anti-war graffiti.[39]

Genocidal rhetoric has marked much of Russia's discussion of the war. In the early days, an article by a Russian pundit first suggested genocidal intent underlying the attack on Ukraine. The author talked about deporting and resettling Ukrainians to re-educate them, while the "nationalist Ukrainian elite" would "need to be liquidated, its re-education is impossible." This communicated intent to destroy the Ukrainian nation led some genocide scholars to conclude that the definitional threshold has been met,[40] while others have said that more evidence is needed.[41] Similar statements have multiplied in Russia's public discourse. Russia's tightly controlled propaganda TV shows feature one guest after the other talking about destroying the Ukrainian nation, stealing and re-educating its children into Russians, murdering everyone who dares defy Russia's "rightful" claims on Ukraine, and punishing each Ukrainian who rejects his or her Russianness by death.[42] Former president Medvedev took to social media to dehumanize Ukrainians by calling them "blood-sucking parasites" and stating that "unterukraine" will disappear because no one needs it. The elite rhetoric has seeped into Russian society's views of the war. Although methodological challenges of opinion polling in authoritarian contexts make it exceedingly hard to estimate exactly what proportion of the Russian public buys into the genocidal rhetoric, analysis of Telegram channels with hundreds of thousands of subscribers has found that many Russians supported the Russian military's execution of civilians in Bucha.[43]

The horrors of Bucha and the destruction of Mariupol have attracted the most attention, but the Russian army has committed war crimes all over the occupied Ukrainian territories. In Yahidne, in the Chernihiv region in the north, the Russian army kept an entire village population in the school basement to control them and use them as human shields for nearly a month. Everyone over eighty years old died.[44] After liberation, mass graves with hundreds of bodies of executed civilians were found in Izyum near Kharkiv in the East.[45] In Kherson, a southern city that Russia occupied in March 2022 and held until the Ukrainian army liberated it in November, investigators have discovered that the Russian occupation authorities set up torture chambers where civilians who were active in civil society or worked for the state were held for weeks, beaten, electrocuted, and sexually abused. In one of the four torture centers operated by Russia in Kherson a "children's cell" was found.[46]

The genocide allegations are supported by evidence that torture chambers in Kherson and elsewhere were not a response to resistance to occupation, but a pre-conceived strategy of the Russian state[47] to identify Ukrainian national activists; the beginning of a plan to destroy the political Ukrainian nation. Other parts of the plan are the systematic destruction of Ukrainian libraries, museums, and national monuments in the occupied territories and the closing down of Ukrainian schools – all steps toward the erasure of the Ukrainian nation in Ukraine. But the action that has attracted the strongest international condemnation is the systematic deportation of Ukrainian children through force or deception to Russia, where some were kept in re-education camps and others were given to Russian families for adoption. The Russian state has neither denied nor hidden the practice, but has claimed that these are "unwanted children," rescued from the war zone and given a new life in Russia. Investigations by the International Criminal Court and the Ukrainian authorities have found evidence to the contrary and President Putin and the Russian children's rights commissioner in charge of the program, Maria Lvova-Belova, have outstanding warrants for their arrest.[48] These warrants are for committing war crimes.

The genocidal rhetoric and genocidal acts have confirmed that Russia's aggression against Ukraine is about controlling Ukraine and about re-imperialization, rather than about Russian insecurity in the wake of NATO expansion. In addition, Russia's actions in response to NATO's latest enlargement wave in 2022–2023 to include Finland and Sweden disproved the claim that Russia sees NATO at its borders as a security threat. If the realist paradigm were correct, we should have seen Russia defensively lashing out against its new NATO member neighbors, taking steps to prevent their accession, or at least fortifying its new 830-mile border with a hostile alliance. Pre-emptive military incursion into Finland and Sweden did not happen, even though some have described the invasion of Ukraine as pre-emptive action to prevent it from joining NATO. Some may counter that in 2022 Russia was tied up in the war in Ukraine already, so it did not have the capacity to attack Finland and Sweden too. But an obvious question reveals itself – why would Russia pre-emptively invade Ukraine, which, as Chapter 4 showed, had only remote chances of joining NATO in some distant future, rather than Finland and Sweden, whose NATO membership was fully plausible all along?

Another way Russia could have reacted in 2022 if it were truly concerned about NATO enlargement was with nuclear threats aimed at deterring Finland and Sweden from making good on their ambition, or aimed at convincing NATO to reject them. Russia did neither in 2022, though propagandists on Russian TV routinely threatened nuclear holocaust on the UK, Germany, and France. At the very least, Russia should have reacted with defensive fortification along the new NATO border. Instead, Putin sent mixed diplomatic signals – vague threats of retaliation coupled with rationalizations that Swedish and Finnish NATO membership was acceptable for Russia. Moreover, Russian troops stationed near the Finnish border were redeployed to other parts of Russia right after Turkey's objection was lifted and Finland's NATO accession became a *fait accompli.* They did not return after Finnish membership became official either. This is not how a leader genuinely fearful of a hostile alliance approaching his country's borders reacts.

Where do we go from here?

Russia and Ukraine are no longer two "post-Soviet states" with similar problems. Putin's fateful decision to launch a full-scale invasion of Ukraine signaled a critical turning point in both Ukraine's and Russia's histories, as well as the place of these states in the European security architecture and its foreseeable future. Regardless of how the war ends – with Ukraine succeeding in de-occupying all or some of its territory or the war morphing into a frozen conflict; with Putin surviving the war or losing power in Russia – the post-war reality will be different for all: for Ukraine, for Russia, and for the West.

Ukraine: European, democratic, no longer "post-Soviet"

Ukraine's determination to distance from Russia in every way and join Western institutions is not simply a reaction to the trauma and should be taken as a deeply held and widely popular foreign and domestic policy position, not as an emotional stance. There are good reasons to recategorize Ukraine geopolitically according to its wishes. As we have argued in this book, long before the war, Russia and Ukraine had diverged fundamentally, and it is high time outsiders separated the two for good when they think of categories of states. The ramifications of this divergence are that we have reason to be fairly optimistic about Ukraine's post-war trajectory. Ukraine is on track to be able to meet the conditionality criteria for EU membership and it would make a contribution to Euro-Atlantic security by joining NATO. At a minimum, the West should treat Ukraine as it did other Eastern European countries in the beginning of their Euro-Atlantic integration process in the 1990s. EU accession will happen through conditionality, monitoring, and support.

Ukraine is a democracy with robust political competition, civil and political rights guarantees, free media, and a vibrant, engaged civil society. Like other European democracies, it wrestles with difficult historical legacies and the challenge of protecting minority rights. To improve and consolidate, it strives to tackle political corruption rooted in the pathologies of the post-communist transition and build stronger foundations for the rule of law. To pursue these processes freely and successfully Ukraine needs to be recategorized decisively as a full-fledged member of the West and not as a buffer between the West and Russia. The best way to ensure that democracy consolidates in Ukraine would be fast EU integration.

NATO accession will also need to happen to bolster not only Ukraine's security, but Europe's security architecture. Most Eastern European states that have already successfully completed their Euro-Atlantic integration are strongly supportive of Ukraine and willing to share their experience and lessons learned. Western European and North American NATO members are moving toward an understanding that the next strategic goal should be Ukraine's entry into the alliance, not only because the Ukrainian army has proven itself on the battlefield as a highly effective force, but because NATO membership for Ukraine is the most obvious way to send a strong message to Russia that its military aggression in Europe will not stand and will not be rewarded with gains.

Post-war Russia: global re-integration will take more than Putin's departure

Russia is an autocracy that has more in common with Iran and China than with Ukraine. It has an extensive surveillance and repression apparatus, no rule of law, a marginal and beleaguered opposition, underdeveloped civil society, and a disempowered citizenry. We should recognize that Putin is not the only, or even the main, obstacle to Russia becoming a European democracy. The future will show whether Russia would remain a personalistic authoritarian regime – be it under Putin or under another hardliner – or whether it would attempt to democratize if a reformer comes to power. Regardless of who governs Russia after the war, they need to commit to a series of measures before relations with the West can be normalized. Until and unless this happens, European security will need to be defined against Russia rather than with it, and Europe will need to continue the economic disengagement from Russia that was accelerated after the 2022 full-scale invasion.

Russia's quick democratization and reintegration into the global economy and the international community are unlikely. Russia faces a host of obstacles, which extend beyond Putin's regime. Even if Putin is replaced, there are alternative elites which are similarly committed to kleptocracy, autocracy, and imperialism and would pursue the same course, only replacing one cadre with their own. Whether it is a well-known cadre of the Putinist regime and inner circle, or a currently unknown mid-range member of the Russian elite, the next Russian president is more likely than not to continue Putin's course both domestically and abroad. Military aggression may be renounced for pragmatic reasons, but the ambition to dominate the "near abroad," and especially Ukraine, through other means is likely to be sustained. After twenty years of Putinism and little cohort renewal, Russian elites are considerably uniform, in background and in ideological orientation.[49] Even if the successor is an outsider, they may still not be a democrat and they may still be an imperialist.

A Russian leader who is a Westernizing liberal, like Alexei Navalny or one of his allies, would, no doubt, be a welcome change from Putin and his cronies. Even then, however, there are good reasons to be cautious and not immediately conclude that Russia has sustainably changed course either in foreign policy or in regime trajectory. It will be important to see whether the new Russian leadership would take concrete steps toward changing the country's course beyond making rhetorical promises. The trust problem cannot be overemphasized, given that Russia unleashed a massive war in Europe, while its leadership repeatedly lied about its intentions before the invasion and continued to lie since, denying its involvement in well-documented acts such as the Bucha massacre and twisting the facts of the mass deportations of Ukrainian children.

To start building trust, a new Russian government will have to send costly signals through concrete actions. Transitional justice measures would be an important test. Russia would have to show its readiness to undo the damage it has done and to atone for the aggression of the Putin regime against Ukraine. The new Russian government would have to return kidnapped Ukrainian children and other civilians, cooperate with Ukraine and the international community on coming up with a fair and just reparations package to help Ukraine's post-war reconstruction, and work with an international tribunal to bring to justice those responsible for the invasion of Ukraine and war crimes committed against Ukrainians. In foreign policy, the new Russian leader would need to quickly and unambiguously lift Russia's objections to Ukraine's NATO and EU accession aspirations. If any other countries in Russia's "near abroad" want to pursue this route, be it Moldova and Georgia, who are already taking steps, or Armenia or Belarus, who have not, a truly renewed Russia would not object and would realize that it is not entitled to a role in the process. Domestically, a new Russian leadership committed to democratization would take concrete steps toward holding free and fair elections, increasing executive accountability, rolling back civil society repression, rebooting the courts to start building the rule of law.

Each of these steps would take time. For comparison on transitional justice, Croatia started surrendering its war criminals to The Hague in 2001, six years after the end of the Yugoslav wars, and entered the EU twelve years later. Serbia has been reluctant to cooperate with The Hague, often glorifying convicted war criminals, and the issue is fraught and far from settled over twenty years after the end of the Milosevic regime. The advocacy of the Russian Westernizing opposition about a swift Russian rapprochement with Europe after Putin is gone should be rejected unless Russia undertakes the above steps.

To change Russia's foreign policy durably, a new Russian government would have to undertake a broader campaign to roll back imperialist attitudes and assumptions broadly held by Russian society. Commonly held ideas include the notion that Russia has never attacked anyone, but it has only been a liberator, that it is entitled to be a great power, that it has always been a benign actor in the neighborhood and has enriched and helped neighbors' development, and need to be re-examined through a national conversation. Without a difficult national conversation about Russian imperialism through the ages and, especially, its recent manifestations, Russia may again perceive it as humiliation and resentment if it loses control over its neighborhood. The aggressive imperialism of Putin's regime should not be replaced by visions for the soft power of the Russian World or a liberal Russian empire. The window of opportunity that may have existed for Ukraine to want to join these projects is now slammed shut.

In addition, a new democratic Russian government would have to reform domestic institutions from scratch. Russia has never had an independent judiciary, has had no free media for over twenty years, civil society has atrophied, and political parties are not functioning vehicles of political competition. Changing this institutional landscape is a tall order. At a minimum, two election cycles without manipulation and producing Russian leaders who promote anti-imperialism abroad and civil and political rights at home would have to take place before we can become sanguine about Russia's democratization prospects. We should not fall into the trap of the early 1990s, when there was too much wishful thinking, despite early signs that Russia's democracy was sputtering and great power ambitions of dominating the neighborhood had never fully abated.

Fears of Russia's possible disintegration if it were to lose the war should not be used as a reason to engage with non-democratic Russia or prevent Ukraine from regaining its internationally recognized territory. Russia's disintegration is not a likely scenario and parallels with the late Soviet Union are tenuous at best. Soviet disintegration followed years of progressive relaxing of political control during Gorbachev's reform period, a round of competitive elections, and then several years of popular mobilization against the union center, with substantial variation in strength across administrative units of the Soviet state. When the Soviet Union finally fell apart, despite inter-ethnic strife, the nightmare scenarios of ubiquitous ethnic violence and failed states in its wake did not materialize. The USSR dissolved into fifteen states, each of which in the common Soviet state was an administrative unit of equal institutional standing and formalized as a quasi-state with a titular ethnic group.

Today's Russia is institutionally arranged as an asymmetric federation consisting of ethnically and non-ethnically designated regions of different institutional status. Many of these regions have never had any separatist sentiment at all and, even at the height of sovereignty movement in the 1990s, only a handful of regions had separatist movements of varying intensity. After two decades of authoritarian state building and Russification under Putin, the potential for separatism has been further weakened and, if this sentiment were to re-emerge, it would be likely to affect only a small number of Russia's regions. Other regions may demand greater autonomy rather than a separate statehood. A democratizing post-war Russia would be best positioned to engage with such demands and transform itself into a true federation, which under Putin it has been only on paper but not in reality. Backing Putin's or another autocrat's rule and endorsing their suppression of a hypothetical separatist mobilization for fear of Russia's disintegration would be a policy driven by problematic parallels that eventually might hasten rather than prevent major destabilization of the Russian state.

Lessons for the West

For the Western allies, but especially for Europe, the implication of this decisive geopolitical rupture between Ukraine and Russia is that Europe's political and security architecture needs a major update. The political engine of the EU since its inception – the Franco-German partnership – needs to rethink its relationship to Ukraine, Russia, and Eastern Europe. It should stop conceiving of Eastern Europe as the EU's periphery or a buffer zone between Europe and Russia. Instead, it should realize that it is an integral part of Europe – diverse and complicated but committed to European integration. Rather than worrying about how to offer security guarantees to Russia and how to re-launch a partnership with it at the first possibility, Europe must focus inward on how to come up with a geopolitical and security strategy that weighs in all European members' and future members' views, concerns, and preferences and prioritizes them over Russia's.

As it prepares to integrate Ukraine, Moldova, and the Western Balkans, Europe must think how to ensure that European governance can work to bolster democracy and the rule of law in all member states. This means figuring out a mechanism for preventing democratic backsliding before it undermines unity, as Hungary has done during the war. To ensure that the next enlargement wave does not later lead to more democratic backsliding in the new member states, the EU should bolster the mechanisms for post-accession monitoring.

The notion of Ukraine as somehow a part of Russia – if not literally then at least culturally and civilizationally – needs to be abandoned for good. Just like European democracies in recent decades have actively questioned their own colonial legacies, they need to acknowledge that the "Ukraine-as-Russia" mental construct is a consequence of centuries of Russian imperialism and a historical narrative cultivated and promoted by the Russian empire, the Soviet Union, as well as post-Soviet Russia – especially but not exclusively under Putin. This mental placement of Ukraine is not an accurate reflection of the past history and is firmly rejected by the vast majority of today's Ukrainian citizens. Ukraine must be free and the empire must finally die.

Notes

Introduction: Russia's invasion and Ukraine's resistance

1 President Putin's address on Ukraine, February 24, 2022. http://en.kremlin.ru/events/president/transcripts/statements/67843
2 *Washington Post*, February 21, 2022. https://www.washingtonpost.com/opinions/2022/02/21/ukraine-invasion-putin-goals-what-expect
3 President Zelensky's address, February 26, 2022. https://www.nbcnews.com/video/president-zelenskyy-sends-video-to-ukrainian-people-134108741773
4 Newsweek, May 23, 2023. https://www.newsweek.com/russia-death-toll-ukraine-already-same-10-years-afghanistan-1708991
5 Sergei Glazyev quoted in D'Anieri, 2019, p. 200.
6 Rating Group poll, February 17, 2022. https://ratinggroup.ua/research/ukraine/dinamika_vneshnepoliticheskih_orientaciy_16-17_fevralya_2022.html, pp. 4–5.
7 Rating Group poll, February 16, 2022. https://ratinggroup.ua/research/ukraine/obschestvenno-politicheskie_nastroeniya_naseleniya_12-13_fevralya_2022.html, p. 9.

1 Entangled histories and identity debates

1 President Putin's address, February 21, 2022. http://en.kremlin.ru/events/president/news/67828
2 Yekelchyk, 2007, p. 24.
3 Himka, 2022.
4 Plokhy, 2015, p. 67.
5 Yekelchyk, 2007, p. 25.
6 Yekelchyk, 2007, p. 26; Plokhy, 2015, p. 70.
7 Yekelchyk, 2007, pp. 24–25.
8 Ibid., p. 27.
9 Plokhy, 2015, pp. 97–98.
10 Yekelchyk, 2007, p. 28; Plokhy, 2015, pp. 100–101.
11 Plokhy, 2015, p. 104.

12 Yekelchyk, 2007, p. 28; Plokhy, 2015, p. 105.
13 Yekelchyk, 2007, p. 30.
14 Ibid., pp. 40–41. For detailed analysis of the emergence of the "Little Russia" idea in the three Ukrainian provinces of the Russian empire on the west bank of the Dnipro (Volyn, Podolia, Kyiv) see Hillis, 2013.
15 Yekelchyk, 2007, pp. 43–44.
16 Ibid., pp. 58–59.
17 Ibid., pp. 68–71.
18 Ibid., pp. 76–78.
19 Ibid., pp. 71–83.
20 Magocsi, 2022, p. 11.
21 Martin, 2001.
22 Magocsi, 2022, p. 15.
23 Pauly, 2014.
24 Applebaum, 2017; Plokhy, 2015, pp. 249–254.
25 Plokhy, 2015, pp. 249–250.
26 Ibid., p. 250.
27 Ibid., pp. 250–251.
28 August 1932 letter of Stalin to Kaganovich, quoted in Plokhy, 2015, pp. 251–252.
29 Plokhy, 2015, p. 253.
30 Graziosi, 2008, p. 147
31 Klid and Motyl, 2012.
32 Plokhy, 2015, p. 254.
33 Marples, 2007.
34 Rossoliński-Liebe and Willems, 2022, p. 3.
35 Plokhy, 2015, p. 282.
36 Ibid., p. 291.
37 Magocsi, 2022, p. 18.
38 Ibid., p. 19.
39 Yekelchyk, 2007, pp. 146–148.
40 Ibid., p. 173.
41 Plokhy, 2015, pp. 313–314.
42 This generation of writers, artists, and other members of the creative intelligentsia adopted the name *shistdesiatnyky* (the "sixtiers," or generations of the sixties). Yekelchyk, 2007, pp. 163–165.
43 Kuzio and Wilson 1994, p. 58.
44 Ibid., p. 143.
45 Plokhy, 2014, p. 54.
46 Ibid., p. 55.
47 Kuzio and Wilson, 1994, p. 125.
48 Plokhy, 2014, p. 220.
49 Poll results in Kuzio and Wilson, 1994, p. 190.
50 Gellner, 1983.
51 Tolz, 1998a, p. 289.
52 Gennadii Zyuganov, leader of the Russian Communist Party, as quoted in Pain, 2009, p. 82.
53 Laruelle, 2008.

54 Poll results in Tolz, 1998b, p. 1015.
55 Novoe Vremia, August 6, 2006.
56 Shevel, 2011c, p. 186.
57 Ibid., pp. 187–188.
58 Morozov, 2009, p. 429.
59 Abdulatipov, Mikhailovskii, and Chichanovskii, 1997.
60 Except for Latvia and Estonia, where citizenship rules excluded most Russian-speakers who arrived during the Soviet occupation from acquiring citizenship, Russian-speakers in other post-Soviet states became citizens of these states at the start of independence automatically.
61 Brudny, 2002; Chubais, 1998.
62 Breslauer and Dale, 1997; Brudny, 2002; Tolz, 1998a.
63 Survey of Russian elites, July 28, 2020, p. 28. https://www.hamilton.edu/documents/SRE2020ReportFINAL.pdf
64 Tolz, 2001, pp. 255–256.
65 Blakkisrud, 2016, 256.
66 Akturk, 2017, p. 1110.
67 Ibid., p. 1111.
68 In Russian – *gosudarstroobrazhujuschii narod.*
69 Nezavisimaia gazeta, January 23, 2012. https://www.ng.ru/politics/2012-01-23/1_national.html. Also Blakkisrud, 2016, p. 255.
70 In Russian, *sistemoobrazuiushcheie iadro.*
71 Shevel, 2011c, pp. 190–191.
72 Gazeta.ru, February 7, 2007. http://www.gazeta.ru/2007/02/07/oa_230946.shtml
73 Putin's address to the Federal Assembly, April 26, 2007. http://archive.kremlin.ru/appears/2007/04/26/1156_type63372type63374type82634_125339.shtml
74 Laruelle, 2015a.
75 Patriarch Kirill's speech at the grand opening of the 3rd Assembly of the Russian World in 2009 (quoted after Metreveli, 2020, p. 102).
76 Nezavisimaia gazeta, December 30, 1999. www.ng.ru/politics/1999-12-30/4_millenium.html
77 Blakkisrud, 2022.
78 Shevel, 2011c.
79 Blakkisrud, 2022, pp. 11–12.
80 Laruelle, 2016.
81 For an in-depth analysis of this narrative, including its constituent elements and nuances, see Kasianov, 2023.
82 Haran' and Maiboroda, 2000; Wilson, 2002.
83 Shevel, 2014, p. 154.
84 Kyïvs'ke naukove tovarystvo imeni Petra Mohyly and "ANOD," 1998, p. 109.
85 Tomenko, Hrebel'nyk, and Vashchenko, 2002, p. 8.
86 Narodnyi Rukh Ukrainy za Perebudovy, 1989, p. 19.
87 Wilson, 2000, p. 185.
88 Ibid., p. 174.
89 Wolczuk, 2000, p. 678.
90 Kuchma's inaugural speech published in *Uriadovyi Kurier*, July 21, 1994.
91 Yekelchyk, 2007, p. 174.
92 Plokhy, 2015, pp. 313–314.

93 *Washington Post*, January 24, 2014. https://www.washingtonpost.com/news/worldviews/wp/2014/01/24/this-is-the-one-map-you-need-to-understand-ukraines-crisis/
94 Golovakha, Panina, and Parakhons'ka, 2011, p. 13. Chapter 3 will offer more detailed analysis of attitudes to state policies on language and historical memory.
95 Schmid and Myshlovska, 2019.
96 Academic literature analyzing and debating the impact of regional, ethnic, and linguistic differences on political attitudes in Ukraine is voluminous. Major studies include Barrington, 2022; Barrington and Faranda, 2009; Onuch and Hale, 2018; Shulman, 2006; Kulyk, 2011; Pop-Eleches and Robertson, 2018.
97 As one scholar put it, increase in Ukrainian self-identification has been occurring simply due to people's "participation in a number of practices prioritizing that identity, from education to travelling with a Ukrainian passport to watching Ukrainian sport teams compete with foreign ones." Kulyk, 2019, p. 176.
98 Golovakha, et al., 2011, p. 33.
99 Brudny and Finkel, 2011. Chapter 3 illustrates these shifts in public opinion in the geographic center of Ukraine on issues such as characterization of the 1932–1933 famine and the Ukrainian nationalist underground.
100 Golovakha, et al., 2011, pp. 13, 33.

2 Regime divergence

1 For the "red–brown coalition" term see: Clover, 1999, p. 9, and for the centrist "swamp" term, see McFaul, 1997.
2 Skillen, 2016.
3 Colton, 2008, p. 208.
4 Yekelchyk, 2005, p. 197.
5 Javeline, 2009.
6 Emery, et al., 2021.
7 Kubicek, 2002.
8 Ibid.
9 Johnson, 2000, p. 231.
10 Darden, 2009.
11 Giuliano, 2017; Gorenburg, 2003.
12 Herrera, 2005.
13 Walker, 2018, p. 47.
14 Colton, 2008, p. 279.
15 Wolczuk, 2001.
16 McFaul, 2000.
17 Nichols, 1999.
18 Bukkvoll, 2001, p. 1143.
19 D'Anieri, 2003; Ishiyama and Kennedy, 2001; McFaul, 2001; Protsyk, 2004
20 Johnson, 2000, pp. 184–185.
21 Hale, 2004.
22 Darden, 2001.
23 Hale, 2004.
24 Kubicek, 2001.

25 Allison, 2002; Fish, 2001.
26 Coppedge, et al., 2023.
27 Ibid.
28 Ibid.
29 Riabchuk, 2002.
30 Popova, 2012.
31 Ibid.
32 Dyczok, 2005.
33 Kuzio, 2005.
34 BBC Russian Service, January 26, 2012. https://www.bbc.com/russian/international/2012/01/120126_putin_russia_west_part_two
35 Huntington, 1991.
36 Karatnycky, 2005, p. 35.
37 Finkel and Brudny, 2014.
38 Radnitz, 2021.
39 Goehring, 2007, p. 748.
40 Larrabee, 2006.
41 Tudoroiu, 2007.
42 Popova, 2012.
43 Oates, 2006.
44 Popova, 2016.
45 Ibid.
46 Way, 2015, p. 80.
47 Kudelia, 2014.
48 Ibid.
49 Smyth, 2020.
50 White and McAllister, 2014.
51 Greene, 2013.
52 CBC, January 19, 2012. https://www.cbc.ca/news/world/russia-s-presidential-candidates-1.1159462
53 Smyth, 2020, p. 6.
54 On stalwarts vs. new protesters see Smyth, Sobolev, and Soboleva, 2013.
55 Greene, 2014.
56 Colton, 2008, p. 307.

3 Historical memory, language, and citizenship

1 Kasianov, 2022a; Portnov, 2013.
2 Korrespondent.net, June 28, 2002. https://korrespondent.net/world/worldabus/49545-izvestiya-vokrug-rossijsko-ukrainskih-uchebnikov-razrazilsya-skandal
3 Maidan-Inform, November 6, 2002. https://maidan.org.ua//arch/hist/1023814416.html
4 NewsRu, November 14, 2008. https://www.newsru.com/russia/14nov2008/history.html
5 Kasianov, 2010, p. 35.
6 Klymenko, 2016.
7 December 14, 2007 statement by the Russian Foreign Ministry. https://mid.ru/ru/foreign_policy/news/1644533/
8 Klymenko, 2016, p. 354.

9 Rating Group poll, November 21, 2012. https://ratinggroup.ua/research/ukraine/priznanie_golodomora_rezultaty_poslednih_issledovaniy.html
10 Newsru.com, November 14, 2008. https://www.newsru.com/russia/14nov2008/history.html
11 Kasianov, 2022b.
12 Malinova, 2017, pp. 45–46.
13 Kasianov, 2022b.
14 Shevel, 2011b, pp. 151–152.
15 Ukrainska Pravda, January 17, 2008. https://www.pravda.com.ua/articles/2008/01/17/3351003/
16 Koposov, 2017, pp. 267–268.
17 Felgenhauer, 2009.
18 Ibid.
19 Kasianov, 2022a, pp. 371–372.
20 Ibid., pp. 373–374.
21 Riabchuk, 2012, p. 445.
22 Motyl, 2010.
23 Korrespondent.net, April 27, 2010. https://korrespondent.net/ukraine/politics/1071204-yanukovich-golodomor-nelzya-priznavat-genocidom-ukraincev
24 Ukrainska Pravda, August 26, 2010. https://www.pravda.com.ua/rus/articles/2010/08/26/5332444/
25 Shevel, 2011b, p. 154.
26 Ibid., p. 154.
27 Kasianov, 2022a, pp. 378–381.
28 Lytvyn as quoted in Dzerkalo Tyzhnia, October 2–8, 2004.
29 For analysis of citizenship policy-making in Ukraine from the late perestroika period see Shevel, 2011a, pp. 143–150.
30 Ibid., p. 146.
31 Ibid., p. 86.
32 Shevel, 2009, p. 290.
33 Zevelev, 2001, p. 137.
34 Tolz, 2001, pp. 254–255; Zevelev, 2001, pp. 132–142.
35 Poll results on the dual citizenship question in Golovakha, et al., 2011, p. 13.
36 Shevel, 2009, p. 282.
37 Zevelev, 2021, p. 21.
38 Grigas, 2016, p. 93.
39 Royal United Services Institute (RUSI), May 1, 2020. https://rusi.org/explore-our-research/publications/commentary/russias-policy-passport-proliferation
40 Luzhkov as quoted in Korrespondent.net, April 28, 2001.
41 Golovakha, et al., 2011, p. 33.
42 Ibid.
43 Arel, 1995, p. 604.
44 Ibid.
45 Shulman, 2005, p. 39.
46 Fournier, 2002.
47 Arel, 1996, p. 77.
48 OSCE High Commissioner on National Minorities, 2001.
49 Shulman, 2005, p. 40.

50 Duma resolution No. 596-III, July 19, 2000. https://duma.consultant.ru/documents/659504?items=1andpage=3
51 RIA Novosti, December 17, 2002. https://ria.ru/20021217/283504.html
52 Gramota.ru, n.d. http://www.gramota.ru/lenta/news/8_1128
53 Podrobytsi.ua, November 8, 2006. https://podrobnosti.ua/365437-lavrov-u-ukrainy-i-rossii-dve-problemy-golodomor-i-jazyki.html
54 Czernicsko and Fedinec, 2016, p. 573.
55 Arel, 2018, p. 251. Also see Moser, 2013.
56 Venice Commission's Opinion on the draft law on languages in Ukraine. Opinion No. 605/2010, March 25–26, 2011.

4 Ukraine, Russia, and the West

1 Colton, 2008.
2 Reddaway and Glinsky, 2001.
3 Fukuyama, 2006.
4 Sakwa, 2018.
5 Radchenko, 2020; Sarotte, 2021.
6 Mearsheimer, 2014.
7 Radchenko, et al., 2020.
8 Smolenski and Dutkiewicz, 2022.
9 Popova and Shevel, 2022.
10 Plokhy, 2014, p. 46.
11 Ibid., p. 49.
12 Plokhy, 2014, pp. 49–50.
13 George H.W. Bush speech, August 1, 1991 https://en.wikisource.org/wiki/Chicken_Kiev_speech
14 Plokhy, 2014, p. 173.
15 Ibid., pp. 173–177.
16 Ibid., p. 171.
17 Ibid., p. 179.
18 D'Anieri, 2019, p. 33.
19 Ibid., p. 34.
20 Ibid., 2019, p. 35.
21 Bukkvoll, 2001.
22 Freeland quoted in D'Anieri, 2019, p. 54.
23 D'Anieri, 2019, p. 41.
24 Ibid., p. 53.
25 Charter of the Commonwealth of Independent States, January 22, 1993. https://treaties.un.org/doc/Publication/UNTS/Volume%201819/volume-1819-I-31139-English.pdf
26 D'Anieri, 2019, p. 35.
27 Dawisha and Parrot cited in Darden, 2009, p. 165.
28 Johnson, 2000, p. 285.
29 D'Anieri, 2019, p. 36.
30 Kuzio, 2022, p. 139.
31 Burant, 1995.
32 Budjeryn, 2022.
33 Sarotte, 2021, pp. 158–160 and 200–203.

34 *RTE*, April 4, 2023. https://www.rte.ie/news/primetime/2023/0404/1374162-clinton-ukraine/
35 Kuzio cited in D'Anieri, 2019, p. 89.
36 Bukkvoll, 2001, p. 1152.
37 Poll results in Tolz 2001, p. 264.
38 Balmaceda, 1998.
39 D'Anieri, 2019, p. 94.
40 Yekelchyk, 2005, p. 202.
41 Sarotte, 2021.
42 Bukkvoll, 2004.
43 Socor, 2018.
44 *The Ukrainian Weekly*, November 2, 2003. http://ukrweekly.com/archive/2003/The_Ukrainian_Weekly_2003-44.pdf, p. 2
45 Radio Free Europe/Radio Liberty, February 21, 2005 https://www.rferl.org/a/1057583.html
46 Politico.eu, February 23, 2005. https://www.politico.eu/article/ukraine-could-join-the-eu-by-2011-says-yushchenko/
47 Larrabee, 2007.
48 Association Agreement between the European Union and Ukraine. https://www.kmu.gov.ua/en/yevropejska-integraciya/ugoda-pro-asociacyu
49 Golovakha, et al., 2011, p. 13.
50 Ibid., pp. 48–49.
51 Decree of President of Ukraine no. 105/2007, February 12, 2007. https://www.zakon2.rada.gov.ua/laws/show/105/2007
52 Mearsheimer, 2014.
53 Gretskiy, 2013.
54 Obkom, June 5, 2008. http://obkom.net.ua/news/2008-06-05/1140.shtml
55 *New York Times*, November 30, 2008. https://www.nytimes.com/2008/11/30/world/europe/30ukraine.html
56 Pothier, 2017, p. 74.
57 Pifer, 2019.
58 Wolczuk, 2005, p. 3.
59 D'Anieri, 2019.
60 Balmaceda, 2013.
61 *Tashkent Times*, January 17, 2023. http://tashkenttimes.uz/national/10383-former-vice-president-of-gazprombank-on-how-russia-is-putting-neighbors-on-a-gas-needle
62 Dragneva-Lewers and Wolczuk, 2015.
63 Marples, 2017.
64 Deutche Welle, May 4, 2010. https://www.dw.com/en/ukraine-scraps-nato-accession-plans/a-5434301
65 BBC, June 3, 2010. https://www.bbc.com/news/10229626
66 Golovakha, et al., 2011, p. 13.
67 D'Anieri, 2019, pp. 195–201.
68 Sherr, 2010.
69 *Glavred*, May 17, 2010. https://glavred.info/stars/175010-medvedev-rasskazal-kak-soskuchilsya-i-poradovalsya-dozhdyu.html
70 Bunce, 1999.

71 Herrera, 2005.
72 Beissinger, 2002.
73 Neumann, 1993.
74 Hill, 2018, pp. 29–31.
75 Kydd, 2007.
76 Schulte, 1997.
77 NATO–Russia Founding Act. May 15, 1997. https://1997-2001.state.gov/regions/eur/fs_nato_whitehouse.html
78 Kostadinova, 2000.
79 Kasekamp, 2020.
80 Radnitz, 2021.
81 Kydd, forthcoming.
82 Epstein, 2005.
83 Lanoszka, 2023.
84 Sarotte, 2021, p. 160.
85 Ibid., pp. 158–159.
86 https://twitter.com/francis_scarr/status/1580066665353519104?s=20
87 Prime Minister of the Russian Federation, August 29, 2008. http://archive.premier.gov.ru/eng/events/news/1758/

5 Euromaidan, Crimea annexation, and the war in Donbas

1 Association Agreement between the European Union and Ukraine. https://eur-lex.europa.eu/eli/agree_internation/2014/295/2022-10-25
2 Wilson, 2014, pp. 54–55.
3 Ibid., p. 64.
4 *Guardian*, September 22, 2013. https://www.theguardian.com/world/2013/sep/22/ukraine-european-union-trade-russia
5 *Guardian*, December 18, 2013. https://www.theguardian.com/world/2013/dec/17/ukraine-russia-leaders-talks-kremlin-loan-deal
6 Wynnyckyj, 2019, p. 54.
7 February 3, 2014 poll by Ilko Kucheriv Democratic Initiatives Foundation and KIIS. https://dif.org.ua/en/article/maidan-december-and-maidan-february-what-has-changed
8 Ibid.
9 Wilson, 2014, p. 68.
10 Wynnyckyj, 2019, pp. 88–89.
11 Wilson, 2014, p. 75.
12 Radio Free Europe/Radio Liberty, January 24, 2014. https://www.rferl.org/a/ukraine-activists-automaidan/25241507.html
13 Civic Solidarity, January 20, 2014. https://www.civicsolidarity.org/article/880/ukraine-brief-legal-analysis-dictatorship-law
14 Wilson, 2014, p. 81.
15 Popova, 2014, p. 68.
16 As quoted in Wilson, 2014, p. 82.
17 Ibid., pp. 82–84.
18 Popova, 2014, p. 66.
19 Wilson, 2014, p. 85.
20 D'Anieri, 2019, p. 217.

21 Wilson, 2014, p. 84.
22 Reuters, February 18, 2014. https://www.reuters.com/article/us-ukraine/ukraine-police-charge-protesters-after-nations-bloodiest-day-idUSBREA1G0OU20140218
23 Wilson, 2014, p. 89.
24 Reuters, February 18, 2014. https://www.reuters.com/article/uk-ukraine/ukraine-police-charge-protesters-after-nations-bloodiest-day-idUKBREA1H0EM20140218
25 Wilson, 2014, p. 87.
26 Ukrainska Pravda, February 19, 2014. https://www.pravda.com.ua/news/2014/02/19/7014963/
27 Wilson, 2014, p. 88.
28 *Guardian*, February 21, 2014. https://www.theguardian.com/world/2014/feb/20/ukraine-dead-protesters-police
29 July 2016 UN High Commissioner for Human Rights report cited in D'Anieri, 2019, p. 219.
30 Ukrainska Pravda, February 20, 2014. https://www.pravda.com.ua/news/2014/02/20/7015164/
31 Ukrainska Pravda, February 20, 2014. https://www.pravda.com.ua/news/2014/02/20/7015330/
32 Way, 2015, p. 85.
33 Wilson, 2014, p. 71.
34 Popova, 2014, p. 69.
35 Wilson, 2014, p. 90.
36 BBC, February 7, 2014. https://www.bbc.com/news/world-europe-26079957
37 Powell and Thyne, 2011.
38 Wilson, 2014, p. 151.
39 Kramer n.d.
40 While here we use the 2001 census data to illustrate the relative share of Russian-speakers in different southeastern regions, as we discuss in Chapter 1, some of those who on the census listed Ukrainian as their native language speak mainly or even exclusively Russian in their daily lives, so as a matter of linguistic practice, nationwide as well as in the southeast, the share of Russian-speakers has been higher than the share of those identifying Russian as their native language on the census.
41 Wilson, 2014, p. 104.
42 Wilson, 1998.
43 Sasse, 2007.
44 Hylton, 2014.
45 Wilson, 2014, p. 105.
46 Arel and Driscoll, 2023, p. 60.
47 Stern, 1994.
48 Wilson, 2014, p. 123.
49 International Republican Institute, Baltic Surveys Ltd., and Rating Group Ukraine poll, May 16–30, 2013. https://www.iri.org/wp-content/uploads/2013/10/201320October20720Survey20of20Crimean20Public20Opinion2C20May2016-302C202013.pdf
50 January–February 2014 KIIS poll: https://kiis.com.ua/?lang=eng&cat=reports&id=231&page=1

51 Malyarenko and Galbreath, 2013.
52 Risch, 2021, p. 16.
53 Arel and Driscoll, 2023, p. 62.
54 Ibid., p. 64.
55 Risch, 2021, p. 17.
56 International Republican Institute, Baltic Surveys Ltd., and Rating Group Ukraine poll, May 16–30, 2013. https://www.iri.org/wp-content/uploads/2013/10/201320October20720Survey20of20Crimean20Public20Opinion2C20May2016-302C202013.pdf
57 Risch, 2021, p. 10.
58 Arel and Driscoll, 2023, p. 82.
59 Risch, 2021.
60 Risch, 2021, p. 25; Giuliano, 2018.
61 January–February 2014 KIIS poll. https://kiis.com.ua/?lang=eng&cat=reports&id=231&page=1
62 Giuliano, 2018, p. 166.
63 Wilson, 2014, p. 110.
64 Arel and Driscoll, 2023, p. 109.
65 Ibid., p. 110.
66 Ibid., p. 114.
67 D'Anieri, 2019, p. 231.
68 Wilson, 2014, p. 113.
69 Ibid., p. 113.
70 Arel and Driscoll, 2023, p. 129.
71 Nitsova, 2021, p. 1845.
72 We use the term rebels rather than separatists to refer to the actors who used force to press demands against the central government. While many of these demands were separatist in nature, the term rebel is still preferable since it captures both the fact that the rebels used force and that the scope of their demands was initially very broad, cacophonic in nature, and not immediately related to separation.
73 Arel and Driscoll, 2023, ch. 6.
74 Ibid., p. 151.
75 Yekelchyk, 2015, p. 144.
76 KIIS poll, April 8–16, 2014. https://dif.org.ua/en/article/opinions-and-views-of-the-citizens-of-southern-and-eastern-regions-of-ukraine-april-2014
77 For analysis of fears and grievances of protesters see Giuliano, 2018; for economic motivations of protests see Zhukov, 2016; for state weakness as an enabling factor see Kudelia, 2014; for the role of local elites see Nitsova, 2021; for the role of Russia see Mitrokhin, 2015; on the agency of street actors see Arel and Driscoll, 2023.
78 Voice of America, January 25, 2023. https://www.voanews.com/a/european-rights-court-rules-dutch-ukraine-cases-against-russia-are-admissible-/6933459.html
79 Vzgliad, March 20, 2014. https://vz.ru/news/2014/3/20/678180.html
80 Reuters, March 17, 2014. https://www.reuters.com/article/ukraine-crisis-group/russia-proposes-international-support-group-on-ukraine-idUSL6N0ME23L20140317
81 Ministry of Foreign Affairs of Ukraine, March 17, 2014. https://mfa.gov.ua/en/news/19760-zajava-mzs-ukrajini

82 Interfax, March 30, 2014. https://www.interfax.ru/russia/368227
83 *Euromaidan Press*, May 16, 2019. https://euromaidanpress.com/2019/05/16/glazyev-tapes-continued-ukraine-presents-new-details-of-russian-takeover-of-crimea-and-financing-of-separatism/
84 Laruelle, 2015b, p. 3.
85 Shandra and Seely, 2019, pp. 53–63.
86 Luhansk was the only exception, but there the local council adopted a radical resolution only *after* armed militants had seized government buildings and pressured the council to pass it. Arel and Driscoll, 2023, 138–139.
87 Ibid.
88 *Economist*, February 21, 2023. https://www.economist.com/briefing/2023/02/21/the-war-is-making-ukraine-a-western-country?
89 D'Anieri, 2019, p. 235; Euractiv, January 30, 2022. https://www.euractiv.com/section/europe-s-east/news/dispatches-from-the-donbas-whats-next-in-ukraines-forever-war/
90 D'Anieri, 2019, p. 245.
91 Ibid.
92 Arel and Driscoll, 2023, p. 168.
93 D'Anieri, 2019, p. 247.
94 Minsk-1 Agreement, September 8, 2014. https://peacemaker.un.org/UA-ceasefire-2014.
95 Minsk-2 Agreement, February 12, 2015. https://www.osce.org/ru/cio/140221. The Minsk-2 agreement was endorsed by United Nations Security Council Resolution 2202 on February 17, 2015.
96 D'Anieri, 2019, p. 249.
97 Allan, 2020.
98 Åtland, 2020.
99 Jacobin, February 13, 2023. https://jacobin.com/2023/02/wolfgang-sporrer-interview-ukraine-war-diplomacy-minsk-agreements

6 The road to full-scale invasion

1 Ukrainska Pravda, May 21, 2015. https://www.pravda.com.ua/news/2015/05/21/7068635/
2 Shevel, 2015.
3 Ibid.
4 OSCE International Election Observation Mission, May 25, 2014. https://www.osce.org/files/f/documents/1/0/119078.pdf
5 Shevel, 2016b.
6 Viatrovych, 2015.
7 Shevel, 2016a; Zhurzhenko 2022
8 Baumann, 2022.
9 Viola, 2022.
10 Berman, 2016.
11 Shevel, 2016a, p. 261.
12 Kononczuk, 2018.
13 Himka, 2015; Human Rights in Ukraine, December 21, 2015. https://khpg.org/en/1450571329
14 Human Rights in Ukraine, October 28, 2019. https://khpg.org/en/1572221946

15 *Media Sapiens*, October 9, 2015. https://ms.detector.media/print/14371/
16 Shevel, 2016b.
17 Kovalov, 2022.
18 Poll results from Rating Group and Razumkov Center/Democratic Initiatives Foundation in Kasianov, 2023, p. 14.
19 *TASS*, May 19, 2015. https://tass.com/world/795614
20 Koposov, 2017, pp. 291–292.
21 International Federation for Human Rights, 2021, pp. 10, 13–14, 16–17.
22 Ibid., p. 6, 15.
23 Wasyliw, 2007.
24 President of Ukraine, September 20, 2018, https://www.president.gov.ua/videos/poslannya-prezidenta-ukrayini-do-verhovnoyi-radi-ukrayini-pr-1006
25 Plokhy, 2017, p. 330.
26 *Economist*, September 9, 2019. https://www.economist.com/erasmus/2019/09/09/taking-sides-in-the-orthodox-churchs-battles-over-russia-and-ukraine
27 Religious Information Service of Ukraine (RISU), October 14, 2018. https://risu.ua/en/russian-security-council-discusses-the-situation-of-russian-orthodox-church-in-ukraine_n93708
28 https://twitter.com/Biz_Ukraine_Mag/status/1619840575045525504/photo/1
29 Bremer, 2016.
30 LB.ua, March 9, 2015. https://lb.ua/society/2015/05/08/304358_predstaviteli_upts_mp_vstali.html
31 Rating Group poll, July 23–25, 2021. https://ratinggroup.ua/research/ukraine/obschestvenno-politicheskie_nastroeniya_naseleniya_23-25_iyulya_2021.html
32 For analysis of the many complexities of Ukrainian Orthodox politics and religious identities, such as prevalence of "just Orthodox" not identifying with any of the competing Orthodox Churches, strong institutional presence of the UOC-MP in central and western Ukraine, traditionally more religious than eastern and southern regions, and differences between UOC-MP leadership, most of whom remain committed to continued union with ROC, and the low-level priests and many parishioners, many of whom have pro-Ukrainian political views, see the following studies: Clark and Vovk, 2020; Krawchuk and Bremer, 2016; Metreveli, 2019; Plokhy and Sysyn, 2003; Wanner, 2020; 2022.
33 KIIS poll, July 6–20, 2022. https://www.kiis.com.ua/?lang=ukrandcat=reportsandid=1129andpage=5
34 Grigas, 2016, p. 87.
35 Human Rights in Ukraine, March 27, 2019. https://khpg.org/en/1553612958
36 Kulyk, 2019.
37 Rating Group poll, March 19, 2022. https://ratinggroup.ua/research/ukraine/language_issue_in_ukraine_march_19th_2022.html
38 Dzerkalo Tyzhnia, July 14, 2017. https://zn.ua/ukr/SOCIUM/ukrayinizaciyi-boyatsya-ne-gromadyani-a-vlada-248439_.html
39 Onuch and Hale, 2023.
40 Sereda, 2023.
41 Popova, 2014.
42 Popova and Beers, 2020.
43 Ibid.
44 Popova, 2020.

45 Popova and Beers, 2020.
46 Ibid.
47 Zaloznaya and Reisinger, 2020.
48 47 Infosapiens Survey, April 1, 2021. https://newjustice.org.ua/wp-content/uploads/2021/06/2021_Survey_Population_Report_ENG.pdf, p. 4
49 Bezruk, 2019.
50 Human Rights in Ukraine, January 27, 2020. https://khpg.org/en/1579909440
51 Popova and Beers, 2020.
52 Marat, 2018.
53 Kovalchuk, et al., 2019.
54 Kaleniuk and Halushka, 2021.
55 Cherviatsova, 2021.
56 Klymenko Time, November 1, 2020. https://klymenko-time.com/novosti/zelenskij-o-reshenii-ksu-demarsh-zagovor-staryh-elit-i-cherti-iz-politicheskogo-ada/
57 https://twitter.com/dkaleniuk/status/1321712758216368128
58 Channell-Justice, 2020.
59 Cherviatsova, 2021.
60 Kyiv Post, May 26, 2021. https://archive.kyivpost.com/ukraine-politics/prosecutors-send-case-against-constitutional-court-head-to-trial.html
61 Ukrainska Pravda, May 26, 2022. https://www.pravda.com.ua/rus/news/2022/05/26/7348760/
62 Kyiv Post, July 14, 2021. https://archive.kyivpost.com/ukraine-politics/supreme-court-overturns-dismissal-of-tupitsky-from-constitutional-court.html
63 Bader, 2020, pp. 261–263.
64 Barbieri, 2020, p. 226.
65 Aasland and Lyska, 2020.
66 Szostek, 2014.
67 Reuters, August 19, 2014. https://www.reuters.com/article/us-ukraine-crisis-television-idUSKBN0GJ1QM20140819
68 Radio Free Europe/Radio Liberty, March 11, 2014. https://www.rferl.org/a/ukrainian-tv-channels-off-the-air/25293466.html; *Guardian*, April 27, 2014. https://www.theguardian.com/world/2014/apr/27/ukraine-donetsk-pro-russian-forces-seize-tv-station-parade-captives; Radio Free Europe/Radio Liberty, June 21, 2022. https://www.rferl.org/a/russia-broadcasting-ukraine-kherson/31907822.html
69 Peisakhin and Rozenas, 2021.
70 Golovchenko, 2022.
71 Erlich, 2021.
72 Erlich, 2023.
73 Forbes, December 16, 2022. https://www.forbes.com/sites/davidaxe/2022/12/16/ukraine-deradicalized-its-extremist-troops-now-they-might-be-preparing-a-counteroffensive/?
74 Gomza, 2022.
75 France24, November 26, 2018. https://www.france24.com/en/20181126-ukraine-president-poroshenko-martial-law-russia
76 Colborne, 2018.

77 NBC News, December 29, 2018. https://www.nbcnews.com/news/world/ukraine-s-martial-law-over-there-s-no-end-sight-n952211
78 Ibid.
79 Dickinson, 2021.
80 Ibid.
81 Ukraine Crisis Media Center, May 14, 2021. https://uacrisis.org/en/court-places-medvedchuk
82 KIIS poll, October, 17–24, 2020. https://www.kiis.com.ua/materials/pr/20201011_soc-politic/polit_orient_oct%202020.pdf
83 *Financial Times*, February 22, 2023. https://www.ft.com/content/80002564-33e8-48fb-b734-44810afb7a49
84 Politico, January 19, 2022. https://www.politico.eu/article/court-decline-jail-poroshenko-treason-case/
85 Infosapiens survey, Apil 1, 2021. https://refubium.fu-berlin.de/bitstream/handle/fub188/21891/EU-STRAT-Working-Paper-No-6.pdf?sequence=1, p. 8.
86 Deutche Welle, September 16, 2014. https://www.dw.com/en/ukraine-ratifies-eu-association-agreement/a-17925681
87 Petrov, 2018, p. 51.
88 Wolczuk, et al., 2017, p. 17.
89 Deutche Welle, September 16, 2014. https://www.dw.com/en/russia-west-delay-key-element-of-eu-ukraine-trade-deal/a-17922830
90 Reuters, March 18, 2014. https://www.reuters.com/article/uk-ukraine-crisis-nato-idUKBREA2H0DO20140318
91 Radio Free Europe/Radio Liberty, December 23, 2014. https://www.rferl.org/a/ukraine-parliament-abandons-neutrality/26758725.html
92 Radio Free Europe/Radio Liberty, February 19, 2019. https://www.rferl.org/a/ukraine-president-signs-constitutional-amendment-on-nato-eu-membership/29779430.html
93 NATO, June 2, 2023. https://www.nato.int/cps/en/natohq/topics_37750.htm
94 Lanoszka and Becker, 2022.
95 Policy Commons, September 30, 2021. https://policycommons.net/artifacts/1898006/making-ukraine-a-nato-member-in-all-but-name/2649141/
96 Blakkisrud, 2016, 2022; Kuzio, 2022.
97 Knott, 2017.
98 Grigas, 2016, pp. 120–121. After 2002 Russia also engaged in massive passportization in South Ossetia and Abkhazia in Georgia. Four years later, according to Russian official statistics, the proportion of Russian citizens in Abkhazia increased from 30% to 80%, and in South Ossetia from 40% to 90%. In 2008, Putin would use passportization as a pretext to invade Georgia – to defend Russian citizens.
99 Rossiiskaia gazeta, September 23, 2014. https://rg.ru/2014/09/22/migranty-site.html
100 Burkhardt, 2020, pp. 1–2.
101 Gazeta.ru, April 24, 2020. https://www.gazeta.ru/social/news/2020/04/24/n_14335717.shtml?updated
102 Zevelev, 2021, p. 25.
103 Burkhardt, 2020, p. 4.
104 There were virtually no independent surveys carried out in occupied Donbas after

2014. Two such surveys carried out in 2019 and in 2021 found that until 2019, before Russian passportization started, a majority (55%) preferred a future within Ukraine, but by 2021 over half wanted to join Russia. O'Loughlin, et al., 2021.

105 AP News, July 11, 2021. https://apnews.com/article/russia-ukraine-terrorism-kharkiv-e334e4b79637a30a0856617c8ee9f390

106 Ministry of Foreign Affairs of Ukraine, July 11, 2022. https://mfa.gov.ua/en/news/zayava-mzs-ukrayini-shchodo-ukazu-prezidenta-rf-pro-sproshchenij-poryadok-nadannya-rosijskogo-gromadyanstva-dlya-gromadyan-ukrayini

107 Zhurzhenko, 2023.

108 Balzer, 2015.

109 Hale, 2018; Hale, 2022.

110 Meduza, October 1, 2022. https://meduza.io/video/2022/10/01/v-2014-godu-posle-prisoedineniya-kryma-putin-uveryal-chto-rossiya-ne-budet-anneksirovat-novye-territorii-ukrainy-vot-kak-eto-bylo

111 Dougherty, 2014.

112 Reuters, April 22, 2014. https://www.reuters.com/article/russia-vkontakte-ceo-idINL6N0NE1HS20140422

113 Reuters, June 5, 2017. https://www.reuters.com/article/us-ukraine-crisis-russia-library-idUSKBN18W12T

114 *Washington Post*, July 22, 2014. https://www.washingtonpost.com/news/worldviews/wp/2014/07/22/meanwhile-in-russia-putin-passes-law-against-protests/

115 Taylor, 2018.

116 Greene and Robertson, 2019; Sharafutdinova, 2020.

117 Pomeranz and Smyth, 2021, pp. 1–5.

118 Pomeranz, 2021.

119 Goode, 2021.

120 Gel'man, 2021.

121 Radio Free Europe/Radio Liberty, April 29, 2005. https://www.rferl.org/a/1058688.html

122 Reuters, April 28, 2021. https://www.reuters.com/world/europe/bulgaria-sees-possible-russian-involvement-munitions-depot-blasts-2021-04-28/

123 Radio Free Europe/Radio Liberty, April 18, 2021. https://www.rferl.org/a/czech-republic-russia-depot-blast-gallery-expulsions/31209726.html

124 *Guardian*, June 23, 2020. https://www.theguardian.com/world/2020/jun/23/skripal-salisbury-poisoning-decline-of-russia-spy-agencies-gru

125 Politico, May 5, 2021. https://www.politico.eu/article/enough-warnings-europe-must-act-on-russian-killings/

126 Radio Free Europe/Radio Liberty, October 2, 2019. https://www.rferl.org/a/what-is-the-steinmeier-formula-and-did-zelenskiy-just-capitulate-to-moscow-/30195593.html

127 Rating Group poll, January 22–26, 2020. http://ratinggroup.ua/en/research/ukraine/obschestvenno-politicheskie_nastroeniya_naseleniya_22-26_yanvarya_2020_goda.html

128 Razumkov Center poll, February 13–17, 2020. https://razumkov.org.ua/napriamky/sotsiologichni-doslidzhennia/gromadska-dumka-pro-sytuatsiiu-na-donbasi-ta-shliakhy-vidnovlennia-suverenitetu-ukrainy-nad-okupovanymy-terytoriiamy-liutyi-2020r?

129 Arel and Driscoll, 2023, p. 189.
130 Deutche Welle, February 3, 2015. https://www.dw.com/en/ukraine-in-appeal-for-international-peacekeeping-force/a-18289480
131 Grono and Brunson, 2018.
132 Ukrinform, December 13, 2019. https://www.ukrinform.ua/rubric-ato/2837221-avakov-ne-viklucae-spilnih-patruliv-policii-z-predstavnikami-ordlo.html
133 Ukrainska Pravda, February 9, 2023. https://www.pravda.com.ua/news/2023/02/9/7388717/
134 *New York Times*, May 5, 2021. https://www.nytimes.com/2021/05/05/us/politics/bidenputin-russia-ukraine.html
135 Article by President Putin "On the historical unity of Russians and Ukrainians," July 12, 2021. http://en.kremlin.ru/events/president/news/66181
136 Pifer, 2021.
137 *Washington Post*, August 16, 2022. https://www.washingtonpost.com/national-security/interactive/2022/ukraine-road-to-war/
138 Ibid.

Conclusion

1 Rating Group, February 21, 2023. https://ratinggroup.ua/en/research/ukraine/kompleksne_dosl_dzhennya_yak_v_yna_zm_nila_mene_ta_kra_nu_p_dsumki_roku.html
2 Ukrainska Pravda, February 13, 2023. https://www.pravda.com.ua/news/2023/02/13/7389111/
3 January 2023 NDI/KIIS poll. https://kiis.com.ua/materials/pr/20230223_6/January_2023_Ukraine_wartime_survey_UKR.pdf
4 May 2022 KIIS poll: https://www.kiis.com.ua/?lang=ukr&cat=reports&id=1112&page=6; July 2022 KIIS poll: https://www.kiis.com.ua/?lang=rus&cat=reports&id=1127&page=1
5 *Euromaidan Press*, February 28, 2023. https://euromaidanpress.com/2023/02/28/what-language-is-the-default-in-ukraine-by-all-means-ukrainian/
6 Bill 8371 Supreme Rada of Ukraine, January 19, 2023. https://itd.rada.gov.ua/billInfo/Bills/Card/41219
7 March–April 2023 KIIS poll. https://kiis.com.ua/?lang=ukr&cat=reports&id=1247&page=1
8 Council of Europe, July 18, 2022. https://www.coe.int/en/web/istanbul-convention/-/ukraine-ratifies-the-istanbul-convention
9 January 2023 KIIS poll. https://kiis.com.ua/materials/pr/20230223_6/January_2023_Ukraine_wartime_survey_UKR.pdf, p. 15.
10 *Guardian*, June 5, 2023. https://www.theguardian.com/world/2023/jun/05/war-brings-urgency-to-fight-for-lgbt-rights-in-ukraine
11 January 2023 KIIS poll. https://kiis.com.ua/materials/pr/20230223_6/January_2023_Ukraine_wartime_survey_UKR.pdf
12 Official Website of Ukraine, March 3, 2023. https://war.ukraine.ua/articles/ukraine-s-road-to-eu-recent-updates-and-future-steps/
13 Kyiv Independent, July 29, 2022. https://kyivindependent.com/explainer-whos-ukraines-new-anti-corruption-prosecutor-and-will-he-deliver-results/
14 RBK-Ukraine, December 8, 2022. https://www.rbc.ua/rus/news/vaks-obrav-zapobizhniy-zahid-eks-glavi-natsbanku-1670516590.html

15 Summer 2022 USAID poll: https://engage.org.ua/eng/cep-2022-surge-in-civic-activism-overwhelming-support-to-resisting-the-enemy-and-fundamental-shift-in-perceiving-corruption/
16 Ibid.
17 De Jure Foundation, December 15, 2022. https://en.dejure.foundation/tpost/pls00yu0d1-we-call-on-the-president-to-veto-the-law
18 De Jure Foundation, December 7, 2022. https://en.dejure.foundation/tpost/rvk2ymb4s1-politically-loyal-composition-of-the-con
19 Center for Democracy and Rule of Law, July 21, 2022. https://cedem.org.ua/en/news/4365-gromadskyh-ta-blagodijnyh/
20 April 2022, Rating Group poll, https://ratinggroup.ua/research/ukraine/vosmoy_obschenacionalnyy_opros_ukraina_v_usloviyah_voyny_6_aprelya_2022.html
21 September 2022, Ilko Kucheriv Democratic Initiatives Foundation poll: https://dif.org.ua/en/article/dovira-do-derzhavi-yak-zberegti-natsionalnu-ednist-zaradi-peremogi
22 Radio Free Europe/Radio Liberty, May 14, 2022. https://www.rferl.org/a/ukraine-law-bans-pro-russia-parties-zelenskiy-signs/31849737.html
23 October–November 2022 Razumkov Centre poll: https://razumkov.org.ua/napriamky/sotsiologichni-doslidzhennia/otsinka-gromadianamy-sytuatsii-v-krainidovira-do-sotsialnykh-instytutiv-politykoideologichni-oriientatsii-gromadian-ukrainy-v-umovakh-rosiiskoi-agresii-veresen-zhovten-2022r
24 Ibid.
25 Ukrainska Pravda, March 15, 2023. https://www.pravda.com.ua/news/2023/03/15/7393584/
26 October–November Razumkov Centre poll: https://razumkov.org.ua/napriamky/sotsiologichni-doslidzhennia/otsinka-gromadianamy-sytuatsii-v-krainidovira-do-sotsialnykh-instytutiv-politykoideologichni-oriientatsii-gromadian-ukrainy-v-umovakh-rosiiskoi-agresii-veresen-zhovten-2022r
27 Politico.eu, January 23, 2023. https://www.politico.eu/article/defense-minister-reznikov-ukraine-corruption-probe-war-russia-zelenskyy/
28 Radio Free Europe/Radio Liberty, January 3, 2023. https://www.rferl.org/a/ukraine-investigation-road-reconstruction-fbi-dnipropetrovsk-public-funds/32205244.html
29 Reuters, March 20, 2022. https://www.reuters.com/world/europe/citing-martial-law-ukraine-president-signs-decree-combine-national-tv-channels-2022-03-20/
30 Espreso, January 13, 2023. https://espreso.tv/mizhnarodna-federatsiya-zhurnalistiv-zaklikae-ukrainskiy-uryad-pereglyanuti-noviy-zakon-pro-zmi
31 *Library of Congress*, April 4, 2022. https://www.loc.gov/item/global-legal-monitor/2022-04-04/ukraine-new-laws-criminalize-collaboration-with-an-aggressor-state/
32 *Guardian*, August 28, 2016. https://www.theguardian.com/world/2016/aug/28/britain-nazi-spies-mi5-second-world-war-german-executed
33 Mylonas and Radnitz, 2022.
34 Stoner, 2023.
35 Ibid.
36 *Guardian*, March 22, 2022. www.theguardian.com/world/2022/mar/22/alexei-navalny-13-years-more-jail-fraud

37 Radio Free Europe/Radio Liberty, December 9, 2022. https://www.rferl.org/a/russia-yashin-guilty-prison-ukraine-discrediting-armed-forces/32169294.html

38 Radio Liberty, April 10, 2023. https://www.svoboda.org/a/vladimir-kara-murza-vystupil-s-poslednim-slovom-v-sude/32357566.html

39 Re:Russia, April 7, 2023. https://re-russia.net/review/231/

40 *Washington Post*, April 5, 2022. https://www.washingtonpost.com/opinions/2022/04/05/russia-is-committing-genocide-in-ukraine/

41 *Time*, March 15, 2023. https://time.com/6262903/russia-ukraine-genocide-war-crimes/

42 *Russian Media Monitor*, April 7, 2023. https://www.youtube.com/watch?v=VMdvtbN7_Fc

43 Garner, 2022.

44 *Time*, February 15, 2023. https://time.com/6255183/ukraine-basement-yahidne-held-captive/

45 Cookman, 2022.

46 Reuters, December 14, 2022. https://www.reuters.com/world/europe/russians-mistreated-kherson-youngsters-childrens-cell-says-ukraine-official-2022-12-14/

47 *Guardian*, March 2, 2023. https://www.theguardian.com/world/2023/mar/02/kherson-torture-centres-were-planned-by-russian-state-say-lawyers

48 International Criminal Court, March 17, 2023. https://www.icc-cpi.int/news/situation-ukraine-icc-judges-issue-arrest-warrants-against-vladimir-vladimirovich-putin-and

49 Snegovaya and Petrov, 2022.

References

Aasland, A. and Lyska, O. (2020). Signs of progress: Local democracy developments in Ukrainian cities. In H. Shelest and M. Rabinovych (eds.), *Decentralization, Regional Diversity, and Conflict: The Case of Ukraine*. Palgrave.

Abdulatipov, R.G., Mikhailovskii, V.A., and Chichanovskii, A.A. (1997). *Natsional'naia politika Rossiiskoi Federatsii : ot kontseptsii k realizatsii*. Moskva: Slavianskii dialog.

Akturk, S. (2017). Post-imperial democracies and new projects of nationhood in Eurasia: Transforming the nation through migration in Russia and Turkey. *Journal of Ethnic and Migration Studies*, 43(7), 1101–1120.

Allan, D. (2020). The Minsk Conundrum: Western policy and Russia's war in eastern Ukraine. *Chatham House*.

Allison, G. (2002). Deepening Russian democracy: Progress and pitfalls in Putin's government. *Harvard International Review*, 24(2), 62–68.

Applebaum, A. (2017). *Red Famine: Stalin's War on Ukraine*. New York: Doubleday.

Arel, D. (1995). Language politics in independent Ukraine: Towards one or two state languages? *Nationalities Papers*, 23(3), 597–622.

Arel, D. (1996). A lurking cascade of assimilation in Kiev? *Post-Soviet Affairs*, 12(1), 73–90.

Arel, D. (2018). Language, status, and state loyalty in Ukraine. *Harvard Ukrainian Studies*, 35(1/4), 233–263.

Arel, D., and Driscoll, J. (2023). *Ukraine's Unnamed War: Before the Russian Invasion of 2022*. Cambridge University Press.

Åslund, A. (2007). *Russia's Capitalist Revolution: Why Market Reform Succeeded and Democracy Failed*. Peterson Institute for International Economics.

Åslund, A. (2009). *How Ukraine Became a Market Economy and Democracy*. Peterson Institute for International Economics.

Åslund, A. and McFaul, M. (2006). *Revolution in Orange: The Origins of Ukraine's Democratic Breakthrough*. Carnegie Endowment for International Peace

Åtland, K. (2020). Destined for deadlock? Russia, Ukraine, and the unfulfilled Minsk agreements. *Post-Soviet Affairs*, 36(2), 122–139.

Bader, M. (2020). Decentralization and a risk of local elite capture in Ukraine. In H. Shelest and M. Rabinovych (eds.), *Decentralization, Regional Diversity, and Conflict: The Case of Ukraine*. Palgrave.

Balmaceda, M. (1998). Gas, oil and the linkages between domestic and foreign policies: The case of Ukraine. *Europe–Asia Studies*, 50(2), 257–286.

Balmaceda, M. (2013). *The Politics of Energy Dependency: Ukraine, Belarus, and Lithuania between Domestic Oligarchs and Russian Pressure*. University of Toronto Press.

Balzer, H. (2015). The Ukraine invasion and public opinion. *Georgetown Journal of International Affairs*,16(1), 79–93.

Barbieri, J. (2020). The dark side of decentralization reform in Ukraine: Deterring or facilitating Russia-sponsored separatism? In H. Shelest and M. Rabinovych (eds.), *Decentralization, Regional Diversity, and Conflict: The Case of Ukraine*. Palgrave.

Barrington, L. (2022). A new look at region, language, ethnicity and civic national identity in Ukraine. *Europe–Asia Studies*, 74(3), 360–381.

Barrington, L. and Faranda, R. (2009). Reexamining region, ethnicity, and language in Ukraine. *Post-Soviet Affairs*, 25(3), 232–256.

Baumann, F. (2022). From war to war: Historical research on Ukraine since 2014. *Osteuropa*, 72(1–3), 309.

Beissinger, M. (2002). *Nationalist Mobilization and the Collapse of the Soviet State*. Cambridge University Press.

Berman, I. (2016). Closing the archives. What Russia's renewed secrecy says about Putin. *Foreign Affairs*.

Bezruk, T. (2019). Who ordered the murder of Katya Handziuk? A year without answers. *Open Democracy*.

Blakkisrud, H. (2016). Blurring the boundary between civic and ethnic: The Kremlin's new approach to national identity under Putin's third term. In P. Kolstø and H. Blakkisrud (eds.), *The New Russian Nationalism: Imperialism, Ethnicity and Authoritarianism, 2000–15* (pp. 249–274). Edinburgh University Press.

Blakkisrud, H. (2022). Russkii as the New Rossiiskii? Nation-building in Russia after 1991. *Nationalities Papers*.

Bremer, T. (2016). Religion in Ukraine: Historical background and the present situation. In A. Krawchuk and T. Bremer (eds.), *Churches in the Ukrainian Crisis* (pp. 3–19). Palgrave Macmillan.

Breslauer, G. and Dale, C. (1997). Boris Yeltsin and the invention of a Russian nation-state. *Post-Soviet Affairs*, 13(4), 303–332.

Brudny, Y. (2002). Politika identichnosti i post-kommunisticheskii vybor Rossii. *Polis* (1), 87–104.

Brudny, Y. and Finkel, E. (2011). Why Ukraine is not Russia: Hegemonic national identity and democracy in Russia and Ukraine. *East European Politics and Societies*, 25(4), 813–833.

Budjeryn, M. (2022). *Inheriting the Bomb: The Collapse of the USSR and the Nuclear Disarmament of Ukraine*. JHU Press.

Bukkvoll, T. (2001). Off the cuff politics – Explaining Russia's lack of a Ukraine strategy. *Europe–Asia Studies*, 53(8), 1141–1157.

Bukkvoll, T. (2004). Private interests, public policy: Ukraine and the Common Economic Space agreement. *Problems of Post-Communism*, 51(5), 11–22.

Bunce, V. (1999). *Subversive Institutions: The Design and the Destruction of Socialism and the State*. Cambridge University Press.

Burant, S. (1995). Foreign policy and national identity: A comparison of Ukraine and Belarus. *Europe–Asia Studies*, 47(7), 1125–1144.
Burkhardt, F. (2020). *Russia's "Passportisation" of the Donbas: The Mass Naturalisation of Ukrainians is More than a Foreign Policy Tool (SWP Comment, 41/2020)*. Berlin: Stiftung Wissenschaft und Politik [German Institute for International and Security Affairs].
Channell-Justice, E. (2020). Ukraine's Constitutional Court crisis, explained. *Ukrainian Research Institute of Harvard University*.
Channell-Justice, E. (2022). *Without the State: Self-Organization and Political Activism in Ukraine*. University of Toronto Press.
Cherviatsova, A. (2021). False dilemma: The president of Ukraine vs. the Constitutional Court. *Verfassungsblog*.
Chubais, I. (1998). *Rossiia v poiskakh sebia: kak my preodoleem ideinyi krizis*: Izd-vo NOK "Muzei bumagi."
Clark, E.A. and Vovk, D. (eds.) (2020). *Religion During the Russian Ukrainian Conflict*. Routledge.
Clover, C. (1999). Dreams of the Eurasian heartland. The reemergence of geopolitics. *Foreign Affairs*, 78.
Colborne, M. (2018). Martial law is a test. Will Ukraine's democracy pass? *Foreign Policy*, November 27.
Colton, T (2008). *Yeltsin: A Life*. Basic Books.
Cookman, L. (2022). Forest of the Dead. Another mass grave in Ukraine reveals the horrors of Russia's occupation. *Foreign Policy* September 19.
Coppedge, M., et al. (2023). V-Dem [Country-Year/Country-Date] Dataset v13. *Varieties of Democracy (V-Dem) Project*.
Czernicsko, I. and Fedinec, C. (2016). Four language laws of Ukraine. *International Journal on Minority and Group Rights*, 23(4), 560–582.
Darden, K. (2001). Blackmail as a tool of state domination: Ukraine under Kuchma. *East European Constitutional Review*, 10: 67.
Darden, K (2009). *Economic Liberalism and its Rivals: The Formation of International Institutions among the Post-Soviet States*. Cambridge University Press.
D'Anieri, P. (2003). Leonid Kuchma and the personalization of the Ukrainian presidency. *Problems of Post-Communism*, 50(5), 58–65.
D'Anieri, P. (2019). *Ukraine and Russia: From Civilized Divorce to Uncivil War*. Cambridge University Press.
Dickinson, P. (2021). Analysis: Ukraine bans Kremlin-linked TV channels. *Atlantic Council*, February 5.
Dougherty, J. (2014). Everyone lies: The Ukraine conflict and Russia's media transformation. Harvard Kennedy School Shorenstein Center on Media, Politics and Public Policy, Discussion Paper.
Dragneva-Lewers, R. and Wolczuk, K. (2015). *Ukraine Between the EU and Russia: The Integration Challenge*. Springer.
Dyczok, M. (2005). Breaking through the information blockade: Election and revolution in Ukraine 2004. *Canadian Slavonic Papers/Revue canadienne des slavistes* 47 (3–4), 241–266.
Emery, N., Ghodsee, K., and Orenstein, M. (2021). *Taking Stock of Shock Database*. University of Pennsylvania.
Epstein, R. A. (2005). NATO enlargement and the spread of democracy: Evidence and expectations. *Security Studies*, 14(1), 63–105.

Erlich, A., Garner, C., Pennycook, G., and Rand, D.G. (2023). Does analytic thinking insulate against pro-Kremlin disinformation? Evidence from Ukraine. *Political Psychology*, 44(1), 79–94.

Erlich, A. and Garner, C. (2023). Is pro-Kremlin disinformation effective? Evidence from Ukraine. *The International Journal of Press/Politics*, 28(1), 5–28.

Felgenhauer, P. (2009). Medvedev forms a commission to protect Russian history. *Eurasia Daily Monitor*, 6(98), 21.

Finkel, E. and Brudny, Y. (2014). Russia and the colour revolutions. In *Coloured Revolutions and Authoritarian Reactions* (pp. 23–44). Routledge.

Finnin, R. (2022). *Blood of Others: Stalin's Crimean Atrocity and the Poetics of Solidarity*. University of Toronto Press.

Fish, S. (2001). Ten years after the Soviet breakup: Putin's path. *Journal of Democracy* 12(4), 71–78.

Fish, S. (2005). *Democracy Derailed in Russia: The Failure of Open Politics*. Cambridge University Press.

Fournier, A. (2002). Mapping identities: Russian resistance to linguistic Ukrainisation in central and eastern Ukraine. *Europe–Asia Studies*, 54(3), 415–433.

Fukuyama, F. (2006). *The End of History and the Last Man*. Simon and Schuster.

Garner, I. (2022). "We've Got to Kill Them": Responses to Bucha on Russian social media groups. *Journal of Genocide Research*, 1–8.

Garner, I. (2023). *Generation Z. Into the Heart of Russia's Fascist Youth*. Oxford University Press.

Gellner, E. (1983). *Nations and Nationalism*. Cornell University Press.

Gel'man, V. (2021). Constitution, authoritarianism, and bad governance: The case of Russia. *Russian Politics*, 6(1), 71–90.

Giuliano, E. (2018). Who supported separatism in Donbas? Ethnicity and popular opinion at the start of the Ukraine crisis. *Post-Soviet Affairs*, 34(2), 158–178.

Giuliano, E. (2017). *Constructing Grievance: Ethnic Nationalism in Russia's Republics*. Cornell University Press.

Goehring, J. ed. (2007). *Nations in Transit 2007: Democratization from Central Europe to Eurasia*. Rowman and Littlefield.

Golovakha, E., Panina, N., and Parakhons'ka, O. (2011). *Ukrainian Society 1992–2010: Sociological Monitoring*. Kyiv: National Academy of Sciences of Ukraine, Institute of Sociology.

Golovchenko, Y. (2022). Fighting propaganda with censorship: A study of the Ukrainian ban on Russian social media. *Journal of Politics*, 84(2), 639–654.

Gomza, I. (2022). Too much ado about Ukrainian nationalists: The Azov Movement and the war in Ukraine. *Krytyka*.

Goode, J.P. (2021). Patriotic legitimation and everyday patriotism in Russia's constitutional reform. *Russian Politics*, 6(1), 112–129.

Gorenburg, D (2003). *Minority Ethnic Mobilization in the Russian Federation*. Cambridge University Press.

Graziosi, A. (2008). Why and in what sense was the Holodomor a genocide? In L. Luciuk and L. Grekul (eds.), *Holodomor: Reflections on the Great Famine of 1932–1933 in Soviet Ukraine* (pp. 139–155). Kashtan Press.

Greene, S. (2013). Beyond Bolotnaia: Bridging old and new in Russia's election protest movement. *Problems of Post-Communism*, 60(2), 40–52.

Greene, S. (2014). *Moscow in Movement: Power and Opposition in Putin's Russia*. Stanford University Press.

Greene, S., and Robertson, G. (2019). *Putin v. the People: The Perilous Politics of a Divided Russia*. Yale University Press.

Gretskiy, I. (2013). Ukraine's foreign policy under Yushchenko. *The Polish Quarterly of International Affairs*, 22(4), 7–28.

Grigas, A. (2016). *Beyond Crimea: The New Russian Empire*. Yale University Press.

Grono, M. and Brunson, J. (2018). Peacekeeping in Ukraine's Donbas: Opportunities and risks. *International Crisis Group*.

Hale, H.E. (2004). The origins of United Russia and the Putin presidency: The role of contingency in party-system development. *Demokratizatsiya*, 12(2), 169–194.

Hale, H.E. (2018). How Crimea pays: Media, rallying round the flag, and authoritarian support. *Comparative Politics*, 50(3), 369–391.

Hale, H.E. (2022). Authoritarian rallying as reputational cascade? Evidence from Putin's popularity surge after Crimea. *American Political Science Review*, 116(2), 580–594.

Haran', O. and Maiboroda, O. (eds.) (2000). *Ukrains'ki livi: mizh leninizmom i sotsial-demokratieiu*: KM Academiia.

Herrera, Y. (2005). *Imagined Economies*. Cambridge University Press.

Hill, F., and Gaddy, C. (2013). *Mr Putin: Operative in the Kremlin*. Brookings Institution Press.

Hill, W. (2018). *No Place for Russia: European Security Institutions since 1989*. Columbia University Press.

Hillis, F. (2013). *Children of Rus'. Right-Bank Ukraine and the Invention of a Russian Nation*. Cornell University Press.

Himka, J.-P. (2015). Legislating historical truth: Ukraine's laws of April 9, 2015. *Ab Imperio*.

Himka, J.-P. (2022). Ten turning points: A brief history of Ukraine. https://ukrainesolidaritycampaign.org/2022/04/13/ten-turning-points-a-brief-history-of-ukraine/

Huntington, S. (1991). Democracy's third wave. *Journal of Democracy*, 2(2), 12–34.

Hylton, G. (2014). Understanding the constitutional situation in Crimea. Marquett University Law School Faculty Blog.

International Federation for Human Rights (2021). *Russia: "Crimes Against History"* (No. 770a).

Ishiyama, J. and Kennedy, R. (2001). Superpresidentialism and political party development in Russia, Ukraine, Armenia and Kyrgyzstan. *Europe–Asia Studies*, 53(8), 1177–1191.

Javeline, D. (2009). *Protest and the Politics of Blame: The Russian Response to Unpaid Wages*. University of Michigan Press.

Johnson, J. (2000). *A Fistful of Rubles: The Rise and Fall of the Russian Banking System*. Cornell University Press.

Kaleniuk, D. and Halushka, O. (2021). Why Ukraine's fight against corruption scares Russia. *Foreign Policy*, December 17.

Karatnycky, A (2005). Ukraine's Orange Revolution. *Foreign Affairs*, 84.

Kasekamp, A. (2020). An uncertain journey to the promised land: The Baltic states' road to NATO membership. *Journal of Strategic Studies*, 43(6–7), 869–896.

Kasianov, G. (2010). The Holodomor and the building of a nation. *Russian Politics and Law*, 48(5), 25–47.

Kasianov, G. (2022a). *Memory Crash: Politics of History in and around Ukraine, 1980s–2010s*. Central European University Press.

Kasianov, G. (2022b). The war over Ukrainian identity. Nationalism, Russian imperialism, and the quest to define Ukraine's history. *Foreign Affairs*.

Kasianov, G. (2023). Nationalist memory narratives and the politics of history in Ukraine since the 1990s. *Nationalities Papers*, 1–20.

Klid, B. and Motyl, A. (eds.) (2012). *The Holodomor Reader: A Sourcebook on the Famine of 1932–1933 in Ukraine*. Canadian Institute of Ukrainian Studies Press.

Klymenko, L. (2016). The Holodomor law and national trauma construction in Ukraine. *Canadian Slavonic Papers*, 58(4), 341–361.

Knott, E. (2017). Quasi-citizenship as a category of practice: Analyzing engagement with Russia's Compatriot policy in Crimea. *Citizenship studies*, 21(1), 116–135.

Kononczuk, W. (2018). The paradoxes of Polish–Ukrainian relations. *Focus Ukraine*. Blog of the Kennan Institute, Wilson Center.

Koposov, N. (2017). *Memory Laws, Memory Wars: The Politics of the Past in Europe and Russia*. Cambridge University Press.

Kostadinova, T. (2000). East European public support for NATO membership: Fears and aspirations. *Journal of Peace Research*, 37(2), 235–249.

Kovalchuk, A., Kenny, C., and Snyder, M. (2019). *Examining the Impact of E-Procurement in Ukraine* (No. 511). Center for Global Development.

Kovalov, M. (2022). When Lenin becomes Lennon: Decommunisation and the politics of memory in Ukraine. *Europe–Asia Studies*, 74(5), 709–733.

Kramer, M. Why did Russia give away Crimea 60 years ago? *CWIHP e-Dossier No. 47*.

Kramer, M. (1998). Neorealism, nuclear proliferation, and East-Central European strategies. *International Politics*, 35(3), 253–304.

Kramer, M. (2008). Russian policy toward the commonwealth of independent states: Recent trends and future prospects. *Problems of Post-Communism*, 55(6), 3–19.

Krawchuk, A. and Bremer, T. (eds.) (2016). *Churches in the Ukrainian Crisis*. Palgrave Macmillan and Springer Nature.

Kubicek, P. (2001). The limits of electoral democracy in Ukraine. *Democratization*, 8(2), 117–139.

Kubicek, P. (2002). Civil society, trade unions and post-Soviet democratisation: Evidence from Russia and Ukraine. *Europe–Asia Studies*, 54(4), 603–624.

Kudelia, S. (2014). The Maidan and beyond: The house that Yanukovych built. *Journal of Democracy*, 25(3), 19–34.

Kudelia, S. (2014). *Domestic Sources of the Donbas Insurgency*: PONARS Eurasia.

Kulyk, V. (2011). Language identity, linguistic diversity and political cleavages: Evidence from Ukraine. *Nations and Nationalism*, 17(3), 627–648.

Kulyk, V. (2019). Identity in transformation: Russian-speakers in post-Soviet Ukraine. *Europe–Asia Studies*, 71(1), 156–178.

Kuzio, T. (2005). Ukraine's Orange Revolution: The opposition's road to success. *Journal of Democracy*, 16(2), 117–130.

Kuzio, T. (2022). *Russian Nationalism and the Russian–Ukrainian War*. New York: Routledge.

Kuzio, T. and Wilson, A. (1994). *Ukraine: Perestroika to independence* (1st ed.). New York: St. Martin's Press.

Kydd, A. (2007). *Trust and Mistrust in International Relations*. Princeton University Press.
Kydd, A. (forthcoming). You can't get there from here.
Kyïvs'ke naukove tovarystvo imeni Petra Mohyly, and "ANOD," A.-d. k. t. (eds.) (1998). *Politychni partii Ukrainy*: Tovarystvo "K.I.S."
Larrabee, S. (2006). Ukraine and the West. *Survival*, 48(1), 93–110.
Larrabee, S. (2007). Ukraine at the crossroads. *Washington Quarterly*, 30(4), 45–61.
Laruelle, M. (2008). *Russian Eurasianism: An Ideology of Empire*. Johns Hopkins University Press.
Laruelle, M. (2015a). *The "Russian World." Russia's Soft Power and Geopolitical Imagination*. Washington, DC: Center on Global Interests.
Laruelle, M. (2015b). The three colors of Novorossiya, or the Russian nationalist mythmaking of the Ukrainian crisis. *Post-Soviet Affairs*, 62(2), 1–20.
Laruelle, M. (2016). Russia as an anti-liberal European civilization. In P. Kolstø and H. Blakkisrud (eds.), *The New Russian Nationalism: Imperialism, Ethnicity and Authoritarianism, 2000–15* (pp. 275–297). Edinburgh University Press.
Lanoszka, A. (2023). Thank goodness for NATO enlargement. In *Evaluating NATO Enlargement: From Cold War Victory to the Russia–Ukraine War* (pp. 307–339). Springer.
Lanoszka, A. and Becker, J. (2022). The art of partial commitment: The politics of military assistance to Ukraine. *Post-Soviet Affairs*, 39 (3), 1–22.
Liber, G. (2016). *Total Wars and the Making of Modern Ukraine, 1914–1954*. University of Toronto Press.
McFaul, M. (1997). *Russia's 1996 Presidential Election: The End of Polarized Politics*. Hoover Press.
McFaul, M. (2000). Yeltsin's legacy. *The Wilson Quarterly*, 24(2), 42–58.
McFaul, M. (2001). *Russia's Unfinished Revolution: Political Change from Gorbachev to Putin*. Cornell University Press.
McFaul, M. (2018). *From Cold War to Hot Peace: An American Ambassador in Putin's Russia*. Houghton Mifflin Harcourt.
McGlynn, J. (2023). *Russia's War*. Polity.
Magocsi, P.R. (2022). *Ukraina Redux. On Statehood and National Identity*. Kashtan Press for the Chair of Ukrainian Studies, University of Toronto.
Malyarenko, T. and Galbreath, D.J. (2013). Crimea: Competing self-determination movements and the politics at the centre. *Europe–Asia Studies*, 65(5), 912–928.
Malinova, O. (2017). Political uses of the Great Patriotic War in post-Soviet Russia from Yeltsin to Putin. In J. Fedor, M. Kangaspuro, J. Lassila, and T. Zhurzhenko (eds.), *War and Memory in Russia, Ukraine and Belarus* (pp. 43–70). Springer.
Marat, E. (2018). *The Politics of Police Reform: Society Against the State in Post-Soviet Countries*. Oxford University Press.
Markus, S. (2015). *Property, Predation, and Protection*. Cambridge University Press.
Markus, S. and Charnysh, V. (2017). The flexible few: Oligarchs and wealth defense in developing democracies. *Comparative Political Studies*, 50(12), 1632–1665.
Marples, D. (2007). *Heroes and Villains. Creating National History in Contemporary Ukraine*. Budapest: Central European University Press.
Marples, D. (2017). *Ukraine in Conflict. An Analytical Chronicle*. E-International Relations.
Martin, T. (2001). *The Affirmative Action Empire: Nations and Nationalism in the Soviet Union, 1923–1939*. Cornell University Press.

Mearsheimer, J.J. (2014). Why the Ukraine crisis is the West's fault: The liberal delusions that provoked Putin. *Foreign Affairs*, 93(5), 77–89.

Metreveli, T. (2019). The making of Orthodox Church of Ukraine: Damocles sword or light at the end of the tunnel? *Religion and Society in East and West*, 47(4–5).

Metreveli, T. (2020). *Orthodox Christianity and the Politics of Transition: Ukraine, Serbia and Georgia*. Routledge.

Mitrokhin, N. (2015). Infiltration, instruction, invasion: Russia's war in Ukraine. *Journal of Soviet and Post-Soviet Politics and Society*, 1(1), 219–250.

Morozov, V. (2009). *Rossiia i drugie. Identichnost' i granitsy politicheskogo soobshchestva*: Novoe literaturnoe obozrenie.

Moser, M. (2013). *Language Policy and the Discourse on Languages in Ukraine under President Viktor Yanukovych* (February 25, 2010 to October 28, 2012). Stuttgart: Ibidem-Verlag.

Motyl, A.J. (2010). Deleting the Holodomor: Ukraine unmakes itself. *World Affairs*, 173(3), 25–33.

Mylonas, H. and Radnitz, S. (2022). *Enemies Within: The Global Politics of Fifth Columns*. Oxford University Press.

Narodnyi Rukh Ukrainy za Perebudovy (1989). *Prohrama. Statut*. Smoloskyp.

Neumann, I. (1993). Russia as Central Europe's constituting other. *East European Politics and Societies*, 7(2), 349–369.

Nichols, T. (1999). *The Russian Presidency: Society and Politics in the Second Russian Republic*. Springer.

Nitsova, S. (2021). Why the difference? Donbas, Kharkiv and Dnipropetrovsk after Ukraine's Euromaidan revolution. *Europe–Asia Studies*, 73(10), 1832–1856.

Oates, S. (2006). *Television, Democracy and Elections in Russia*. Routledge.

O'Loughlin, J., Sasse, G., Toal, G., and Bakke, K.M. (2021). A new survey of the Ukraine-Russia conflict finds deeply divided views in the contested Donbas region. *The Washington Post*.

Onuch, O. (2014). The Maidan and beyond: Who were the protesters? *Journal of Democracy*, 25(3), 44–51.

Onuch, O., and Hale, H. (2018). Capturing ethnicity: The case of Ukraine. *Post-Soviet Affairs*, 34(2–3), 84–106.

Onuch, O. and Hale, H. (2023). *Zelensky Effect*. Oxford University Press.

OSCE High Commissioner on National Minorities. (2001). Letter of January 12, 2001 to the Minister of Foreign Affairs of the Republic of Ukraine, Mr. Anatoly M. Zlenko, and the letter of reply, dated April 6, 2001.

Orttung, R. (2004). Business and politics in Russia's regions. *Problems of Post-Communism*, 51(2) (March/April 2004), 48–60.

Pain, E. (2009). Russia between empire and nation. *Russian Politics and Law*, 47(2), 60–86.

Pauly, M. (2014). *Breaking the Tongue: Language, Education, and Power in Soviet Ukraine, 1923–1934*. University of Toronto Press.

Peisakhin, L. and Rozenas, A. (2018). Electoral effects of biased media: Russian television in Ukraine. *American Journal of Political Science*, 62(3), 535–550.

Petrov, R. (2018). EU common values in the EU–Ukraine association agreement: Anchor to democracy? *Baltic Journal of European Studies*, 8(1), 49–62.

Pifer, S. (2019). NATO's Ukraine challenge: Ukrainians want membership but obstacles abound. *Brookings*.

Pifer, S. (2021). Russia's draft agreements with NATO and the United States: Intended for rejection? *Brookings*.

Pisano, J. (2023). *Staging Democracy. Political Performance in Ukraine, Russia, and Beyond*. Cornell University Press.

Plokhy, S. (2006). *The Origins of the Slavic Nations: Premodern Identities in Russia, Ukraine, and Belarus*. Cambridge University Press.

Plokhy, S. (2014). *The Last Empire: The Final Days of the Soviet Union*. Basic Books.

Plokhy, S. (2015). *The Gates of Europe: A History of Ukraine*. Basic Books.

Plokhy, S. (2017). *Lost Kingdom: The Quest for Empire and the Making of the Russian Nation, from 1470 to the Present*. Basic Books.

Plokhy, S., and Sysyn, F. (2003). *Religion and Nation in Modern Ukraine*. Canadian Institute of Ukrainian Studies Press.

Pomeranz, W.E. and Smyth, R. (2021). Russia's 2020 constitutional reform: The politics of institutionalizing the status-quo. *Russian Politics*, 6(1), 1–5.

Pomeranz, W.E. (2021). Putin's 2020 constitutional amendments: What changed? What Remained the same? *Russian Politics*, 6(1), 6–26.

Pop-Eleches, G. and Robertson, G. (2018). Identity and political preferences in Ukraine – before and after Euromaidan. *Post-Soviet Affairs*, 34(2–3), 107–118.

Popova, M. (2012). *Politicized Justice in Emerging Democracies: A Study of Courts in Russia and Ukraine*. Cambridge University Press.

Popova, M. (2014). Why the Orange Revolution was short and peaceful and Euromaidan long and violent. *Problems of Post-Communism*, 61(6), 64–70.

Popova, M. (2016). Ukraine's politicized courts. In R. Orttung and H. Hale (eds.), *Beyond the Euromaidan: Comparative Perspectives on Advancing Reform in Ukraine* (pp. 143–161). Stanford University Press.

Popova, M. (2020). Can a leopard change its spots? Strategic behavior versus professional role conception during Ukraine's 2014 court chair elections. *Law and Policy*, 42(4), 365–381.

Popova, M. and Beers, D.J. (2020). No revolution of dignity for Ukraine's judges: Judicial reform after the Euromaidan. *Demokratizatsiya: Journal of Post-Soviet Democratization*, 28(1), 113–142.

Popova, M. and Shevel, O. (2022). Russia's invasion of Ukraine is essentially not about NATO. *Just Security*.

Portnov, A. (2013). Memory wars in post-Soviet Ukraine (1991–2010). In U. Blacker, A. Etkind, and J. Fedor (eds.), *Memory and Theory in Eastern Europe* (pp. 233–254). Palgrave Macmillan.

Pothier, F. (2017). An area-access strategy for NATO. *Survival*, 59(3), 73–80.

Powell, J. and Thyne, C. (2011). Global instances of coups from 1950 to 2010: A new dataset. *Journal of Peace Research*, 48(2), 249–259.

Protsyk, O. (2004). Ruling with decrees: Presidential decree making in Russia and Ukraine. *Europe–Asia Studies*, 56(5), 637–660.

Radchenko, S. (2020). "Nothing but humiliation for Russia": Moscow and NATO's eastern enlargement, 1993–1995. *Journal of Strategic Studies*, 43(6–7), 769–815.

Radchenko, S., Sayle, T., and Ostermann, C. (2020). Introduction to the special issue, NATO: past and present. *Journal of Strategic Studies*, 43(6–7).

Radnitz, S. (2021). *Revealing Schemes: The Politics of Conspiracy in Russia and the Post-Soviet Region*. Oxford University Press.

Reddaway, P. and Glinski, D. (2001). *The Tragedy of Russia's Reforms: Market Bolshevism Against Democracy*. US Institute of Peace Press.
Remy, J. (2018). *Brothers or Enemies: The Ukrainian National Movement and Russia from the 1840s to the 1870s*. University of Toronto Press.
Riabchuk, M. (2002). Ukraine: One state, two countries? *Transit Europäische Revue*, 23.
Riabchuk, M. (2012). Ukraine's "muddling through": National identity and post-communist transition. *Communist and Post-Communist Studies*, 45(3), 439–446.
Risch, W. J. (2021). Prelude to war? In D. Marples (ed.), *The War in Ukraine's Donbas: Origins, Contexts, and the Future* (pp. 7–28). Central European University Press.
Rossoliński-Liebe, G. and Willems, B. (2022). Putin's abuse of history: Ukrainian "Nazis," "genocide," and a fake threat scenario. *Journal of Slavic Military Studies*, 35(1), 1–10.
Sakwa, R. (2018). One Europe or none? Monism, involution and relations with Russia. *Europe–Asia Studies*, 70(10), 1656–1667.
Sasse, G. (2007). *The Crimea Question: Identity, Transition, and Conflict*. Harvard University Press.
Sarotte, M. (2021). *Not One Inch: America, Russia, and the Making of Post-Cold War Stalemate*. Yale University Press, 2021.
Schmid, U. and Myshlovska, O. (eds.) (2019). *Regionalism without Regions: Reconceptualizing Ukraine's Heterogeneity*. Central European University Press.
Schulte, G. L. (1997). Former Yugoslavia and the new NATO. *Survival*, 39(1), 19–42.
Sereda, V. (2023). *Displacement in War-Torn Ukraine. State, Displacement, and Belonging* (Elements in Global Studies). Cambridge University Press.
Shandra, A. and Seely, R. (2019). *The Surkov Leaks: The Inner Workings of Russia's Hybrid War in Ukraine*. Royal United Services Institute for Defence and Security Studies.
Sharafutdinova, G. (2020). *The Red Mirror: Putin's Leadership and Russia's Insecure Identity*. Oxford University Press.
Shekhovtsov, A. and Umland, A. (2014). The Maidan and beyond: Ukraine's radical right. *Journal of Democracy*, 25(3), 58–63.
Sherr, J. (2010). *The Mortgaging of Ukraine's Independence*. London: Chatham House, 2010.
Shevel, O. (2009). The politics of citizenship policy in new states. *Comparative Politics*, 41(3), 273–291.
Shevel, O. (2011a). *Migration, Refugee Policy, and State Building in Postcommunist Europe*. Cambridge University Press.
Shevel, O. (2011b). The politics of memory in a divided society: A comparison of post-Franco Spain and post-Soviet Ukraine. *Slavic Review*, 70(1), 137–164.
Shevel, O. (2011c). Russian nation-building from Yel'tsin to Medvedev: Civic, ethnic, or purposefully ambiguous? *Europe–Asia Studies*, 63(2), 179–202.
Shevel, O. (2014). Memories of the past and visions of the future: Remembering the Soviet era and its end in Ukraine. In M. H. Bernhard and J. Kubik (eds.), *Twenty Years after Communism: the Politics of Memory and Commemoration* (pp. 147–167). Oxford University Press.
Shevel, O. (2015). The parliamentary elections in Ukraine, October 2014. *Electoral Studies*, 39, 159–163.
Shevel, O. (2016a). The battle for historical memory in postrevolutionary Ukraine. *Current History*, 115(783), 258–263.

Shevel, O. (2016b). Decommunization in post-Euromaidan Ukraine. Law and practice. *PONARS Eurasia Policy Memo No. 411*.

Shulman, S. (2005). Ukrainian nation-building under Kuchma. *Problems of Post-Communism*, 52(5), 32–47.

Shulman, S. (2006). Cultural comparisons and their consequences for nationhood in Ukraine. *Communist and Post-Communist Studies*, 39(2), 247–263.

Skillen, D. (2016). *Freedom of Speech in Russia: Politics and Media from Gorbachev to Putin*. Routledge.

Smoleński, J. and Dutkiewicz, J. (2022). The American pundits who can't resist "Westsplaining" Ukraine. *New Republic, 4*.

Smyth, R., Sobolev, A., and Soboleva, I. (2013). Patterns of discontent: Identifying the participant core in Russian post-election protest. In *Russia's Winter of Discontent: Taking Stock of Changing State Society Relationships*. Uppsala University.

Smyth, R. (2020). *Elections, Protest, and Authoritarian Regime Stability: Russia 2008–2020*. Cambridge University Press.

Snegovaya, M. and Petrov, K. (2022). Long Soviet shadows: The nomenklatura ties of Putin elites. *Post-Soviet Affairs*, 38(4), 329–348.

Socor, Vladimir. (2018). Azov Sea, Kerch Strait: Evolution of their purported legal status (Part One). *Eurasia Daily Monitor*, 15(169).

Szporluk, R. (2000). *Ukraine, Russia, and the Breakup of the Soviet Union*. Hoover Institution Press.

Stern, J. (1994). Moscow meltdown: Can Russia survive? *International Security*, 18(4), 40–65.

Stoner, K (2020). *Russia Resurrected: Its Power and Purpose in a New Global Order*. Oxford University Press.

Stoner, K. (2023). The Putin myth. *Journal of Democracy*, 34(2), 5–18.

Szostek, J. (2014). Russia and the news media in Ukraine: A case of "soft power"?. *East European Politics and Societies*, 28(03), 463–486.

Taylor, B. (2018). *The Code of Putinism*. Oxford University Press.

Tolz, V. (1998a). Conflicting "homeland myths" and nation-state building in postcommunist Russia. *Slavic Review*, 57(2), 267–294.

Tolz, V. (1998b). Forging the nation. National identity and nation building in post-communist Russia. *Europe–Asia Studies*, 50(6), 993–1022.

Tolz, V. (2001). *Russia. Inventing the Nation*. Oxford University Press.

Tomenko, V., Hrebel'nyk, V., and Vashchenko, K. O. (eds.) (2002). *Pravo vyboru: politychni partiï ta vyborchi bloky: dovidnyk*. Heoprynt.

Tudoroiu, T. (2007). Rose, orange, and tulip: The failed post-Soviet revolutions. *Communist and Post-Communist Studies*, 40(3), 315–342.

Uehling, G.L. (2023). *Everyday War: The Conflict over Donbas, Ukraine*. Cornell University Press.

Viatrovych, V. (2015). "Decommunization" and academic discussion. *Krytyka*.

Viola, L. (2022). Putin's war on history is another form of domestic repression. *The Conversation*.

Walker, M. (2018). Do the people rule? The use of referenda in Russia. In Sperling, V., *Building the Russian State: Institutional Crisis and the Quest for Democratic Governance*. Routledge.

Wanner, C. (2020). An affective atmosphere of religiosity: Animated places, public spaces, and the politics of attachment in Ukraine and beyond. *Comparative Studies in Society and History*, 62(1), 68–105.

Wanner, C. (2022). *Everyday Religiosity and the Politics of Belonging in Ukraine*. Cornell University Press.

Wasyliw, Z.V. (2007). Orthodox Church divisions in newly independent Ukraine, 1991–1995. *East European Quarterly*, 41(3), 305–322.

Way, L. (2015). *Pluralism by Default: Weak Autocrats and the Rise of Competitive Politics*. Johns Hopkins University Press.

White, S. and McAllister, I. (2014). Did Russia (nearly) have a Facebook revolution in 2011? Social media's challenge to authoritarianism. *Politics*, 34(1), 72–84.

Wilson, A. (1998). Politics in and around Crimea: A difficult homecoming. In E. Allworth (ed.), *The Tatars of the Crimea: Return to the Homeland. Studies and Documents* (pp. 281–322). Duke University Press.

Wilson, A. (2000). *The Ukrainians. Unexpected Nation*. Yale University Press.

Wilson, A. (2002). Reinventing the Ukrainian left: Assessing adaptability and change, 1991–2000. *Slavonic and East European Review*, 80(1), 21–59.

Wilson, A. (2014). *Ukraine Crisis: What it Means for the West*. Yale University Press.

Wolczuk, K. (2000). History, Europe and the "national idea." The "official" narrative of national identity in Ukraine. *Nationalities Papers*, 28(4), 671–694.

Wolczuk, K. (2001). *The Moulding of Ukraine: The Constitutional Politics of State Formation*. Central European University Press.

Wolczuk, K. (2005). *Ukraine after the Orange Revolution*. Centre for European Reform.

Wolczuk, K., Delcour, L., Dragneva, R., Maniokas, K., and Žeruolis, D. (2017). The association agreements as a dynamic framework: Between modernization and integration. EU-STRAT Working Paper.

Wynnyckyj, M. (2019). *Ukraine's Maidan, Russia's war: A Chronicle and Analysis of the Revolution of Dignity*. Stuttgart: bidem-Verlag.

Yekelchyk, S. (2007). *Ukraine: Birth of a Modern Nation*. Oxford University Press.

Yekelchyk, S. (2015). *The Conflict in Ukraine: What Everyone Needs to Know*. Oxford University Press.

Zaloznaya, M. and Reisinger, W.M. (2020). Mechanisms of decoupling from global regimes: The case of anticorruption reforms in Russia and Ukraine. *Demokratizatsiya: The Journal of Post-Soviet Democratization*, 28(1), 77–111.

Zevelev, I. (2001). *Russia and its New Diasporas*. United States Institute of Peace.

Zevelev, I. (2021). Russia in the post-Soviet space: Dual citizenship as a foreign policy instrument. *Russia in Global Affairs*, 19(2), 10–37.

Zhukov, Y. M. (2016). Trading hard hats for combat helmets: The economics of rebellion in eastern Ukraine. *Journal of Comparative Economics*, 44(1), 1–15.

Zhurzhenko, T. (2021). Fighting empire, weaponising culture: The conflict with Russia and the restrictions on Russian mass culture in post-Maidan Ukraine. *Europe–Asia Studies*, 73(8), 1441–1466.

Zhurzhenko, T. (2022). Legislating historical memory in post-Soviet Ukraine. In *Memory Laws and Historical Justice: The Politics of Criminalizing the Past* (pp. 97–130). Springer.

Zhurzhenko, T. (2023). Terror, collaboration, and resistance. Russian rule in the newly occupied territories of Ukraine. *Osteuropa* (6–8), 179–200.

Index